This important book explores critic
national Law and the nonhuman in the contemporary
bold interdisciplinary approach exposes the limitations of the Humanism and
Anthropocentrism inherent to International Law, while re-asserting the Law's
commitment to face the challenges of the posthuman predicament. Foremost
among them, the regulation of human-machine interaction in military technologies and the status of nature in Environmental Law.

Pragmatic, but theoretically savvy, Jones combines critique with creativity
by proposing alternative sources that many help overcome legal liberalism.
Posthuman Feminism, Queering the Nonhuman, Indigenous Epistemologies, New Materialism and the Rights of Nature movement are just some of
the toolkits this remarkable book provides as a way forward.

Emily Jones holds legal discourse accountable but also confirms its ability
to change and construct more inclusive, sustainable and just worlds. A major
work that will leave a mark.

Rosi Braidotti, Distinguished Professor Emerita, Utrecht University,
the Netherlands

Anchoring us in new possibilities, this impressive work explains what posthuman feminist perspectives offer to the urgent task of superseding international law's deadly imperial anthropocentrism by fostering legal systems
capable of sustaining life in all its forms. Drawing on a staggering array
of interdisciplinary critical scholarship, Jones illustrates some of the paradigm shifts that are necessary if we, and the planet, are to survive (let
alone flourish) in these posthuman times. To illustrate, she engages adeptly
with current debates in two areas of international law – the regulation of
lethal military technologies and international environmental law. Along the
way Jones remains cognisant of the many tensions that can compromise or
co-opt feminist efforts to change international law's neoliberal humanist
orientation from within, readily acknowledging that posthuman feminist
change is also necessary outside the law and may even require a turning
away from law.

Dianne Otto, Melbourne Law School, Australia

In this meticulously researched and beautifully written book, Emily Jones
draws on posthuman feminism to both highlight and question international
law's constitutive boundaries: human/nature, human/technology and, perhaps above all, the boundaries imposed upon feminist legal theory in the

field. By applying a radically egalitarian feminist framework to the laws of war and international environmental law, Jones reveals that some of the most urgent problems of our times, war, climate change and anti-feminist backlash, are much more interconnected than we might have thought.

Ntina Tzouvala, Associate Professor, ANU College of Law, Australian National University

FEMINIST THEORY AND INTERNATIONAL LAW

Feminist approaches to international law have been mischaracterised by the mainstream of the discipline as being a niche field that pertains only to women's lived experiences and their participation in decision-making processes. Exemplifying how feminist approaches can be used to analyse all areas of international law, this book applies posthuman feminist theory to examine the regulation of new and emerging military technologies, international environmental law and the conceptualisation of the sovereign state and other modes of legal personality in international law.

Noting that most posthuman scholarship to date is primarily theoretical, this book also contributes to the field of posthumanism through its application of posthuman feminism to international law, working to bridge the theory and practice divide by using posthuman feminism to design and call for legal change. This interdisciplinary book draws on an array of fields, including philosophy, queer and feminist theories, postcolonial and critical race theories, computer science, critical disability studies, science and technology studies, marine biology, cultural and media studies, Indigenous onto-epistemologies, critical legal theory, political science and beyond to provide a holistic analysis of international law and its inclusions and exclusions.

This interdisciplinary book will appeal to students and scholars with interests in legal, feminist and posthuman theory, as well as those concerned with the contemporary challenges faced by international law.

Dr Emily Jones is a NUAcT Fellow based in Newcastle Law School, Newcastle University, UK.

FEMINIST THEORY AND INTERNATIONAL LAW

Posthuman Perspectives

Emily Jones

Routledge
Taylor & Francis Group

LONDON AND NEW YORK

Designed cover image: © Getty Images

First published 2023
by Routledge
4 Park Square, Milton Park, Abingdon, Oxon OX14 4RN

and by Routledge
605 Third Avenue, New York, NY 10158

a GlassHouse book

Routledge is an imprint of the Taylor & Francis Group, an informa business

© 2023 Emily Jones

British Library Cataloguing-in-Publication Data
A catalogue record for this book is available from the British Library

ISBN: 978-1-032-04389-0 (hbk)
ISBN: 978-1-032-42690-7 (pbk)
ISBN: 978-1-003-36379-8 (ebk)

DOI: 10.4324/9781003363798

Typeset in Bembo
by SPi Technologies India Pvt Ltd (Straive)

CONTENTS

Acknowledgements   *viii*

Note on the Text   *x*

List of Acronyms   *xi*

Introduction: Posthuman Feminism and International Law   1

1   International Law and the Nonhuman   27

2   Human and Machine: Lethal Autonomous Weapons Systems   56

3   Regulating Military Technologies: Between Resistance and Compliance   84

4   Queering the Nonhuman: Engaging International Environmental Law   110

5   The Subjectivity of Matter: The Rights of Nature in International Law   128

6   Posthuman Feminism: Reworlding Exits from Liberal Legalism   153

Bibliography   *165*

Index   *197*

ACKNOWLEDGEMENTS

While I am listed as the sole author, I could not have written this book without the support and inspiration of many others. Thank you to Gina Heathcote for her unwavering support of my work, both when writing my thesis and then when transforming that thesis into this book. Enormous thanks must also go to Rosi Braidotti, who was not only a brilliant PhD examiner but also took it upon herself to become a mentor to me. My deep gratitude also extends to Dianne Otto, who has likewise mentored me, always believing in me, my work and this book. I have learnt a great deal from these three feminist women and am deeply indebted to each of them.

Thank you to Rosi Braidotti, Dianne Otto, Alice Finden, Ntina Tzouvala, Anna Grear, Noam Lubell, John Williams and Gina Heathcote for providing extremely helpful feedback on some of the later versions of the chapters of this book. Passages of this book were also inspired by conversations with and the feedback of Yoriko Otomo and Vanja Hamzić, both of whom provided poignant guidance at key moments when I was writing my thesis. With thanks to both.

I wrote various parts of this book while visiting other institutions. In 2019, I was lucky enough to be a Kathleen Fitzpatrick Visiting Fellow at the Laureate Program in International Law at Melbourne Law School, hosted by Anne Orford. Parts of this text were written there while other parts were inspired by conversations with colleagues on the programme. With special thanks to Anne for the opportunity and for her support.

During the course of my PhD, I undertook a visiting research position at Sciences Po Paris. Thank you to Emmanuelle Tourme-Jouannet for her guidance during that time, and for being so welcoming and generous.

I also wrote parts of this text while undertaking a visiting research position at the Institute for Cultural Inquiry (ICON) at Utrecht University in 2020. Thank you to Rosi Braidotti for the invitation which provided me with invaluable research time.

I am very lucky to have met many people who have been willing to help guide me in this project over the years, including Ratna Kapur, Christine Chinkin, Louise Arimatsu, Loveday Hodson, Grietje Baars, Rahul Rao, Hilary Charlesworth, Matilda Arvidsson and Keina Yoshida. With thanks to each for their guidance and for the many inspiring conversations.

Thank you to all my colleagues at the University of Essex for being so welcoming, friendly and supportive and for seeing my potential before I had even finished my PhD. With special thanks to Patricia Palacios Zuloaga for her friendship, Meagan Wong for being my international law co-conspirator and to Kai Yin Low, Daragh Murray and Carla Ferstman for their belief in and support of my research.

I am grateful to Jérémie Gilbert, Elizabeth Macpherson and Julia Dehm for our conversations on the rights of nature, many of which informed the writing of Chapter 5.

I would like to thank my PhD colleagues at SOAS University of London, for being part of the journey with me and for being there to support and guide me when needed. My thanks go to Jana Cattien, Sheri Labenski, Akanksha Mehta, Sabiha Allouche, Haje Keli, Siavash Eshghi, Hanns Kendal and Jacquelyn Strey and, at the time postdoctoral researcher, Bérénice K. Schramm.

Thank you to Goda Klumbytė, Ruth Clemens, Fiona Hillary and Kay Sidebottom, my fellow posthuman kin, for being such a great source for support and for always reminding me of the importance of reworlding.

I have come to learn that one cannot underestimate the value of a supportive editor. Thank you to my editor, Colin Perrin at Routledge, for his enthusiasm right from the moment I reached out to him to the concluding stages of writing this book.

I am grateful to all my students at SOAS University of London and the University of Essex, from 2014 until the present, for teaching me more than I could ever have taught them.

I would also like to thank my A level teachers who pushed me to believe in myself, properly, for the first time. Special thanks to Dave Brock, my first ever law teacher, who put up with cheeky teenage Emily, his belief in my potential never wavering.

Thank you to my friends and family. In particular, I am deeply grateful to my parents and to Rachel, Anneke, Rosi, Hamida, Di, Jana, Patricia, Gina, Hanns, Miranda, Sheri, Steph and Jasper.

Thank you, Alice, for the best of times.

NOTE ON THE TEXT

Some sections of this book are drawn from material published elsewhere. Over the years, they have transformed into something often quite different to their originals. However, these previously published works are: Emily Jones 'Posthuman International Law and the Rights of Nature', *Journal of Human Rights and the Environment* (2021) 12(0): 76–101; and Emily Jones, 'A Posthuman-Xenofeminist Analysis of the Discourse on Autonomous Weapons Systems and Other Killing Machines', *Australian Feminist Law Journal* (2018) 44(1): 93–118.

ACRONYMS

AI	Artificial Intelligence
BWC	Biological Weapons Convention
CBD	Convention on Biological Diversity
CCW	Convention on Certain Conventional Weapons
DARPA	Defense Advanced Research Projects Agency (US)
DoD	Department of Defense (US)
ECS	Engagement Control Centre
ECtHR	European Court of Human Rights
EIA	Environmental Impact Assessment
GARN	Global Alliance for the Rights of Nature
GDP	Gross Domestic Product
GGE	Group of Governmental Experts
HETs	Human Enhancement Technologies
IA	Intelligence Amplification
ICCPR	International Covenant on Civil and Political Rights
ICESCR	International Covenant on Economic, Social and Cultural Rights
ICJ	International Court of Justice
ICRC	International Committee of the Red Cross
IEL	International Environmental Law
IHL	International Humanitarian Law
LARS	Lethal Autonomous Robotic Systems
LAWS	Lethal Autonomous Weapons Systems
LGBTIQ+	Lesbian, Gay, Bisexual, Transgender, Intersex, Queer +
NGO	Non-Governmental Organisation
OOO	Object-Orientated Ontology
PAAC-4	Patriot Advanced Affordable Capability-4

PAC	Patriot Advanced Capability
PAC-2	Patriot Advanced Capability-2
PCIJ	Permanent Court of International Justice
PTSD	Post-Traumatic Stress Disorder
RoN	Rights of Nature
SAT	Situation Awareness Technology
SIPRI	Stockholm International Peace Research Institute
STS	Science and Technology Studies
TWAIL	Third World Approaches to International Law
UDRME	Universal Declaration of the Rights of Mother Earth
UN	United Nations
UNEA	United Nations Environment Assembly
UNFCCC	United Nations Framework Convention on Climate Change
UNEP	United Nations Environment Programme
UNGA	United Nations General Assembly
VCLT	Vienna Convention on the Law of Treaties
WILFP	Women's International League for Peace and Freedom
WPS	Women, Peace and Security

INTRODUCTION

Posthuman Feminism and International Law

Faced with the climate crisis, the perpetuation of global inequalities in gendered, raced, classed and other forms, the use of ever more dystopian military technologies and technologies of surveillance to monitor populations and borders, and much more, it is clear that human lives are deeply entwined with our environments and the technologies we use. We are living in posthuman times.

International law has played, in some instances, an important role in providing aspirational frameworks for those seeking to create a better future. However, international law is also based upon a series of normative underpinnings, including anthropocentrism and exclusionary humanism, i.e. the centring of the white male subject. International law subsequently plays a core role in structuring and maintaining an unequal global order.

This book argues that posthuman feminism can be used to analyse international law and to provide alternative ways of doing international law; ways that better rise to the challenges of the present. Posthuman feminism seeks to dismantle exclusionary humanist hierarchies upheld between humans, such as those of gender, race and class, while also re-thinking the anthropocentric idea that humans sit in hierarchy over nonhuman subjects, such as the environment and nonhuman animals. Posthuman feminism is my chosen theoretical framework precisely because it engages with the central issues of the contemporary moment including those raised by growing inequalities, new technologies and the environmental crisis. Through examining the regulation of military technologies in Chapters 2 and 3, and the way that international law regulates the environment in Chapters 4 and 5, I analyse whether and how international law can be re-thought to address the challenges of the posthuman present.

DOI: 10.4324/9781003363798-1

Beginning with a discussion of feminist approaches to international law, this Introduction reflects on the way feminist approaches have been taken up, first, by the mainstream of the discipline of international law and second, by international institutions. I argue that feminist approaches, despite their frequent mischaracterisation as being niche, provide fundamental and necessary analyses of international law that insist on its re-thinking.

This book draws on two central case studies to apply posthuman feminism: international environmental law and the regulation of military technologies. Given this focus, the second section of this Introduction provides an outline of existing feminist international legal engagements with the two areas, noting the contribution this book makes to both.

The third section of this Introduction turns to defining posthuman feminism. Here, I situate posthuman feminism within the wider posthuman turn, noting differences and similarities between an array of posthuman theories, including transhumanism and new materialism. I then move on, in the following section, to provide a brief genealogy of posthuman theory within legal scholarship, before focusing more specifically on the emerging but limited take-up of these theories within international law. Finally, I conclude by outlining the structure of the book and the book's central arguments.

Feminist Approaches to International Law

Feminist approaches to international law have always cut across many layers, as Hilary Charlesworth and Christine Chinkin show in their metaphorical excavational dig:

> One obvious sign of power differentials between women and men is the absence of women in international legal institutions. Beneath this is the vocabulary of international law ... Digging further down, many apparently 'neutral' principles and rules of international law can be seen to operate differently with respect to women and men. Another, deeper, layer of the excavation reveals the gendered and sexed nature of the basic concepts of international law ... Permeating all stages of the dig is a silence from and exclusion of women ... [this is] an integral part of the structure of the international legal order, a critical element of its stability. The silences of the discipline are as important as its positive rules and rhetorical structures.[1]

Feminist approaches to international law have long drawn attention to a variety of issues at varying levels of the excavational dig, from topics which pertain to women's lived experiences to issues of general international law, providing

---

1 Hilary Charlesworth and Christine Chinkin, *The Boundaries of International Law: A Feminist Analysis*, (Manchester University Press, 2000), p. 49.

analyses of core concepts such as the sovereign state,[2] of international humanitarian law,[3] the law of treaties[4] or the law on the use of force.[5] Over the past three decades since Charlesworth, Chinkin and Wright's seminal 1991 article,[6] a multitude of feminist approaches to international law have emerged and much work has been done to bring women into the international legal system.[7] However, the majority of feminist approaches have come, today, to focus primarily on the first few layers of Charlesworth and Chinkin's excavation: on women's representation and the need to include them in decision-making.[8] More critical feminist approaches, such as postcolonial feminism and queer feminism, which dig further down into the basic concepts and assumptions of international law, have been relegated to the periphery of both the scholarly field and institutional take-up.[9]

As noted, one reason why critical feminist approaches remain on the periphery of the discipline of international law is related to how feminist approaches are seen by the mainstream of the discipline itself. Therefore, while:

2 Karen Knop, 'Why Rethinking the Sovereign State is Important for Women's International Human Rights Law,' in Rebecca J. Cook (ed.), *Human Rights of Women*, (Pennsylvania University Press, 1994): 153–164; Hilary Charlesworth and Christine Chinkin, 'The Idea of the State,' in *The Boundaries of International Law: A Feminist Analysis*, (Manchester University Press, 2000) 124–170; Hilary Charlesworth, 'The Sex of the State in International Law,' in Ngaire Naffine and Rosemary Owens (eds.), *Sexing the Subject of Law*, (LBC Information Services, 1997): 251–268. For more recent analyses, see: Yoriko Otomo, 'Of Mimicry and Madness: Speculations on the State,' *Australian Feminist Law Journal* (2014) 28(1): 53–76; Gina Heathcote, 'Sovereignty,' in *Feminist Dialogues on International Law: Successes, Tensions, Futures*, (Oxford University Press, 2019): 103–132.

3 Judith Gardham, 'A Feminist Analysis of Certain Aspects of International Humanitarian Law,' *Australian Yearbook of International Law* (1988) 12: 265–278.

4 Hilary Charlesworth and Christine Chinkin, 'The Law of Treaties,' in *The Boundaries of International Law: A Feminist Analysis*, (Manchester University Press, 2000): 96–123.

5 Gina Heathcote, *The Law on the Use of Force: A Feminist Analysis*, (Routledge, 2012); Christine Chinkin, 'Gendered Perspective to the International Use of Force,' *Australian Yearbook of International Law* (1992) 12: 279–293; Hilary Charlesworth and Christine Chinkin, 'The Use of Force in International Law,' in *The Boundaries of International Law: A Feminist Analysis*, (Manchester University Press, 2000): 250–274.

   For an overview of the development of feminist approaches to international law, see: Dianne Otto, 'Feminist Approaches to International Law,' in Anne Orford and Florian Hoffman (eds.), *Oxford Handbook of International Legal Theory*, (Oxford University Press, 2016): 488–450.

6 Hilary Charlesworth, Christine Chinkin and Shelley Wright, 'Feminist Approaches to International Law,' *American Journal of International Law* (1991) 85(4): 613–645.

7 For a short list of some of the key ways women have been brought into international law since 1991 'from the vantage point of 2004,' see: Doris Buss and Ambreena Manji, 'Introduction,' in Doris Buss and Ambreena Manji (eds.), *International Law: Modern Feminist Approaches*, (Hart, 2014): 1–16, p. 3–4.

8 Hilary Charlesworth, Gina Heathcote and Emily Jones, 'Feminist Scholarship on International Law in the 1990s and Today: An Inter-Generational Conversation,' *Feminist Legal Studies* (2019) 27: 79–93.

9 Karen Engle, Vasuki Nesiah and Dianne Otto, 'Feminist Approaches to International Law,' in Jeffrey N. Dunoff and Mark A. Pollack (eds.), *International Legal Theory: Foundations and Frontiers*, (Cambridge University Press, 2022): 174–195.

> [m]uch feminist international legal scholarship presents itself as being in conversation with the mainstream of international law … [t]his conversation is, however, almost completely one sided … It is very hard to find any response from international legal scholars to feminist questions and critiques; feminist scholarship is an optional extra, a decorative frill on the edge of the discipline.[10]

Charlesworth therefore continues that, while some scholars occasionally reference feminism in the 'whispers'[11] of their work in an attempt to show that they are 'broadminded' or 'have kept up with their reading', in the end, feminist ideas are 'almost never treated seriously; they are not acknowledged, debated or refuted'.[12] Work that does critique feminist scholarship tends to dismiss and disparage it for doing precisely what it aims to do; critiquing traditional international law and its claim to objectivity.[13] All in all, while international lawyers now seem willing to 'tolerate feminists at their side' they mostly do so as long as they do not have to change '*what* they do or *how* they do it'.[14]

This book challenges the way that feminist approaches are categorised by the majority of international lawyers as an optional add on or as a "niche" field. Rather, by directly engaging with core issues of general international law, including the regulation of military technologies and international environmental law, I show how feminist approaches, and specifically posthuman feminism, can provide central insights for analysing *all* areas of international law.

In contrast to the response of international legal scholarship, non-governmental organisations (NGOs) and international institutions have taken up the feminist

---

10 Hilary Charlesworth, 'Talking to Ourselves? Feminist Scholarship in International Law,' in Sari Kouvo and Zoe Pearson (eds.), *Feminist Perspectives on Contemporary International Law: Between Resistance and Compliance?* (Hart, 2014): 17–32, p. 17–18.

11 Hilary Charlesworth, 'Cries and Whispers: Responses to Feminist Scholarship in International Law,' *Nordic Journal of International Law* (1996) 65: 557–568.

12 Charlesworth, above note 10, p. 18.

13 Charlesworth, above note 11. See also; Hilary Charlesworth, 'Feminist Critiques of International Law and Their Critics,' *Third World Legal Studies* (1995) 13(1): 1–16. For examples of these critiques, see; Fernando R. Tesón, 'Feminism and International Law: A Reply,' *Virginia Journal of International Law* (1992–1993) 33: 647–684; Aaron Xavier Fellmeth, 'Feminism and International Law: Theory, Methodology, and Substantive Reform,' *Human Rights Quarterly* (2000) 22(3): 658–733.

14 Buss and Manji, above note 7, p. 3. Emphasis is the authors' own. See also, Charlesworth, Heathcote and Jones, above note 8. While Charlesworth's critique remains largely true in the contemporary, there are, however, two notable recent exceptions to the failure of international legal scholarship to engage with feminist perspectives, these being a chapter on 'Feminism' by Andrea Bianchi in his book *International Law Theories*, and a chapter on feminist approaches to international law in the updated second edition of B.S. Chimni's book, *International Law and the World Order*. See: Andrea Bianchi, 'Feminism,' in *International Law Theories: An Inquiry into Different Ways of Thinking*, (Oxford University Press, 2017): 183–204; B.S. Chimni, 'Feminist Approaches to International Law: The Work of Hilary Charlesworth and Christine Chinkin,' *International Law and the World Order: A Critique of Contemporary Approaches*, (Cambridge University Press, 2nd edn, 2017): 358–439.

mantle with more enthusiasm.[15] As Janet Halley argues, '[F]eminists now walk the halls of power'.[16] However, this by no means applies to all feminists or feminisms;[17] there has been a 'selective engagement' with feminist ideas by institutions.[18] Feminist voices in institutions are usually associated with and heard only when discussing issues of representation and sexual violence, with occasional reference to women's lived experiences beyond this. Feminist critiques of core international legal issues, such as the feminist work mentioned above on the law of treaties or the concept of the sovereign state, have not been adopted in the same manner.[19] This limited take-up by institutions has, in turn, impacted upon scholarship. Most contemporary feminist scholarship in international law now focuses on one of four themes: women's participation and representation, the recognition of women's human rights, sexual violence in conflict and the development of the Women, Peace and Security agenda. While these themes are each important, they lie within shallower layers of the excavational dig. It is evident that these are themes that best fit existing institutional agendas and therefore the power to challenge those agendas is limited. Feminist perspectives which analyse issues of international law outside of these frames remain peripheral.

There have, of course, always been feminist scholars whose work has focused on a broader array of topics outside issues of representation and women's lived experiences, focusing on the deeper layers of the feminist excavational dig and often drawing on gender theories from outside the law to inform their work. Notable examples include Ratna Kapur's and Vasuki Nesiah's work on postcolonial feminist approaches,[20] Anne Orford's work on the gendered narratives of humanitarian intervention,[21] Gina Heathcote's work on the law on the use of force[22] and on structural bias feminism,[23] Yoriko Otomo's feminist psychoanalytic analysis of state sovereignty,[24] Dianne Otto's work on dismantling the gender

---

15 Charlesworth, above note 10, p. 18, 20.

16 Janet Halley, 'Introducing Governance Feminism,' in Janet Halley et al., *Governance Feminism: An Introduction*, (Minnesota University Press, 2018): ix–xxi, p. ix.

17 As Halley herself qualifies. See: Ibid., p. ix.

18 Kerry Rittich, 'The Future of Law and Development: Second Generation Reforms and the Incorporation of the Social,' *Michigan Journal of International Law* (2004) 26(1): 199–243, p. 233.

19 This is a point also made by Chimni. See; Chimni, above note 14, p. 359.

20 See, for example: Ratna Kapur, *Gender, Alterity and Human Rights: Freedom in a Fishbowl*, (Edward Elgar, 2018); Ratna Kapur, 'The Tragedy of Victimization Rhetoric: Resurrecting the "Native" Subject in International/Post-Colonial Feminist Legal Politics,' *Harvard Human Rights Journal* (2002) 15(1): 1–38; Vasuki Nesiah, 'The Ground Beneath Her Feet: TWAIL Feminisms,' in Antony Anghie et al. (eds.), *The Third World and International Order*, (Brill, 2003): 133–143.

21 Anne Orford, 'Muscular Humanitarianism: Reading the Narratives of the New Interventionism,' *European Journal of International Law* (1999) 10(4): 679–711.

22 Heathcote, above note 5.

23 Gina Heathcote, *Feminist Dialogues on International Law: Successes, Tensions, Futures*, (Oxford University Press, 2019).

24 Otomo, above note 2.

binary[25] and Irini Papanicolopulu's edited collection which provides a gender analysis of the law of the sea,[26] among others.[27] While feminist approaches, as I have argued, have been mischaracterised by the mainstream of international law, feminist approaches provide unique insights into how international law operates and how it can be re-thought. It is thereby in the vein of authors such as these that this monograph is written, arguing that feminist approaches can be used to analyse all areas of international law, including, as per the focus of this monograph, international environmental law and the regulation of new and emerging military technologies.

Feminist Approaches to the Environment and Military Technologies in International Law

Given the mischaracterisation of feminist approaches to international law that I described above, the regulation of military technologies and international environmental law are not fields that are generally associated with such approaches. However, there have been some feminist international legal engagements with both these fields. As such, this book seeks to add to this existing scholarship. In this section, I provide an outline of the scholarship in these two areas before explaining what this book adds to each in turn.

As the climate crisis and environmental degradation become ever more urgent issues, feminist international lawyers have begun to focus with greater urgency on international environmental law and the need to apply feminist analyses. Most of this work has also been limited or shaped by institutional agendas, focusing either

---

25 See, for example: Dianne Otto, 'Queering Gender [Identity] in International Law,' *Nordic Journal of Human Rights* (2015) 33(4): 299–318; Dianne Otto, 'International Human Rights Law: Towards Rethinking Sex/Gender Dualism,' in Margaret Davies and Vanessa E. Munro (eds.), *The Ashgate Research Companion to Feminist Legal Theory*, (Routledge, 2013): 197–216.

26 Irini Papanicolopulu (ed.), *Gender and the Law of the Sea*, (Brill, 2019). While some chapters in this book focus more on women's lived experiences and issues of representation, there are other chapters which use gender, less to focus on women's lives and more to interrogate the mainstream legal framework and its epistemic basis. In particular, see: Loveday Hodson, 'Mermaids and Utopias: The High Seas as Feminist Space?' in Irini Papanicolopulu (ed.), *Gender and the Law of the Sea*, (Brill, 2019): 122–143; Liesbeth Lijnzaard, 'The UN Fish Sticks Agreement as a Metaphor, or the Law of the Sea as a Gendered Process,' in Irini Papanicolopulu (ed.), *Gender and the Law of the Sea*, (Brill, 2019): 149–161; Gina V. Heathcote, 'Feminism and the Law of the Sea: A Preliminary Inquiry,' in Irini Papanicolopulu (ed.), *Gender and the Law of the Sea*, (Brill, 2019): 83–105; Alice Ollino, 'Feminism, Nature and the Post-Human: Towards a Critical Analysis of the International Law of the Sea Governing Marine Living Resources Management,' in Irini Papanicolopulu (ed.), *Gender and the Law of the Sea*, (Brill, 2019): 204–228.

27 See, for example: Loveday Hodson and Troy Lavers (eds.), *Feminist Judgments in International Law*, (Bloomsbury, 2019).

The 2019 *Research Handbook of Feminist Engagement with International Law* can also be seen as part of this phenomenon, with many chapters, again, focusing on issue pertaining to women's lives but with a few chapters focusing on different issues, such as climate change or the field of global constitutionalism. See: Susan Harris Rimmer and Kate Ogg (eds.), *Research Handbook on Feminist Engagement with International Law*, (Edward Elgar, 2019).

on the need to include women and gender issues further in decision-making processes[28] or on the impacts of environmental degradation on women's lives.[29] While
these forms of inclusion are vitally important, with women's experiences of environmental issues such as climate change having been side-lined for far too long
in global debates on the environment, this is not the vein in which this book is
written. My argument is that feminist approaches can be used to analyse all areas of
international law, and not just areas that pertain directly to women's lives. Feminist
approaches can, I argue, be used to challenge the assumptions underpinning international law.

There is, however, an increasing body of work that focuses less on environmental
impacts and women's lives and more on challenging the masculinist underpinnings
of international environmental law.[30] For example, Katie Woolaston argues that
international law treats wildlife as a commodity, calling for feminist theories of relationality to be used to underly this field instead.[31] In turn, Anne Rochette argues
that the gendered difference in the value given to 'hard' as compared to 'soft' law
in international law, and the fact that most international environmental law agreements are consensual and thus deemed to be 'soft' law, means that their 'formal legal
status is often devalued' within this gendered system.[32] She argues that this ensures
that any move to tackle the root causes of environmental issues are 'off-set by the
much "harder" legal recognition of a state's sovereign right to exploit its resources'.[33] Heathcote, focusing on the Law of the Sea, a separate field of international
law though one that also tackles issues of environmental concern, draws specifically
on posthuman feminism to begin to question the prioritisation of human interests

28 See, for example: Keina Yoshida, 'The Protection of the Environment: A Gendered Analysis,'
    Goettingen Journal of International Law (2020) 10(1): 283–305; Rowena Maguire, 'Gender, Climate
    Change and the United Nations Framework Convention on Climate Change,' in Susan Harris
    Rimmer and Kate Ogg (eds.), *Research Handbook on Feminist Engagement with International
    Law*, (Edward Elgar, 2019): 63–80; Anne Rochette, 'Transcending the Conquest of Nature
    and Women: A Feminist Perspective on International Environmental Law,' in Doris Buss and
    Ambreena Manji (eds.), *International Law: Modern Feminist* Approaches, (Hart, 2005): 203–235;
    Karen Lesley Morrow, 'Tackling Climate Change and Gender Justice – Integral; not Optional,'
    Oñati Socio-Legal Series (2021) 11(1): 207–230; Carol Cohn and Claire Duncanson, 'Women,
    Peace and Security in a Changing Climate,' *International Feminist Journal of Politics* (2020) 22(5):
    742–762.
29 See, for example: Maguire, Ibid.; Rochette, Ibid.; Rowena Maguire and Bridget Lewis,
    'Women, Human Rights and the Global Climate Regime,' *Journal of Human Rights and the
    Environment* (2018) 9(1): 51–67; Jody M. Prescott, *Armed Conflict, Women and Climate Change*,
    (Routledge, 2019).
30 Linda A. Malone, 'Environmental Justice Reimagined through Human Security and Post-
    Modern Ecological Feminism: A Neglected Perspective on Climate Change,' *Fordham
    International Law Journal* (2015) 38(5):1445–1472.
31 Katie Woolaston, 'Wildlife and International Law: Can Feminism Transform Our Relationship
    with Nature?' in Susan Harris Rimmer and Kate Ogg (eds.), *Research Handbook on Feminist
    Engagement with International Law*, (Edward Elgar, 2019): 44–62.
32 Rochette, above note 28, p. 204.
33 Ibid.

in the Law of the Sea.[34] Likewise, Alice Ollino draws on posthuman feminism to argue that the regulation of marine living resources is anthropocentric and thereby systematically 'reinforces patterns of ecological degradation'.[35] Furthermore, scholars such as Anna Grear, Dianne Otto and myself have begun to bring posthuman feminism to bear on questions of environmental law, drawing links between the marginalisation of gendered, raced and classed human subjects and the exploitation of the environment.[36]

While the latter examples of the use of posthuman feminism represent an emerging shift in feminist approaches to environmental law issues, much of the feminist work on international environmental law either focuses, as noted, on women's participation or their vulnerabilities. This book shifts that focus. Instead, I ask what deeper excavations of feminist theory, and specifically posthuman feminism, can bring to thinking through some of the core environmental challenges of our times, including climate change and environmental degradation. This is done in particular in Chapters 4 and 5, where I incorporate queer theories of the nonhuman into my posthuman feminist frame to challenge the anthropocentric norms that underly international environmental law.

The other key topic of focus in this book is the regulation of military technologies. Feminist international lawyers have previously engaged with questions of international law and technology, from the use of technology to store and distribute information and collect evidence,[37] to challenges in relation to how big data is used in gendered ways in refugee management.[38] Interestingly, however, one of the strongest feminist international legal engagements with technology has been within the context of armed conflict, where posthuman feminism has carved out a foothold. Posthuman feminism has informed scholarships analysing drone warfare,[39] questioning the human subject of international humanitarian law,[40] and analysing the gendered use of exoskeletons on the battlefield.[41] There has, however, as far as I

---

34 Heathcote, above note 26.

35 Ollino, above note 26.

36 Emily Jones and Dianne Otto, Thinking through Anthropocentrism in International Law: Queer Theory, Posthuman Feminism and the Postcolonial, LSE Women, Peace and Security blog (January 2020); Dianne Otto and Anna Grear, 'International Law, Social Change and Resistance: A Conversation Between Professor Anna Grear (Cardiff) and Professorial Fellow Dianne Otto (Melbourne),' *Feminist Legal Studies* (2018) 26: 351–363.

37 Clare Brown, 'The Use of ICTs in Conflict and Peacebuilding: A Feminist Analysis,' *Australian Feminist Law Journal* (2018) 44(1): 137–153.

38 Kristin Bergtora Sandvik, 'Technology, Dead Male Bodies, and Feminist Recognition: Gender ICT Harm,' *Australian Feminist Law Journal* (2018) 44(1): 49–69.

39 See, for example: Lauren Wilcox, 'Embodying Algorithmic War: Gender, Race and the Posthuman in Warfare,' *Security Dialogue* (2016) 48(1): 1–18; Lauren Wilcox, 'Drone warfare and the making of bodies out of place,' *Critical Studies on Security* (2015) 3(1): 127–131.

40 Matilda Arvidsson, 'Targeting, Gender, and International Posthumanitarain Law and Practice: Framing the Question of the Human in International Humanitarian Law,' *Australian Feminist Law Journal* (2018) 44(1): 9–28.

41 Gina Heathcote, 'War's Perpetuity: Disabled Bodies of War and the Exoskeleton of Equality,' *Australian Feminist Law Journal* (2018) 44(1): 71–91.

am aware, not yet been an attempt to understand what a posthuman feminist analysis could add to debates on legal change. This book, through its critique of mainstream debates on lethal autonomous weapons systems (Chapter 2), and its discussion of providing posthuman feminist regulatory solutions for military technologies (Chapter 3), exemplifies, not only how posthuman feminism can be used to critically analyse existing law, but also how it can be used to design and foster legal change.

Feminist approaches to international law have been mischaracterised as pertaining solely to issues of women's experiences of discrimination and their lack of representation in decision-making. This book, through its deeper excavation of mainstream issues of international law, rebuts this mischaracterisation, arguing that feminist theories can be used to analyse and can provide a unique perspective on multiple areas of international law, including those areas that do not seemingly directly pertain to women's lives. In the next section, I turn to define posthuman feminism in further detail.

Posthuman Feminism

This monograph will be of interest, not only to international lawyers and legal theorists, including feminist legal theorists, but also to those interested in posthuman theory and posthuman feminism (more on the differences between the two below). While posthuman theory has developed rapidly across many disciplines over the past decade (albeit primarily, but not solely, in the humanities), much of this scholarship remains theoretical: there is little work that seeks to *apply* posthuman theory, with some of the scholarship on posthuman pedagogies, fashion studies and art perhaps providing the best examples of exceptions.[42] International law, however, is inherently tied to the material conditions of the world. By applying posthuman feminism to international law and seeking posthuman feminist solutions to international legal problems, this monograph adds substantially to the field of posthuman theory, providing an example of how these theories can be applied to shape practice.

Posthuman feminist theory sits at the convergence between post-humanism and post-anthropocentrism, seeking to dismantle hierarchies of privilege between humans, such as gender, race and class (post-humanism), a well as the idea that the human sits in hierarchical supremacy over other subjects – including the environment and nonhumans (post-anthropocentrism).[43] Posthuman feminist theory stretches 'in multiple, rhizomic and tentacular directions',[44] bringing critiques of humanism as

---

42 See, for example: Carol A. Taylor and Annouchka Bayley (eds.), *Posthumanism and Higher Education*, (Palgrave Macmillan, 2019): Carola A. Taylor and Christina Hughes (eds.), *Posthuman Research Practices in Education*, (Palgrave Macmillan, 2016); Oron Catts, 'Biological Arts/Living Arts,' in Rosi Braidotti and Maria Hlavajova (eds.), *Posthuman Glossary*, (Bloomsbury, 2018): 66–68; Anneke Smelik, 'Wearable Technology,' in Rosi Braidotti and Maria Hlavajova (eds.), *Posthuman Glossary*, (Bloomsbury, 2018): 455–458.

43 This is the definition Braidotti uses throughout her work on the posthuman. See, for example, Rosi Braidotti, *Posthuman Feminism*, (Polity Press, 2022).

44 Ibid., p. 6.

found, for example, in intersectional feminist theory, postcolonial theory, queer theory and critical disability studies,[45] together and alongside fields such as critical animal and environmental studies and science and technology studies.[46] Situated at the conjunction of these areas, posthuman feminism provides a critique of the exclusionary nature of the elite masculinist (so-called human) subject situated at the centre of western philosophy (and international law). I thereby use posthuman feminism, following Rosi Braidotti, as 'both a marker of present conditions and as a navigational tool'.[47] Posthuman feminism is used in this book as an interdisciplinary (or postdisciplinary[48]) method, bringing multiple areas of study together to challenge the exclusionary humanism and anthropocentrism upheld by and through international law.

Given that interdisciplinarity is a central component of posthuman feminism, while this book speaks most directly to international law, it draws on international law and feminist approaches to it alongside work from philosophy, science and technology studies, queer and feminist theories, marine biology, postcolonial and critical race theories, computer science, critical disability studies, cultural and media

45 For examples on some of the literatures in these fields that best speak to (or sit within) posthumanism, see:On intersectional feminism: Ibid.; Cecilia Åsberg and Rosi Braidotti (eds.), *A Feminist Companion to the Posthumanities*, (Springer International, 2018); Stacy Alaimo, *Bodily Natures: Science, Environment, and the Material Self*, (Indiana University Press, 2010); Stacy Alaimo and Susan Heckman (eds.), *Material Feminisms*, (Indiana University Press, 2008); Karen Barad, 'Posthumanist Performativity: Toward an Understanding of How Matter Comes to Matter,' *Signs* (2003) 28(3): 801–831; Donna Haraway, *Simians, Cyborgs and Women: The Reinvention of Nature*, (Routledge, 1991).

　　On critical race studies, the postcolonial and posthumanism: Zakiyyah Iman Jackson, 'Animal: New Directions in the Theorization of Race and Posthumanism,' *Feminist Studies* (2013) 29(3): 669–685; Ramon Amaro, 'Afrofuturism,' in Rosi Braidotti and Maria Hlavajova (eds.), *Posthuman Glossary*, (Bloomsbury, 2018); Simone Bignall and Daryle Rigney, 'Indigeneity, Posthumanism and Nomad Thought: Transforming Colonial Ecologies,' in Rosi Braidotti and Simone Bignall (eds.), *Posthuman Ecologies*, (Rowman & Littlefield, 2019): 159–182.

　　On queer theory: Noreen Giffney and Myra J. Hird (eds.), *Queering the Non/Human* (Routledge, 2008); Dana Luciano and Mel Y. Chen, 'Has the Queer even been Human?,' *GLQ: A Journal of Lesbian and Gay Studies* (2015) 21(203): 183–207.

　　On critical disability studies: Dan Goodley, Rebecca Lawthom and Katherine Runswick-Cole, 'Posthuman Disability Studies,' *Subjectivity* (2014) 7: 342–361; Heathcote, above note 41.

46 For examples on some of the literatures in these fields that best speak to (or sit within) posthumanism, see:

　　On critical environmental studies/posthumanism: Stacy Alaimo, *Exposed: Environmental Politics and Pleasures in Posthuman Times*, (Minnesota University Press, 2016).

　　On STS: Donna Haraway, 'A Cyborg Manifesto,' in David Bell and Barbara M. Kennedy (eds.), *The Cybercultures Reader*, (Routledge, 2001): 291–324.

47 Braidotti, above note 43, p. 3.

48 Cecilia Åsberg and Rosi Braidotti, 'Feminist Posthumanities: An Introduction' in Cecilia Åsberg and Rosi Braidotti (eds.), *A Feminist Companion to the Posthumanities*, (Springer International, 2018): 1–22, p. 15; Nina Lykke, 'Passionately Posthuman: From Feminist Disidentifications to Postdisciplinary Posthumanities,' in Cecilia Åsberg and Rosi Braidotti (eds.), *A Feminist Companion to the Posthumanities*, (Springer International, 2018): 23–33; Cecilia Åsberg, 'The Timely Ethics of Posthumanist Gender Studies,' *Feministische Studien* (2013) 31(1): 7–12, p. 10. On posthuman interdisciplinarity and transversality, see: Rosi Braidotti and Matthew Fuller, 'The Posthumanities in an Era of Unexpected Consequences,' *Theory, Culture & Society* (2019) 36(6) 3–29.

studies, Indigenous onto-epistemologies, critical legal theory, political science and beyond. By bringing a variety of critical perspectives to bear on the topics discussed, innovative analyses and solutions start to take shape. However, working across disciplines comes with its own challenges, with different disciplines sometimes providing contrasting or contradictory analyses of the same problem. This is best exemplified in Chapter 3, where I propose regulatory alternatives to address the challenges posed by new military technologies. My discussion here becomes conceptually split down the middle, with the first half seeking posthuman feminist solutions that can be forged within existing international legal and institutional frames, and the second half looking beyond the law to Indigenous, critical disability and feminist approaches to artificial intelligence (AI) design. This is part of a wider tension that runs throughout the book: the tension between what feminist international lawyers have termed resistance and compliance.[49] This terminology describes the tension feminists face when working within the international legal system, seeking change from within, versus working beyond the constraints of that system to completely reimagine international law. This tension permeates discussions throughout the book and is a topic I return to in detail in the concluding chapter.

I have chosen posthuman feminism as my central theoretical framework for two reasons. First, posthuman feminist theory, as outlined above, brings together multiple different areas of study, providing for a complex and integrated analysis of the structural underpinnings of international law. Second, posthuman feminist theory has a strong focus on environmental issues and on techno-scientific innovation. Broadly, in relation to the environment, posthuman feminism provides a framework to re-think anthropocentrism, bringing nonhuman and environmental concerns to the forefront of thought and insisting on the interconnections between humans, nonhuman subjects and matter.[50] In relation to science and technology, posthuman feminism challenges the idea that humans are somehow in charge of and separate from their innovations, highlighting how 'humans are entangled in intricate relationships with technology and science'.[51] Given these focal points, posthuman feminism provides a distinct set of navigational tools for developing a critical analysis of key emerging issues in international law in relation to both the environment and technological innovation.

Positioning my analysis in posthuman feminism enables me to engage with both feminist approaches to international law and the wider field of posthuman studies. Posthuman theory now has many branches, with the term 'posthuman' having become an 'umbrella term' for a diverse range of theories including transhumanism, new materialisms, anti-humanisms, 'agential realism'[52] and the 'ahuman',[53] among

---

49 Sari Kouvo and Zoe Pearson (eds.), *Feminist Perspectives on Contemporary International Law: Between Resistance and Compliance?* (Hart, 2014).
50 Åsberg and Braidotti, above note 48.
51 Ibid., p. 7.
52 Karen Barad, *Meeting the Universe Halfway: Quantum Physics and the Entanglement of Matter and Meaning*, (Duke University Press, 2007).
53 Patricia MacCormack, *The Ahuman Manifesto: Activism for the End of the Anthropocene*, (Bloomsbury, 2020).

others. Braidotti outlines the various origins and strands of posthuman theory, identifying:

> three major strands in contemporary posthuman thought: the first comes from moral philosophy and develops a reactive form of the posthuman; the second, from science and technology studies, enforces an analytic form of the posthuman; and the third, from my own tradition of anti-humanist philosophies of subjectivity, proposes a critical post-humanism.[54]

I do not align myself with the first 'reactive' form of posthumanism that Braidotti describes. This strand is typified by scholars who defend humanism and reject its historical decline by looking at contemporary developments such as globalisation and technological advancement and using these phenomena to reinstate an updated form of liberalism.[55] I am nervous of any project that aims to reinstate liberal internationalism,[56] especially given the role liberal ideologies have played in perpetuating colonialism and other global inequalities.

Braidotti is also critical of the second strand of posthumanism which comes from science and technology studies, noting that this scholarship often upholds humanistic values with little critical analysis of the possible perils of doing do.[57] Transhumanism perhaps best exemplifies this mode of thought. While there are multiple transhumanisms, the differences between which are beyond the scope of this chapter,[58] transhumanism broadly seeks to move humans beyond their current physical limitations by drawing on a mixture of human-machine and biomedical enhancements. Transhumanism is a broad label which includes ideas such as attempts to prevent the aging process and creating stronger, faster and more efficient human beings.[59] Transhumanism sits, in many ways, in opposition to the posthuman stance I take in this monograph. Transhumanism seeks to perfect 'man,' make him [sic] faster, stronger, and unable to die.[60] This approach, which is based upon Enlightenment thought,[61] is a form of 'ultra-humanism',[62] reifying 'a particular normative version of humanity that enables distinctions between more or less worthy forms of life'.[63] In short, transhumanism contrasts to posthuman feminism in

---

54 Rosi Braidotti, *The Posthuman*, (Polity Press, 2013), p. 38.
55 Ibid., p. 38–39.
56 As is Braidotti. See: Ibid., p. 38–39.
57 Ibid., p. 42.
58 For a more detailed exploration of transhumanisms, see: Francesca Ferrando, *Philosophical Posthumanism*, (Bloomsbury, 2020), p. 31–33.
59 Nick Bostrom, 'In Defence of Posthuman Dignity,' *Bioethics* (2005), 19(3): 202–214. See also; Mark O'Connell, *To Be a Machine: Adventures Among Cyborgs, Utopians, Hackers and the Futurists Solving the Modest Problem of Death*, (Granta, 2017).
60 Though as Ferrando explains, there are forms of transhumanism which do seek to think more about social inequalities, such as democratic transhumanism. See: Ferrando, above note 58, p. 31–33.
61 Ibid., p. 32–34.
62 Ibid., p. 33.
63 Lauren Wilcox, 'Embodying …,' above note 39, p. 5.

that, not only does it ignore the inequalities between humans but, by seeking to create a super-human (masculinised) race, it strengthens these inequalities by creating two tiers of humanity, those with tech and those without.[64] It is no coincidence that the majority of transhumanists are white men from the global north.

The third stand of posthuman thought that Braidotti identifies is critical posthumanism. This is where I, like Braidotti, align my work and where posthuman feminism sits within the wider field of posthuman studies. This form of posthumanism seeks to dismantle the hierarchies upheld by both exclusionary humanism (i.e. the central focus in western thought on the white male subject) and anthropocentrism.[65] However, there are multiple strands of differing critical posthumanisms.[66] While I engage many strands of thought from within the critical posthumanities, I have chosen specifically to focus on posthuman feminism precisely because this body of work, unlike certain other strands of posthuman work, refuses to side-line the issue of inequalities between humans when focusing on the nonhuman. As outlined above, some forms of posthuman theory, such as transhumanism, uphold and even create new hierarchies between humans. There are other strands of posthuman thought that have similarly been critiqued. Some versions of new materialism, for example, which broadly seeks to challenge dominant understandings of subjectivity by stressing the force and agency of matter, has been subject to different, but related critiques.[67] The charge here is that, in seeking to re-centre matter (objects, the environment, etc), questions of epistemology can be side-lined, producing a theory of matter that, ultimately, thinks about matter alone, displacing important issues surrounding the inequalities that remain between humans.[68]

There are many examples where moves towards the nonhuman have worked to displace a focus on the inequalities between humans. Such moves treat the question of epistemology as *passé*, transcendence being (re)posed as found in the nonhuman other. This is one critique of transhumanism, as I outlined above, but other strands,

---

64 Calum Chace, *The Economic Singularity: Artificial Intelligence and the Death of Capitalism*, (Three Cs, 2016), p. 5.

65 Rosi Braidotti and Maria Hlavajova, 'Introduction,' in Rosi Braidotti and Maria Hlavajova (eds.), *The Posthuman Glossary*, (Bloomsbury, 2018): 1–14, p. 1. See also: Rosi Braidotti and Emily Jones, 'Critical Posthuman Theory,' in Rosi Braidotti, Emily Jones and Goda Klumbytė (eds.), *More Posthuman Glossary*, (Bloomsbury, forthcoming 2023): 28–30.

66 This is exemplified well by the *Posthuman Glossary* which contains over 160 entries, with the forthcoming *More Posthuman Glossary* containing over 60. See: Rosi Braidotti and Maria Hlavajova (eds.), *Posthuman Glossary*, (Bloomsbury, 2018); Rosi Braidotti, Emily Jones and Goda Klumbytė (eds.), *More Posthuman Glossary*, (Bloomsbury, forthcoming 2023).

67 See: Rosi Braidotti, 'A Theoretical Framework for the Critical Posthumanities,' *Theory, Culture & Society* (2019) 36(6): 31–61, p. 42–43; Simon Choat, 'Science, Agency and Ontology: A Historical Materialist Response to New Materialism,' *Political Studies* (2017) 66(4): 1027–1042; Alaimo, above note 45, p.178–188; Sheila Jasanoff, 'Future Imperfect: Science, Technology, and the Imaginations of Modernity,' in Sheila Jasanoff and Sang Hyun Kim (eds.), *Dreamscapes of Modernity: Sociotechnical Imaginaries and the Fabrication of Power*, (University of Chicago Press, 2015): 1–33, p. 17.

68 Braidotti, Ibid, p. 42–43.

such as object-orientated ontology (OOO),[69] likewise side-line central questions of epistemology. As scholars such as Rebekah Sheldon and Braidotti have noted,[70] in seeking to re-centre objects, OOO works to centre objects alongside an unquestioned human subject, that subject being white, male, Eurocentric, heterosexual and middle class. For critics, this neglect of epistemology thereby results in an inadequate account of how such perspectives apply in a world where inequalities between humans remain.[71] For example, Zakiyyah Iman Jackson warns against appeals to merely moving 'beyond the human,' arguing that such appeals, detached from the critiques of humanism made by black people, risk reinforcing racism and Eurocentric ideas of transcendentalism, asking '*Whose* conception of humanity are we moving beyond?'[72] Jackson thus concludes that 'any movement towards the nonhuman' must inherently be simultaneously 'a movement towards blackness, as blackness constitutes the very matter at hand'.[73]

However, not all strands of posthumanism can be fairly critiqued in this way. New materialist Jane Bennett, for example, consistently refuses to side-line the inequalities between humans in her work on vibrant matter.[74] Likewise feminist new materialism works explicitly to situate understandings of matter alongside and in relation to intersectional feminist analyses of the differences between humans.[75] Thus, as Sheldon argues, it is the displacement of epistemology as being a 'second-order representation' in OOO which contrasts starkly to the relational way feminist new materialism regards what Karen Barad has astutely termed 'onto-epistemology'.[76] On the other hand, posthuman feminist theory, in bringing together critiques of both humanism and anthropocentrism, ensures that the question of matter's significance can be thought without risking the displacement of important epistemological turns that have come about through feminist, queer, critical race, postcolonial and crip theory, among others. This move requires challenging the 'Universal (Hu) man' and its 'Eurocentric construction', this being a central tenet of the critical posthuman project.[77] Thus, as Braidotti notes, while it 'may be difficult for people who have never been considered socially and politically [and legally] fully human to adopt an affirmative relation to the posthuman predicament', including '[w]omen,

---

69 Which is sometimes classed as being part of the new materialist turn, sometimes not. Examples of OOO include: Ian Bogost, *Alien Phenomenology, or What's It Like to be a Thing?* (Minnesota University Press, 2012); Graham Harman, *Tool-Being: Heidegger and the Metaphysics of Objects*, (Open Court, 2002).

70 Braidotti, above note 67; Rebekah Sheldon, 'Form / Matter / Chora: Objected-Orientated Ontology and Feminist New Materialism,' in Richard Grusin (ed.), *The Nonhuman Turn* (Minnesota University Press, 2015): 193–222.

71 See: Braidotti, Ibid, p. 42–43; Choat, above note 67; Alaimo, above note 45, p. 178–188; Jasanoff, above note 67, p. 17.

72 Zakiyyah Iman Jackson, 'Outer Worlds: The Persistence of Race in Movement "Beyond the Human",' *GLQ: A Journal of Lesbian and Gay Studies* (2015) 21(2–3): 215–218, p. 215.

73 Ibid., p. 217.

74 See: Jane Bennett, *Vibrant Matter*, (Duke University Press, 2010).

75 Sheldon, above note 70.

76 Ibid., p. 196. On 'onto-epistemology', see: Barad, above note 52.

77 Lykke, above note 48, p. 26.

LGBTQ+ people, the colonized, Indigenous peoples, people of colour and a multitude of non-Europeans who historically have had to fight for the basic right to be considered and treated as human', this 'exclusionary notion of the human' is 'precisely what is challenged by' posthuman feminism.[78]

In this book, I read new materialism as part of my posthuman feminist convergence between post-anthropocentrism and post-humanism, although new materialism, which broadly seeks to re-situate the importance of matter in western thought, lies more squarely within post-anthropocentrism. I draw, however, on new materialism within the wider frame of posthuman feminist theory precisely to again ensure that critiques of humanism are not lost when undertaking a new materialist shift: leaning into posthuman feminist theory brings the question of who is seen as a subject and questions of matter together. While new materialism is used throughout the book, it comes to the fore more prominently in Chapters 4 and 5, where I discuss the implications of thinking matter and the environment as agentic for re-imagining international environmental law.

Posthuman feminism adds to the wider field of critical posthumanism.[79] Unfortunately, mainstream posthuman scholarship has neglected feminist theory, with critical posthumanism increasingly ignoring its feminist roots despite the fact that feminist theory was one of the precursors of the posthuman turn.[80] There is much to be learnt by engaging with feminist theory, including queer theory, as part of the posthuman turn. Posthuman feminism, through its deployment of key feminist theoretical interventions such as intersectionality, and through feminism's long engagement with critiques of humanism,[81] provides a holistic account of the multiple ways that exclusionary humanist and anthropocentric modes of thought centre a particular human subject, de-centring marginalised human subjects and nonhumans. As Braidotti argues:

> mainstream posthuman scholarship must make an effort to move beyond its self-referential insular tendencies and engage openly with feminist theories, including the minoritarian strands that may not be as central to the canonical Anglo-American tradition. Posthuman critical theories cannot continue to indulge in their masculinist and Eurocentric solipsism. It would be mutually beneficial if feminist theory and posthuman theory would exchange and dialogue more systematically.[82]

It is therefore this ethical commitment to de-centring the dominant human subject that makes posthuman feminism so central to my project of disrupting mainstream accounts of feminism in international law.[83]

---

78 Braidotti, above note 43, p. 6–7.
79 For more on defining posthuman feminism, see; Braidotti, Ibid.; Åsberg, above note 48.
80 Braidotti, Ibid.
81 Ibid.
82 Ibid., p. 7.
83 Rosi Braidotti, for example, argues that posthuman feminism disrupts mainstream feminist accounts, including liberal and socialist feminisms. See: Ibid., p. 6.

Posthuman Legal Theory

This is the first monograph to apply posthuman feminism, or posthuman theory for that matter, to international law. While scholarship on posthuman theory and international law has begun to emerge in an array of journal articles and book chapters, as I detail below, this monograph provides a more sustained analysis of how posthuman theories can be applied to analyse international law. It draws on theories which have been rarely or, in some cases, never applied to international law, this perhaps being best exemplified by Chapter 4's use of queer theories of the nonhuman to analyse international environmental law. Yet despite the emerging nature of posthuman theory as applied to international law, posthuman legal theory, or legal materiality,[84] is now a fairly well-established field, although it is a relatively new one. In this section, I provide a brief overview of some of the core elements of posthuman legal theories before outlining the embryonic posthuman interventions in international law.

Posthuman legal theory, a term I am using to broadly encompass legal theories of materiality and the nonhuman, covers a broad array of subjects, from posthuman data[85] to military technologies[86] to environmental issues.[87] Key trends within this scholarship include: work that focuses on the agency and vibrancy of matter, voices that focus primarily on connections between the law and space, analyses of nonhuman subjects in the law and, finally, work on objects and the law.[88] While I briefly map each of these approaches below, it is important to note that these approaches often blend into one another, with scholars regularly using multiple forms of each approach in a text. The mapping below, therefore, is not an overview of distinct

---

84 See: Hyo Yoon Kang and Sara Kendall (eds.), Special Issue on Legal Materiality, *Law Text Culture* (2019b) 43: 1–293; Hyo Yoon Kang, 'Law's Materiality: Between Concrete Matters and Abstract Forms, or How Matter Becomes Material,' in Andreas Philippopoulos-Mihalopoulos (ed.), *Routledge Handbook for Law and Theory*, (Routledge, 2018): 453–474.

85 On posthuman data, see: Jannice Käll, 'The Materiality of Data as Property,' *Harvard International Law Journal Frontiers* (2020) 61: 1–11; Jannice Käll, 'A Posthuman Data Subject? The Right to be Forgotten and Beyond,' *German Law Journal* (2017) 18(5): 1145–1162.

86 On conflict and military technologies, see: Arvidsson, above note 40; Heathcote, above note 41; Emily Jones, 'A Posthuman-Xenofeminist Analysis of the Discourse on Autonomous Weapons Systems and Other Killing Machines,' *Australian Feminist Law Journal* (2018) 44(1): 93–118; Wilcox, 'Embodying …,' above note 39; Lauren Wilcox, 'Drones, Swarms and Becoming-Insect: Feminist Utopias and Posthuman Politics,' *Feminist Review* (2017) 116: 25–45.

87 See, for example: Anna Grear, '"Anthropocene, Capitalocene, Chthulucene": Re-encountering Environmental Law and Its "Subject" with Haraway and New Materialism,' in Louis J. Kotzé (ed.), *Environmental Law and Governance for the Anthropocene*, (Hart, 2017): 77–95; Emily Jones, 'Posthuman International Law and the Rights of Nature,' *Journal of Human Rights and the Environment* (2021) 12(0): 76–101; Sam Adelman, 'A Legal Paradigm Shift towards Climate Justice in the Anthropocene,' *Oñati Socio-Legal Series* (2021) 11(1): 44–68.

88 Similar categories are also drawn by Johnson, albeit in relation to legal materiality as applied to legal history. See: Tom Johnson, 'Legal History and The Material Turn,' in Markus D. Dubber and Christopher Tomlins (eds.), *The Oxford Handbook of Legal History*, (Oxford University Press, 2018): 497–514.

approaches but is, rather, an attempt to outline some of the ways people have begun to undertake posthuman analyses of the law.

As noted, one strand of work in the field of posthuman law and legal materiality addresses questions concerning how the law can better account for the agency of matter.[89] For example, Joanne Conaghan examines and finds hope in what new materialism can add to legal feminism.[90] The inherent yet invisible materiality of the law is central is here,[91] with scholarship broadly focusing on how materials come to matter.[92] For example, Margaret Davies draws on new materialisms and posthuman theory alongside feminist legal theory, legal geographies and socio-legal theory to ask the question: What is law?[93] Davies notes that the law relies on creating distinctions between objects and subjects. This means that, while the law does define objects, for instance through the regulation of property, 'humans remain as the sole source of law while objects are simply objects – passive Cartesian matter'.[94] Challenging this human centrism, Davies examines how material factors produce the law, noting the relationships between humans and matter and concluding that '*law is essentially material*'.[95]

A second strand of thought focuses on questions of law and space. Andreas Philippopoulos-Mihalopoulos, for example, analyses the link between the law and the material world, focusing on what he terms 'lawscapes', that is, the connection between law and space. Lawscapes, he argues, 'are constantly conditioned by each other, allowing one to emerge from within its connection to the other'.[96] This relationship, he continues, is not dialectical, as law and space continually fold into one another.[97] He gives the example of a no smoking sign which is a 'visibilisation of the law' in a certain space, as contrasted to the open space of an art gallery which performs an 'invisibilisation of the law'.[98] In both instances, law and space are entwined, albeit in different ways.[99] Philippopoulos-Mihalopoulos thereby calls for a focus on

89 See: Andreas Philippopoulos-Mihalopoulos, *Spatial Justice: Body, Lawscape, Atmosphere*, (Routledge, 2015); Gunther Teubner, 'Rights of Non-humans? Electronic Agents and Animals as New Actors in Politics and Law,' *Journal of Law and Society* (2006) 33: 497–521; Grear, above note 87; Oscar Guardiola-Rivera, 'Return of the Fetish: A Plea for a New Materialism,' *Law and Critique* (2007) 18: 275–307; Daniela Gandorfer, 'Introduction to Research Handbook on Law and Literature. What is your Power?' in Peter Goodrich and Daniela Gandorfer (eds.), *Research Handbook on Law and Literature*, (Edward Elgar, 2022): 1–13.

90 Joanna Conaghan, 'Feminism, Law and Materialism: Reclaiming the Tainted Realm,' in Margaret Davies and Vanessa Munro (eds.), *The Ashgate Research Companion to Feminist Legal Theory*, (Routledge, 2013): 31–50.

91 Alain Pottage, 'The Materiality of What?,' *Journal of Law and Society* (2012) 39: 167–183.

92 See also: Hyo Yoon Kang and Sara Kendall, 'Legal Materiality' in Simon Stern et al. (eds.), *The Oxford Handbook of Law and Humanities*, (Oxford University Press, 2019a): 21–38.

93 Margaret Davies, *Law Unlimited*, (Routledge, 2017).

94 Ibid., p. 67.

95 Ibid., p. 44 – author's own emphasis.

96 Philippopoulos-Mihalopoulos, above note 89, p. 4.

97 Ibid., p. 4.

98 Ibid., p. 4.

99 Ibid., p. 4.

spatial justice through the recognition of the multiple, competing and shared bodies, human and nonhuman, that occupy the same space at the same time. While his focus differs slightly from that of Davies, Philippopoulos-Mihalopoulos likewise notes the need for the law to better visibilise the role of nonhuman actants.[100]

A third strand focuses more squarely on law and the nonhuman agent, with questions arising around the legal status of animals,[101] of the environment[102] and of machines,[103] including questions about how machines and bodies interact through, for example, the bionic body, and how the law then responds to these bodies.[104] Work here tends to analyse both the status of the nonhuman in the law, while also seeking to recast these subjects through, for example, a focus on nonhuman rights.[105] This is an approach that has been taken up in some literature in international law[106] and is an approach I return to in more detail specifically in Chapters 4 and 5, where I discuss the rights of nature.

The fourth strand of posthuman legal scholarship is the reading of law through materials and objects.[107] These approaches focus on objects to understand the law, noting how objects are situated in legal relationships.[108] For example, James Leach examines the documents that record custom and Indigenous knowledge on the Rai Coast of Papua New Guinea. Leach notes the role documents have played in colonial governance while simultaneously examining how documents have also been used as a mode of resistance.[109] In a similar vein, Mahmoud Keshavarz and Amin Parsa situate military uniforms as central in legal relations, marking some bodies as targetable.[110] Another strand of thought within this field focuses on the evidential role of matter. For example, Kamari Maxine Clarke and Sara Kendall analyse how geospatial materials, such as satellite imagery, are conscripted as evidence in international criminal

---

100 Ibid., p. 5.
101 Yoriko Otomo and Edward Mussawir (eds.), *Law and the Question of the Animal*, (Routledge, 2013); Edward Mussawir, 'A Modification in the Subject of Right: Deleuze, Jurisprudence and the Diagram of Bees in Roman Law,' in Rosi Braidotti and Simone Bignall (eds.), *Posthuman Ecologies: Complexity and Process after Deleuze*, (Rowman & Littlefield, 2019): 243–263.
102 Jones, above note 87.
103 Teubner, above note 89; Jones, above note 86.
104 Sabrina Gilani, 'Bionic Bodies, Posthuman Violence and the Disembodied Criminal Subject,' *Law and Critique* (2021) 32: 171–193.
105 Jones, above note 87.
106 Ibid.
107 See, for example: Andreas Philippopoulos-Mihalopoulos, 'Flesh of the Law: Material Legal Metaphors,' *Journal of Law and Society* (2016) 43: 45–65; Kathryn McNeilly, 'Documents and Time in International Human Rights Law Monitoring: Artefacts, Objects, Things,' in Kathryn McNeilly and Ben Warwick (eds.), *The Time and Temporalities of International Human Rights Law*, (Bloomsbury, 2022): 85–102.
108 Jessie Hohmann and Daniel Joyce, *International Law's Objects*, (Oxford University Press, 2018).
109 James Leach, 'Documents against 'Knowledge'; immanence and transcendence and approaching legal materials,' *Law Text Culture* (2019) 23: 16–39.
110 Mahmoud Keshavarz and Amin Parsa, 'Targeted by Persuasion: Military Uniforms and the Legal Matter of Killing in War,' *Law Text Culture* (2019) 23: 223–239.

trials.[111] A similar theme comes through in some of the work of the forensic architecture group, with Susan Schuppli, for example, examining the processes and procedures through which matter, such a photographs and videos, comes to bear witness.[112]

As I noted above, while I have identified four strands of posthuman law, these approaches often overlap, with scholars regularly adopting several approaches at the same time. These approaches are not distinct but, rather, represent different ways of doing posthuman legal theory. In this book, I similarly draw on all of the above approaches at different moments. However, I focus primarily on issues of the human and nonhuman and the relationships between the two, including the agency of matter (the first and third strands of legal materialism outlined above), and less on questions of space and of objects in international law. There are a few reasons for this focus. The first is related to my posthuman feminist framework. Posthuman feminism has focused more squarely on questions of the nonhuman and the agency of matter and less on objects and space. The second reason, however, is more personal. For me, focusing on the recasting of human–nonhuman relations and thinking about agency differently provides both a theoretical starting point as well as, potentially, and as I explore in this book, a model for re-thinking how international lawyers "do" (international) law. I wanted this book to focus, not just on the theoretical, but also on thinking through how international law may be imagined and practised otherwise. I found that these approaches best served this aim precisely because they call for a recasting of the law itself.

Another element that distinguishes the present text from the above-mentioned works is its focus on feminism. With the exception of Davies and Conaghan and, to a lesser extent, Philippopoulos-Mihalopoulos, the above-mentioned texts do not focus on feminist theory nor do they reference feminism. This is concerning. As I noted above, Braidotti warns that the posthuman turn is erasing its feminist theoretical origins,[113] and it seems that the field of legal materiality is following suit. In this book, I centre intersectional feminist ideas throughout as part of my posthuman feminist framework, working to re-centre feminism within legal engagements with posthumanism and refusing to side-line the feminist origins of the posthuman turn.

This book also seeks to contribute to the broader field of posthuman engagements with the law through its focus on practice. While the above-mentioned scholarship on posthuman theory and law has been successful in challenging the humanist and anthropocentric underpinnings of legal frames, the application of these theories to the law itself – to legal practice – is the next step that needs to be taken. This monograph, through its application of posthuman feminism to international law, uses this body of thought, not only to analyse the law, but also to think through concrete legal solutions to contemporary challenges. This book is therefore a call to

---

111 Kamari Maxine Clarke and Sara Kendall, 'The Beauty ... is that It Speaks for Itself': Geospatial Materials as Evidentiary Matters,' *Law Text Culture* (2019) 23: 91–118.
112 Susan Schuppli, *Material Witness: Media, Forensics, Evidence*, (MIT Press, 2020). See also: Helene Kazan, 'The Architecture of Slow, Structural, and Spectacular Violence and the Poetic Testimony of War,' *Australian Feminist Law Journal* (2018) 44(1): 119–136.
113 Braidotti, above note 43.

apply posthuman feminist legal theory to re-think the law beyond the realm of legal theory, a call that I hope will continue to expand well beyond the pages of this book.

Posthuman Theory and International Law

While posthuman legal theory is now a thriving field, the take-up of posthuman ideas in international law remains relatively new. Publications in this area tend to focus on specific areas of international law and are consequently harder to distinguish by approach. There are, however, a few exceptions where scholars have focused more generally on international law as opposed to a specific field. I will discuss these more general posthuman interventions before turning to those in specific fields, notably the laws of armed conflict, international environmental law and human rights law. Unlike the posthuman engagements within legal theory outlined in the previous section, posthuman engagements within international law often draw on feminist ideas.[114]

A recent article by Jessie Hohmann begins to explore the implications of new materialism for international law in general. Hohmann highlights the materiality of the world, from climate change to the poor material living conditions of much of the world's population, arguing that it is time to question Enlightenment ideas which position 'humans as sole agents, acting over a passive nature'.[115] Hohmann calls for new materialist insights into international law, recognising 'wider views of agency that stress the relation of all entities, the entanglements between and among human and non-human, and the vibrancy of matter'.[116] Writing to map an emerging research agenda, Hohmann identifies several key areas where she sees potential in applying new materialist theory to international law, including new technologies (including military technologies, AI and automation),[117] international legal work on contingency and international law[118] and scholarship on commodification and international law.[119] Serendipitously, this book engages in each of these areas, with discussions of military technologies in Chapters 2 and 3, its general focus on (re-) imagining international law throughout, and its efforts to challenge the commodification of international law, particularly when thinking about extractive capitalism and the environment in Chapters 1, 4 and 5.

Another text that engages more generally with international law is *International Law's Objects*, a collection edited by Daniel Joyce and Hohmann. This text fits squarely into the law and objects strand of posthuman scholarship discussed in the previous section, shining a light on how objects shape and are shaped by

---

114 See, for example: Jones, above note 86; Arvidsson, above note 40; Heathcote, above note 41.
115 Jessie Hohmann, 'Diffuse Subjects and Dispersed Power: New Materialist Insights and Cautionary Lessons for International Law,' *Leiden Journal of International Law* (2021) 34: 585–606, p. 586.
116 Ibid., p. 587.
117 Ibid., p. 597.
118 Ibid., p. 604.
119 Ibid., p. 605.

international law.[120] In a similar vein, Salter has edited two volumes that focus on how ordinary objects shape our imagination of the international.[121]

Daniel R. Quiroga-Villamarín has also written more generally about international law and posthuman ideas. He has published three articles on the theme of legal materialism and international law. Two of these sit squarely in the law and objects literature. The first explores how the 'material turn' and, specifically, readings of law and objects, can contribute to the field of international legal histories,[122] while the second article focuses on the materiality of shipping containers, situating these containers as central to debates within the International Organisation for Standardisation (ISO) in the late fifties and early sixties.[123] The third article focuses less on law and objects, providing instead a comprehensive overview of the wider material turn in social theory, concluding that these theories may prove useful for analysing international law. Quiroga-Villamarín warns, however, against the conflation of different forms of new materialism, noting their differing ontologies, politics and methodologies, echoing a concern I raised earlier when defining posthuman feminism.[124] Overall, Quiroga-Villamarín provides insight into how the field of law and objects can be used to develop international legal histories, while also finding promise in applying theories of legal materiality to international law more generally.

A key discussion that is emerging in international legal engagements with posthumanism centres around a fear that "old" materialism is being left behind. Quiroga-Villamarín, for example, expresses a concern that the term 'new materialism' risks hiding the 'enormous inheritance that these new movements have from the "old" materialists'.[125] Hohmann expresses a similar concern, arguing that new materialist critiques need to be brought into conversation with older materialisms, such as Marxism and TWAIL (third world approaches to international law), to ensure that global inequalities are not side-lined in new materialist analyses.[126] These fears map onto some of the wider critiques I outlined above which call into question the depoliticising nature of some strands of posthuman thought. While these fears may be well placed when thinking about, for example, the application of transhumanism or OOO to international law, I do not share these fears when it comes to the application of posthuman feminism to international law. This is

---

120 Hohmann and Joyce, above note 108.

121 Mark B. Salter (ed.), *Making Things International 1: Circuits and Motion*, (Minnesota University Press, 2015); Mark B. Salter (ed.), *Making Things International 2: Catalysts and Reactions*, (Minnesota University Press, 2016).

122 Daniel Ricardo Quiroga-Villamarín, 'Beyond Texts? Towards a Material Turn in the Theory and History of International Law,' *Journal of the History of International Law* (2020) 23: 466–500.

123 Daniel R. Quiroga-Villamarín, 'Normalising Global Commerce: Containerisation, Materiality, and Transnational Regulation (1956–68),' *London Review of International Law* (2020) 8(3): 457–477.

124 Daniel R. Quiroga-Villamarín, 'Domains of Objects, Rituals of Truth: Mapping Intersections between International Legal History and the New Materialisms,' *International Politics Reviews* (2020) 8: 129–151.

125 Ibid., p. 130.

126 Hohmann, above note 115.

because posthuman feminism, as outlined above, *must* and *does* engage with postcolonial and Marxist theories, as well as feminist and queer theories, critical analyses of disability, Indigenous onto-epistemologies and much more, through its intersectional feminist alignment. This book, in turn, likewise engages these theories throughout as part of its posthuman feminist framework.

Beyond the above-mentioned texts, posthuman engagements with international law have largely emerged in conversation with specific fields of international law, namely the laws of armed conflict, international environmental law and human rights. In the following paragraphs, I will provide a brief outline of each of these fields before turning to the last and final section of this Introduction which outlines the structure of the book.

A key voice working on posthuman engagements with the laws of armed conflict is Matilda Arvidsson. Arvidsson applies posthuman feminism to argue that international humanitarian law, the law that regulates conflict, needs to pay more attention to the material and digital conditions of warfare, asking who, and what the 'human' at the centre of international humanitarian law is. She calls for a greater understanding of what she terms *posthumanitarian international law*.[127] Elsewhere, Arvidsson has analysed swarming drones, seeking to disrupt transhuman desires in warfare by calling for a posthuman politics of ontological becoming to be applied to understandings of contemporary warfare.[128] Taking a slightly different turn, Heathcote analyses the use of exoskeletons in armed conflict, using posthuman feminism together with critical disability studies. She argues that exoskeletons, when understood in the context of the US military's aim of getting injured soldiers back on the battlefield, perpetuate ideas of the modernist man in warfare.[129] Scholars in international relations have also contributed to this field. Lauren Wilcox, for example, has also analysed the material elements of drones,[130] drawing on posthuman theory to examine how bodies are gendered and racialised in drone warfare,[131] marking some people as more "killable" than others.[132] Finally, I too have published in this field, drawing on posthuman feminism to analyse debates on lethal autonomous weapons systems,[133] a discussion I develop further in Chapters 2 and 3 of this volume.

A second field where posthuman theory has been applied to international law is in the realm of environmental law. Due to the transnational nature of international environmental law, some of these texts focus less squarely on international law, though they each speak back to international law in their own way. A key

---

127 Arvidsson, above note 40.
128 Matilda Arvidsson, 'The Swarm that We Already Are: Artificially Intelligent (AI) Swarming 'Insect Drones', Targeting and International Humanitarian Law in a Posthuman Ecology,' *Journal of Human Rights and the Environment* (2020) 11(1): 114–137.
129 Heathcote, above note 41.
130 Wilcox, above note 86.
131 Wilcox, 'Embodying …', above note 39.
132 Wilcox, 'Drone warfare', above note 39.
133 Jones, above note 86.

voice here is Anna Grear, who applies posthuman theory, including posthuman feminisms, to highlight human-nonhuman connections, fostering new legal imaginaries.[134] Likewise, Marie-Catherine Petersmann has analysed what re-thinking human-nonhuman relations may mean for environmental governance and care.[135] Emille Boulot and Joshua Sterlin take a similar approach, applying what they term the 'legal ontological turn' to look towards an environmental law for all beings,[136] while Matt Harvey and Steve Vanderheiden draw on theories of the 'more-than-human' to question who speaks for nature in law.[137] In other disciplines, social scientists Nick J. Fox and Pam Alldred have applied posthuman theory to challenge the sustainable development paradigm[138] and to re-think climate change policies,[139] while Sam Adelman has used new materialist concepts of agency and mattering to re-think climate justice.[140] Furthermore, as noted above, scholars such as Heathcote and Ollino have applied posthuman feminism to analyse the treatment of nature in the Law of the Sea.[141] Another strand of scholarship provides posthuman or material analyses of the nonhuman animal,[142] including work which focuses on their legal status, noting how animals are already part of legal relations.[143] I have also published in this area. First, in a co-authored piece with Otto which examines new materialism and the links between the marginalisation of gendered, raced and classed subjects and the exploitation of the environment,[144] and second on what posthuman theory and the rights of nature movement may learn from one another[145] – a theme I return to in more detail in Chapter 5 of this book.

Human rights law is the third area of international law where posthuman theory has been deployed. An example is Upendra Baxi's *Human Rights in a Posthuman*

---

134 Anna Grear, 'Legal Imaginaries and the Anthropocene:"'Of" and "For",' *Law and Critique* (2020) 31: 351–366; Grear, above note 87; Anna Grear, 'Resisting Anthropocene Neoliberalism: Towards New Materialism Commoning?,' in Anna Grear and David Bollier (eds.), *The Great Awakening: New Modes of Life Amidst Capitalist Ruins*, (Punctum Books, 2020): 317–355.

135 Marie-Catherine Petersmann, 'Sympoietic Thinking and Earth System Law: The Earth, Its Subjects and the Law,' *Earth System Governance* (2021) 9: 1–8; Marie-Catherine Petersmann, 'Response-Abilities of Care in More-Than-Human Worlds,' *Journal of Human Rights and the Environment* (2021) 12: 102–124.

136 Emille Boulot and Joshua Sterlin, 'Steps Towards a Legal Ontological Turn: Proposals for Law's Place Beyond the Human,' *Transnational Environmental Law*, (2022) 11(1): 13–38.

137 Matt Harvey and Steve Vanderheiden, '"For the trees have no tongues": eco-feedback, speech, and the silencing of nature,' *Journal of Human Rights and the Environment* (2021) 12: 38–58.

138 Nick J. Fox and Pam Alldred, 'Climate Change, Environmental Justice and the Unusual Capacities of Posthumans,' *Journal of Human Rights and the Environment* (2021) 12: 59–75.

139 Nick J. Fox and Pam Alldred, 'Re-Assembling Climate Change Policy: Materialism, Posthumanism, and the Policy Assemblage,' *British Journal of Sociology* (2020) 17(2): 269–283.

140 Adelman, above note 87.

141 Heathcote, above note 26; Ollino, above note 26.

142 Maneesha Deckha, 'Toward a Postcolonial, Posthumanist Feminist Theory: Centralizing Race and Culture in Feminist Work on Nonhuman Animals,' *Hypatia* (2012) 27(3): 527–545.

143 Andrew Lang, 'Purse Seine Net,' in Jessie Hohmann and Daniel Joyce (eds.), *International Law's Objects*, (Oxford University Press, 2018): 377–386.

144 Jones and Otto, above note 36.

145 Jones, above note 87.

World.[146] Focusing primarily on issues in human rights such as countering terrorism and the right to development, Baxi concludes his book with some reflections on posthumanism as applied to human rights. He argues that posthuman theory is useful when it comes to the important work of challenging the white, male, Enlightenment idea of the universal subject that lies at the heart of human rights law, reflecting in particular on how technological innovation is challenging this subject.[147] Grear's scholarship has also been key in this area, drawing on new materialism to re-imagine human rights in a way that may address anthropocentrism.[148] Birgit Schippers, writing from the discipline of politics, likewise argues that posthumanism challenges the focus on the atomistic individual human of human rights. Schippers thereby welcomes the re-configuring of human rights through human-nonhuman assemblages that applying posthuman theory to rights entails.[149]

As discussed, both posthuman feminism and posthuman theory more broadly have been little applied to international law. While some literature is beginning to emerge in journal articles and book chapters, a stronger engagement between posthuman theories, including posthuman feminism, and international law is required if international law is to engage productively with the pressing problems of this posthuman world wherein life in its many forms is under serious threat.

Overview of the Book

This book applies posthuman feminist theory to a variety of areas of international law, examining what international law can learn from posthuman feminism while exemplifying how feminist theory can be used to analyse all areas of international law – and not just the areas of international law that are seen to pertain to women's lives. In this endeavour, I also seek to contribute to posthuman studies more broadly. As I noted above, the vast majority of posthuman work thus far is theoretical. This book, in applying posthuman feminism to international law, makes a contribution to bridging the theory and practice divide.

I have attempted to write this book in a way that makes it accessible to as many people as possible. This comes from a political commitment to making academia accountable but is also linked to the book's focus on practice. My hope is that this book can be picked up by a legal theorist, a posthuman theorist, an activist or a doctrinal international lawyer alike, and that each may be able to gain something from reading it. At times, I fear I have been less successful in this aim than in others, particularly when trying to condense large bodies of complex theory or when trying to explain technical points in international law. My focus on accessibility also, at times, means that I end up using language to get my message across, as opposed to

---

146 Upendra Baxi, *Human Rights in a Posthuman World*, (Oxford University Press, 2009).
147 Ibid., p. 197–239.
148 Anna Grear, 'Human Rights and New Horizons? Thoughts toward a New Juridical Ontology,' *Science, Technology and Human Values* (2018) *43*(1): 129–145.
149 Birgit Schippers, 'Towards a Posthumanist Conception of Human Rights?', in Birgit Schippers (ed.), *Critical Perspectives on Human Rights*, (Rowman & Littlefield, 2019): 63–82.

using language in a way that challenges dominant humanistic and anthropocentric uses of language. This use of language was, however, a choice, and one that speaks back to the themes and aims of the book.

Chapter 1 begins with a discussion of the nonhuman and international law. While, formally, international law has always been concerned with nonhuman subjects, the most important being the sovereign state, this does not mean that international law is post-human. In fact, I argue that while international law has long accepted multiple nonhuman entities as legal persons, such as international organisations, this has occurred only when such entities are compatible with the liberal humanist, anthropocentric, gendered and racialised underpinnings of the international legal project, including neoliberal economics. This chapter examines, first, international law's exclusionary humanism through an analysis of the concept of the sovereign state in international law and the way capitalist ideologies structure the inequitable global order. Second, it examines the anthropocentrism of international law, focusing on an area of international law which has supposedly been designed to protect the environment: international environmental law. I argue that while *some* subjects that are not human, such as the state or the global corporation, have rights and duties under international law, other entities that do not fit the hierarchical and imperial liberal internationalist underpinnings of the global order, such as marginalised human subjects and the environment, have been denied this status. I argue that, despite international law's formal focus on the nonhuman, international law's impacts are all-too-human. I thereby conclude that posthuman feminism provides an important framework through which to move beyond the humanist and anthropocentric structures of international law.

Given that one of the aims of this book is to apply posthuman feminism to reform international law, the next few chapters examine a series of case studies. Chapter 2 considers the regulation of military technologies and the current global focus on the need to regulate lethal autonomous weapons systems, the central question of concern here being whether machines should be involved in making life/death decisions. I argue that military technologies are currently viewed, defined and regulated through a humanist and anthropocentric lens. In debates on these technologies, the human is situated as being in control of and separate from the machine. Furthermore, autonomous systems are defined as being distinct from automated systems – with concerns being raised over the former but not the latter. Drawing on a series of examples of existing technologies and technologies under development, I argue that machines and humans are already working together to make life/death decisions. I thereby problematise the binary opposition prevalent in discussions in the field between autonomy and automation, arguing that autonomy and automation are not distinct: it is hard to determine where one ends and the other starts. It is thereby argued, drawing on posthuman feminism, that any possible regulation or ban of new and emerging military technologies will be ineffective if the distinctions between the human and the machine and autonomy and automation are upheld.

Chapter 3 provides some tentative alternative posthuman feminist inspired proposals for the regulation of military technologies. Considering the tensions between resistance and compliance, that is, the need to work inside the system of international law while also seeking to move beyond it, this chapter makes two sets of proposals. The first applies posthuman feminism to provide alternative proposals for the regulation of military technologies that use existing international legal and institutional frameworks. The second set of proposals seeks to provide an alternative way of thinking about military technology regulation beyond the narrow framework of contemporary international law, drawing on feminist and Indigenous approaches to AI.

Chapters 4 and 5 both focus on posthuman analyses of international environmental law. Chapter 4 picks up from Chapter 1, where I examined the anthropocentrism inherent in international environmental law, moving on to examine whether and how queer theories of the nonhuman may be used to re-imagine international environmental law in the posthuman. Chapter 5 goes on to apply these theories to seek legal reform by bringing them into conversation with the emerging rights of nature (RoN) movement. I thereby examine whether the RoN movement may be one way in which to apply posthuman feminist ideas. I conclude by finding hope in the emerging RoN movement, while outlining a series of concerns that must be thought through as this movement develops. These concerns include the challenges of universalism and the need to ensure that nature is not merely included within the existing frame of liberal international law but, rather, that nature is used to transform international law in the posthuman.

The concluding chapter discusses the challenges of applying posthuman feminist theory to international law. Drawing primarily on the scholarship of critical feminist international lawyer, Ratna Kapur, I return to the discussion in Chapter 3 around resistance and compliance and whether feminists should seek legal change from within the law or whether there is a need instead to look beyond the law, given international law's problematic exclusionary humanist and anthropocentric underpinnings. I discuss the challenges faced when seeking to move international law beyond liberal legalism. While I have offered a series of more practical proposals for legal change in earlier chapters, in this concluding chapter, I emphasise the need to see and define the law in new ways. I argue that western legal scholars, including myself, have a lot to learn from Indigenous jurisprudence.

Driven by a profound conviction that the law, legal discourse and critical legal theories have a crucial role to play in the posthuman re-composition of subjectivity and legal knowledge production, I argue that posthuman feminist analyses can enhance our individual and collective ability to deal with the urgent challenges of our times. Overall, this book is an attempt to both analyse international law from a posthuman feminist perspective and to apply posthuman feminism to international law in practice. I make some central advancements in both these areas – exemplifying how feminist approaches are not just about 'women's issues', as the mainstream of international law would have it, but, rather, feminist approaches can be used to analyse and re-frame *all* areas of international law.

1

INTERNATIONAL LAW AND THE NONHUMAN

While, formally, international law has always focused on the nonhuman, the central subject of international law being the state, this does not mean that international law is posthuman. In fact, and as I argue in this chapter, while international law has long accepted multiple nonhuman entities as legal persons, such as the state or international organisations, this has occurred only when such entities are compatible with the liberal humanist, anthropocentric, gendered and racialised underpinnings of the international legal project and neoliberal economics.

As I noted in the Introduction, I use posthuman feminism both as an analytical tool and as a 'navigational tool'[1] or interdisciplinary method, using the posthuman feminist umbrella to bring multiple areas of study together to challenge exclusionary humanism and anthropocentrism. In this vein, this chapter draws on feminist, postcolonial and other critical international legal scholarship alongside posthuman feminist theories, bringing these bodies of work into conversation with one another to examine the exclusionary humanism and anthropocentrism which underlies and is perpetuated by international law.

The chapter focuses, first, on the exclusionary humanism of international law, conducting an analysis of the concept of the sovereign state and of the role of capitalism in the global order. Here, multiple examples are drawn on, from the role of the corporation in international law, to international law's role in perpetuating global inequalities, to the phenomenon of land grabbing. The second part of this chapter provides an analysis of the anthropocentrism of international law. Here, I argue that international law defines the environment as a resource, justifying environmental damage and extraction in the name of human interests. My analysis of this anthropocentrism is gradually built into the chapter, emerging at key moments in the first half and coming to the fore in the discussion on land

---

1 Rosi Braidotti, *The Posthuman*, (Polity Press, 2013), p. 3.

DOI: 10.4324/9781003363798-2

grabbing. This has been done purposefully, to allow the links between exclusionary humanism and anthropocentrism to unfold as the text develops. The final section of this chapter, however, focuses squarely on international law and anthropocentrism, examining the anthropocentrism of the area of international law which has supposedly been designed to protect the environment: international environmental law. Consequently, it is argued that while *some* subjects that are not human, such as the state or the global corporation, have rights and duties under international law, other entities that do not fit the (neo)liberal, humanist, anthropocentric, gendered and racialised underpinnings of the global order have been denied this status. These denied subjects differ in terms of how they have been denied legal status, with some gaining a more limited recognition than others, but include, for example, marginalised and oppressed human subjects including the poor, women and racialised subjects, and the environment and nonhuman animals, among others. It is thereby argued that, despite international law's formal focus on the nonhuman, there is a need for further analyses that seek to challenge and re-think the exclusionary humanist and anthropocentric ideas that underpin international law. Posthuman feminist theory, I argue, can be used in this aim.

Is International Law Already Posthuman?

In theory, international law is not primarily about humans, at least in terms of the legal subject of international law. Most courses on international law begin with: international law is based on state consent and the state is the central subject of international law.[2] International law is therefore deemed to be a horizontal legal system that is made up of multiple sovereign states which are all said to be formally equal: there is no one overarching law-making authority in international law, such as a Parliament. That is not to say, however, that the state is the only subject of international law. Other entities, including international organisations and individuals are also formally recognised as international legal subjects. This means that they, too, have legal personality, defined as the capacity to have rights and duties under international law.[3] However, the legal status of entities other than the state derives

---

2 This was affirmed in the *Lotus* case where the Permanent Court of International Justice declared that international law is the law 'govern[ing] relations between independent States.' *Case of the SS Lotus* (Judgment), 1927 PCIJ Series A No. 10, at 18.

3 *Reparation for Injuries Suffered in the Service of the United Nations* (Advisory Opinion), International Court of Justice,11th April 1949, ICJ Rep 174, ICGJ 232 (ICJ 1949), p. 9. See also; James Crawford, *The Creation of States in International Law*, (Oxford University Press, 2006), p. 32.

   Note, however, that there is no clear list of the rights and duties that form international personality. For a failed attempt to define these rights and duties, see; United Nations, UNGA Res A/RES/375 (1949).

from states consenting to them having personality.[4] In this model, the state therefore remains the central subject of international law, being the entity upon which authority in international law is derived. Entities other than the state thereby hold more limited forms of personality, the rights and duties they hold depending on those granted to them by states. This can be seen in the example of the individual, who may have rights when their human rights have been violated but who cannot, for example, sign a Treaty like a state can.[5] The state therefore remains the only entity in international law that wields the full array of rights and duties.

However, scholars increasingly dispute the fact that the state is *the* source of all power in international law. Janne Nijman, for example, argues that the well-functioning state derives its legal personality from its citizens.[6] Others have argued that domestic courts also play a role in international law making,[7] or argue that the

---

4 This was determined, for example, in relation to international organisations in the *Reparations* Advisory Opinion of the International Court of Justice (ICJ) in 1949. In this case, the ICJ discussed whether the newly formed United Nations (UN) had international personality. The Court concluded that the UN did indeed possess such personality, this personality being derived from the UN Charter, a document drafted and signed by states. The Court thereby concluded that, to be able to 'carry out the intentions of its founder' (states), the UN must be deemed to have international legal personality. Overall, the UN (and subsequently other international organisations) was deemed to have legal personality because states had given it such. See: *Reparations* Advisory Opinion, above note 3, p. 9. See also: *Legality of the Threat or Use of Nuclear Weapons* (Advisory Opinion), International Court of Justice, 8 July 1996, I.C.J. Reports 1996, p. 226, para 19.

In relation to individual legal personality, it is key to note that this form of personality has a long and potted history. It was, however, recognised explicitly in the Toyko and Nuremburg tribunals (see, for example: *Trial of Major War Criminals Before the International Military Tribunal*, Judgement: The Law of the Charter, International Military Tribunal for Germany, 1st October 1946 citing ex parte Quirin), as well as by the the Permanent Court of International Justice (PCIJ – the precursor to the ICJ) in 1928 (see: *Jurisdiction of the Courts of Danzig*, Advisory Opinion, 1928, PCIJ, Ser B, No 15, p. 17–18). Individuals in the contemporary, however, now gain competence through a wide array of sources, including, of course, international human rights instruments. See: Robert McCorquodale, 'The Individual and the International Legal System,' in Malcom Evans (ed.), *International Law*, (Oxford University Press, 5th edn, 2018): 259–288.

5 United Nations, Vienna Convention on the Law of Treaties, 23 May 1969, U.N.T.S. vol. 1155.

6 Janne Elisabeth Nijman, *The Concept of International Legal Personality: An Inquiry into the History and Theory of International Law*, (Asser Press, 2004), p. 465–73. Critical scholars have, however, critiqued Nijman's approach. For example, Rose Parfitt argues that while, on the face of it, Nijman seems to promote greater individual participation in international law, promoting democratic values, her perspective also resonates strongly with widely criticised calls for humanitarian intervention. See: Rose Parfitt, 'Theorizing Recognition and International Personality,' in Anne Orford and Florian Hoffmann (eds.), *The Oxford Handbook of the Theory of International Law* (Oxford University Press, 2016): 583–599, p. 593. For a detailed discussion of the relationship between sovereignty and the individual, both historically but also critically (from a TWAIL perspective), see: Rose Parfitt, 'Item No. 2 State, Colony, Individual: The *Longue Durée* of International Legal Reproduction,' in *The Process of International Legal Production: Inequality, Historiography, Resistance*, (Cambridge University Press, 2019): 77–153. For critiques of humanitarian intervention, see: Anne Orford, 'Muscular Humanitarianism: Reading the Narratives of the New Interventionism,' *European Journal of International Law* (1999) 10: 679–711; Anne Orford, *Reading Humanitarian Intervention: Human Rights and the Use of Force in International Law*, (Cambridge University Press, 2008).

7 Karen Knop, 'Here and There: International Law in Domestic Courts,' *N.Y.U. Journal of International Law and Politics* (1999–2000) 32: 501–535.

corporation, although not formally being a legal subject in international law, wields some law-making authority,[8] while others have made clear the role that non-governmental organisations (NGOs) play in the global order.[9] Furthermore, building on the indeterminacy thesis of international law, which essentially points out that there are no fixed outcomes in international law and highlights international law's deeply political nature,[10] scholars such as David Kennedy and Gina Heathcote examine the role that expert decision-makers play in interpreting and making the law.[11] Critical international legal scholars therefore argue for a wider array of actors to be recognised as decision-making entities in international law,[12] with scholars such as Roland Portmann arguing that there should be 'a presumption that all effective actors of international relations' may have personality.[13] These positions, however, sit starkly in contrast with the formalist position that is taken in most textbooks of international law, that the only entities with legal personality are the state,[14] the individual and international organisations, with a few *sui generis* entities also having limited personality.[15] The rights and duties of all these entities, other than the state itself, are deemed to derive from state consent. Formally, therefore, the central subject of international law is not the human but is the state, a nonhuman subject.

The fact that international law's main subject has always been nonhuman does not, however, make it posthuman. As I noted in the Introduction, while posthuman feminism focuses on the nonhuman, rendering previously invisiblised nonhuman subjects visible, these theories also challenge the multiple hierarchies between relational human and nonhuman entities, focusing both on the hierarchies within the label "humanity" (such as gender, race and class) and the hierarchical positioning of the human over nonhuman others. Given this, it becomes clear that international law certainly is *not* posthuman, despite its formal focus on the nonhuman subject.

---

8 Dan Danielsen, 'Corporate Power and Global Order,' in Anne Orford (ed.), *International Law and Its Others*, (Cambridge University Press, 2006): 85–99; Grietje Baars, *The Corporation, Law and Capitalism: A Radical Perspective on the Role of Law in the Global Economy*, (Brill, 2019).

9 See: Karen Knop, 'Why Rethinking the Sovereign State is Important for Women's International Human Rights Law,' in Rebecca J. Cook (ed.), *Human Rights of Women*, (Pennsylvania University Press, 1994): 153–164; Pierre-Marie Dupuy and Luisa Vierucci (eds.), *NGOs in International Law: Efficiency in Flexibility?* (Edward Elgar, 2008); Steve Charnovitz, 'Nongovernmental Organizations and International Law,' *American Journal of International Law* (2017) 100(2): 348–372.

10 Martti Koskenniemi, *From Apology to Utopia. The Structure of International Legal Argument*, (Cambridge University Press, 2005 [1989]).

11 David Kennedy, *A World of Struggle: How Power, Law and Expertise Shape Global Political Economy*, (Princeton University Press, 2016); Gina Heathcote, 'Expertise,' in Gina Heathcote, *Feminist Dialogues on International Law: Successes, Tensions, Futures*, (Oxford University Press, 2019): 30–70.

12 Danielsen, above note 8.

13 Roland Portmann, *Legal Personality in International Law*, (Cambridge University Press, 2010), p. 14.

14 With insurgents sometimes having limited personality, depending on the circumstances. See Antonio Cassese, *International Law*, (Oxford University Press, 2nd edn, 2005), p. 124–131.

15 Examples include the Holy See and the International Committee of the Red Cross. See: Ibid., p. 131–134.

This is because international law is based upon both exclusionary humanist and anthropocentric values.

One way we can think about the exclusionary humanism of international law and its all-too-human impacts is by looking at the concept of the sovereign state, international law's central (supposedly nonhuman) subject. Focusing in particular on how sovereignty is framed in international law, Antony Anghie has shown how the concept of state sovereignty was historically shaped by and through colonialism, having been used to justify which states should be sovereign and which should not.[16] In the contemporary, sovereignty is deemed to operate differently, with all states being absolute in their internal sovereignty and thereby fully independent and autonomous and completely in control of their own decision-making processes. This conceptualisation is exemplified by the doctrine of state consent, which presumes that the state can freely consent to international law-making. The way the independence and autonomy of the sovereign state is constructed creates a sovereign state that is based upon 'isolation and separation'.[17] International law, however, is made up of multiple sovereign states, all of whom, being sovereign, are supposedly equal in their absolute power over their territory and decision-making – this, of course, being a legal fiction.[18] Sovereign equality is the doctrine used to manage this contradiction, alongside its partner, state consent. Sovereign equality declares that all sovereign states are equal under international law and thus all equal to choose whether or not to consent to international law. In reality, states are not equal.[19] States differ in power greatly and this impacts the real meaning of consent in international law.

Critical work on unequal treaties in international law unpacks some of these issues of consent, examining the real inequalities between states. Unequal treaties commonly refer to a series of treaties made between Japan and China and western powers in the nineteenth and early twentieth centuries either following military defeat or the threat of force. Such treaties were created to force these countries to agree to policies imposed by the west, including the opening up of closed and

---

16 Antony Anghie, 'Finding the Peripheries: Sovereignty and Colonialism in Nineteenth Century International Law,' *Harvard International Law Journal*, (1999), 40: 1–71.

17 Hilary Charlesworth, 'The Sex of the State in International Law,' in Ngaire Naffine and Rosemary Owens (eds.), *Sexing the Subject of Law*, (LBC Information Services, 1997): 251–268, p. 261.

18 For a wider discussion of different conceptualisations of sovereignty or "relational sovereignty", see: Christine Chinkin, Gina Heathcote, Emily Jones and Henry Jones, '*Bozkurt* Case, aka the *Lotus Case (France v Turkey)*: Ships that Go Bump in the Night,' in Loveday Hodson and Troy Lavers (eds.), *Feminist Judgments in International Law*, (Bloomsbury, 2019): 27–51 (on imagining international law as based on community as opposed to individual sovereignty); Simone Bignall, 'Relational Sovereignty,' in Rosi Braidotti, Emily Jones and Goda Klumbytė (eds.), *More Posthuman Glossary*, (Bloomsbury, forthcoming 2023) (on relational sovereignty).

19 See: Gerry Simpson, *Great Powers and Outlaw States: Unequal Sovereigns in the International Legal Order*, (Cambridge University Press, 2004).

regulated markets to foreign trade.[20] Most international lawyers, have, however, long abandoned talking about unequal treaties, treating them as a relic of international law's colonial past. In the contemporary, and as I outlined above, sovereign states are deemed to be equal, each consenting to the making of international law. Unequal treaties are now deemed to have been eradicated following the implementation of S.51 and 52 of the Vienna Convention on the Law of Treaties 1969 (VCLT) which bans the use or threat of military force as a means of procuring an unequal Treaty.[21] However, while international lawyers no longer talk about unequal treaties *per se*, treaties remain very unequal. As Matthew Craven notes, 'every treaty, in some respect, is a manifestation of inequality – whether understood in terms of a substantive lack of equilibrium in the respective burdens and benefits, or in terms of the unequal bargaining power of the contracting parties'.[22] While the banning of the use of force to gain the upper hand was indeed implemented under the VCLT, this does not mean that coercion was banned. There are many forms of coercion which continue, including economic and political coercion.[23] Furthermore, colonialism is not a mere relic of the past but continues to structure global inequalities to the present day.[24] By ignoring these realities and 'flattening out' the inequalities in treaties through promoting a formally equal yet 'fictitious' discourse of international law,[25] international lawyers prove that they are 'unwilling … to engage effectively with the problem of inequality'.[26] This lack of willingness to deal with real inequality can be seen across the conceptual framework of international law, in that, in proclaiming sovereign equality and state consent, international lawyers apply false, idealised concepts of equality to an unequal reality. The nature of state consent can clearly be questioned, with many treaties being signed under some form of implicit duress, often reflecting global inequalities.[27] Therefore, while states may be formally equal, all sovereign, and all consenting parties in the making of international law, it is evident that this is a legal fiction.

---

20 For example, see: The Treaty of Nanking, 29ᵗʰ August 1842. For more on unequal treaties, see China Miéville, *Between Equal Rights: A Marxist Theory of International Law*, (Pluto Press, 2006), p. 248; Ntina Tzouvala, 'The Standard of Civilisation in the Nineteenth Century: Between the 'Logic of Improvement' and the 'Logic of Biology',' in *Capitalism as Civilisation: A History of International Law*, (Cambridge University Press, 2020): 44–87. For an excellent analysis of the Treaty of Nanking and the Treaty of Tientsin, see: Rose Parfitt, *The Process of International Legal Production: Inequality, Historiography, Resistance*, (Cambridge University Press, 2019), p. 136–144.

21 Vienna Convention on the Law of Treaties, above note 5.

22 Matthew Craven, 'What Happened to Unequal Treaties? The Continuities of Informal Empire,' *Nordic Journal of International Law* (2005) 74: 335–382, p. 337–338.

23 Tzanakopoulos examines the role of economic coercion in international law in more detail, arguing that, while economic coercion is currently permitted in international law, there are strong arguments as to why it should not be. See: Antonios Tzanakopoulos, 'The Right to be Free from Economic Coercion,' *Cambridge Journal of International and Comparative Law* (2015) 4(3): 616–633.

24 Craven, above note 22; Anghie, above note 16.

25 Craven, Ibid., p. 340.

26 Ibid., p. 382.

27 Ibid.

Another example of the all-too-human impacts of international law can be seen when examining the concept of the state in international law. The state is an artificial legal person made up of individuals who are supposed to act on behalf of all. In reality, the state promotes certain human interests. As feminist scholars have pointed out, those interests are often those of the male elite with power in the state in question.[28] After all, according to the Montevideo Convention – the instrument that defines what a state is under international law,[29] a state must a have a clear and in control government, i.e. a clear voice of authority and power.[30] The construction of the sovereign state as a whole entity 'allows the state to be seen as a complete, coherent, bounded entity that speaks with one voice, obliterating the diversity of voices within the state'.[31] This set-up leads, in the words of Iris Marion Young, reflecting on the use of so-called impartiality in political theory, to the creation of a structure where 'the particular perspectives of dominant groups claim universality, and help … justify hierarchical decision-making structures'.[32] International law perpetuates existing inequalities in society by promoting a unified, hierarchical structure, consequently ensuring that those least heard in society remain least heard in international law too.

Yet the state is not only an all-too-human concern in terms of *who* it represents, it is also an all-too-human concern in terms of *what* it represents. Feminist, queer and postcolonial scholars have provided various critiques of the concept of the sovereign state, arguing that how the state is constructed in international law is both gendered and racialised. Much of this work begins by deconstructing the model of subjectivity that underpins the concept of the state, noting that '[t]he State is described in international law as a whole, inhabited body with stable and inviolate borders. Jurisdictional force transforms this creature into a "legal person"'.[33] Critical scholars have deconstructed the model of personhood which has been used to conceptualise the state in international law, arguing that this model is based upon a liberal idea of the supposedly universal subject, that subject being, in reality, male and white.

The personification of the sovereign state in international law has a long history, with personification models being used as early as in the work of Grotius in the fifteenth century.[34] Moving further along the timeline, in 1688, Pufendorf described

28 Hilary Charlesworth and Christine Chinkin, 'The Idea of the State,' in Hilary Charlesworth and Christine Chinkin, *The Boundaries of International Law: A Feminist Analysis*, (Manchester University Press, 2000): 124–170. See also: Wendy Brown, *Politics Out of History*, (Princeton University Press, 2001), p. 10.
29 While the Montevideo Convention was initially a regional Treaty, its provisions on the definition of statehood are now accepted as customary international law.
30 Montevideo Convention on the Rights and Duties of States, 26 December 1933, Article 1(c).
31 Hilary Charlesworth and Christine Chinkin, *The Boundaries of International Law: A Feminist Analysis*, (Manchester University Press, 2000), p. 133.
32 Iris Marion Young, *Justice and the Politics of Difference*, (Princeton University Press, 1990), p. 97.
33 Yoriko Otomo, *Unconditional Life: The Postwar International Law Settlement*, (Oxford University Press, 2016), p. 71.
34 For a discussion of this, see: Helen M. Kinsella, 'Gendering Grotius,' *Political Theory*, (2006) 34(2): 161–191, p. 161.

the state's legal status in terms of personality, arguing that the state is 'a single person with intelligence and will, performing other actions peculiar to itself and separate to those of the individuals'.[35] Moving on to the 1990s, Louis Henkin submitted that 'states are to be seen like individuals in the state of nature'. States, he continues, like humans, are equal, have rights and duties, morality and the ability to make decisions. They have a right to life (to exist) and a right to property (territory). They enter into relations with one another, creating a 'political system reflecting a social contract'.[36]

The personification thesis has been a key starting point for critical scholars when highlighting the gendered and racialised biases that underly the conceptualisation of the state in international law. For example, Hilary Charlesworth argues that 'the character of the central person in international law, the nation state, rests on particular beliefs about sexual difference'.[37] The sovereign state is constructed as both symbolically male and female at different points,[38] the female construction being seen as the oddity.[39] For example, according to the Montevideo Convention, a state must have a 'defined territory'.[40] Entities that do not fulfil this requirement are often feminised and racialised in different ways. As Rose Parfitt notes, many states and nonstate groups, including Indigenous peoples, have been unable to construct a claim to boundedness.[41] Indigenous groups do not always have a bounded territory that they hold absolute control over, either because they have been colonised (and thus had that control taken from them) or, in some instances, because they are nomadic peoples without clear state-like boundaries. In a similar vein, Teemu Ruskola argues that the normative masculinity associated with states fosters a system whereby the 'deviant masculinities' of global south states 'render them rapable', this logic being used to justify colonial and neocolonial exclusions and interventions.[42] This is made clear when examining how states that are unable to maintain their bounded individual status, what Gerry Simpson terms 'outlaw states',[43] are often deemed to be deviant others, the 'mad', the 'bad' and the 'dangerous'[44] and are thus feminised (and

35 Samuel von Pufendorf, *De Iure Naturae et Gentium*, Libri Octo, Vol. I, 1688.

36 Louis Henkin, 'The Mythology of Sovereignty,' in *State Sovereignty: The Challenge of a Changing World: Proceedings of the 1992 Conference of the Canadian Council on International Law*, (1992), p. 15 and 18.

37 Hilary Charlesworth, 'The Sex of the State in International Law,' in Ngaire Naffine and Rosemary Owens (eds.), *Sexing the Subject of Law*, (LBC Information Services, 1997): 251–268, p. 253.

38 Ibid., p. 253.

39 Charlesworth and Chinkin, above note 28. See also; Teemu Ruskola, 'Raping Like a State,' *UCLA Law Review* (2009–10) 57: 1477–-1536. Much of this work on personification came from and drew on feminist legal theoretical work around the domestic legal person. See: Ngaire Naffine, 'The Body Bag,' in Ngaire Naffine and Rosemary Owens (eds.), *Sexing the Subject of Law*, (LBC Information Services, 1997): 73–93.

40 Montevideo Convention, above note 30, Article 1(b).

41 Parfitt, above note 20, p. 596; Charlesworth and Chinkin, above note 31, p. 129–130.

42 Ruskola, above note 39.

43 Simpson, above note 19.

44 Ibid., p. ix–xi.

often racialised), sometimes being labelled as "failed states".[45] Non-state groups or "failed states" are all seen as having 'permeable, negotiable, penetrable, vulnerable boundaries',[46] this narrative being used to feminise states, particularly those in the global south, in all too familiar, neocolonial and racialised ways.[47]

However, the sovereign state is not the only legal subject in international law which, through its conceptualisation, perpetuates real inequalities. Other scholars have examined how the legal subject in international law, whether applied to the state or other legal entities, centres around a universalised vision of human subjectivity that is classed, gendered and white.[48] This can be seen when looking at the corporate form in international law. Anna Grear, for example, highlights how the legal person of the law is very much *not* an 'embodied, corporeally "thick", flesh and blood human being at all, but a highly selective *construct*'.[49] The legal subject, she argues, is based upon 'the construct of a white, property owning, acquisitive, broadly Eurocentric masculinity'.[50] While the construct of the legal subject may be 'too impossibly embodied for *any* corporeally specific human' to fit, including even the 'white, European, male property-owner' himself (given the 'abstract, rational knower' of the Cartesian subject upon which this subject is based), 'the same is *not* true … of the corporate juridical form' which perfectly fits, argues Grear, 'the structural and ideological features of a fully capitalistic legal subject'.[51] Grear thereby argues that the global corporation in many ways best fits the concept of legal personhood precisely because it is the ultimate (neo)liberal, rational, independent actor that legal personhood has been framed around.[52]

While Grear draws primarily on US domestic law to exemplify her argument, with the US being the first jurisdiction to recognise the corporation as a legal

45 Charlesworth and Chinkin, above note 31, p. 133–134.

46 Ibid., p. 129–130.

47 Rose Parfitt, above note 20, p. 9; Sara Kendall has also noted this, focusing in particular on how these dynamics play out in the "war on terror." See: Sara Kendall, 'Cartographies of the Present: "Contingent Sovereignty" and Territorial Integrity,' in Martin Kuijer and Wouter Werner (eds.), *Netherlands Yearbook of International Law* (2016) 47: 83–105, p. 100.

48 For more on the gendered and racialised form of the legal person in domestic law, see; Ngaire Naffine, 'Women and the Cast of Legal Persons,' in Jackie Jones, Anna Grear, Rachel Anne Fenton and Kim Stevenson (eds.), *Gender, Sexualities and Law*, (Routledge, 2011): 15–25; Anna Grear, '"Sexing the Matrix": Embodiment, Disembodiment and the Law – towards the Re-Gendering of Legal Rationality,' in Jackie Jones, Anna Grear, Rachel Anne Fenton and Kim Stevenson (eds.), *Gender, Sexualities and Law*, (Routledge, 2011): 39–52. These domestic frameworks have then, as Rose Parfitt shows, been transposed into international law. See: Parfitt, above note 6.

49 Anna Grear, 'Deconstructing Anthropos: A Critical Legal Reflection on "Anthropocentric" Law and Anthropocene "Humanity",' *Law and Critique* (2015) 26(3): 225–249, p. 237 – author's own emphasis.

50 Ibid., p. 236.

51 Ibid., p. 237 – author's own emphasis. For more on the Cartesian formation of this subject, see the same article, p. 233–237.

52 Ibid.; Anna Grear, *Redirecting Human Rights: Facing the Challenge of Corporate Legal Humanity*, (Palgrave Macmillan, 2010). See also: Elena Blanco and Anna Grear, 'Personhood, Jurisdiction and Injustice: Law Colonialities and the Global Order,' *Journal of Human Rights and the Environment* (2019) 10(1): 86–117.

person,[53] she and others have noted how this US legal turn was then replicated in international law.[54] The corporation has long played a role in international law,[55] this role often being deeply tied to the colonial project. For example, the 1602 Charter of the Dutch East India Company stated that the corporation could 'keep armed forces, install Judicial officers … as well as jointly ensure the enforcement of the law and justice, all combined so as to promote trade'.[56] It is evident from this statement from the Charter alone that the corporation was already assigned rights and duties in international law in the seventeenth century, and that the legal status of the corporation was thereby '*pivotal* to the colonial development of the international legal order and remains a core – if not *the central* – feature of the contemporary global order'.[57]

Thinking further about the parallels between the domestic personhood granted to the corporate form and some of the transpositions of this form into international law, Fleur Johns contends that the global corporate form in international law, like the domestic frameworks described by Grear, is also based on individualism. The corporation, however, as noted above, is not a widely accepted international personality in international law. Rather, corporations are registered in domestic law and are thus governed by that law. Johns, however, notes that the assignation of a nationality to a corporation resonates with 'Anglo-American corporate law doctrine' which theorises 'the corporation in ways consonant with individualism'.[58] Despite its lack of recognition as an international personality, many authors have argued that the corporation does wield great power in the global order.[59] For example, Grietje Baars, referring to the difficulty in holding corporations to account in international law, argues that international law actually protects the corporate

---

53 Grear, above note 49, p. 237–245. This recognition in US law can be traced back to the US case of *County of Santa Clara v Southern Pacific Railroad*, 118 US 394 (1886), in which the US Supreme Court declared, in a surprisingly mundane, matter-of-fact manner, that, for the purposes of the Fourteenth Amendment to the US Constitution, the corporation is a person without 'argument,' stating that 'we are all of the opinion that [the Fourteenth amendment] does' apply. See also; Gregory A. Mark, 'The Personification of the Business Corporation in American Law,' *University of Chicago Law Review* (1987) 54(4): 1441–1483; Carl J. Mayur, 'Personalizing the Impersonal: Corporations and the Bill of Rights,' *Hastings Law Journal* (1990) 41(3): 577–667; Cary Federman, 'Constructing Kinds of Persons in 1886: Corporate and Criminal,' *Law and Critique* (2003) 14(2): 167–189.

54 Grear, above note 49, p. 241; Fleur Johns, 'Theorizing the Corporation in International Law,' in Anne Orford and Florian Hoffmann (eds.), *The Oxford Handbook of the Theory of International Law* (Oxford University Press, 2016): 635–654; Grietje Baars, 'From the Dutch East India Company to the Corporate bill of Rights: Corporations and International Law,' in Ugo Mattei and John D. Haskell (eds.), *Research Handbook on Political Economy and Law*, (Edward Elgar, 2017): 260–279.

55 See: Doreen Lustig, *Veiled Power: International Law and the Private Corporation 1996–1981*, (Oxford University Press, 2020).

56 Rupert Gerritson (ed.), trans. Peter Reynders, 'A Translation of the Charter of the Dutch East India Company (Verenigde Oostindische Compagnie or VOC): Granted by the States General of the United Netherlands, 20 March 1602,' Australia on the Map Division of the Australasian Hydrographic Society Canberra (2009), p. 6.

57 Grear, above note 49, p. 238 – emphasis in the original.

58 Johns, above note 54, p. 641.

59 Baars, above note 8; Danielsen, above note 8.

form and its role in the global order by constricting 'corporate impunity, while at the same time keeping this fact largely hidden from us through its promise of accountability forever deferred'.[60] This, as Doreen Lustig argues, is part of a wider history of the co-construction of the state and the corporation in international law.[61] For example, the quote above from the 1602 Charter of the Dutch East India Company shows how the corporation and the state were already working together to co-govern in the seventeenth century. Lustig argues that these relations continue to the present day. Therefore, while the corporation is often deemed to be outside the realm of public international law, operating instead in the private domain, in reality, the corporation and the state continue to work in tandem to govern. This legal construction operates to insulate companies from responsibility while also sustaining 'hierarchical economic and political power relations'.[62] Thus, as Baars concludes, even those areas of international law that should be about protecting people, such as international criminal law, international human rights law and the field of business and human rights, have helped, and continue 'to help, corporations gain and maintain a legitimate role in the management of global affairs'.[63] By fostering a veneer of legitimacy, these frameworks actually justify the ultimately illegitimate power wielded by global corporations.[64] What becomes clear, therefore, is that while international law is formally based on nonhuman subjects, primarily the state, several other nonhuman subjects, such as the corporation, play a key role in the global order. The thing that both these nonhuman subject formations share, beyond their ability to wield power in the global order, is their consistent privileging of elite human interests over others.

The above discission of the sovereign state, sovereign equality, state consent and the corporate legal person in international law clearly exemplifies that the concept of the (nonhuman) sovereign state is all-too-human, being deeply embedded in constructions of power, gender and race in international law. International law's central focus on the state works to create hierarchies between so-called civilised and

---

60 Baars, Ibid., p. 13.

61 Lustig, above note 55.

62 Ibid., p. 4.

63 Baars, above note 8, p. 2. See also: Susan Marks, *A False Tree of Liberty: Human Rights in Radical Thought*, (Oxford University Press, 2019); Grietje Baars, '"It's not Me, It's the Corporation": The Value of Corporate Accountability in the Global Political Economy,' *London Review of International Law* (2016) 4(1): 127–163.
    Upendra Baxi has also warned against the emergence of a new paradigm of human rights that is more 'trade-related and market-friendly,' noting how this transformation helped 'justify corporate well-being and dignity over that of the human person.' See: Upendra Baxi, 'Voice of Suffering and the Future of Human Rights,' *Transnational Law and Contemporary Problems* (1998): 315–325, p. 321–322. Similarly, Susan Marks has argued that human rights discourses were actually complicit in the rise of neoliberal capitalism. See: Susan Marks, Four Human Rights Myths, LSE Law, Society and Economy Working Papers 10/2012. In addition, for a further analysis of the relationship between human rights and neoliberalism, see: Jessica Whyte, *The Morals of the Market: Human Rights and the Rise of Neoliberalism*, (Verso, 2019).

64 For more on how international law operates to allow corporations exert influence in international law while obscuring their agency, see: Lustig, above note 55.

uncivilised states while obliterating the diversity of voices within a state, working to represent the interests of a male elite.

International Law as All-Too-Human: Capitalism, Colonialism and Exclusion

While international law is formally based primarily around nonhuman entities, such as the state or international organisations, it is all-too-human, playing a central role in upholding and fostering global inequalities. In this section, I argue that the capitalist and neoliberal ideologies that underpin international law play a central role in the maintenance of an unequal global order.

Political economy 'has become the dominant discourse' in the contemporary global order.[65] While the story of industrialisation is often told through a narrative of progress,[66] in reality, it is clear that political economy is a form of 'global imperialism',[67] having been used to justify 'why some people have entitlements to land, resources and profits, and other people do not'.[68] This is exemplified by Ntina Tzouvala, who argues that progress in contemporary international law is often linked to a state's ability to conform with 'the basic tenets of capitalist modernity',[69] the 'standard of civilisation' in international law therefore being narrated through capitalist narratives of progress.[70] This means that, while, on the one hand, there is a scepticism around whether predominantly non-white communities can be equally included in international law (one that relies upon racism), on the other, their inclusion is considered desirable and possible depending on their ability to conform with capitalist modernity.[71] However, capitalist modernity wielded in the name of 'good governance' is neither a neutral nor an inevitable measure of progress.[72] As Anne Orford concludes, reflecting on free trade, neoliberal policies, while being touted as the "best" way to structure global economics, produce 'a system in which poorer countries continue to export vital resources even during periods of scarcity, investments are protected even during periods of civil war, and the people who

---

65 Anne Orford, 'Theorizing Free Trade,' in Anne Orford and Florian Hoffmann (eds.), *The Oxford Handbook of the Theory of International Law*, (Oxford University Press, 2016): 701–737, p. 701.

66 Ibid., p. 701.

67 B.S. Chimni, 'Capitalism, Imperialism, and International Law in the Twenty-First Century,' *Oregon Review of International Law* (2012) 14(1): 17–45.

68 Orford, above note 65, p. 702.

69 Ntina Tzouvala, *Capitalism as Civilisation: A History of International Law*, (Cambridge University Press, 2020), p. 2.

70 Ibid. See also Parfitt, above note 20, p. 381–392.

71 Tzouvala, Ibid., p. 22. Rose Parfitt also makes a similar argument, drawing on Tzouvala and applying her work specifically to the criteria for statehood. See: Parfitt, Ibid.

72 Tzouvala, Ibid.; James T. Gathii, 'Good Governance as a Counterinsurgency Agenda to Oppositional and Transformative Social Projects in International Law,' *Buffalo Human Rights Law Review* (1999) 5: 107–174; Orford, above note 65; See also: Parfitt, Ibid., p. 381–388. For an analysis of contemporary shifts/continuities in relation to the narrative of 'good governance,' see: Luis Eslava, *Local Space, Global Life: The Everyday Operation of International Law and Development*, (Cambridge University Press, 2015), p. 14–15.

labour to produce key commodities remain impoverished and undernourished'.[73] Overall, capitalist and neoliberal ideologies have worked to foster, perpetuate and legitimise global inequalities.[74]

Discussing more directly the role international law has played in the perpetuation of inequalities through political economy, Marxist international lawyers highlight international law's role in the functioning of capitalism. These scholars argue that international law is structured around capitalist accumulation and that this accumulation depends upon 'the exploitation and dispossession inflicted upon domestic working classes and colonial territories'.[75] Soviet legal thinker Pashukanis, for example, defined law, and international law, as being the intermediary in commodity exchange, this commodity exchange being deeply tied to imperialism.[76] International law is, he concludes, 'the legal form of the struggle of the capitalist states among themselves for domination over the rest of the world'.[77] States are therefore, according to Pashukanis, either capitalist states or the object of capitalist states.[78] This can be seen, he argues, in the fact that 'states have equal rights yet in reality they are unequal in their significance and in their power'[79] – a point I made above.

However, Marxist international lawyers disagree about the exact relationship between international law and capitalism. While scholars such as China Miéville argue that international law is a capitalist structure, stating that the 'chaotic and bloody world around us *is the rule of law*',[80] thereby finding little hope or promise in international law's transformative potential, others remain more hopeful. Tzouvala, for example, disputes the linking of the 'penultimate essence of law' to the 'penultimate essence of capitalism'.[81] Tzouvala thus highlights the close relationship between international law and capitalism without 'attempting to explain the entirety of the relationship between international law and capitalism'.[82] This seems like a sensible approach, and one that allows for a wider array of structurally oppressive forces to be made visible in the history of international law, including class and race but also gender. This is vital. For example, Robert Knox has shown how race and capitalism are mutually constitutive[83] while feminist socialists

---

73 Orford, Ibid., p. 702.

74 Orford, Ibid., p. 703. See also; Ingo Venzke, 'The Law of the Global Economy and the Spectre of inequality,' *London Review of International Law* (2021) 9(1): 111–134.

75 Tzouvala, above note 69, p. 21. See also: Robert Knox, 'Marxist Approaches to International Law, in Anne Orford and Florian Hoffmann (eds.), *The Oxford Handbook of the Theory of International Law*, (Oxford University Press, 2016): 306–326.

76 Evgeny B. Pashukanis, 'The General Theory of Law and Marxism,' in Piers Beirne and Robert Sharlet (eds.), *Pashukanis: Selected Writings on Marxism and Law*, (Academic Press London, 1980), p. 58, 77.

77 Ibid., p. 169.

78 Ibid., p. 172. See also: Miéville, above note 20.

79 Pashukanis, Ibid., p. 178.

80 Miéville, above note 20, p. 319 – author's own emphasis.

81 Tzouvala, above note 69, p. 41.

82 Tzouvala, Ibid., p. 42.

83 Robert Knox, 'Valuing Race? Stretched Marxism and the logic of imperialism,' *London Review of International Law* (2016) 4(1): 81–126.

have highlighted the gendered nature of contemporary capitalism,[84] including how capitalist ideologies uphold the gender binary.[85] Overall, what is clear is that international law is permeated by a series of structures and values, including 'the standard of civilisation,' capitalism and patriarchy. These values are neither inevitable nor neutral,[86] and, as I argue and exemplify in later chapters of this book, international law *can* be imagined otherwise.

International law, alongside and as part of other forces, such as political economy, plays a role in fostering global inequalities: and these inequalities are vast. In 2019, the world's billionaires, only 2153 people, shared more wealth than the bottom 4.6 billion people (who make up 60 percent of the world's population).[87] While the billionaires in question are mostly men, the unpaid care work undertaken by women globally is estimated to be worth US$10.8 trillion, this being three times the size of the global tech industry.[88] In addition, Oxfam International found that the world's 22 richest men have more wealth than all of the women in the African continent.[89] The COVID-19 pandemic has exacerbated this, with 97 million more people being put into poverty in 2020.[90] This sits in contrast to statistics from April to July of the same year that show that total billionaire wealth climbed by 27.5 percent.[91] While global poverty is often associated with the global south, another notable recent phenomenon is the exacerbation of global inequalities in wealthy, global north states. For example, during a country visit to the UK, the world's fifth largest economy, the former UN Special Rapporteur on extreme poverty and human rights, Philip Alston, found that a fifth of the population of the UK now live in poverty.[92]

84 Christine Delphy, trans. Diana Leonard, 'A Materialist Feminism is Possible,' *Feminist Review* (1980) 4: 79–105; Tzouvala, above note 69, p. 32; Anne McClimtock, *Imperial Leather: Race, Gender and Sexuality in the Colonial Context*, (Routledge, 1995), p. 207–208; Rosemary Hennessey and Chrys Ingraham, 'Introduction: Reclaiming Anticapitalist Feminism,' in Rosemary Hennessey and Chrys Ingraham (eds.), *Materialist Feminism: A Reader in Class, Difference and Women's Lives*, (Routledge 1997): 1–14.

85 Jules Joanne Gleeson and Elle O'Rourke (eds.), *Transgender Marxism*, (Pluto Press, 2021); Mario Meili, *Towards a Gay Communism: Elements of a Homosexual Critique*, (Pluto Press, 2002); Holly Lewis, *The Politics of Everybody: Feminism, Queer Theory and Marxism at the Intersection*, (Zed Books, 2016).

86 See also: Parfitt, above note 20.

87 Oxfam International, 'Time to Care: Unpaid and Underpaid Care Work and the Global Inequality Crisis,' 20 January 2020.

88 Ibid.

89 Ibid.

90 Daniel Gerszon Mahler et al., Updated Estimates of the Impact of COVID-19 on Global Poverty: Turning the Corner on the Pandemic in 2021?, World Bank Blogs, 24 June 2021, https://blogs.worldbank.org/opendata/updated-estimates-impact-covid-19-global-poverty-turning-corner-pandemic-2021 (last accessed 11 July 2022).

91 UBS, 'Riding the Storm: Market Turbulence Accelerates Diverging Fortunes,' *Billionaires Insight* 2020, p. 36, www.ubs.com/content/dam/static/noindex/wealth-management/ubs-billionaires-report-2020-spread.pdf (last accessed 28 September 2022).

92 UN Human Rights Council, Report of the Special Rapporteur on Extreme Poverty and Human Rights: Visit to the United Kingdom of Great Britain and Northern Ireland, 30 May 2019, A/HRC/41/39.

What these factors expose is the all-too-human nature of international law. International law claims to be objective. However, the capitalist, colonial and gendered values that underpin international law have deeply biased impacts, creating categories of people who are more human than others. While, as Martti Koskenniemi notes, 'nobody denies that extreme poverty ought to be eradicated',[93] the former UN Special Rapporteur on extreme poverty and human rights argued in 2015 that the 'international human rights community' has largely ignored 'the consequences of extreme inequality'.[94] While this may be true, it is also not the fault, entirely, of the human rights community. Human rights remain difficult to enforce,[95] particularly in relation to economic and social rights, whereas international economic law provisions are rarely plagued by the same issues of enforceability. Therefore, as Jason Beckett argues, it becomes clear that extreme poverty is both 'a man-made phenomenon' and a 'legal regime'.[96] International law helps uphold poverty, sustaining and perpetuating hierarchies within humanity.

"The human" has never been a neutral term, however. Drawing on Michel Foucault's critique of the epistemological construct of "man",[97] anticolonial thinker Sylvia Wynter critiques the overrepresentation of man and the creation of a central subject of thought that is based upon the white, wealthy man of the global north, noting how this construction also creates 'subjugated Human Others'.[98] Other scholars have made similar points, with Frantz Fanon, for example, analysing the dehumanisation or 'damned' status of the colonial subject[99] and with Ayça Çubukçu examining the problematic way that 'humanity' still operates as a category

---

93 Martti Koskenniemi, *International Law and the Far Right: Reflection of Law and Cynicism*, Annual T.M.C Asser Lecture Series (T. M. C. Asser Press, 2019), p. 20.

94 UN Human Rights Council, Report of the Special Rapporteur on Extreme Poverty and Human Rights, Philip Alston, 27 May 2015, A/HRC/29/31, para 3.

95 Ingo Venzke likewise argues that the issue surrounding the enforcement of human rights is an example of how international law is complicit in perpetuating global inequalities. See: Venzke, above note 74.

96 Jason Beckett, 'Creating Poverty,' in Anne Orford and Florian Hoffmann (eds.), *The Oxford Handbook of the Theory of International Law*, (Oxford University Press, 2016): 985–1010, p. 985.

97 Michel Foucault, *The Order of Things*, (Routledge, 2001 [1966]).

98 Sylvia Wynter, 'Unsettling the Coloniality of Being/Power/Truth/Freedom: Towards the Human/After Man, Its Overrepresentation – An Argument,' *The New Centennial Review* (2003) 3(3): 257–337, p. 288. See also: Sylvia Wynter and Katherine McKittrick, 'Unparalleled Catastrophe for Our Species? Or, to Give Humanness a Different Future: Conversations,' in Katherine McKittrick (ed.), *Sylvia Wynter: On Being Human as Praxis*, (Duke University Press, 2015): 9–89; Sylvia Wynter, 'On How We Mistook the Map for the Territory, and Re-Imprisoned Ourselves in Our Unbearable Wrongness of Being, of Désêtre: Black Studies Toward the Human Project,' in Lewis R. Gordon and Jane Anna Gordon (eds.), *Not Only the Master's Tools: African-American Studies and Theory in Practice*, (Paradigm Publishers, 2006): 107–169.

For more on situating anticolonial theories of the human, such as that of Wynter but also others, alongside posthuman thought, see: Zakiyyah Iman Jackson, 'Animal: New Directions in the Theorization of Race and Posthumanism,' *Feminist Studies* (2013) 39(3): 669–685.

99 Frantz Fanon, trans Constance Farringdon, *The Wretched of the Earth*, (Grove Press, 1963). For a discussion of Fanon's conceptualisation of humanity and the damned as applied to international law, see: Kojo Koram, '"Satan is Black" – Frantz Fanon's Juridico-Theology of Racialisation and Damnation,' *Law, Culture and the Humanities* (2017): 1–20.

to include and exclude both subjects but also alternative modes of thought.[100] In a similar vein, queer scholars have noted the inhuman or less-than-human nature of the queer subject, a point I will return to in more detail in Chapter 3.[101] This critique of "man" has led Rosi Braidotti to declare that the end of humanity 'has been *leitmotif* in European philosophy ever since Friedrich Nietzsche proclaimed the "death of God" and of the idea of Man that was built upon it'.[102] In fact 'humanity', she continues, 'is very much the male of the species: it is a he' who is 'white, European, handsome and able-bodied'.[103]

This scholarship echoes much of the analysis I have provided of international law above, including the way international law perpetuates capitalism, colonialism and patriarchy, creating some subjects that are less human, at least in terms of political status, than others. Turning to international legal history, this categorisation of people as more or less than human (with the human, here, in fact being the white, European man) can be seen clearly when looking at the League of Nations Mandate System which was set up in the aftermath of the Great War. Under the Mandate System, territories were categorised as class 'A', 'B' or 'C' Mandates, depending on an array of factors including, most notably, 'the stage of development of the people'.[104] 'A' Mandates were deemed to have reached the highest 'stage of development', thus being 'provisionally recognised' until 'able to stand alone', with 'B' Mandates being those deemed less ready for independence and 'C' Mandates being territories defined as so unable to self-govern that they were 'best administered under the law of the Mandatory', i.e. another state such as the UK or France.[105] Yet this levelled categorisation of human and less-than-human peoples has a much longer history in international law, with the eighteenth and nineteenth centuries seeing some peoples having been denied political status entirely, their land being declared *terra nullius*, 'nobody's land', which could therefore, according to this logic, be occupied and colonised without even the pretence of an exploitative agreement or Treaty made in bad faith.[106] The Earth's colonised have long known the exclusive nature of the category of the "human" and international law's role in enforcing such exclusions through violence, domination and exploitation. Colonialism is at the

---

100 Ayça Çubukçu, 'Thinking Against Humanity,' *London Review of International Law* (2017) 5(2): 251–267.

101 Dana Luciano and Mel Y. Chen, 'Has the Queer ever been Human?' *GLQ: A Journal of Lesbian and Gay Studies* (2015) 21(203): 183–207; Gloria Anzaldúa, *Borderlands/La Frontera: The New Mestiza*, (Aunt Lute Books, 2012), p. 40.

102 Braidotti, above note 1, p. 6.

103 Ibid., p. 24.

104 League of Nations, Covenant of the League of Nations, 28 April 1919, Article 22.

105 Ibid.. For an analysis of the Mandate system, see Ntina Tzouvala, 'The Institutionalisation of Civilisation in the Interwar Period,' in Ntina Tzouvala, *Capitalism as Civilisation: A History of International Law* (Cambridge University Press, 2020): 88–128. For an analysis of more and less than human statuses during the wider colonial era, see: Anghie, above note 16.

106 For an Indigenous perspective on this, see: Irene Watson, 'Buried Alive,' *Law and Critique* (2002) 13: 253–269.

founding core of the international legal project[107] and international law continues to enforce an exclusionary model of humanity.[108] In short, while international law may be formally based on nonhuman actors, the impact of the law and the way it operates in determining which lives are more worthy than others, more grievable than others,[109] is deeply human in all too familiar ways.

Colonialism, Anthropocentrism and Land Grabbing

Another factor that is exposed through the above analysis of the role of corporations and capitalism in international law as compared to statistics on global poverty, is the deeply *material* nature of the law and the way that the law situates the particular (white, male) human in hierarchical priority over the nonhuman environment. This is a phenomenon that Jason Moore terms the capitalocene, describing, in Donna Haraway's words, the 'system of power, profit and re/production in the web of life',[110] in other words, describing capitalism's role in the objectification of the environment and the nonhuman animal for profit.[111] Adding another layer of analysis, Carmen G. Gonzalez helpfully uses the framework of racial capitalism to think through the relationship between 'environmental degradation, racial subordination, and the capitalist world economy'.[112] After all, colonialism and the capitalist domination of nature and nonhuman animals have long been intertwined: rapid industrialisation under colonialism worked in assemblage with racism and other imposed hierarchies to ensure that Europe made a profit at the expense of peoples *and* their environments.[113] The links between capitalism, poverty and anthropocentrism can also be seen when looking at the 2019 Report of the Special Rapporteur on extreme poverty and human rights entitled 'Climate Change and Poverty'. In this report, the Special Rapporteur notes how climate change will not only make things worse for those already living in poverty, but will also 'pull vast numbers into poverty'.[114] Exclusionary humanism and anthropocentrism go hand in hand.

107 Anghie, above note 16.
108 Koram, above note 99; Çubukçu, above note 100.
109 Judith Butler, *Frames of War: When is Life Grieveable?* (Verso, 2009).
110 Jason Moore, 'The Capitalocene, Part I: On the Nature and Origins of Our Ecological Crisis,' *The Journal of Peasant Studies* (2017) 44(3): 594–630, p. 594.
111 Donna Haraway, *Staying with the Trouble: Making Kin in the Chthulucene*, (Duke University Press, 2016), p. 47-51.
112 Carmen G. Gonzalez, 'Racial Capitalism and the Anthropocene,' in Sumudu A. Atapattu, Carmen G. Gonzalez and Sara L. Seck (eds.), *The Cambridge Handbook of Environmental Justice and Sustainable Development*, (Cambridge University Press, 2021): 72–85, p. 72. See also: Angela P. Harris, 'Toward a Law and Political Economy Approach to Environmental Justice,' in Sumudu A. Atapattu, Carmen G. Gonzalez and Sara L. Seck (eds.), *The Cambridge Handbook of Environmental Justice and Sustainable Development*, (Cambridge University Press, 2021): 453–469.
113 See, for example, Anna Grear, 'Human Rights, Property and the search for 'Worlds Other," *Journal of Human Rights and the Environment* (2012) 3(2): 173-195.
114 UN Human Rights Council, 'Report of the Special Rapporteur on Extreme Poverty and Human Rights: Climate Change and Poverty,' 17 July 2019, A/HRC/41/39.

The phenomenon of land grabbing exemplifies these links between exclusionary humanism and anthropocentrism. Land grabbing is the large-scale appropriation of land, either through buying or leasing it, by various entities including corporations, states and individuals. Land grabbing has a long history rooted in colonialism.[115] However, land grabbing became a particular phenomenon in the contemporary global order following the 2008 global spike in food prices.[116] This spike caused many entities to seek to acquire land with the objective of making a profit in case of future spikes.[117] While food production is the most prominent reason for land grabbing,[118] other reasons include, for example, the production of biofuel. Land grabbing was estimated by the World Bank in 2010 to have resulted in the acquisition of around 45 million hectares of land,[119] with the Land Matrix, a global and independent land monitoring initiative, citing a figure of 42 million between 2012 and 2016.[120] As the World Bank has noted, land grabs tend to happen in places where government controls are weaker, often due to government indebtedness, with land grabs generally occurring in areas where the poorest rural people live, 'expelling people with non-traditional land title from their land'.[121] Further, while 'some of this land had been cleared of existing inhabitants and users' much of it has subsequently 'not yet [been] put into production; in many cases buyers and investors are simply preparing for the next global crisis'.[122]

An example of the all-too-human impact of land grabbing can be seen by looking at a land grabbing project which began in 2011 in Senegal. The land in question was leased to grow biofuel, given the increasing demand for low carbon solutions

115 See; GRAIN, Seized: The 2008 Landgrab for Food and Financial Security, 24 October 2008, www.grain.org/article/entries/93-seized-the-2008-landgrab-for-food-and-financial-security (last accessed 11 July 2022); Marc Edelman et al.,, 'Global Land Grabs: Historical Processes, Theoretical and Methodological Implications and Current Trajectories,' *Third World Quarterly* (2013) 34(9): 1517–1531. In addition, Surabhi Ranganathan has highlighted the fact that land grabs apply at sea, discussing the phenomenon of ocean floor grabbing. See: Surabhi Ranganathan, 'Ocean Floor Grab: International Law and the Making of an Extractive Imaginary,' *European Journal of International Law* (2019) 30(2): 573–600.

116 See: GRAIN, Ibid.; Marc Edelman, et al., (eds.). *Global Land Grabs: History, Theory and Method*, (Routledge, 2015).

117 This phenomenon is defined by the World Bank as having been massively impacted by the 2008 crisis. See: World Bank, 'Rising Global Interest in Farmland: Can It Yield Sustainable and Equitable Benefits?' World Bank, 2011, https://documents1.worldbank.org/curated/en/998581468184149953/pdf/594630PUB0ID1810Box358282B01PUBLIC1.pdf (last accessed 28 September 2022).

118 Kerstin Nolte et al.; "International Land Deals for Agriculture: Fresh Insights from the Land Matrix: Analytical Report II,' Centre for Development and Environment, University of Bern, and German Institute of Global and Area Studies, University of Pretoria, Bern Open Publishing, 2016, www.landmatrix.org/media/filer_public/ab/c8/abc8b563-9d74-4a47-9548-cb59e4809b4e/land_matrix_2016_analytical_report_draft_ii.pdf (last accessed 11 July 2022).

119 World Bank, above note 117.

120 Nolte et al. above note 118.

121 Saturnino M. Borras Jr. et al., 'Towards a Better Understanding of Global Land Grabbing: An Editorial Introduction,' *The Journal of Peasant Studies* (2011) 38(2): 209–216, p. 210.

122 Ibid., p. 209.

in Europe.[123] The ongoing project led by Italian Tampieri Financial Group and the Senegalese Senethanol, resulted in many in the local community losing access to grazing land, land for the collection and cultivation of timber and access to water collection points.[124] Nine thousand community members and 40 villages had been affected as of 2016.[125] Further to this 'villagers living in close proximity to the project are under constant threat of eviction by company representatives and local police'.[126] Again, the nexus between sovereign state power and the protection of private and corporate financial interests at the expense of real lives is clear in this example, as is the displacement of climate change, this land grab having occurred as part of a biofuel project that seeks to address the environmental concerns of Europe through the displacement of people in the global south.

North/south politics play out in complex ways in the context of land grabbing.[127] Most land grabs happen in the global south: the vast majority of land grabs occur within the African continent, the second next biggest site being Asia.[128] There are clear undertones of colonialism in the story of land grabbing with many of these corporations coming from the global north.[129] It must be noted, however, that many of the rich in the global south are grabbing land in the global south too,[130] with Malaysian companies being the biggest corporate land grabbers according to the Land Matrix.[131] The vast majority of land grabs (over 70 percent) occur at the hands of private companies.[132] Land grabbing thereby provides a contemporary example of how corporations continue to colonise,[133] exploiting the land of people and nonhuman animals who were formerly colonised by European states.[134]

Rosi Braidotti has identified the role 'advanced capitalism' plays in the contemporary posthuman convergence, exposing the interlinking ways that the social injustices fostered by capitalism work alongside other vectors, such as the threat to humanity posed by climate change, to 'simultaneously unit[e] … humanity in the

123 See: Climate Diplomacy, Protest Against the Senhuile-Senethanol Project in Senegal, https://climate-diplomacy.org/case-studies/protest-against-senhuile-senethanol-project-senegal#-fact_sheet_toc-actors (last accessed 11 July 2022).
124 See: Ibid.; Nolte et al, above note 118, p. 43.
125 Nolte et al., Ibid.
126 Ibid.
127 For a discussion of land grabbing in post-colonial states, see: Ntina Tzouvala, 'A False Promise? Regulating Land-Grabbing and the Post-Colonial States,' *Leiden Journal of International Law* (2019) 32(2): 235–253.
128 Nolte et al, above note 118, p. 9, 16.
129 Ibid.
130 Saturnino M. Borras Jr. et al., above note 121, p. 209.
131 Nolte et al, above note 118, p. 22.
132 Ibid., p. 26.
133 Some land grabs have occurred in the global north, e.g. Australia, New Zealand, Spain – though these are in the minority. See: Ibid.
134 See also: Penelope Simons, 'International Law's Invisible Hand and the Future of Corporate Accountability for Violations of Human Rights,' *Journal of Human Rights and the Environment* (2013) 3(1): 5–43. For a Marxist analysis of the international legal issues related to land grabbing, see: Umut Özsu, 'Grabbing Land Legally: A Marxist Analysis,' *Leiden Journal of International Law* (2019) 32: 215–233.

threat of extinction' while also 'dividing it by controlling access to the resources needed to meet the challenge'.[135] Thus, she concludes, '[t]he economically dispossessed and impoverished are missing out on the advantages and profits of advanced capitalism and are in fact the most exposed to the lethal effects of ecological depletion and global pandemics'.[136] It is clear from the above examples that international law, too, is marked by the dynamics of the posthuman convergence described by Braidotti. International law, despite its formal primary focus on nonhuman legal subjects, is all-too-human. International law is deeply humanist, protecting certain elite human interests over all others. Furthermore, the exclusionary humanism of international law goes hand in hand with anthropocentrism and the exploitation of the environment. In the next section, I will delve deeper into my evaluation of the anthropocentrism of international law, providing a critical analysis of the area of international law that is supposed to protect against environmental exploitation: international environmental law.

The Anthropocentrism of International (Environmental) Law

Globally, groups are declaring that we have reached an era of "climate emergency".[137] Environmental damage is increasing yet not enough action is being taken. The impacts of climate change and environmental degradation are global, impacting on human and nonhuman life. Climate change has already displaced communities, rendering their homes uninhabitable,[138] while over one million plant and animal species are currently threatened by extinction.[139] It is clear, however, that while we are, as Braidotti notes, 'all in this together, we are not', she continues, 'one and the same'.[140] The impacts of cryosphere (the frozen parts of the Earth) change, for example, are being felt in particular by communities who live in close connection with the ocean and cryosphere, including those in coastal environments, on small islands, in polar areas or in the high mountains, with the impacts on Indigenous communities being most prominent.[141] In the meantime,

135 Rosi Braidotti, *Posthuman Feminism*, (Polity Press, 2022), p. 4–5.

136 Ibid

137 W. J. Ripple et al., 'World Scientists' Warning of a Climate Emergency,' *Bioscience* (2020) 70(1): 8–12; Climate Emergency and Declaration and Mobilisation in Action, Climate Emergency Declaration Datasheet,' https://www.cedamia.org/global/ (last accessed 11 July 2021).

138 This can be seen, for example, in Fiji. See: Annah E. Piggott-McKellar et al., 'Moving People in a Changing Climate: Lessons from Two Case Studies in Fiji,' *Social Sciences* (2019) 8(133): 1–17.

139 Intergovernmental Science-Policy Platform on Biodiversity and Ecosystem Services (IPBES), 'The Global Assessment Report on Biodiversity and Ecosystem Services: Summary for Policymakers,' 2019, https://ipbes.net/sites/default/files/2020-02/ipbes_global_assessment_report_summary_for_policymakers_en.pdf (last accessed 11 July 2022).

140 This is a phrase Braidotti uses throughout her work. However, see: Rosi Braidotti, '"We" Are in *This* Together, but We Are Not One and the Same,' *Journal of Bioethical Inquiry* (2020) 17: 465–468.

141 IPCC, 'Summary for Policymakers,' IPCC Special Report on the Ocean and Cryosphere in a Changing Climate, 2019, p. 15, https://www.ipcc.ch/srocc/chapter/summary-for-policymakers/ (last accessed 29 September 2022).

climate change displacement will primarily affect people in the global south.[142] Further, as noted above, '[c]limate change will have devastating consequences for people in poverty'.[143] Women are also at the receiving end of a disproportionate number of the impacts of climate change, with many policies to tackle these impacts upholding male norms and thereby failing to address the needs of women.[144] Furthermore, people with disabilities are also some of the most adversely impacted people when it comes to environmental impacts, yet this issue receives little attention.[145]

Greater environmental action is urgently needed. Lawyers have long sought recourse through the law. The main area of international law that focuses on protecting the environment is international environmental law. Despite this, 'it is striking how little international environmental law does, in fact, regulate' with many environmental issues being governed, not by international environmental law, but by other areas of law, including agricultural practices and the slaughter of animals for food.[146] While scholars have provided a critical analysis of these areas of law and their anthropocentric nature elsewhere, in this section, I outline how international environmental law, the body of law supposedly most squarely targeted at environmental protection, is anthropocentric.

International environmental law is made up of a series of focused instruments that govern different parts of the environment, with different principles and approaches emerging accordingly. Examples include treaties that focus on conservation and sustainable use of natural resources and biodiversity,[147] the obligation to preserve the marine environment,[148] instruments to decrease pollution[149] and so forth. Positive obligations focus on specific areas: there is no general obligation in international

---

142 Sawkat Alam et al. (eds.), *International Environmental Law and the Global South*, (Cambridge University Press, 2015). Usha Natarajan, 'Third World Approaches to International Law (TWAIL) and the Environment' in Andreas Philippopoulos-Mihalopoulos and Victoria Brooks (eds.), *Research Methods in Environmental Law: A Handbook*, (Edward Elgar, 2017): 207–235.

143 UN Human Rights Council, above note 114. See also; Sumudu Atapattu and Carmen G. Gonzalez, 'The North-South Divide in International Environmental Law', in Sawkat Alam et al. (eds.), *International Environmental Law and the Global South*, (Cambridge University Press, 2015): 1–20.

144 Joane Nagel, *Gender and Climate Change: Impacts, Science, Policy*, (Routledge, 2016).

145 Sumudu A. Atapattu et al., 'Intersections of Environmental Justice and Sustainable Development: Framing the Issues,' in Sumudu A. Atapattu et al. (eds.), *The Cambridge Handbook of Environmental Justice and Sustainable Development*, (Cambridge University Press, 2021): 1–20, p. 15; Global Greengrants Fund, Why the Environmental Justice Movement Must Include Persons with Disabilities, 18 March 2019, www.greengrants.org/2019/03/18/disability-and-environment (last accessed 11 July 2022).

146 Stephen Humphreys and Yoriko Otomo, 'Theorizing International Environmental Law,' in Anne Orford and Florian Hoffman (eds.), *The Oxford Handbook of the Theory of International Law*, (Oxford University Press, 2016): 797–819, p. 798.

147 United Nations, Convention on Biological Diversity, 5 June 1992, 1760, U.N.T.S. vol. 69.

148 United Nations General Assembly, Convention on the Law of the Sea, 10 December 1982, Article 192.

149 Conference of the Parties, Adoption of the Paris Agreement, 12 December 2015, U.N. Doc. FCCC/CP/2015/L.9/Rev/1.

law to protect the environment.[150] While the UN General Assembly has taken up the task of environmental protection, most notably through the work of the UN Environment Programme (UNEP), there is no single organisation that has the competence over all environmental matters.[151] The issue of fragmentation within public international law generally[152] is a key challenge within international environmental law too,[153] and while certain areas of this field of law are moving towards a more integrated approach, changes are occurring only within specific areas.[154]

There have been some attempts to create a stronger international legal basis for environmental protection. One obvious site for international lawyers in this regard, given the lack of Treaty provision, is customary international law. Customary international laws are laws that states may not have signed up to *per se*, at least not necessarily in the form of a formal legal document such as a Treaty, but are said to exist and apply universally first, because of state practice, i.e. states are generally following the rule, and second, through *opinio juris* – states believe that this rule is the law. If both the elements of state practice and *opinio juris* can be shown, a rule can be deemed to be a source of international law,[155] meaning, for the most part, it applies to all states.[156] However, while the 1972 Stockholm Conference on the Human Environment and 1992 Rio Conference on Environment and Development were both political attempts at creating universal rules and principles, and while 'some of the principles contained in' the instruments that came about from these conferences 'are of sufficiently norm-creating character' to potentially be deemed customary international law,[157] an overall customary international legal obligation to protect

150 For example, looking at the Stockholm Declaration, it seems Principle 2 comes closest to seeking to protect the environment overall. However, environmental protection is named as needed for the sake of 'future generations', retaining an anthropocentric stance. See: UN General Assembly, Stockholm Declaration, United Nations Conference on the Human Environment, 15 December 1972, A/RES/2994.

151 The UN Environment Assembly (UNEA) does do some important work here, however.

152 Martti Koskenniemi, 'Fragmentation of International Law: Difficulties Arising from the Diversification and Expansion of International Law,' International Law Commission 2006, A/CN.4/1.682.

153 This has been noted by the UN Secretary General as well as the Ecological Law and Governance Association in the Oslo Manifesto. See: UN General Assembly, Report of UN Secretary General, Gaps in International Environmental Law and Environment-Related Instruments: Towards a Global Pact for the Environment, 30 November 2018, A/73/419; Ecological Law and Governance Association, Oslo Manifesto, https://elgaworld.org/oslo-manifesto (last accessed 11 July 2022).

154 Redgwell argues that ongoing developments within the remit of the UN Convention on Biological Diversity 1992 are possibly the strongest example of attempts at integration. See: Catherine Redgwell, 'International Environmental Law,' in Malcolm D. Evans (ed.), *International Law*, (Oxford University Press, 5th edn, 2018): 675–716, p. 677.

155 United Nations, Statute of the International Court of Justice, 18 April 1946, Article 38(1).

156 Subject to the persistent objector rule.

157 Redgwell, above note 154, p. 680.
      Some of these principles have indeed been recognised as customary international law. For example, the principle of prevention has been recognised by the ICJ in its 1966 Advisory Opinion on *The Legality of the Threat or Use of Nuclear Weapons*, above note 4, para 29; *Pulp Mills on the River Uruguay, Argentina v Uruguay*, International Court of Justice, 2006 ICJ Rep 113, para 101.

the environment cannot easily be deemed to exist. This is due, in part, to the fact that most state practice promotes economic interests over environmental protection, with states believing this to be permissible. To some extent the law supports them in this line of thought. For example, while international environmental law is often plagued by enforcement issues, with many of the key instruments of international environmental law being soft law provisions and therefore more difficult to enforce, in contrast, international economic law has much stronger structures of both adjudication and enforcement, thereby creating incentives to comply with the latter when these two bodies of law clash.

The principle of sustainable development provides an example of a principle that prioritises economic need over environmental need. This principle, often deemed to be 'the über-principle' of international environmental law,[158] is made up of several components, including the general need to exploit resources in a manner that is 'sustainable', the need to preserve resources for future generations, the equitable use of resources between states and the need to consider economic and development plans and objectives.[159] Originally a principle put in place, in part, to seek to balance the economic differences between states, in the contemporary, the need to balance sustainability against economic and development objectives is supposed to be applied to ensure that states, and especially states with stronger development needs, can continue to draw on their natural resources[160] (though the principle also has a longer and darker colonial history).[161] Overall, the principle purports that economic growth, human development and environmental protection can co-exist.[162] Critics, however, argue that sustainable development is impossible while capitalist economic growth remains embedded within the principle itself.[163] In short, the sustainable development approach ultimately allows environmental exploitation to continue. While sustainable development seeks, in part, to account for economic imbalances (many of which are the result of colonialism and the ways European powers profited, and continue to profit from, the extraction of resources from the places they colonised) there are risks presented by this approach, which is used by states to justify environmental damage. Speaking specifically about global north/south inequalities, Usha Natarajan and Kishan Khoday argue that sustainable

---

158 Humphreys and Otomo, above note 146, p. 800.
159 For a history of sustainable development, see: Sumudu A. Atapattu et al., above note 145, p. 3–9.
   Sustainable development concretised recently through its use in the 2015 Paris Agreement to the UN Framework Convention on Climate Change (UNFCCC) and the 2017 Resolution of the UN General Assembly, 'Our Ocean, Our Future: Call to Action.' See: United Nations, UNGA Res A/Res/71/312 (2017).
160 See: Ruth Gordon, 'Unsustainable Development' in Shawkat Alam et al. (eds.), *International Environmental Law and the Global South*, (Cambridge University Press, 2015): 50–73.
161 Humphreys and Otomo, above note 146, p. 816.
162 John C. Bernbach and Fererico Cheever, 'Sustainable Development and Its Discontents,' *Transnational Environmental Law* (2015) 4(2): 247–287.
163 Gordon, 'above note 160; Sumudu A. Atapattu et al., above note 145, p. 5.

development is seldom used 'to call for less development'.[164] They subsequently conclude that the concept of sustainable development ensures that the status quo remains, helping to 'naturalize and obfuscate the process whereby some people systemically under-develop others', resulting in the continued deepening of global inequalities.[165]

Principles that potentially invoke a more universal nature have, however, been used in specific Treaty regimes, such as the concept of the common heritage of humankind (tellingly originally referred to as 'mankind'). However, it is key to note that this principle has mostly been invoked in relation to resources within international territories not owned by one state alone, such as the high seas, with invocation being most prominent notably in relation to resources in the deep seabed.[166] While some have argued that the principle should be applied more broadly to that which is essential to the shared interest of all humans, with arguments also being made around the need to preserve it for future generations,[167] the application of the principle within the territorial jurisdiction of sovereign states has proven controversial.[168] Overall, 'no fully agreed definition' of the common heritage principle exists, with the application of the principle varying in the 'different legal regimes referring to it or being based upon it'.[169] While the principle has been invoked in more general international environmental law, the term more commonly used here is the 'common concern of mankind',[170] which, as Rüdiger Wolfrum points out, 'seems to call predominantly for co-operation and equitable burden sharing, and does not cover the full spectrum of the common heritage principle'.[171] It is evident that the principle of the common heritage of humankind is by no means universally understood and applied. For example, reflecting on outer space law,

---

164 Usha Natarajan and Kishan Khoday, 'Locating Nature: Making and Unmaking International Law,' *Leiden Journal of International Law* (2014) 27(3): 573–593, p. 589.

165 Ibid.

166 See, for example; United Nations, above note 147, Preamble; UN General Assembly, above note 148, Article 136; UN General Assembly, Resolution 2749, Declaration of Principles Governing the Seabed and the Ocean Floor, and the Subsoil Thereof, beyond the Limits of National Jurisdiction, 17 December 1970, UNGA 118, A/RES/2749 (XXV); Agreement Relating to the Implementation of Part XI of the United Nations Convention on the Law of the Sea of 10 December 1982, adopted July 28, 1994, 1836 U.N.T.S. 3. See: Rüdiger Wolfrum, Common Heritage of Mankind, Max Planck Encyclopaedias of International Law,https://opil.ouplaw.com/view/10.1093/law:epil/9780199231690/law-9780199231690-e1149> (last accessed 11 July 2022).

167 Philippe Sands and Jacqueline Peel, *Principles of Environmental Law*, (Cambridge University Press, 4th edn, 2018), p. 552.

168 See: Wolfrum, above note 166; John E. Noyes, 'The Common Heritage of Mankind: Past, Present, and Future,' *Denver Journal of International Law and Policy* (2011) 40: 447–471, p. 450.

169 Wolfrum, Ibid.

170 See, for example, Protection of Global Climate for Present and Future Generations of Mankind, UNGA Res 43/53, 6 December 1988, GAOR 43rd Session Supp 49 vol. 1, 133.

171 Wolfrum, above note 166.

under which space has traditionally been treated as part of the commons,[172] Craven argues that the 'commons' has come to be understood in a way that justifies the commercial exploitation of nature in the name of societal interests.[173] Likewise, Surabhi Ranganathan has argued that the marking of the deep seabed as part of the 'common heritage of mankind'[174] was likewise used to mark the ocean floor as a site of extraction.[175] Given these insights, while the idea of using the principle of common heritage to protect the environment in and of itself may seem both necessary and, in some ways ideal, legally, it is clear that this is not the dominant understanding of the common heritage principle which, rather, has been used to mask extractive interests.

Furthermore, as a specialised area of general international law, international environmental law is formed by laws arising from the sovereign will of states – a framework for international law-making that ensures that state interests, and thereby economic interests, must be balanced against environmental damage and may even be protected over environmental interests (as exemplified through the above discussion of sustainable development). International environmental law perpetuates this structure. This can be seen, for example, by looking at some of the early core environmental law instruments that shored up the state's sovereignty over its natural resources, situating the environment and nonhuman animals as resources, objects to be exploited. For example, the 1992 Convention on Biological Diversity

---

172 The legal principle which states that outer space is part of the global commons to be held by all mankind is to be found in, for example: UNGA, The Treaty on Principles Governing the Activities of States in the Exploration and Use of Outer Space, Including the Moon and Other Celestial Bodies (The Outer Space Treaty), 27 January 1967, UNGA Resolution 2222 (XXI); UNGA, Agreement Governing the Activities of States on the Moon and Other Celestial Bodies (The Moon Agreement), 18 December 1979, UNGA Resolution 34/68. However, this position is itself already being challenged, with NASA's release of the Artemis Accords in 2020. The Accords followed an Executive Order by President Trump a few months earlier which called for the inclusion of commercial partners in space exploration and encouraging exploration of space mining. The Accords aim to 'establish a common set of principles to govern the civil use of outer space', seeking to 'facilitate exploration, science and *commercial activities* for the benefit of humanity'. The Accords propose a series of bilateral agreements in which 'partner nations' agree to follow US-drafted rules. This represents a move away from ideas of shared cooperation and ownership, towards a property-based model which sees outer space as the next commercial frontier. See: NASA, 'The Artemis Accords: Principles for a Safe, Peaceful, and Prosperous Future,' 2020, https://www.nasa.gov/specials/artemis-accords/img/Artemis-Accords_v7_print. pdf (last accessed 11 July 2022); US Federal Register, 'Encouraging International Support for the Recovery and Use of Space Resources,' Executive Order 13914 of 6 April 2020, https://www. federalregister.gov/documents/2020/04/10/2020-07800/encouraging-international-support-for-the-recovery-and-use-of-space-resources (last accessed 11 July 2022). See also: Cait Storr, "Space is the Only Way to Go': The Evolution of the Extractivist Imaginary of International Law,' in Shane Chalmers and Sundhya Pahuja (eds.), *Routledge Handbook of International Law and the Humanities*, (Routledge, 2021): 290–301.

173 Matt Craven, '"Other Spaces": Constructing the Legal Architecture of a Cold War Commons and the Scientific-Technical Imaginary of Outer Space,' *European Journal of International Law* (2019) 30(2): 547–572.

174 UN General Assembly, above note 148, Part XI, Section 2, Article 136.

175 Ranganathan, above note 115.

(CBD) notes that 'States have sovereign rights over their own biological resources'.[176] Similarly, Principle 21 of the 1972 Stockholm Declaration affirms that 'States
have ... the sovereign right to exploit their own resources pursuant to their own
environmental policies',[177] with both the International Covenant on Economic,
Social and Cultural Rights (ICESCR) and the International Covenant on Civil and
Political Rights (ICCPR), two of the central texts in international human rights
law, affirming 'permanent sovereignty over natural resources'.[178] These instruments,
among others, were central in ensuring 'the categorical establishment, in international law, of human sovereignty over nature, as codified into and channelled
through the ... state',[179] essentially shoring up an arrangement for global environmental governance based around '*humanism-as-statism*'.[180]

   While some efforts to unite international environmental law are being made
through the ongoing negotiations to create a Global Pact for the Environment,[181]
the aim of the Pact is to consolidate existing principles, with new principles being
created only as required for consolidation purposes.[182] This means that the principles that Pact negotiations are seeking to consolidate are existing environmental
regimes. However, as exemplified above, these existing regimes are fundamentally anthropocentric, meaning that their consolidation in the creation of a Global
Pact will, inevitably, lead to an anthropocentric outcome document. Overall, and
despite integrative developments, of which some examples have been given above,
international environmental law remains highly fragmented. Different parts of the
environment remain subject to different legal regimes and obligations.[183] These

---

176 United Nations, above note 147.
177 Stockholm Declaration, above note 150.
178 Common article 1(2) of both: UN General Assembly, International Covenant on Civil and
     Political Rights, 16 December 1966, U.N.T.S. vol. 999; UN General Assembly, International
     Covenant on Economic, Social and Cultural Rights, 16 December 1966, U.N.T.S. vol. 993.
     See also: United Nations, UNGA Res A/RES/3171 (1973). Of course, part of the original
     intent behind this principle was also to prevent global north states continuing to exploit the
     natural resources of the global south. However, the post-colonial and highly capitalist pat-
     terns of political economy that emerged in the twentieth and twenty-first centuries have scup-
     pered this hope, with contemporary patterns of trade and investment following much the same
     power dynamics as upheld in colonial times. See: Anthony Burke, 'The Absent Presence of
     Biodiversity in International Law,' *International Political Sociology* (2019) 13: 333–351, p. 342;
     Sumudu Atapattu and Carmen G. Gonzalez, above note 143.
179 Burke, Ibid., p. 341.
180 Ibid. – author's own emphasis.
181 United Nations, UNGA Res A/Res/72/277 (2018). For a good overview of ongoing negotia-
     tions on the Pact, see: Yann Aguila and Jorge E. Viñuales, 'A Global Pact for the Environment:
     Conceptual Foundations,' *Review of European, Comparative and International Environmental Law*
     (2019) 28(1): 3–12.
182 On the balance in the negotiations between consolidation and innovation and the ability of the
     Pact to put forward provisions which may go beyond those found in existing Treaty regimes,
     see: Ibid., p. 8.
183 See: Usha Natarajan and Julia Dehm, Where is the Environment? Locating Nature in
     International Law, TWAILR, 2019, https://twailr.com/where-is-the-environment-locating-
     nature-in-international-law (last accessed 11 July 2022).

structural formations work to ensure that the central subject of international environmental law remains stubbornly anthropocentric.

Attempts have been made to ensure greater environmental protection, however, in other areas of international law. One attempt at bringing a more integrated or holistic approach to environmental protection invokes international human rights law standards. The intersections between human rights and the environment are wide-ranging, from the issue of environmental refugees to the environmental impacts of conflict.[184] One of the most promising and rapidly developing convergences between human rights and the environment is to be found in the right to a healthy environment. The human right to a healthy, clean and sustainable environment was recognised at the global level for the first time by the Human Rights Council in October 2021.[185] The right was then subsequently recognised by the UN General Assembly (UNGA) in July 2022.[186] While neither the Human Rights Council nor the UNGA defined the right, the UN Special Rapporteur on Human Rights and the Environment, taking stock of the way the right has been defined regionally and domestically, has noted that the right to a healthy environment includes many elements, including 'the right to breathe clean air, [and to have] access to clean water and adequate sanitation, healthy and sustainable food, a safe climate, and healthy biodiversity and ecosystems'.[187] While the right is potentially transformative, providing a more integrated means by which a locality and its overall 'health' can be protected, the right remains limited in its framing. This is because the right protects *human* rights to *live* within a healthy environment. The right does not protect the rights of the environment, therefore, to its own health, nor the rights of animals to live in a healthy environment. This means that environmental damage that does not (at first glance) impact on humans but may, for example, impact on other species or cases where environmental damage is occurring a long way from human occupants (such as in the high seas) is not addressed by the right in its current framing.[188] Accordingly, while the human right to a healthy environment is indeed one of the most promising areas of global environmental protection it,

184 The relationship between the enjoyment of rights and the quality of the human environment was first recognised in 1968. See: UN General Assembly, 1968, UNGA Res 2398, A/RES,2398 (XXII). On environmental refugees see: UNHCR, Climate Change and Disaster Displacement, https://www.unhcr.org/uk/climate-change-and-disasters.html (last accessed 11 July 2022); On the environmental impacts of conflict, see: Eliana Cusato, 'International Law, the Paradox of Plenty and the Making of Resource-Driven Conflict,' *Leiden Journal of International Law* (2020) 33(3): 649–666; Karen Hulme, *War Torn Environment: Interpreting the Legal Threshold* (Brill, 2004); Eliana Cusato, *The Ecology of War and Peace: Marginalising Slow and Structural Violence in International Law,* (Cambridge University Press, 2021).

185 UN General Assembly, Resolution Adopted by the Human Rights Council on the Human Rights to a Clean, Healthy and Sustainable Environment 18 October 2021, A/HRC/48/13.

186 UN General Assembly, Resolution Adopted by the Human Rights Council on the Human Rights to a Clean, Healthy and Sustainable Environment 18 October 2021, A/HRC/48/13.

187 Report of the Special Rapporteur Ibid., para 17.

188 This is a point Neimanis has raised, albeit in relation to the right to water. See: Astrida Neimanis, 'Bodies of Water, Human Rights and the Hydrocommons,' *TOPIA: Canadian Journal of Cultural Studies* (2009) 21: 161–182, p. 161, 173.

like international environmental law more broadly, continues primarily to promote human interests and is marked by the deep anthropocentrism that pervades the fragmented way that interests are protected in international environmental law.[189]

As Stephen Turner argues on the basis of related concerns, 'the very design of the law itself is fundamentally predisposed to environmental degradation and forms part of a dysfunctional global legal architecture which cannot achieve environmental sustainability'.[190] International environmental law reproduces a problematic subject/object binary under which humans are the central subject of the law and 'the environment' is mere object. This remains the case both when the environment is being protected (where it is still seen as an object) and when it is being exploited, i.e. as an economic resource. Nonhumans and the environment thus range along what Grear calls a 'spectrum of objectifications'.[191]

Above, I outlined how international law creates some entities and people that are better recognised or are deemed to be more human than others. I then moved on to examine the anthropocentrism embedded into international law, exemplifying how international law also renders other entities, such as the environment, as objects. International law's exclusionary humanist and anthropocentric underpinnings are connected, enforcing and sustaining inequalities between humans while prioritising elite human needs over those of the nonhuman. Overall, the interlocking way these multiple structures of power work together to inform and structure the global order has led Baars to aptly call for a tackling of the 'whitesupremacistableistspeciesistimperialistcapitalistcisheteropatriarchy'[192] – a phrase that well summaries the multiple, interlocking forms of inequality and oppression that are upheld by and through international law.

Conclusion

While international law is formally based primarily around nonhuman subjects, international law is all-too-human. This is the case in terms of how the law is structured and what interests it represents, and in terms of the inequalities international law fosters and helps to uphold. International law is also stubbornly anthropocentric, this being the case even in areas of international law that seek to protect the environment, such as international environmental law and human rights and the environment. Various interlocking vectors of inequality and oppression play out in this system, including gender, race, class, capitalism, colonialism and

---

189 For a wider discussion of the anthropocentrism of human rights, see: Anna Grear, 'Human Rights and New Horizons? Thoughts toward a New Juridical Ontology,' *Science, Technology & Human Values* (2018) 43(1): 129–145.

190 Stephen J. Turner, *A Global Environmental Right*, (Routledge, 2014), p. 32.

191 Anna Grear, '"Anthropocene, Capitalocene, Chthulucene": Re-Encountering Environmental Law and Its "Subject" with Haraway and New Materialism,' in Louis J. Kotzé (ed.), *Environmental Law and Governance for the Anthropocene*, (Hart, 2017): 77–95, p. 87.

192 Grietje Baars, '#Lesbiansarehot: On Oil, Imperialism, and What It Means to Queer International Law,' *feminists@law* (2017) 7(1): 1–9, p. 9.

anthropocentrism. Overall, international law works to render some entities subjects of the law and others objects, creating hierarchies between humans and between humans and nonhumans.

There is a need to challenge, in Donna Haraway's words, our 'dark bewitched commitment to the lure of Progress' which 'lashes us to endless infernal alternatives, as if we had no other ways to reworld, reimagine, relive, and reconnect with one another, in multispecies well-being'.[193] Exclusionary humanism and anthropocentrism have come to condition our collective imagination of what international law is and can be. Posthuman feminism, as a theory that challenges hierarchies upheld by both exclusionary humanism and anthropocentrism, can be used, as I will show in the following chapters, to analyse and re-think international law, allowing for a reworlding for an international law otherwise.

193 Haraway, above note 111, p. 50–51.

2

HUMAN AND MACHINE

Lethal Autonomous Weapons Systems

The global order has changed vastly over the course of the past century, with technological development being one of the core drivers of this change.[1] While the Cold War of the twentieth century saw the evolution of proxy wars, the late twentieth and the early twenty-first centuries saw the emergence of 'new wars'[2] and the phenomenon of drone warfare. This transformation of armed conflict has not only led to debates on targeting methods and decisions[3] and the remoteness of warfare,[4] but also had a serious impact on people's lives, with those living under drones experiencing health repercussions due to the constantly present threat of the buzzing objects above them.[5]

The twentieth and twenty-first centuries also saw an increase in global military spending which was estimated by the Stockholm International Peace Research

1 Yoriko Otomo, *Unconditional Life: The Postwar International Law Settlement*, (Oxford University Press, 2016), p. 118.
2 Christine Chinkin and Mary Kaldor, *International Law and New Wars*, (Cambridge University Press, 2017).
3 See, for example: Lauren Wilcox, 'Embodying Algorithmic War: Gender, Race and the Posthuman in Warfare,' *Security Dialogue* (2016) 48(1): 1–18; Laurie Calhoun, *We Kill Because We Can*, (Zed Books, 2016).
4 Grégoire Chamayou, *A Theory of the Drone*, trans. Janet Lloyd, (The New Press, 2015), p. 37; Ian Graham Ronald Shaw and Akhter Majed, 'The Unbearable Humanness of Drone Warfare in FATA, Pakistan,' *Antipode*, (2011) 44(4): 1490–1509, p. 1496.
5 Drone warfare has been shown to cause post-traumatic stress disorder (PTSD) in both operators and those living in areas where drones are used. See, for example: The International Human Rights and Conflict Resolution Clinic, Stanford Law School and Global Justice Clinic, NYU School of Law, 'Living Under Drones: Death, Injury and Trauma to Civilians from US Drone Practices in Pakistan,' 2012); Atef Abu Saif, *The Drone Eats with Me: A Gaza Diary* (Beacon Press, 2016).

DOI: 10.4324/9781003363798-3

Institute (SIPRI) to be around US$1.96 trillion in 2020.[6] Military spending in 2020 as a percentage of GDP was just below 10 per cent in Oman and Saudi Arabia[7] and US military spending was $801 billion in 2021.[8] The weapons business is a lucrative one to be in. US defence and aerospace companies generated an estimated $874 billion in total industry sales revenue in 2020.[9] The military economy is also a fast moving one, allowing constant, continuous profits as weapons and machinery need regular replacement and technological advancement means that there is always a race to have the most up-to-date systems.[10] Businesses are not the only thing on which the military economy has an impact, however. Studies have shown that the US military is one of the largest polluters in history, being the forty-seventh largest emitter of greenhouse gases in the world.[11]

Technological developments have led to discussions of the use of artificial intelligence (AI) by the military and the development of lethal autonomous weapons systems (LAWS) – broadly defined as systems that can independently select and engage targets. For example, in 2017, the US launched Project Maven, seeking to 'integrate artificial intelligence and machine learning more effectively across operations to maintain advantages over increasingly capable adversaries and competitors'.[12] The main work of Project Maven has been to use machine learning to enhance drone targeting,[13] with vast amounts of funding being given to Silicon Valley companies in this vein.[14] This led staff at Google to famously denounce

6 Stockholm International Peace Research Institute (SIPRI), Military Expenditure Database, www.sipri.org/research/armaments/milex/milex_database/milex_database (last accessed 11 July 2022). Statistic taken from global military expenditure from the year 2020 (latest figure in current US$).

7 Ibid. Statistic taken from global military expenditure from the year 2020.

8 Ibid. Statistic taken from global military expenditure from the year 2021 (latest figure in current US$). Figure slightly rounded up.

9 Aerospace Industries Association, '2021 Facts and Figures,' 2021, https://www.aia-aerospace.org/wp-content/uploads/2021-Facts-and-Figures-U.S.-Aerospace-and-Defense.pdf (last accessed 27 September 2022).

10 Miroslav Nincic and Thomas R. Cusack, 'The Political Economy of US Military Spending,' *Journal of Peace Research* (1979) 6(2): 101–115, p. 112; P. Dunne, 'The Political Economy of Military Expenditure: An Introduction,' *Cambridge Journal of Economics* (1990) 14: 395–404, p. 398.

11 Oliver Belcher et al., 'Hidden Carbon Costs of the "Everywhere War": Logistics, Geopolitical Ecology, and the Carbon Boot-Print of the US Military,' *Transactions of the Institute of British Geographers* (2020) 45(1): 65–80.

12 Robert O. Work, 'Establishment of an Algorithmic Warfare Cross-Functional Team (Project Maven),' Memorandum from the US Deputy Secretary of Defence, 26 April 2017, https://www.govexec.com/media/gbc/docs/pdfs_edit/establishment_of_the_awcft_project_maven.pdf (last accessed 11 July 2022).

13 See: Ibid.

14 See: Thomas Brewster, Project Maven: Startups Backed by Google, Peter Thiel, Eric Schmidt and James Murdoch are Building AI and Facial Recognition Surveillance Tools for the Pentagon, Forbes, 8 September 2021, https://www.forbes.com/sites/thomasbrewster/2021/09/08/project-maven-startups-backed-by-google-peter-thiel-eric-schmidt-and-james-murdoch-build-ai-and-facial-recognition-surveillance-for-the-defense-department/?sh=4f29385a6ef2 (last accessed 11 July 2022).

Google's link to Project Maven, with Google subsequently ending its contract with the project in 2019.[15] In March 2021, the National Security Commission on Artificial Intelligence in the US, a bipartisan commission of experts, released a report arguing that the US needs to do more to stay on top of the AI game in 'the race for AI supremacy'.[16] These developments have all occurred against the backdrop of a radically uneven global order, in which existing inequalities in terms of gender, class and race, but also between states and regions, are perpetuated. LAWS play a central role in the race for military AI supremacy and are rightly controversial. Many organisations and now over 30 states (notably all from the global south apart from the Holy See, Austria and New Zealand) have called for a pre-emptive ban on these systems.[17]

The previous chapter analysed international law's formal focus on nonhuman subjects, concluding that international law is permeated by both exclusionary humanism and anthropocentrism. This chapter will delve into discussing international law's anthropocentric humanism in more detail through a focus on the regulation of military technologies. The way military technologies are viewed, defined and regulated is deeply humanist, situating the machine and the human as distinct. These humanist underpinnings – which paradoxically reiterate human exceptionalism while undermining the very premises of human survival – are challenged in this chapter. This is done, first, through a focus on existing military technologies which are deemed "automated", such as drone technologies, missile interception systems and wearable military technologies. These examples are drawn on to deconstruct the false binary line that is drawn within debates on LAWS between automated and autonomous systems. Second, the humanist underpinnings of the debate are challenged by looking at trends in the research and development of new military technologies, which focus increasingly on human enhancement technologies (HETs), literally blurring the boundaries between human and machinic bodies. Existing HETs, many of which are already in use, are described in this chapter to problematise humanist distinctions made, once again, between automation and autonomy – a key value in liberal individualism – and the tendency to uphold distinctions between the human and the machine. It is thereby argued, drawing on posthuman

---

15 Janet Burns, Google Employees Denounce Company's Military Drone Work in Letter to CEO, Forbes, 10 April 2018, https://www.forbes.com/sites/janetwburns/2018/04/10/google-employees-denounce-companys-military-drone-work-in-letter-to-ceo/?sh=20e1ace1ef0d (last accessed 11 July 2022); Janet Burns, Google Employees Resign over Company's Pentagon Contract, Ethical Habits, Forbes, 14 May 2018, https://www.forbes.com/sites/janetwburns/2018/05/14/google-employees-resign-over-firms-pentagon-contract-ethical-habits/?sh=5d74f1874169 (last accessed 11 July 2022).

16 National Security Commission on Artificial Intelligence, 'Final Report,' March 2021, https://www.nscai.gov/wp-content/uploads/2021/03/Full-Report-Digital-1.pdf (last accessed 11 July 2022), p. 7.

17 Human Rights Watch, Stopping Killer Robots: Country Positions on Banning Full Autonomous Weapons and Retaining Human Control, 10 August 2020, https://www.hrw.org/report/2020/08/10/stopping-killer-robots-country-positions-banning-fully-autonomous-weapons-and#_ftn12 (last accessed 11 July 2022).

feminist theory, that any possible regulation or ban on new and emerging military technologies will be ineffective if these distinctions continue to structure the debate on regulation.

Posthuman feminism has long worked to challenge the exclusionary and anthropocentric humanism that permeates dominant understandings of technology. Applying posthuman feminism to ongoing debates on the regulation of LAWS, this chapter seeks to understand what these theories can add to the debate. Posthuman feminism has largely taken a utopian stance when it comes to technological change, posing technology as a means by which to construct a redemptive feminist future. By applying posthuman feminist theory to the law, a different picture is painted. Many technologies are, after all, first developed for military purposes.[18] In addition, LAWS directly challenge posthuman feminist technological utopianism because LAWS are systems that, by definition, select targets and decide themselves whether or not to firet, i.e. dystopian killing machines. This chapter, through applying posthuman feminism, speaks back to the realities of feminist technological utopianism in a militarised world.

The chapter also contributes to existing literature on posthuman theory and conflict. Existing posthuman analyses of conflict included literatures on more general posthuman evaluations of warfare[19] or security,[20] to posthuman analyses of drone warfare,[21] to posthuman feminist examinations of international humanitarian law[22] and of exoskeletons,[23] to discussions of the erasure of nonhuman animals from discourses on conflict.[24] Despite this, very little has been written about LAWS from a posthuman perspective.[25] This chapter adds to the emerging field of posthuman analyses of LAWS while also adding to the wider field of posthumanism and conflict.

18 Sat Nav is an example of this. See: Aeronautics and Space Engineering Board et al., *The Global Positioning System: A Shared National Asset*, (National Academies Press, 1995).
19 Joanna Bourke, 'Killing in a Posthuman World: The Philosophy and Practice of Critical Military History,' in Bolette Blaagaard and Iris van der Tuin (eds.), *The Subject of Rosi Braidotti: Politics and Concepts*, (Bloomsbury, 2004): 29–37.
20 Audra Mitchell, '"Posthuman Security": Reflections from an Open-ended Conversation,' in Clara Eroukhmanoff and Matt Harker (eds.), *Reflections on the Posthuman in International Relations*, (E-International Relations Publishing, 2017): 10–18.
21 See, for example: Wilcox, above note 3; Matilda Arvidsson, 'The Swarm that We Already Are: Artificially Intelligent (AI) Swarming 'Insect Drones', Targeting and International Humanitarian Law in a Posthuman Ecology,' *Journal of Human Rights and the Environment* (2020) 11(1): 114–137.
22 Matilda Arvidsson, 'Targeting, Gender, and International *Posthumanitarain* Law and Practice: Framing the Question of the Human in International Humanitarian Law,' *Australian Feminist Law Journal* (2018), 44(1): 9–28.
23 Gina Heathcote, 'War's Perpetuity: Disabled Bodies of War and the Exoskeleton of Equality,' *Australian Feminist Law Journal* (2018) 44(1): 71–91.
24 See: Erika Cudworth and Steve Hobden, 'The Posthuman Way of War,' *Security Dialogue* (2015) 46(6): 513–529.
25 With the exception here being my own preliminary investigations into this topic. See: Emily Jones, 'A Posthuman-Xenofeminist Analysis of the Discourse on Autonomous Weapons Systems and Other Killing Machines,' *Australian Feminist Law Journal* (2018) 44(1): 93–118.

Finally, this chapter speaks to scholarship on gender and LAWS. While there is significant literature on gender and drones,[26] there have been far fewer gender analyses of LAWS.[27] The scholarship that does exist has, so far, focused either on the inclusion of women in debates, on the impact on women's lives and the gendered discourses perpetuated by LAWS,[28] or on the problems of potential discrimination that could ensue if LAWS are deployed.[29] While this important work informs this chapter greatly, my focus differs. Rather than evaluating the gendered dynamics of LAWS, this chapter engages directly in debates on their regulation. One of the aims of this book is to show the ways that gender theory, through the application of posthuman feminism, can be used to analyse all areas of international law, not just those areas that pertain specifically to women's lives. I thereby draw on posthuman feminism to re-think the humanist underpinnings of the debate on LAWS before, in the following chapter, moving on to propose alternative posthuman feminist inspired proposals for regulation.

26 See, for example: Lindsay C. Clark, 'Grim Reapers: Ghostly Narratives of Masculinity and Killing in Drone Warfare,' *International Feminist Journal of Politics* (2018) 20(4): 602–623; Wilcox, above note 3; Lauren Wilcox, 'Drones, Swarms and Becoming-Insect: Feminist Utopias and Posthuman Politics,' *Feminist Review* (2017) 116: 25–45; Eric Blanchard, 'The Technoscience Question in Feminist International Relations: Unmanning the US War on Terror' in J. Ann Tickner Laura Sjoberg (eds.), *Feminism and International Relations: Conversations About the Past, Present, and Future,* (Routledge, 2011): 146–165; Lauren Wilcox, 'Drone Warfare and the Making of Bodies out of Place,' *Critical Studies on Security* (2015) 3(1): 127–131; Cara Daggett, 'Drone Disorientations: How "Unmanned" Weapons Queer the Experience of Killing in War,' *International Feminist Journal of Politics* (2015) 17(3): 361–379.

27 As above note 25. Arvidsson has also begun to consider what a feminist posthuman approach to International Humanitarian Law (IHL) may look like and does consider LAWS briefly in her paper. See: Arvidsson, above note 22.

28 See: Juliana Santos de Carvalho, 'A "Male" Future: An Analysis of the Gendered Discourses Regarding Lethal Autonomous Weapons,' *Amsterdam Law Forum* (2018) 2: 41–61; Gina Heathcote, 'LAWS, UFOs and UAVs: Feminist Encounters with the Law of Armed Conflict,' in Dale Stephens and Paul Babie (eds.), *Imagining Law: Essays in Conversation with Judith Gardham,* (University of Adelaide Press, 2017): 153–170; Ray Acheson, 'Autonomous Weapons and Gender-Based Violence,' Campaign to Stop Killer Robots and Women's International League for Peace and Freedom 2020, https://reachingcriticalwill.org/images/documents/Publications/aws-and-gbv.pdf (last accessed 11 July 2022).

Manjikian also touches on the gendere.d dynamics of LAWS, though she mostly focuses in her article on drones. See: Mary Manjikian, 'Becoming Unmanned: The Gendering of Lethal Autonomous Warfare Technology,' *International Feminist Journal of Politics* (2014) 16(1): 48–65. See also: Heather M. Roff, 'Gendering a Warbot,' *International Feminist Journal of Politics* (2016) 18(1): 1–18. Similarly, Heyns and Borden also touch on LAWS though their focus on unmanned weapons largely centres on drones. See: Christof Heyns and Tess Borden, 'Unmanned Weapons: Looking for the Gender Dimensions,' in Fionnuala Ní Aoláin et al. (eds.) *The Oxford Handbook of Gender and Conflict* (Oxford University Press, 2018): 376–389.

29 Ray Acheson, 'Autonomous Weapons and Patriarchy,' Campaign to Stop Killer Robots and Women's International League for Peace and Freedom 2020, https://reachingcriticalwill.org/images/documents/Publications/aws-and-patriarchy.pdf (last accessed 11 July 2022).

Posthuman Feminism: Techno-Utopianism or Militarised Masculinity?

Posthuman feminism is broadly positive about the feminist potentials of new technologies.[30] Donna Haraway, for example, in her *Cyborg Manifesto*, highlights the possibilities technology poses for women. Focusing on the figure of the cyborg, the idea that the human and machine are already one, Haraway argues that technology calls the human subject into question, challenging the exclusionary and anthropocentric humanism that has long dominated western thought.[31] For Haraway, the 'cyborg myth is about transgressed boundaries, potent fusions and dangerous possibilities'.[32] Therefore, while, for Haraway, 'cyborg unities are monstrous and illegitimate', she sees this as a positive thing from the perspective of feminism, concluding that 'in our present political circumstances, we could hardly hope for more potent myths for resistance and recoupling'.[33] The cyborg inherently challenges exclusionary and anthropocentric humanism, including the gendered and racialised assumptions that underly it and therefore, for Haraway, the cyborg holds promise.

Feminist science and technology studies elsewhere have likewise shown an optimism around the feminist potentials of technology, with Cecilia Åsberg and Nina Lykke describing this field as sharing a basic assumption that science and technology are entangled with societal interests and thus 'can be held as politically and ethically accountable'.[34] Similarly, xenofeminism, another strand of posthuman feminism, finds promise in technological advancement, viewing science and technology 'as an activist tool';[35] a site where feminist intervention is required in the aim of shaping scientific and technological developments through feminist ethics.[36] A central idea in much of the literature is the need and technology's ability to disrupt long-held gendered dualisms between nature and culture.[37] There is subsequently a strong focus in both xenofeminism and the wider field of feminist science and technology studies on reproductive technologies.[38]

However, while posthuman feminism has found hope in technological change, there are those who remain more cautious. Haraway, for example, is all too aware of

---

30 Contemporary posthuman feminism is also intimately connected to cyberfeminism which sprang out of the 1980s, as well as feminist technoscience studies. For a more on these different feminisms and how they link in to posthuman feminism, see: Rosi Braidotti, *Posthuman Feminism*, (Polity Press, 2022), p. 149–176; Maureen McNeil, *Feminist Cultural Studies of Science and Technology*, (Routledge, 2007).

31 Donna Haraway, 'A Cyborg Manifesto,' in David Bell and Barbara M. Kennedy (eds.), *The Cybercultures Reader*, (Routledge, 2001): 291–324.

32 Ibid., p. 295.

33 Ibid., p. 295.

34 Cecilia Åsberg and Nina Lykke, 'Feminist Technoscience Studies,' *European Journal of Women's Studies* (2010) 17(4): 299–305, p. 299.

35 Helen Hester, *Xenofeminism*, (Polity Press, 2018), p. 7.

36 See: Ibid.; Laboria Cuboniks, *The Xenofeminist Manifesto*, (Verso, 2018).

37 See: Haraway, above note 31; Ibid.; Braidotti, above note 30.

38 Hester, above note 35. See also: Sophie Lewis, *Full Surrogacy Now: Feminist Against the Family*, (Verso, 2021).

the dangers and risks technology poses.[39] Haraway states that technology is already embedded within capitalism, noting that the people usually making these machines are often exploited, poor women from the global south.[40] This is something the Xenofeminist Manifesto (the founding text of xenofeminism) notes too, adding that 'a large amount of the world's poor is adversely affected by the expanding technological industry (from factory workers labouring under abominable conditions to the Ghanaian villages that have become a repository for the e-waste of the global powers)'.[41] Technological disparity is no longer just about who makes the technology and who has access to it but is also about who dismantles it, with much of this deeply toxic labour being done without adequate safety protection, training or knowledge.

The xenofeminists, like Haraway, are wary of the links between technology and capital, noting that technology has, until now, mostly been used 'in the exclusive interests of capital, which, by design, only benefits the few'.[42] However, the Xenofeminist Manifesto remains positive about the possible futures of technology, arguing that there are 'radical opportunities afforded by developing (and alienating) forms of technological mediation'.[43] The manifesto therefore notes that, although there are ongoing problems around accessibility, 'digital tools have never been more widely available or more sensitive to appropriation than they are today'.[44] Consequently, for the xenofeminists, the dark sides of technology and the ways it has been used up until now do not make technology's use futile. Rather, the xenofeminists note the need to politicise technology. Technology is a tool for revolution: xenofeminism 'seeks to strategically deploy existing technologies to re-engineer the world'.[45]

While technology holds great potential for feminists, the dark sides of technological development cannot be forgotten, with technologies designed to kill perhaps best representing the possible dystopias that technology may help to construct.[46] Rosi Braidotti, for example, focusing on drones, calls these new technologies of war 'necro-technologies',[47] drawing on Archille Mbembe's concept of necropolitics and applying it to drones to define them as technologies that give the power to decide who may live and who may die.[48] Furthermore, feminist security studies have long highlighted the gendered underpinnings of the military technology

---

39 Haraway, above note 31, p. 295.
40 Ibid., p. 295.
41 Laboria Cuboniks, above note 37, Interrupt 0×08.
42 Ibid., Interrupt 0×08.
43 Ibid., Interrupt 0×08.
44 Ibid., Interrupt 0×08.
45 Ibid., Zero 0×02.
46 Emily Jones, 'Feminist Technologies and Post-Capitalism: Defining and Reflecting Upon Xenofeminism,' *Feminist Review* (2019) 123: 126–134.
47 Rosi Braidotti, *The Posthuman*, (Polity Press, 2013), p. 9.
48 Achille Mbembe, 'Necropolitics,' trans. Libby Meintjes, *Public Culture*, 2003, 15(1): 11–40. See also: Achille Mbembe, *Necropolitics*, (Duke University Press, 2019).

world.[49] For example, political scientist Mary Manjikian concludes that technology is more likely to create a more militarised, hyper-masculine world,[50] this conclusion contrasting starkly with the techno-utopic ideals of the posthuman feminist scholars above.[51] Similarly, Cristina Masters questions how much technology can be used to challenge social constructions of gender. Focusing on the figure of the cyborg soldier, Masters argues that gender is in fact reinscribed through this figure which both represents a particular post-human future while remaining in the frame of modern humanism.[52]

While posthuman feminism may see potential in technology, reading this literature alongside feminist security studies reminds us that technology is deeply entwined with militarism and, thereby, exclusionary humanism. Furthermore, technology is largely created by a capitalist elite that is, for the most part, white, male and situated in the global north.[53] It is clear that the techno-utopianism of posthuman feminism must be held in tension alongside the militarised nature of technology. The techno-utopianism of posthuman feminism does not mean, however, that it cannot contribute to security debates. As Ruha Benjamin reminds us, 'a black feminist approach to posthumanism and all of its technoscientific promises … is an approach to world-building in which myriad life forms can flourish'.[54] In the following sections, I will outline some of the legal and ethical debates on LAWS before applying posthuman feminism to analyse these debates. I exemplify how both the human and the machine and autonomy and automation are being treated as falsely distinct in the debates on LAWS, this operating to centre anthropocentric and humanist perspectives. In the next chapter, heeding Benjamin's words, I put forward some tentative legal solutions to address these concerns, exemplifying the usefulness of posthuman feminism, not only in analysing the contemporary technologically mediated moment, but also in constructing legal change.

---

49 See, for example, Cohn's 1987 study of defence intellectuals: Carol Cohn, 'Sex and Death in the Rational World of Defence Intellectuals,' *Signs*, (1987), 12(4): 687–718.

50 Manjikian, above note 28.

51 This is a point Heyns and Borden also raise in relation to unmanned weapons more generally. See: Heyns and Borden, above note 28.

52 Cristina Masters, 'Bodies of Technology: Cyborg Soldiers and Militarized Masculinities,' *International Feminist Journal of Politics* (2005) 7(1): 112–132.

53 This can be exemplified by the way that facial recognition technology has a problem with recognising black faces. Made by the white elite, the technology itself has been built based on whiteness, forcing some, such as coder Joy Buolamwini, to wear a white mask when using the software. See: The Algorithmic Justice League, https://www.ajlunited.org/ (last accessed 11 July 2022). In addition, Sandvik has discussed how the use of technology and data collection to manage refugees works to render invisible black male refuges. See; Kristin Bergtora Sandvik, 'Technology, Dead Male Bodies, and Feminist Recognition: Gendering ICT Harm Theory,' *Australian Feminist Law Journal* (2018) 44(1): 49–69.

54 Ruha Benjamin, 'Discriminatory Design, Liberating Imagination,' in Ruha Benjamin (ed.), *Captivating Technology: Race, Carceral Technoscience, and Liberatory Imagination in Everyday Life,* (Duke University Press, 2019): 1–22, p. 10.

The Legal and Ethical Debates on Lethal Autonomous Weapons Systems

LAWS have been called by many names, including autonomous weapons, autonomous weapons systems and fully-autonomous weapons systems. However, in this chapter I have chosen to use the language of LAWS, this being the term the parties to the Convention on Certain Conventional Weapons (CCW) – the arena where a series of diplomatic meetings on the regulation of LAWS have been held since 2014 – seem to have settled on over the past few years. This term is, however, problematic in its own way, with the terms 'lethal' and 'autonomous' both being, as yet, undefined and with their definitions being vital to debates on regulation, as we shall see. The term LAWS is therefore used with those caveats and discussions in mind.

The US and UK governments, the UN Special Rapporteur on Summary or Arbitrary Executions and Human Rights Watch have all previously defined LAWS as: 'robotic weapon systems that, once activated, can select and engage targets without further intervention by a human operator'.[55] Since this early definition, other definitions have been put forward, with, for example, the UK using the language of systems that are 'capable of understanding higher level intent and direction'.[56] The definition of LAWS is still being debated at CCW meetings. The terms of this definition will be extremely important in relation to any future regulation. While it is broadly agreed that autonomy has yet to be achieved, research is ongoing in this area.[57] While most agree that LAWS do not yet exist, this is somewhat debatable depending on the way autonomy is defined, as I will come on to discuss in the following sections.

Many groups have called for a pre-emptive ban or a moratorium on LAWS. These groups include multiple NGOs, the UN Special Rapporteur on Summary or Arbitrary Executions,[58] over 30 states, notably all from the global south (bar the Holy See, Austria and New Zealand) and a group of over 70 religious leaders.[59] A number of philosophers have also joined this grouping, arguing that machines

---

55 UN General Assembly, Report of the Special Rapporteur on Extrajudicial, Summary or Arbitrary Executions, 9 April 2013, A/HRC/23/47, para. 38. See also U.S. Department of Defense, Autonomy in Weapons Systems, Directive 3000.09 (21 November 2012); UK Ministry of Defence, The UK Approach to Unmanned Aircraft Systems Joint Doctrine Note 2/11 (30 March 2011); Human Rights Watch, 'Losing Humanity: The Case Against Killer Robots,' 2012, p. 2, https://www.hrw.org/report/2012/11/19/losing-humanity/case-against-killer-robots (last accessed 28 September 2022).

56 Ministry of Defence, 'Human-Machine Teaming,' Joint Concept Note 1/18, 2018, p. 60.

57 Convention on Certain Conventional Weapons, Meeting of State Parties, 25 November 2014, CCW/MSP/2014, para 21.

58 'Report of the Special Rapporteur on extrajudicial …', above note 55.

59 Pax for Peace, Religious Leaders Call for a Ban on Killer Robots, 12 November 2014, https://www.paxforpeace.nl/stay-informed/news/religious-leaders-call-for-a-ban-on-killer-robots (last accessed 11 July 2022).

should not be able to make life/death decisions,[60] and multiple texts have been published by the European Parliament calling for a pre-emptive ban.[61] However, as we shall see, there are various actors that argue, in contrast, that LAWS will prove to be more accurate and therefore will make more just decisions on the battlefield, with some even arguing that the use of LAWS will better support the upholding of the laws of armed conflict.

There are various legal and ethical debates around LAWS.[62] Arguments include that the removal of humans from the field could drastically increase states' willingness to go to war due to the heavily reduced risk of military casualties.[63] Others submit that LAWS could lead to a reduction in casualties as they do not have emotions and will therefore never feel the need to uphold a 'shoot first ask questions later' policy.[64] However, the larger legal concern about these systems is whether LAWS are compatible with and/or able to uphold international humanitarian law (IHL), the law that governs what parties can and cannot do in conflict. Article 36 of Additional Protocol I of the Geneva Conventions states that all weapons systems must be verified as compatible with IHL before being used,[65] making the question of compatibility essential. Some, including roboticist Ron Arkin, argue that machines may better uphold the standards of IHL than humans currently can and do.[66] Arkin and others thereby argue that if a system can be shown to be able to respect the laws of war as well or better than a human in similar circumstances, there is a moral obligation to deploy that system.[67] However, this approach fails to account for how IHL applies in practice.

---

60 Robert Sparrow, 'Robots and Respect: Assessing the Case Against Autonomous Weapon Systems,' *Ethics and International Affairs* (2016) 30(1): 93–116; Peter Asaro, 'On Banning Autonomous Weapons Systems: Human Rights, Automation, and the Dehumanization of Lethal Decision-Making,' *International Review of the Red Cross* (2012) 94(886): 687–709.

61 See, for example: European Parliament, 'Guidelines for Military and Non-Military Use of Artificial Intelligence: Press Release,' 20 January 2021, https://www.europarl.europa.eu/news/en/press-room/20210114IPR95627/guidelines-for-military-and-non-military-use-of-artificial-intelligence, (last accessed 11 July 2022); European Parliament Resolution on Autonomous Weapons Systems 12 September 2018 2018/2752(RSP); European Parliament Resolution on the Use of Armed Drones 25 February 2014 2014/2567(RSP) Section 2(d).

62 See for example: Jack M. Beard, 'Autonomous Weapons and Human Responsibilities' (2014) 45(3): 617–681.

63 'Report of the Special Rapporteur on Extrajudicial ...,' above note 55.

64 Ron Arkin, 'Lethal Autonomous Systems and the Plight of the Non-Combatant,' *AISB Quarterly* (2013): 137–236.

65 Protocol Additional to the Geneva Conventions of 12 August 1949, and Relating to the Protection of Victims of International Armed Conflicts, 8 June 1977, 1125 U.N.T.S. 3, 8 June 1977, Article 36.

66 Arkin, above note 64.

67 Ronald Arkin, *Governing Lethal Behaviour in Autonomous Robots* (Routledge, 2009); Ronald Arkin, 'The Case for Ethical Autonomy in Unmanned Systems,' *Journal of Military Ethics* (2010) 9(4): 332–341; George R. Lucas, 'Automated Warfare,' *Stanford Law & Policy Review* (2001) 25(2): 317–340, p. 322, 326, 336. See also Sparrow's critique of this stance: Sparrow, above note 60, p. 16.

First, Arkin's approach assumes that IHL provides the only standard that must be upheld, thereby ignoring debates on how human rights also apply in conflict alongside IHL, as well as wider ethical concerns and non-legal standards. Furthermore, this argument, in purporting that IHL is the only standard that must be complied with, fails to account for critiques of IHL that argue that this body of law upholds gendered and racialised stereotypes. For example, various scholars have critiqued the way that, in the context of counter-terrorism, gender and racial profiling have been used to determine whether a subject is a legitimate target under IHL or not, with the 'military aged brown man' becoming essentially inherently targetable.[68] The risk here is that, by making IHL the only standard with which LAWS must comply, the gendered and racialised assumptions that haunt IHL will be imported into the regulation of LAWS.

The second critique of Arkin's approach, and as exemplified in part by the first point, is the fact that IHL does not apply through binary choices but rather requires a balanced assessment of principles, perspectives and ethical standpoints. As Vilmer argues 'roboticists often exaggerate their ability to program IHL and convert legal rules into algorithms. Non-jurists often have a simplistic understanding of the rules, reducing them to univocal commands'.[69] This can be seen when exploring the rules of IHL themselves and how they apply. For example, the principle of proportionality is central in IHL. This principle requires that 'incidental loss of civilian life, injury to civilians, damage to civilian objects' is to be balanced against 'the concrete and direct military advantage anticipated'.[70] Yet determining what is proportionate or not is not simply a matter of logic but rather, a subjective evaluation is required.[71] Proportionality requires a deep understanding of nuance, as shown by the number of legal debates surrounding this principle.[72]

Despite this, there are many lawyers who argue that IHL is adequate to regulate LAWS. This position has been put forward by some members of the Group

---

68 Wilcox, above note 3; Wilcox, 'Drone Warfare ...,' above note 26; Lucy Suchman, 'Algorithmic Warfare and the Reinvention of Accuracy,' *Critical Studies on Security* (2020) 8(2): 175–187, p. 176; Louise Amoore, 'Algorithmic War: Everyday Geographies of the War on Terror,' *Antipode* (2009) 41(1): 49–69, p. 54. See also: Laurie Calhoun, *We Kill Because We Can*, (Zed Books, 2016).

69 Jean-Baptiste Jeangène Vilmer, Terminator Ethics: Should We Ban 'Killer Robots'?, Ethics and International Affairs, 2015, https://www.ethicsandinternationalaffairs.org/2015/terminator-ethics-ban-killer-robots/ (last accessed 11 July 2022).

70 Protocol Additional ..., above note 65, Article 51(5)(b); Rome Statute of the International Criminal Court, 17 July 1998 ISBN No. 92-9227-227-6, Article 8(2)(b)(iv).

71 Claude Pilloud and Jean Pictet, 'Protocol I – Article 57 – Precautions in Attack,' in Yves Sandoz et al. (eds.), *Commentary on the Additional Protocols of 8 June 1977 to the Geneva Conventions on 12 August 1949*, (Martinus Nijhoff, 1987) 683.

72 See in general: Michael Newton and Larry May, *Proportionality in International Law*, (Oxford University Press, 2014).

of Governmental Experts (GGE) at the CCW, as well as by some legal scholars[73] and some governments, including those of the UK[74] and Russia.[75] To analyse this position, it is necessary to examine the application of IHL in more detail. This section by no means provides a comprehensive overview of IHL as applied to LAWS. Rather, it focuses on some of the key elements of applicability and the debates that surround them, working to challenge the claim that IHL is, as it stands, adequate to regulate LAWS.[76]

Article 35 of the First Additional Protocol of the Geneva Conventions 1949 sets out what are now seen to be the foundational principles of weapons law.[77] Article 35(1) provides the right of the parties to a conflict to choose the means and methods of warfare, noting that that choice 'is not unlimited', whereas Article 35(2) prohibits means and methods of warfare that cause 'superfluous injury or unnecessary suffering'. Article 35(4) then goes on to outline the prohibition of indiscriminate attacks.[78] These provisions provide what is known as the principle of distinction,[79] which affirms that all those involved in armed conflict must distinguish between combatants and civilians.[80] Article 57(2), which has been argued to be customary international law,[81] then provides further detail on the obligation to ensure that

---

73 Human-Machine Interaction in the Development, Deployment and Use of Emerging Technologies in the Area of Lethal Autonomous Weapons Systems, Submitted by the United States, CCW/GGE.2/2018/P.4, p. 6–7. Tim McFarland, while providing a fairly neutral analysis of LAWS and IHL, broadly likewise argues that these systems could be compatible with IHL. See, generally: Tim McFarland, *Autonomous Weapons Systems and the Law of Armed Conflict*, (Cambridge University Press, 2020). Peter Margulies makes a related argument, albeit focusing more specifically on AI-based situation awareness technology (SAT), arguing that this technology should be used as it will make target selection more accurate. See: Peter Margulies, 'The Other Side of Autonomous Weapons: Using Artificial Intelligence to Enhance IHL Compliance,' in Eric Talbot and Ronald T.O. Alcala (eds.), *The Impact of Emerging Technologies on the Law of Armed Conflict*, (Oxford University Press, 2019): 147–174. In addition, Pablo Kalmanovitz argues that LARS can be conceivably developed and deployed in a way that is compatible with IHL. See: Palo Kalmanovitz, 'Judgement, Liability and the Risks of Riskless Warfare,' in Nehal Bhuta et al. (eds.), *Autonomous Weapons Systems: Law, Ethics, Policy* (Cambridge University Press, 2016):147–176.
74 In 2015, the UK government opposed a ban on LAWS, stating that 'international humanitarian law already provides sufficient regulation for this area', adding also that all weapons employed by UK armed forces would be 'under human oversight and control.' See: Owen Bowcott, UK Opposes International Ban on Developing 'Killer Robots', *The Guardian*, 13 April 2015.
75 Russian Federation, Potential Opportunities and Limitations of Military Uses of Lethal Autonomous Weapons Systems: Working Paper Submitted by the Russian Federation, UN Doc. CCW/GGE.1/2019/WP.1, 15 March 2019, p. 5.
76 For a more comprehensive overview of the law as applied to LAWS, see: McFarland, above note 73.
77 See: Ibid., p. 16–17.
78 Protocol Additional ..., above note 65, Article 35. These provisions echo the Regulations annexed to the Forth Hague Convention of 1907 (expect the term 'methods of warfare' was not used in the Hague Convention). See: Convention Respecting the Law and Customs of War on Land and Its Annex: Regulations Concerning the Laws and Customs of War on Land, 26 January 1910.
79 Protocol Additional ..., above note 65 – along with other articles, mainly Article 48.
80 This ICJ has described this principle as a 'cardinal' principle of humanitarian law. See: *Legality of the Threat or Use of Nuclear Weapons* (Advisory Opinion) [1996] ICJ Reports 226, 257 [78].
81 For example, see: *Prosecutor v Kupreškić (Judgment)* (International Criminal Tribunal for the Former Yugoslavia, Trial Chamber, Case No IT-95-16, 14 January 2000, para 524.

the risk to civilian life is minimised at all times and, in line with this, states must review the different forms an attack may take.[82] In order to abide by these international legal obligations, LAWS would have to be able to distinguish between military objectives and civilian objects and between combatants (including members of organised armed groups and those taking a direct part in the hostilities) and civilians.[83] These are complex decisions. For example, determining whether something is a rifle or an umbrella from a distance can be difficult.[84] Such a dilemma could not be evaded easily. While a system could read codes on the side of a weapon and use this to determine whether someone is a combatant or not, such a system could still feasibly decide that an armed civilian is a combatant. After all, in conflict situations, it is common for civilians to carry weapons for self-defence, and if peacekeepers are present, they may also carry weapons, thus complicating identification further.[85] In addition, even if a system were able to distinguish effectively between a combatant and a non-combatant, it would then also need to be able to assess whether someone is *hors de combat* and therefore may not be attacked.[86] It would furthermore need to be able to determine when someone is seriously injured and split off from their group, thus making them an illegitimate target under IHL.[87] While seeing that a person is seriously wounded is often a good indication that they are defenceless and no longer able to engage in a hostile act, this does not always follow. It is difficult to imagine a machine being able to make determinations such as these without it having full AI, i.e. a decision-making process capability of a similar or higher level than humans. This point is, however, essential, as the decision about whether someone is *hors de combat* or not is not only difficult but, if a person or a machine gets it wrong, attacking a person who is *hors de combat* is a grave breach of the Geneva Conventions.[88] Given the complexity of these rules, it seems very unlikely that a machine would have the ability to make such a decision effectively. Of course, humans also struggle with these decisions, rendering this question, in the end, as much ethical as legal – do we want machines to be making these decisions?[89]

Despite claims that IHL can be easily programmed into a machine, it is clear that IHL is as much a system of ethics as it is of law. After all, the basic premise of IHL is an acceptance that warfare does and will exist, with IHL seeking to make warfare more ethical and humane. Given this context, the Martens Clause is also of relevance here. The Martens Clause states that 'civilians and combatants remain under the protection and authority of the principles of international law derived

82 Protocol Additional ..., above note 65, Article 57(2).
83 Ibid., see generally Article 57.
84 Sparrow, above note 60.
85 Ibid., p. 101–102.
86 Protocol Additional ..., above note 65, Article 41.
87 Ibid.
88 Ibid.
89 For more on LAWS and the principle of distinction, see: Roff, above note 28; Michael W. Meir, 'Emerging Technologies and the Principle of Distinction: A Further Blurring of the Lines Between Combatants and Civilians,' in Eric Talbot and Ronald T.O. Alcala (eds.), *The Impact of Emerging Technologies on the Law of Armed Conflict*, (Oxford University Press, 2019): 211–234.

from established custom, from the principles of humanity and from the dictates of public conscience'.[90] This clause is generally deemed to have attained the status of customary international law,[91] however there is no single legal interpretation, the Clause representing the recognition of the fact that what is acceptable and what is not may change over time.[92] While there may be debate as to what the Martens Clause means and how it exactly applies, it is questionable whether a machine being allowed to make life/death decisions can ever have been deemed to be in line with the principles of humanity and public conscience, with scholars taking positions on both sides of the debate.[93]

In the context of the ongoing debates around the applicability of the Martens Clause, Tim McFarland argues that the Martens Clause 'does not, at present, place any special restrictions on the incorporation of autonomous control capabilities into weapon systems'.[94] McFarland analyses the different ways the Martens Clause could be interpreted in its application to LAWS. One interpretation views the Martens Clause as not enough, in itself, of a basis to prohibit a weapon. Rather, a customary or conventional prohibition is needed. The second position views the Clause as an interpretative tool, providing guidance on existing rules. The final interpretation of the applicability of the Martens Clause is the idea that the Clause is an independent source of law.[95] However, as McFarland notes, while this latter interpretation of the applicability of the Martens Clause has long existed, the extent to which such an interpretation of the Clause has influenced the development of the law is 'unclear'.[96] This fact, alongside the rather vague and debatable language of the Clause itself, makes it difficult to see how the Martens Clause could be used, for example, to ban LAWS. However, the status of the Clause and its role in providing a space for ethical debate on issues of 'the principles of humanity' and 'the dictates of public conscience' is key,[97] reminding all that the laws of armed conflict are by no means neutral nor objective but are, rather, deeply entwined with complex ethical questions.

Another key issue here is accountability. Accountability when the laws of armed conflict are violated may be difficult to determine where LAWS are involved, as

90 The Martens Clause is found in several treaties relating to international humanitarian law but was incorporated into the body of the main 1949 Geneva Conventions as well as in the First Additional Protocol. See: Protocol Additional …, above note 65.

It is generally acknowledged that the principle now applies throughout the whole scope of international humanitarian law.

91 *Legality of the Threat or Use of Nuclear Weapons* (Advisory Opinion), International Court of Justice, 8 July 1996, I.C.J. Reports 1996, 226. See in particular the judgment of Judge Weeramantry.

92 See: Ibid. – Judge Shahabuddeen; McFarland, above note 73, p. 102–103.

93 For various submissions as to what the Martens Clause means, see, for example, *Legality of the Threat of Use of Nuclear Weapons*, Ibid. See also Peter Asaro, '*Jus nascendi*, robotic weapons and the Martens Clause' in Ryan Calo et al. (eds.), *Robot Law*, (Edward Elgar Publishing, 2016): 367–386.

94 McFarland, above note 73, p. 103.

95 Ibid., p. 104–105.

96 Ibid., p. 105.

97 For a discussion on what 'the principles of humanity' and 'the dictates of public conscience' may mean, see: Ibid., p. 106–112.

the responsibility may lay across many actors. This is perhaps most poignant when considering the application of international criminal law or tort law. For example, if a machine kills an innocent person independently, should the military commanding the robot be held accountable? Or rather the manufacturer, the inventor, the commander, the programmer or, even, in the case of AI machines, the system itself? Accountability is a central issue in this area, with many authors having raised concerns over the accountability gap.[98]

Other scholars have warned of the discriminatory potentials of LAWS. Machines are programmed by humans and human biases can be transposed into technologies. Researchers have, for example, raised issues with AI, data collection and racial[99] and gender bias,[100] including issues with the use of data collection in refugee situations which ends up discriminating against black, male refugees in particular.[101] In addition, the discriminatory use of algorithms and data that adversely impact the poor, and particularly racialised poor communities, has been highlighted.[102] Researchers such as Safiya Umoja Noble have also revealed the ways that algorithms perpetuate stereotypes about black women.[103] As Ray Acheson highlights, it is very likely, given this wider context, that LAWS, if deployed, will also make decisions in ways that are discriminatory. LAWS, to select targets, will have to categorise different people and distinguish between different groups, rendering it highly likely that existing societal bases for oppression, including patriarchy, racism and ableism, will be further entrenched through the use of these systems.[104]

Given the many legal and ethical debates, it will come as no surprise that there are many proposals on the table when it comes to the regulation of LAWS. However, pressure is increasing for GGE at the CCW, who have been mandated to produce a final outcome. So far, no agreement has been made, through the GGE did, in

---

98 For a wider discussion of these issues, see: Ibid., p.127–174; Marta Bo, 'Autonomous Weapons and the Responsibility Gap in the of the *Mens Rea* of the War Crime of Attacking Civilians in the ICC Statute,' *Journal of International Criminal Justice* (2021) 19(2): 275–299; Laura A. Dickinson, 'Lethal Autonomous Weapons Systems: The Overlooked Importance of Administrative Accountability,' in Eric Talbot and Ronald T.O. Alcala (eds.), *The Impact of Emerging Technologies on the Law of Armed Conflict*, (Oxford University Press, 2019): 69–97; Daniel N. Hammond, 'Autonomous Weapons and the Problem of State Accountability,' *Chicago Journal of International Law* (2015) 15: 652–687; Beard, above note 62; Hin-Yan Liu, 'Refining Responsibility: Differentiating Two Types of Responsibility Issues Raised by Autonomous Weapons Systems,' in Nehal Bhuta et al. (eds.), *Autonomous Weapons Systems: Law, Ethics, Policy* (Cambridge University Press, 2016): 325–344.

99 See: Ramon Amaro, *The Black Technical Object: On Machine Learning and the Aspiration of Black Being*, (MIT Press, 2022); Ruha Benjamin, *Race After Technology*, (Polity Press, 2019).

100 Ilinca Barson, Reseach Reveals Inherent AI Gender Bias: Quantifying the Accuracy of Vision/ Facial Recognition on Identifying PPE Masks, Wunderman Thompson 2021, https://www. wundermanthompson.com/insight/ai-and-gender-bias (last accessed 11 July 2022).

101 Sandvik, above note 53.

102 Virgina Eubanks, *Automating Inequality: How High-Tech Tools Profile, Police, and Punish the Poor*, (St Martin's Press, 2018).

103 Safiya Umoja Noble, *Algorithms of Oppression: How Search Engines Reinforce Racism*, (NYU Press, 2018).

104 Acheson, above note 29. See also: Suchman, above note 68.

2019, produce 11 non-binding Guiding Principles.[105] As noted above, while some have argued that IHL alone will be enough to regulate LAWS, others have called for a pre-emptive ban through binding legal agreements. Over the past few years, and in the process of seeking to articulate a ban, it has become clear that defining autonomy and meaningful human control will be at the crux of any agreement. This is epitomised by the International Committee of the Red Cross (ICRC)'s current position on the issue – recommending that states adopt legally binding rules to regulate LAWS based on three core pillars: that humans are not targeted, that systems with a high degree of unpredictability are not deployed and that human control is retained.[106] Given the centrality of autonomy and meaningful human control to ongoing debates, the following section unpicks definitions of autonomy by focusing on the difference between autonomy and automation, concluding that the distinction between the two is essentially meaningless. I then move on to question both the concept of autonomy and of meaningful human control through a focus on recent developments in HETs.

Autonomy and Meaningful Human Control

Robotic systems of varying levels of autonomy/automation and lethality have already been deployed in numerous states. To understand how autonomy can be defined for the purpose of regulating LAWS, it is necessary to analyse these existing systems, allowing for an unpacking of the difference between existing systems and LAWS. As I will argue, the distinction between autonomy and automation, however, is unclear, rendering the debate on LAWS far more complex than often portrayed. The distinctions being made between autonomy and automation, I will argue, underly a false humanist presumption that the machine and the human are distinct.[107]

One weapon system already in use is the Patriot Advanced Capability (PAC) system. The Patriot system can select, target and hit incoming missiles, small aircraft and drones, without human intervention. The system does not operate entirely independently: up to three officers watch over it from what is called an Engagement Control Centre (ECS). The operators can let the system run in automatic mode, but they are able to intervene to deselect or choose targets. Both the operator and computer can make decisions on whether an incoming entity is a friend or an enemy. However, as John Hawley has noted, the 'nuts and bolts of the ballistic missile engagements process are too complex and time-limited for direct … human participation'.[108] Human involvement is therefore present, but largely as a backup,

---

105 Meeting of the High Contracting Parties to the Convention on Prohibitions or Restrictions on the Use of Certain Conventions Weapons Which May Be Deemed to Be Excessively Injurious or to Have Indiscriminate Effects, 13–15 November 2019, CCW MSP/2019/9, Annex III.

106 ICRC, Position on Autonomous Weapons Systems, 12 May 2021, https://www.icrc.org/en/document/icrc-position-autonomous-weapon-systems (last accessed 11 July 2022).

107 Jones, above note 25.

108 John K. Hawley, 'Patriot Wars: Automation and the Patriot Air and Missile Defense System, Voices from the Field,' Center for New American Security 2017, p. 4.

with operators being trained to supervise as opposed to being trained to understand precisely how the technology works.[109] Human operators are subsequently being asked to undertake 'increasingly minimal but at the same time inherently complex roles'[110] when operating this system. This has led to errors in the past, with various air defence systems having made targeting mistakes, including firing on allies or even civilian targets, as exemplified by a Buk air defence system firing on Malaysian Airlines flight MH17 in 2014.[111] While the previous PAC-2 system relied on the ECS for guidance once launched, the latest PAC-3 and PAAC-4 systems include their own radar transmitter and guidance computer, allowing the missile to guide itself once launched, meaning it can itself change course if necessary.[112] This system operates similarly to other systems, such as Phalanx, a system used on ships which automatically detects, evaluates and engages anti-ship missiles.

Another system that calls into question the line between autonomy and automation is the SGR-A1, an immobile sentry gun deployed on the border between North and South Korea.[113] The system can detect potential enemies using infra-red up to 4km away. It uses a low light camera and pattern recognition software to determine whether a target is human, animal or matter. The SGR-A1 also uses voice recognition software to identify approaching persons. It can command someone to surrender and to not move closer. It can then, accordingly, when the person gets within 10m of the system, choose to sound an alarm or fire either rubber or real bullets. While this decision is usually to be made by a human who watches over the system, the system does have a fully automatic mode where it can be set to decide itself.[114]

While some automatic or semi-autonomous weapons systems are clearly already in use, full autonomy is a long way off. Autonomy is often distinguished from automation – with automated systems being pre-programmed machines used to perform specific tasks and autonomous machines being defined as able to make decisions themselves in changing and diverse conditions, thus being able to select from multiple options as opposed to being predictable in their processes.[115] Therefore, while

---

109 Dan Saxon, 'A Human Touch: Autonomous Weapons, DoD Directive 3000.09 and the Interpretation of 'Appropriate Levels of Human Judgment over Force',' in Nehal Bhuta et al. (eds.), *Autonomous Weapons Systems: Law, Ethics, Policy* (Cambridge University Press, 2016): 185–208, p. 191–192.

110 Ingvild Bode and Tom Watts, 'Meaning-*less* Human Control: Lessons from Air Defence Systems on Meaningful Human Control for the Debate on AWS,' Centre for War Studies 2021, https://dronewars.net/wp-content/uploads/2021/02/DW-Control-WEB.pdf (last accessed 11 July 2022), p. 39.

111 See: Bode and Watts, Ibid., p. 42–59.

112 Global Security, Patriot Advanced Capability-3, www.globalsecurity.org/space/systems/patriot-ac-3.htm (last accessed 11 July 2022).

113 Jean Kamagai, A Robotic Sentry for Korea's Demilitarized Zone IEEE, Spectrum, 2007, http://spectrum.ieee.org/robotics/military-robots/a-robotic-sentry-for-koreas-demilitarized-zone (last accessed 11 July 2022).

114 Global Security, Samsung Techwin SGR-A1 Sentry Guard Robot, /www.globalsecurity.org/military/world/rok/sgr-a1.htm (last accessed 11 July 2022).

115 M.L. Cummings, 'Artificial Intelligence and the Future of Warfare,' Chatham House, 2017, p. 3.

automated machines may be 'making decisions' whether to fire or not, they do not make thought out decisions as they ultimately work through binary algorithms in a specific, set environment, never learning themselves from their behaviour. Automated systems supposedly do what they are told to do: they are predictable in as much as they will act as told to within the set of conditions predicted when they were made. This has led some experts to argue that the sorts of systems discussed above are automated, not autonomous.[116] Despite this, the debate as to whether these machines are automated or autonomous is contentious. Ambassador Michael Biontino of Germany has highlighted the difficulties of definition here, noting that

> there are a number of different proposals as to where to draw the line between "autonomous" and "automated" … and probably, our understanding as to where to draw this line will even evolve over time as technological advances are made.[117]

At the international level, levels of autonomy are discussed in terms of whether the system includes the human in/on/out of the loop.[118] Human-out-of-the-loop machines are machines that independently select targets without supervision. Scholars argue that these machines currently only exist as used against solely material targets, with electronic jamming systems being an example.[119] These types of systems are then distinguished from human-in-the-loop systems and human-on-the-loop systems. Human-in-the-loop systems are deemed to be systems where the decision to fire is made by a human, whereas human-on-the-loop systems are defined as those which independently designate and process tasks while fully under the supervision of a human who can interrupt their actions, the Patriot system being an example here. All these categories sit somewhere between the lines of autonomy and automation. The debate around LAWS at the international level, therefore, is mostly about whether human-out-of-the-loop systems should be allowed and to what extent. Human-out-of-the-loop systems are thereby considered to be the types of machines that are dangerous, the assumption being that these systems do not yet exist.

However, whether LAWS exist or not depends on one's perspective. Vilmer, for example, defines the Patriot system as a human-on-the-loop system. This is

---

116 Vilmer, above note 69.
117 General Statement made by Ambassador Michael Biontino, Representing Germany, Swiss Ambassador's Conference, Security in Uncertainty: New Approaches to Disarmament, Arms Control and Non-Proliferation, 26 January 2016.
  See also: Gregor Noll, 'War by Algorithm: The End of War?' in Max Liljefors et al. (eds.), *War and the Algorithm*, (Rowman & Littlefield, 2019): 75–104.
118 For a detailed discussion of what autonomy can mean in terms of LAWS, see; Giovanni Sartor and Andrea Omicini, 'The Autonomy of Technological Systems and Responsibilities for Their Use,' in Nehal Bhuta et al. (eds.), *Autonomous Weapons Systems: Law, Ethics, Policy*, (Cambridge University Press, 2016): 39–74.
119 Vilmer above note 69.

because, he argues, it is fully automated yet always supervised by a human.[120] The Patriot system, however, can independently select targets, decide whether a target is an enemy target or not, fire and accurately target once released. Such a system could be defined as autonomous depending on how autonomy is defined. While the human does remain on the loop, the system does not require this to work and, as noted above, the role of the human supervisor is increasingly diminishing as the technology develops, with the time periods in which decisions must be made decreasing. On the other hand, Patriot could arguably not be deemed autonomous because it works in specific conditions based on a set of algorithms. However, it is unclear at what point algorithmic programming may become so advanced that it becomes, in effect, a complex decision-making process. In addition, noting that a machine works on algorithms does not make that machine predictable,[121] as exemplified by the AI black box dilemma whereby AI systems now often give an input and output without showing how a decision was made. As Louise Amoore notes, algorithms often give an incomplete account of themselves. Machines learn through human relationships and therefore exist in a very different way to that predicted by their source code.[122] Machines and algorithms do not always work as they are supposed to, begging the question at which point unexpected algorithmic behaviour may amount to autonomy. It becomes clear that the three descriptions of human in/on/out of the loop 'simplif[y] matters and do ... not take into account the fact that autonomy does not consist of three levels, but rather it is a continuum of many degrees'.[123] The same can be said of definitions of autonomy and automation. Autonomy and automation are not mutually exclusive but operate as part of a continuum.[124] Patriot and SGR-A1 systems, for example, are already bridging this automated/autonomous distinction in that their programming is so complex that it can be seen as a very low-level decision-making process. In short, given these difficulties, it is questionable whether making distinctions between autonomy and automation is helpful at all when thinking about how to regulate contemporary military technologies.

Part of the problem with the autonomy debate is that it tries to separate the machine from the human from the outset. Either the human is in the loop and thus controlling the machine, or on the loop, prevailing with ultimate control, or out of the loop, which poses the machine as 'other', distinct and separate from the human. Ultimately, these machines are all deeply connected to and work with the human in various ways, either through being operated by a human or, at the more advanced level, having at least been programmed by a human. Technology is changing the way we delegate tasks and make decisions but there is still always a

---

120 Ibid.
121 See, for example: Frank Pasquale, *The Black Box Society: The Secret Algorithms that Control Money and Information*, (Harvard University Press, 2015).
122 Louise Amoore, *Cloud Ethics: Algorithms and the Attributes of Ourselves and Others*, (Duke University Press, 2020).
123 Vilmer, above note 69.
124 Ibid.

human choice being made at some stage of the development or deployment of a system. However, for a system to be *fully* autonomous, it seems that some form of high-level intelligence is needed. What intelligence means for the purpose of AI is, however, debatable.[125] While many companies and institutions now claim to be using AI systems, there is a big difference between narrow AI systems or machine learning, which mostly make choices between binaries, albeit sometimes adapting in a certain set of conditions, and strong or general AI systems, which would be able to make complex and nuanced decisions. If algorithms work on binaries between 0 and 1, it seems that general AI, which would be needed for any system to be fully autonomous, in making choices, would either navigate these binaries or work beyond these binaries altogether. As noted above, however, the point at which binaries become so complex that they may constitute intelligence remains unclear.

Complex or general AI purposefully embedded in weapons technology would clearly move weapons systems towards 'full' autonomy of the kind where machines may not only be able to make their own decisions and learn but where they may also be able to create and programme themselves. AI of this kind does not yet exist in the realm of LAWS (or possibly at all – depending on one's definition of AI), although there are a number of AI programmes and machines (arguably) in existence that are being developed and tested.[126] For the most part these programmes remain limited, lagging far behind what could feasibly be dubbed human intelligence with most machines able to perform only one specific task (even if they often perform that task very well). Overall, the difference between autonomy and automation is not clear cut. This poses great problems when it comes to regulating LAWS, calling into question exactly what needs to be regulated.

This dilemma can be further unpacked by examining the UK's position on LAWS. The UK argues that LAWS will be 'capable of understanding higher level of intent and direction'.[127] This definition sets the bar so high that it ultimately means that the UK defines LAWS as, for the foreseeable future, technologically infeasible. Despite this, the UK has identified what it terms 'human-machine teaming' as the future of warfare.[128] This position is paradoxical, given that each of the systems outlined above presents questions around where the line between autonomy and automation and the human and the machine should be drawn. The UK's definition rests upon problematic distinctions between autonomy and

---

125 See: Matt Ginsberg, *Essentials of Artificial Intelligence*, (Morgan Kaufmann, 2013); Jones, above note 25.

126 Elon Musk and Mark Zuckerberg, for example, disagree as to the definition of AI, with Zuckerberg defining AI broadly and thus stating that it exists already and with Musk seeing AI as being much more advanced and more akin to what some call a General Artificial Intelligence (AGI), i.e. something which is intelligent across all areas, not just for one specific purpose. See; Artur Kiulian, Elon Musk and Mark Zuckerberg are Arguing about AI – but they're Both Missing the Point, Entrepreneur, 2017, https://www.entrepreneur.com/article/297861 (last accessed 11 July 2022).

127 Ministry of Defence, above note 56, p. 60.

128 Ibid.

automation, the human and the machine. This definition allows the UK to promote itself as being concerned about LAWS while, in the meantime, deploying increasingly autonomous systems.

The autonomy/automation distinction plays out in one of the central concepts under discussion in the regulatory debate on LAWS, that is, meaningful human control. A term initially proposed by NGO Article 36,[129] this term has since been embraced by groups including the ICRC.[130] What meaningful human control means, however, remains debatable. While, for example, the UK government has declared that 'human control'[131] will always be present in any future systems they develop, with the US focusing more on 'human judgment',[132] the actual degree of human involvement has not been clarified.[133] There have been attempts by others to define meaningful human control, with philosopher Peter Asaro, for example, arguing that meaningful human control must include sufficient opportunity for human supervisors to morally reason before the deployment of force.[134] It is clear, however, that meaningful human control is being posed either as the opposite to autonomy or as a controller of and over autonomy.

John Williams has problematised the term 'meaningful human control', arguing that the human envisaged by the term is ultimately a Eurocentric subject; the 'rational, rights-holding, masculine individual' of liberal thought.[135] This model, warns Williams, risks the 'epistemical marginalization' of forms of knowledge beyond the Eurocentric liberal tradition. Williams thereby notes that the debate on LAWS largely excludes the voices of the people most likely to be subject to them, including those currently living under drones, these people being based primarily in the global south. This is a concern, as these people are the ones who 'have the greatest experience of the effects of key LAWS precursors' such as drones.[136] This debate harks back to the discussions in Chapter 1, where I questioned the central subject of the law, arguing that international law is based on both exclusionary humanism (and thereby gender, race, class and ableism) and anthropocentrism.

---

129 Richard Moyes, Key Elements of Meaningful Human Control, Article 36, April 2016, www.article36.org/wp-content/uploads/2016/04/MHC-2016-FINAL.pdf (last accessed 11 July 2022).

130 ICRC, 'Autonomous Weapon Systems: Implications of Increasing Autonomy in the Critical Functions of Weapons,' Geneva, 2016, https://www.icrc.org/en/publication/4283-autonomous-weapons-systems (last accessed 29 September 2022); US Department of Defense, above note 55.

131 See: Ministry of Defence, Letter to Maiara Folly, 4 January 2021, https://article36.org/wp-content/uploads/2021/01/UK-govt-reply-2020-LAWS.pdf (last accessed 11 July 2022).

132 US Department of Defense, above note 55.

133 See: Saxon, above note 109; Noel Sharkey, 'Staying in the Loop: Human Supervisory Control of Weapons,' in Nehal Bhuta et al. (eds.), *Autonomous Weapons Systems: Law, Ethics, Policy* (Cambridge University Press, 2016): 23–38, p. 26.

134 Peter Asaro as quoted in Saxon, Ibid., p. 202.

135 John Williams, 'Locating LAWS: Lethal Autonomous Weapons, Epistemic Space, and "Meaningful Human Control",' *Journal of Global Security Studies* (2021) 6(4): 1–18, p. 2.

136 Ibid., p. 3.

The second concern with the increasing focus on meaningful human control is that the human continues to be situated at the centre of the paradigm.[137] This human is not only the white, male subject of European liberalism but, furthermore, the machine is very much the 'other' to the human in this paradigm, an entity to be controlled by humans. This can be seen in the way autonomy is discussed in relation to the human who is imagined as either in/on/out of the loop. This paradigm does not account for how humans and machines work in connection.[138] In contrast, posthuman feminism challenges the centrality of the human within western thought, working to re-think the human/machine binary. Posthuman feminism argues that a new way of defining subjectivity is needed, one that sees the complexities and interconnections between the human and the nonhuman. Rejecting the human as the central paradigm, posthuman feminism notes that human is located 'in the flow of relations with multiple others'.[139] As Bruno Latour puts it: 'You are different with a gun in your hand; the gun is different with you holding it'.[140] The gun and the person are neither a subject nor an object but rather, as Karen Barad argues, agency switches from being something someone has to being relational, part of the 'ongoing reconfigurings of the world'.[141] The humanist discourse around LAWS ignores the posthuman reality that humans and machines are already working in connection with one another[142] and that life/death decisions are already being made by human-machine combinations.

A further example of the way humans and machines already work together to make life/death decisions can be seen when examining drone warfare. The use of drones in conflict has increased dramatically over the past decade.[143] While drones are defined as distinct from LAWS, because they require a human operator, the distinction becomes less clear when evaluating the realities of how targeting decisions are made in drone warfare. While many drone strikes are conducted as 'personality strikes' – i.e. strikes on a particular, key, well-known person – these occur only a few times a year, with 'signature strikes' happening regularly.[144] These attacks are conducted on the basis of a 'pattern of life' analysis. 'Pattern of life' analyses develop a profile of an individual or a network of individuals by drawing on all

---

137 See: Connal Parsley, 'Automating Authority: The Human and Automation in Legal Discourse on the Meaningful Human Control of Lethal Autonomous Weapons Systems,' in Shane Chalmers and Sundhya Pahuja, *Routledge Handbook of International Law and the Humanities*, (Routledge, 2021): 432–445.

138 Haraway, above note 31.

139 Braidotti, above note 47, p. 50; see also; Lucy Suchman and Jutta Weber, 'Human-Machine Autonomies,' in Nehal Bhuta et al. (eds.), *Autonomous Weapons Systems: Law, Ethics, Policy*, (Cambridge University Press, 2016): 75–101.

140 Bruno Latour, *Pandora's Hope: Essays on the Reality of Science Studies*, (Harvard University Press, 1999), p. 179.

141 Karen Barad, *Meeting the Universe Halfway: Quantum Physics and the Entanglement of Matter and Meaning*, (Duke University Press, 2007), p. 141.

142 See also: Suchmand and Weber, above note 139.

143 Bourke, above note 19, p. 29–37.

144 Wilcox, 'Drone Warfare …', above note 26, p. 128–129.

the intelligence available, including drone and other aerial surveillance intelligence, communications interceptions, phone tapping and GPS tracking information.[145] The drone itself is only one part of a broader system which includes big data, algorithms, intelligence collection, chains of command and bureaucratic formations, among other technologies and practices.[146] The gathering of this information builds up to create a file of information collected by humans and machines which, as Grégoire Chamayou has noted, 'once it becomes thick enough, will constitute a death warrant'.[147] This is an example of human-machine life/death decision-making. Part of the decision-making process here is already done by machines which gather this data and predict the likelihood of an individual's involvement with terrorist organisations. While humans are clearly involved, in that they then must note the results of the data collected, deem it enough to act upon and then operate the drone to kill the subject in question, the machine and the human are making life/death decisions *together*.[148] Furthermore, as Lauren Wilcox has shown, this data is often interpreted in racialised and gendered ways.[149]

The difficulty in determining autonomy is a problem that has been recognised by the US Military Defense Science Board who, upon reviewing some of the definitions of levels of autonomy being used by the Department of Defense (DoD) and noting that these definitions 'are not particularly helpful', recommended that 'the DoD abandon the use of "levels of autonomy"' and focus instead on 'the explicit allocation of cognitive functions and responsibilities between the human and computer to achieve specific capabilities'.[150] In a similar vein, Ingvild Bode and Tom Watts have argued that, upon an analysis of 'how automated and autonomous features have already been integrated into the critical functions of air defence systems … in some situations, human control has become effectively meaningless'.[151] While the DoD report was published in 2012, it seems the concern was not heeded, and states continue to align with calling for the need for meaningful human control without actually defining that control, begging the question whether states really care about meaningful human control at all or whether, rather, they prefer to position themselves in a way that makes them look ethical, while manipulating definitional ambiguities to continue to develop increasingly advanced technologies. After all, while even lower-end technologies such as drones do indeed challenge the distinction between human and machine decision-making, these technologies

---

145 Ian Shaw, 'Predator Empire: The Geopolitics of US Drone Warfare,' (2013) 18(3): *Geopolitics*: 536–559, p. 550.
146 Wilcox, above note 3, p. 5.
147 Chamayou, above note 4, p. 49.
148 For a discussion of how technology is also changing how humans make decisions, with human reasoning becoming increasingly automated in an era of cognitive capitalism, see: Luciana Parisi, 'Automated Thinking and the Limits of Reason,' *Cultural Studies ↔ Critical Methodologies* (2016) 16(5): 471–481.
149 Wilcox, above note 3.
150 DoD Defense Science Board, 'The Role of Autonomy in DoD Systems,' Task Force Report 2012, https://irp.fas.org/agency/dod/dsb/autonomy.pdf (last accessed 11 July 2022), p. 4.
151 Bode and Watts, above note 110, p. 3.

are certainly not the technologies being discussed when debating autonomy and meaningful human control for the purpose of regulating LAWS. By trying to define autonomy and meaningful human control instead of working to understand automation and autonomy, the human and the machine, as in continuum, debates on LAWS operate in a void, denying the fact that machines are already making life/death decisions alongside humans. This has led Dan Saxon to argue that calls for maintaining appropriate levels of judgement will ultimately be rendered useless as 'decision-making cycles ... shrink to micro-seconds', this being justified as 'common sense ... in situations where lives depend on the fastest possible actions and reactions'.[152] In short, the humanist framing of the debate on LAWS deflects attention from the central ethical question which is, do we want machines making life/death decisions and, if some level of involvement is justifiable, how much?

Human Enhancement Technologies

As noted, there are many definitions of AI. However, as science fiction author and computer scientist, Vernor Vinge has noted, 'in humans, the hardest development problems have already been solved. Building up from within ourselves ought to be easier than figuring out first what we really are and then building machines that are all of that'.[153] Superintelligence, Vinge thereby concludes, seems more likely to occur through intelligence amplification (IA), that is, through 'computer/human interfaces [that] may become so intimate that users may reasonably be considered superhumanly intelligent'.[154] In short, while a genuinely intelligent and therefore fully autonomous system may be hard to create, upgrading the human is much easier as we already have biology on our side.

Seeking to enhance a soldier's capabilities is by no means a new approach. Amphetamines and similar drugs have been used for decades, with 225 million stimulant tablets being used by the US military in the space of only three years in the Vietnam War era, between 1966 and 1969.[155] Emerging trends in the development of military technologies show that upgrading the human through HETs, including through the use of technologies such as brain-computer interface systems and wearable technologies, is one way that developers are seeking to create ever more advanced and efficient military technologies. Enhanced soldiers would not, however, be included in any proposed ban of LAWS. This, I argue, is concerning. While, on the one hand, it is hard to argue that an upgraded soldier is a weapon system, at least when looking at current technologies in use on the battlefield,

---

152 Saxon, above note 109, p. 209.
153 Vernor Vinge, The Coming Technological Singularity: How to Survive in the Post-Human Era, paper presented at Vision 21: Interdisciplinary Science and Engineering in the Era of Cyberspace Conference, NASA Lewis Research Centre, 1993, NASA Publication CP-10129, https://ntrs.nasa.gov/archive/nasa/casi.ntrs.nasa.gov/19940022855.pdf (last accessed 11 July 2022).
154 Ibid.
155 Lucasz Kamieński, Shooting Up: A History of Drugs and War, (Oxford University Press, 2016), p. 189.

developments in this field will increasingly challenge this distinction. Furthermore, and as we have already seen above through my posthuman feminist analysis of military technologies already in use, when machines are so deeply embedded in life/death decision-making, the central ethical question around whether or not LAWS should be used, that is, whether machines should be making life/death decisions, is likewise relevant when applied to HETs. This is not to say that HETs create soldiers that are the equivalent of LAWS. The soldier, is, ultimately, human, possibly (and hopefully) retaining human choice capacity and empathy,[156] these being some of the values those calling for the regulation of LAWS are keen to retain. At the same time, the cyborg soldier that is part human and part machine is the ultimate transhuman subject critiqued in the Introduction to this volume, coinciding with Kantian and Cartesian discourses that separate mind and body, reason and emotion,[157] posing challenges, again, to those concerned about retaining something meaningfully human. For example, as noted above, emotions in military contexts are often deemed to be a weakness by many who then use this argument to justify LAWS.[158] Following this line of argument, it is feasible to consider that attempts may be made to render soldiers emotionless. An uncertainty thereby remains around at what point a technologically enhanced human may be deemed to be as much or even more machine than human. In short, drawing on examples of existing HETs in use and technologies in development, in this section, I argue that, similar to some of the existing weapons systems outlined above, HETs exemplify the false binaries drawn between autonomy and automation and the human and the machine. This calls into question the effectiveness of regulating LAWS. If the central concern in the debate on LAWS is whether life/death decisions should be delegated to machines, regulating LAWS alone is not and cannot be enough.

One example of a HET which, as I previously noted, has long been in use, is pharmaceuticals.[159] In the US, the Defense Advanced Research Projects Agency (DARPA) has been key in funding various HET projects, including the development of pharmaceuticals. Funded projects include, for example, seeking to prevent

---

156 Anxieties around what and who counts as human in relation to human enhancement technologies are already garnering attention, such anxieties being only set to increase in intensity as human enhancement technologies advance. Contemporary anxieties were expressed, for example, over the debate around whether Oscar Pistorius, an athlete with prosthetic legs below the knee, could compete in the Olympics as opposed to the Paralympics. See Leslie Swartz, 'Cyborg Anxieties: Oscar Pistorius and the Boundaries of What It Means to Be Human,' *Disability & Society* (2008) 23(2): 187–190.

157 Masters, above note 52, p. 114.

158 Arkin, above note 64.

159 There is a debate as to what HETs include and whether or not they must physically change the subject or whether wearables should be included. For the purposes of this chapter, HETs are defined broadly, the point being not to engage in the debate on the definition of HETs per se but, rather, to show the ways that technology and the human are already deeply intertwined in multiple ways. For more on defining HETs see: Ioana Maria Puscas, 'Military Human Enhancement,' in William H. Boothby (ed.), *New Technologies and the Law in War and Peace*, (Cambridge University Press, 2018):182–229, p. 184–187.

blood loss,[160] pharmaceuticals that aim to prevent muscle fatigue[161] and seeking to enhance cognitive performance.[162] Nanotechnologies, i.e. science and technology conducted on the nano scale, likewise already exist. These technologies, if used, could be adopted for similar ends to, for example, edit a soldier's genes to spread biological diseases and thereby to 'protect soldiers from means of methods of warfare that may then kill those without the modification'.[163] As Kobi Leins astutely puts it, 'no public literature exists regarding military uses of this type', yet 'the technology exists'.[164]

Wearable military technologies are also already in use. While it is debatable whether or not these technologies are HETs, depending on how one defines human enhancement,[165] I have chosen a broad definition here because these technologies also raise issues around decision-making, this being my central concern. Exoskeletons are a good example here. Originally designed to make soldiers stronger and faster and to help disabled soldiers get back to work,[166] many of these wearable military technologies are being used, not only to increase strength but to make life/death decision-making more efficient. An example of such a technology can be seen in the Boomerang gunfire location system. Boomerang pinpoints the exact location of incoming small arms fire using acoustic detection and sophisticated algorithms. This information is then relayed directly to the soldier who can choose whether or not to fire.[167] Initially mounted onto trucks, there is now also a wearable system called the Boomerang Warrior-X. While the system still requires a soldier to use the information given to choose whether to fire, the Boomerang system provides another example of how the human and the machine are already working together to make life/death decisions. If one combines these systems and, for example, merges the data collection and profiling used in drone warfare and gives this to a soldier in an exoskeleton using a system such as Boomerang Warrior-X, questions again arise around how much the human at the centre of all this technology has a choice about whether or not to fire on a target.

The above is an example of a combination of fairly low-tech systems. However, HETs are developing rapidly. Brain-computer interface applications likewise challenge

---

160 Ibid., p. 192–194.
161 Ibid., p. 194–195.
162 Ibid., p. 195–197.
    For an analysis of the historical, present and future use of drugs to enhance soldiers in the US military, see: Andrew Bickford, *Chemical Heroes: Pharmacological Supersoldiers in the US Military*, (Duke University Press, 2020).
163 Kobi Leins, *New War Technologies and International Law: The Legal Limits to Weaponising Nanomaterials*, (Cambridge University Press, 2022), p. 35. See also this book generally for a wider discussion of the legal limits of the military use of nanotechnolgoies.
164 Ibid., p. 35.
165 See above note 159.
166 For more on exoskeletons and military use from a gender perspective see: Heathcote, above note 23.
167 Raytheon, Boomerang, www.raytheon.co.uk/capabilities/products/boomerang (last accessed 11 July 2022).

distinctions between the human and the machine.[168] These systems may be external or implanted into the subject. HRL's Information & System Sciences Laboratory's transcranial direct current stimulation project is an example of an external brain-computer interface system.[169] The researchers in this project 'measured the brain activity patterns of six commercial and military pilots and then transmitted these patterns into novice subjects as they learned to pilot an airplane in a realistic flight stimulator'.[170] The study found that 'subjects who received brain stimulation via electrode-embedded head caps improved their piloting abilities'.[171] This example demonstrates a possible way to decrease the time it takes to learn complex skills, given that 'commercial and military pilot training programs [already] now utilize flight simulation extensively for training basic flight and combat skills'.[172] As the researchers on the project note, such a study could have enormous 'benefits for commercial and military applications'.[173]

There are multiple other HETs that further challenge the distinction between the human and the machine, including technologies that enhance vision beyond 20/20 vision or technologies that may allow for soldiers to use their devices while simultaneously focusing on one's surroundings. Such technologies are already being developed in partnership with the US military.[174] Furthermore, in 2015, a quadriplegic woman was able to pilot a flight stimulator with her mind alone.[175] Later, in 2018, a pilot with a brain chip was able to fly a swarm of drones.[176] These examples, alongside the other examples given above, each show a further way that technology is being developed to enhance soldier capabilities. These various measures are a

---

168 For an overview of Brain Computer Interfaces and the legal and ethical issues raised, see: Noam Lubell and Katya Al-Khateeb, 'Cyborg Soldiers: Military Use of Brain-Computer Interfaces and the Law of Armed Conflict,' in Laura Dickenson and Eiki Berg (eds.), *Big Data and Armed Conflict*, (Oxford University Press, forthcoming 2023).

For an analysis of neurotechnology and its legality under IHL, see: Gregor Noll, 'Weaponising Neurotechnology: International Humanitarian Law and the Loss of Language,' *London Review of International Law* (2014) 2(2): 201–231.

169 Jaehoon Choe et al., 'Transcranial Direct Current Stimulation Modulates Neuronal Activity and Learning in Pilot Training,' *Frontiers in Human Neuroscience* (2016) 10(34): 1–25.

170 Matthew Phillips as quoted in HRL Laboratories, HRL Demonstrates the Potential to Enhance the Human Intellect's Existing Capacity to Learn New Skills, 2016, www.hrl.com/news/2016/0210 (last accessed 11 July 2022).

171 Choe et al., above note 169.

172 Ibid., p. 2.

173 Ibid., p. 2.

174 See: eMacula, Applications, https://www.emacula.io/home/applications (last accessed 11 July 2022).

175 Nick Stockton, Woman Controls a Fighter Jet Sim Using Only Her Mind, WIRED, 5 March 2015, https://www.wired.com/2015/03/woman-controls-fighter-jet-sim-using-mind/ (last accessed 11 July 2022).

176 Patrick Tucker, It's Now Possible to Telepathically Communicate with a Drone Swarm, Defence One, 6 September 2018, https://www.defenseone.com/technology/2018/09/its-now-possible-telepathically-communicate-drone-swarm/151068 (last accessed 11 July 2022). For an overview of DARPA funded efforts to develop brain-computer interface technologies, see: Robbin A. Miranda et al., 'DARPA-Funded Efforts in the Development of Novel Brain-Computer Interface Technologies,' *Journal of Neuroscience Methods* (2015) 244: 52–67.

long way off being defined as a weapons system[177] and therefore, while invoking similar ethical questions to those invoked by LAWS, remain off the radar when it comes to international weapons regulation.

Conclusion

Many of the technologies that are already being used on the battlefield or that are under development, including HETs, the Patriot system, the SGR-A1 and even the technologies used in drone warfare, already call into question the boundaries between the human and the machine and autonomy and automation when it comes to life/death decision-making. Discussions on LAWS, however, continue to assert autonomous systems as the machinic 'other', seeking to define the limits of meaningful human control over the machine. This means that while a vast amount of time and energy is going into regulating LAWS, in the meantime, technologies that already call into question whether and how much a machine should be making life/death decisions are in use, these systems flying under the radar of the LAWS debate. A posthuman feminist approach that pays attention to the relationship between the human and the machine is needed to ensure that the full range of technologies which may kill may be captured through legal regulation.

While this chapter has exemplified how posthuman feminism can be used to challenge the humanist assumptions that underly debates on the regulation of LAWS, noting that this challenge must be heeded if LAWS and other military technologies are to be regulated appropriately, the next chapter draws on this analysis to look towards alternative regulatory solutions for LAWS and other new and emerging military technologies.

177 See: Puscas, above note 159, p. 203–205.

3

REGULATING MILITARY TECHNOLOGIES

Between Resistance and Compliance

This book aims to show how gender theory can be used to analyse all areas of international law. This was exemplified in the previous chapter, where I drew on posthuman feminism to re-think some of the debates surrounding the regulation of LAWS. I argued that the current debate on LAWS relies on problematic humanist assumptions that create false binaries between the human and the machine and between understandings of autonomy and automation.

A second core aim of this volume is to exemplify how posthuman feminism can be used, not only as a theoretical framework to re-think international law, but also as a tool to design and foster legal change. As noted in the Introduction, this is a core challenge for posthuman theory. The application of these theories to practice is the much-needed next step in the field.[1] This chapter focuses on the application of posthuman feminism to practice, drawing on the work of the previous chapter to propose alternative posthuman feminist inspired legal frameworks for the regulation of new military technologies.

The chapter is written in conversation with feminist approaches to international law, particularly speaking to debates on how feminists can engage in making legal change. Feminist international legal scholars have widely discussed the need to balance the tension between what is termed resistance and compliance, that is, the need to seek change within international law while also working to imagine beyond international law and its gendered normative underpinnings. In this chapter, I outline these debates, exemplifying the core tensions through the example of feminist engagements with the UN Security Council's Women, Peace and Security agenda. Given the feminist call for approaches that both resist and comply, this chapter subsequently makes two sets of proposals. The first set is written in the vein of compliance. These proposals engage with existing debates in international

---

1 Margaret Davies, *Law Unlimited*, (Routledge, 2017).

DOI: 10.4324/9781003363798-4

law, drawing on frameworks already in place and reading them through posthuman feminism to provide alternative proposals for the regulation of military technologies. The second set of proposals focuses more on resistance methods and on challenging the exclusionary humanist nature of the debate on LAWS. Here, I draw on literatures including posthuman feminisms and xenofeminism, data feminism and Indigenous knowledge as applied to AI, and as inspired by black, postcolonial and crip analyses of technology, to reconfigure human relationships with technology. These theories are used to provide an alternative way of thinking about regulating military technologies – seeking understandings and solutions beyond the narrow framework of thought that international law can provide as currently configured.

There is, however, another tension that underlies this chapter, one that maps onto the resistance and compliance conundrum. That tension is anti-militarism. Feminist engagements with international law have long centred an anti-militarist perspective, from the Women's Peace Conference held in the Hague in 1915, to the feminist activism of Greenham Common. This anti-militarism has also long included a strong focus on disarmament, the work of the Women's International League for Peace and Freedom being essential here. This chapter, in seeking to provide alternative proposals for the regulation of military technologies, at times sits in tension with these feminist aims. After all, working to regulate weapons systems is a very different goal from resisting their use. This tension is one that lies between resistance and compliance, between challenging the justification of conflict and the use of weapons versus engaging in debates on the regulation of weapons, seeking to shape those debates for the better. The concern is that the latter risks legitimising the use of weapons, marking some weapons as illegal and thereby some as legal. In engaging in these debates, I do not wish to displace feminist anti-militarist positions that I align with politically. Rather, this chapter represents an attempt, to use Donna Haraway's words, to 'stay with the trouble',[2] to work between and across resistance and compliance modes of feminism, proposing multiple modes of resistance that work within international law while seeking futures beyond it.

Feminist Strategies in International Law: Between Resistance and Compliance

Sari Kouvo and Zoe Pearson argue that the tension between resistance and compliance is 'built into the heart of the feminist project within international law'.[3] This tension is framed around the choice feminists must make between either using international law as a tool to change women's immediate circumstances or challenging the normative structures of international law. For the most part, feminist approaches have turned towards what can be deemed more of a compliance

---

2 Donna Haraway, *Staying with the Trouble: Making Kin in the Chthulucene*, (Duke University Press, 2016).
3 Sari Kouvo and Zoe Pearson (eds.), *Feminist Perspectives on Contemporary International Law: Between Resistance and Compliance?*, (Hart, 2014), p. 5.

mode, working within the system to seek change, remaining hopeful of 'international law's potential for women'.[4] This, as I argued in the Introduction, is often a choice that is shaped by the demands of institutions. In short, feminist international lawyers have a limited array of choices when engaging with international law. In seeking to foster change, feminists have often reverted to complying with or working within the normative framework of international law to find feminist solutions.

This dilemma can be seen through the example of feminist engagements with the Women, Peace and Security (WPS) agenda. Made up of a series of Security Council resolutions, the WPS agenda seeks to ensure that gender equality and women's participation are promoted through work on peace and security.[5] While there have been many gains made through the WPS agenda, providing an authoritative framework through which, for example, women's grassroots organisations can 'claim a role in peace negotiations and postconflict decision making',[6] the WPS agenda has been widely critiqued. Criticisms have included questions around which women are included and excluded,[7] challenges to the focus on women and girls as opposed to wider constructions of gender, including the needs of LGBTIQ+ persons,[8] and the lack of focus on hegemonic masculinities.[9] Other voices have challenged the

---

4 Ibid., p. 5.
5 Security Council Resolution 1325, 31 October 2000, S/RES/1325.; Security Council Resolution 1820, 18 June 2008, S/RES/1820; Security Council Resolution 1888, 30 September 2009, S/RES/1888; Security Council Resolution 1889, 5 October 2009, S/RES/1889; Security Council Resolution 1960, 16 December 2010, S/RES/1960; Security Council Resolution 2106, 24 June 2013, S/RES/2106; Security Council Resolution 2122,18 October 2013, S/RES/2122; Security Council Resolution 2242, 13 October 2015, S/RES/2242; Security Council Resolution 2467, 23 April 2019, S/RES/2467; Security Council Resolution 2493, 29 October 2019, S/RES/2493.
6 Dianne Otto, 'The Security Council's Alliance of Gender Legitimacy: The Symbolic Capital of Resolution 1325' in Hilary Charlesworth and Jean-Marc Coicaud (eds.), *Fault Lines of International Legitimacy* (Cambridge University Press, 2010): 239–287, p. 240. For more on the usefulness of the resolutions for feminist organisations, see also: Dianne Otto, 'Contesting Feminism's Institutional Doubles: Troubling the Security Council's Women, Peace and Security Agenda,' in Janet Halley et al. (eds.), *Governance Feminism: Notes from the Field*, (Minnesota University Press, 2019): 200–229.
7 Maria Martin de Almagro, 'Producing Participants: Gender, Race, Class, and Women, Peace and Security,' *Global Society* (2018) 32(4): 395–414; Sara Bertotti et al., *The Law of War and Peace: A Gender Analysis Volume One*, (Bloomsbury, 2021), p. 22; Gina Heathcote, 'Security Council Resolution 2242 on Women, Peace and Security: Progressive Gains or Dangerous Developments?' *Global Society* (2018) 32(4): 374–394, p. 378.
8 See: Tamsin Phillipa Paige, 'The Maintenance of ~~International Peace and Security~~ Heteronormativity,' in Dianne Otto (ed.), *Queering International Law: Possibilities, Alliances, Complicities, Risks*, (Routledge 2018): 91–109; Lisa Davies and Jessica Stern, 'WPS and LGBTI Rights,' in Sara E. Davies and Jacqui True (eds.), *The Oxford Handbook of Women, Peace, and Security* (Oxford University Press 2019) 658–668; Jamie J. Hagen, 'Queering Women, Peace and Security,' *International Affairs* (2016) 92(2): 313–332.
9 Heathcote, above note 7.

dominant focus in the agenda on tackling conflict-related sexual violence,[10] or have questioned the essentialism present in the agenda and the suggestion that women should have a place at the table because of their innate peacefulness.[11] Feminists have also problematised the adoption of provisions which pertain to countering terrorism in the WPS agenda,[12] noting that the agenda risks 'being co-opted into the civilising tropes that surround the work of countering terrorism'.[13] I do not have the space to outline all of the critiques of the WPS agenda in detail here. Rather, I will focus on the critiques that relate particularly to the resistance and compliance conundrum, the purpose being to understand the ways that (posthuman) feminism can be used to engage with international law in a way that bridges the theory and practice divide.

The first WPS resolution, 1325, has its origins in feminist civil society.[14] A group of feminist NGOs, facilitated by the Women's International League for Peace and Freedom (WILPF),[15] played a key role in calling for this first resolution, having drafted an initial text for the Security Council to consider. WILPF is an organisation which evolved out of the 1915 Women's Peace Congress and is committed to fostering peace through promoting feminist ideas. The initial drafts of the resolution reflected WILPF's and other feminist organisation's wider aims to end conflict and militarism, alongside other issues such as strengthening the protection of women

---

10 Sara Bertotti et al., above note 7, p. 25 Dianne Otto, 'Contesting.'., above note 6, p. 204–210.
     For literature that more generally problematises the focus on sexual violence in international law and victimisation narratives, see: Ratna Kapur, 'The Tragedy of Victimization Rhetoric: Resurrecting the "Native" Subject in International/Post-Colonial Feminist Legal Politics,' *Harvard Human Rights Journal* (2002) 15(1): 1–38; Gina Heathcote, 'Laws, UFOs and UAVs: Feminist Encounters with the Law of Armed Conflict,' in Dale Stephens and Paul Babie (eds.), *Imagining Law: Essays in Conversation with Judith Gardam*, (University of Adelaide Press, 2016): 153–170, p. 158.
     For a wider discussion of how the focus on sexual violence in conflict came about and how this focus works to sideline other important issues, see; Karen Engle, *The Grip of Sexual Violence in Conflict*, (Stanford University Press, 2020).

11 Dianne Otto, 'The Security Council's …,' above note 6; Sara Bertotti et al., above note 7, p. 22, 28.
     See also, more generally on the stereotypes that haunt women in the international order: Laura Sjoberg and Caron E. Gentry, *Mothers, Monsters, Whores: Women's Violence in Global Politics*, (Zed Books, 2007).

12 See: Fionnuala Ní Aoláin, 'The "War on Terror" and Extremism: Assessing the Relevance of the Women, Peace and Security Agenda,' *International Affairs* (2016) 9(2): 275–291; Heathcote, above note 7.

13 Heathcote, Ibid., p. 387.

14 For more background see; Bertotti et al., above note 7, p. 20–21; Cornelia Weiss, 'Creating UNSCR 1325: Women who served as initiators, drafters, and strategists,' in Rebecca Adami and Dan Plesch (eds.), *Women and the UN: A new history of women's international human rights*, (Routledge, 2021): 139–160.

15 Cohn et al. note that 'The NGO Working Group on Women, Peace and Security initially consisted of Amnesty International, International Alert, the Hague Appeal for Peace, the Women's International League for Peace and Freedom, the International Peace Research Association and the Women's Commission for Refugee Women and Children.' See: Carol Cohn et al., 'Women, Peace and Security: Resolution 1325,' *International Feminist Journal of Politics* (2004) 6(1): 130–140, p. 130, note 1.

in conflict and supporting women's grassroots peacebuilding efforts.[16] However, in 'order to present a common position among the Working Groups' participants, and to make the proposal more acceptable to states, WILPF had to preventatively accept not to put forward its historical forte of disarmament and anti-militarism'.[17] Furthermore, states have the last say on the content of resolutions. The resolution subsequently adopted by the Security Council has been highly criticised for being a watered-down version of WILPF's, and the coalition's, original vision.[18] From this example alone, the tensions between resistance and compliance and working within powerful institutions can already be seen.

Writing almost two decades after the adoption of 1325, Dianne Otto argues that the initial ideas which informed WILPF and the coalition's vision, which were based around peace, can now be seen as at odds with the subsequent trajectory of the agenda.[19] The resolutions, Otto notes, do not limit the 'justifications for the use of arms'. Rather, instead of focusing on peace, Otto argues that the WPS agenda may provide a 'new trigger for the collective use of force', having the potential to support new justifications for so doing.[20]

Overall, these critiques have led scholars to question whether feminists can ever really make gains when working with powerful institutions such as the Security Council. Sara E. Davies and Jacqui True, for example, note the underlying tensions presented by seeking to 'transform power relations' by engaging with the 'political and economic institutions ... that have marginalised women's representation and livelihoods'.[21] As Otto notes, 'the Security Council's approach to peace supports the continued expansion of the international market for arms, increased powers of state security institutions, and more coercive policing of sexuality and gender'.[22] These aims, which sit in antithesis with feminist aims, render working with the Security Council inherently contestable.[23]

Further risks presented by engaging with powerful institutions such as the Security Council include the impact on feminist thought. One cost of the WPS agenda has been 'a softening of feminist opposition to war' as feminist peace

---

16 Cohn et al., Ibid., p. 131–132.

17 Otto, 'The Security Council's ...', above note 6, p. 255.

18 Cynthia Cockburn, *From Where We Stand: War, Women's Activism and Feminist Analysis*, (Zed Books, 2007), p. 147.

19 Dianne Otto, 'Women, Peace and Security: A Critical Analysis of the Security Council's Vision,' in Fionnuala Ní Aoláin et al. (eds.), *The Oxford Handbook of Gender and Conflict*, (Oxford University Press, 2018): 106–118, p. 111.

20 Otto, Ibid., p. 112.

21 Sara E. Davies and Jacquie True, From Pillars to Progress in Women, Peace and Security, LSE Blog, 26 November 2018, https://blogs.lse.ac.uk/wps/2018/11/26/from-pillars-to-progress-in-women-peace-and-security (last accessed 11 July 2022).

22 Otto, above note 19, p. 107. See also; Ratna Kapur, 'Gender, Sovereignty and the Rise of a Sexual Security Regime in International Law and Postcolonial India,' *Melbourne Journal of International Law* (2014) 14(2): 317–345.

23 For a discussion of these 'faultlines', see: Otto, 'The Security Council's ...', above note 6.

advocates shift from focusing on ending war to 'making wars safer for women'.[24] This shift has not only impacted the focus of civil society but also scholarship. As I outlined in the Introduction, the majority of feminist scholarship in international law has come to focus on a narrower array of issues as compared to the wide variety of topics this body of work analysed at the time of its inception. Therefore, while working with the Security Council may provide some legitimacy, some access to power, overall, questions are raised by what is lost through this collaboration.

The tensions feminists face between working to change international law from within versus wanting to resist the normative and gendered structure of international law, are complex. The risks of working within problematic systems of power must be balanced against the potential gains to be made through working with powerful institutions. The WPS agenda provides an example of the wider tension, to return to Kouvo and Pearson, of resistance and compliance.[25] In the meantime, the take-up of *some* feminist ideas by the international system has worked to ensure that liberal and dominance feminist perspectives (and their contemporary configurations through carceral feminism[26]), have been given a platform in international law, this occurring at the expense of alternative feminist visions or 'unorthodox, "outsider" ideas'[27] including, for example, postcolonial feminisms.[28] Furthermore, it can never be ensured that feminist engagements with institutions will be taken up in the way initially anticipated, as the above example highlights. As Nancy Fraser argues, feminist engagements with mainstream power can often be transformed into a 'strange shadowy version' or an 'uncanny double' of the original.[29]

The debate between resistance and compliance is by no means unique to feminist approaches. A similar phenomenon has been noted by Marxist international lawyer, Susan Marks. Marks highlights how the focus of many international lawyers on human rights has pushed aside other issues, including structural concerns.[30] While human rights may focus on many important issues, human rights also 'engender and sustain' the status quo of the global order.[31] This can be seen, for example,

---

24 Otto, above note 19, p. 107.
  This is a phenomenon Nesiah has also discussed, noting the turn to what she terms 'International Conflict Feminism,' i.e. the focus of many feminist initiatives on women as victims of conflict, which she problematises for presenting only a partial gender perspective. See: Vasuki Nesiah, 'Gender and Forms of Conflict: The Moral Hazards of Dating the Security Council,' in Fionnuala Ní Aoláin et al. (eds.), *The Oxford Handbook of Gender and Conflict*, (Oxford University Press, 2018): 289–302.
25 Kouvo and Pearson, above note 3.
26 Karen Engle, 'Feminist Governance and International Law: From Liberal to Carceral Feminism,' in Janet Halley et al. (eds.), *Governance Feminism: Notes from the Field*, (Minnesota University Press, 2019): 3–20.
27 Janet Halley, 'Introducing Governance Feminism,' in Janet Halley et al. (eds.), *Governance Feminism: An Introduction* (Minnesota University Press, 2018): ix–xxxviii, p. xi.
28 Engle, above note 26.
29 Nancy Fraser, 'Feminism, Capitalism, and the Cunning of History,' *New Left Review* (2009) 56: 97–117, p. 114.
30 Susan Marks, 'Human Rights and Root Causes,' *Modern Law Review* (2011) 74: 57–78, p. 71. See also: Susan Marks, 'False Contingency,' *Current Legal Problems* (2009) 62: 1–21.
31 Marks, 'Human Rights and Root Causes,' Ibid., p. 71.

when looking at how human rights define struggles for liberation as an individual issue. The focus on individual victims and their rights silences the need for collective struggles against, for example, racism, patriarchy or capitalism.[32] In short, scant attention is given to the larger framework within which those conditions that helped foster the injustice in question are systematically reproduced. This works, as Robert Knox adds, to ensure that 'the "practical" focus on human rights is profoundly *depoliticizing*', silencing broader, structural critiques of the law by containing such critique within a fundamentally liberal discourse.[33] Overall, these authors note similar concerns to those that arise in the feminist resistance and compliance thesis, analysing the difficulty all critical international lawyers face when deciding whether to change the system from within or seek to challenge the system from the outside – with the risk of having a limited impact accordingly.

I do not mean, however, to suggest that those working with or within institutions are inherently complying while others are resisting, nor to create an unhelpful binary between civil society actors and critical academics (especially as so many bridge the two). After all, the feminist values of the multiple groups which have, over the past few decades, sought to utilise the WPS agenda, are 'continually produced, contested, reconsidered, and reenvisioned', as groups work to negotiate between complying with governmental methods while resisting the 'inequitable, masculinist, imperial, and military framework that is institutionally embedded'.[34] Otto, for example, while deeply critical of the WPS agenda, remains hopeful that feminists can continue to transform it from within. While the Security Council and other institutions have only 'selectively engaged' with feminist ideas thus far,[35] Otto finds recourse to hope in the contestable nature of significations,[36] identifying a series of 'footholds' in the WPS resolutions where postcolonial and materialist

---

32 Emily Jones, 'Gender and Reparations: Seeking Transformative Justice,' in Carla Ferstman and Mariana Goetz (eds.), *Reparations for Victims of Genocide, War Crimes and Crimes Against Humanity: Systems in Place and Systems in the Making*, (Brill, 2020): 86–118.

33 Robert Knox, 'Marxist Approaches to International Law,' in Anne Orford and Florian Hoffmann (eds.), *The Oxford Handbook of the Theory of International Law*, (Oxford University Press, 2016): 306–326, p. 321. This is a point Knox has also made elsewhere in relation to wider engagements with international law (not just human rights). See: Robert Knox, 'Strategy and Tactics,' *Finnish Yearbook of International Law* (2010) 21: 193–229 – emphasis in the original.

Similar themes are discussed by many others, including, for example, Bonaventura de Sousa Santos who, discussing Erik Olin Wright's work, seeks to find grounded, real utopias, moving utopian thinking beyond theory and into practice. See; Boaventura de Sousa Santos, 'The Alternative to Utopia is Myopia,' *Politics & Society* (2020) 48(4): 567–584.

In a related yet different vein, the edited collection *Contingency in International Law* seeks to re-imagine international law, providing insight into the possibility of alternative legal pasts and thereby of transformative futures. See; Ingo Venzke and Kevin Jon Heller (eds.), *Contingency in International Law: On the Possibility of Different Legal Histories*, (Oxford University Press, 2021).

34 Otto, 'Contesting …', above note 6, p. 201.

35 Ibid., p. 201.

36 Here, Otto draws on Judith Butler's work on re-signification. See; Judith Butler, 'Contingent Foundations: Feminism and the Question of "Post-Modernism"' in Judith Butler and Joan W. Scott (eds.), *Feminists Theorize the Political*, (Routledge, 1992): 3–21.

feminist ideas could be more radically inserted.[37] While it is useful to contest the forms of feminism that Halley and others have termed 'governance feminism',[38] resistance and compliance are not binary modes of engagement. While 'feminist activism outside legal and governmental institutions is crucial, feminists must also work inside of those institutions to transform them'.[39] Both approaches are needed and do not necessarily sit in antithesis with one another. Different stories to the binary narratives told between victory and danger, activism and scholarship, are required.[40]

There is a need for multiple strategies. Working within the system of international law and seeking to transform it from within can be a useful strategy, yet there are risks presented by co-optation. At the same time, there is clearly a need for feminist imaginaries beyond international law. Moving to scholarship outside international law can provide insight here, noting the need to balance these tensions and 'stay with the trouble' (to return to Haraway's words).[41] For example, the rejection of the separation between theoretical and practical knowledge was central to the work of French post-structuralist theorist Michel Foucault,[42] his work having strongly influenced critical posthumanism and explaining, in part, why critical posthuman theory is so keen to critique *and* engage in the world.[43] As Marieke de Goede notes, this position challenges understandings in international relations that tend to position critical engagements and practical knowledge as separate.[44] Focusing specifically on the tension between Science and Technology Studies (STS) and its engagement with the critical study of security politics, a tension that is, of course, highly relevant to this chapter, de Goede highlights that '[c]ritique cannot lay claim to a position *outside* of the practices it aims to challenge'.[45] De Goede thereby calls for more nuanced understandings of practice and critique that work across contradictory positions.[46] This is, after all, an essential part of living in the world as a critical thinker.[47] There are very few who

37 Otto, Ibid. Gina Heathcote, drawing on Otto's concept of 'footholds', undertakes a similar turn through focusing on resolution 2242 and proposing an 'alternative future' for the resolution through the application of intersectional and postcolonial feminisms. See: Heathcote, above note 7, p. 390–394.

38 Janet Halley et al., *Governance Feminism: An Introduction*, (Minnesota University Press, 2018).

39 Otto, 'Contesting ...', above note 6, p. 221–222.

40 Dianne Otto, 'Beyond Stories of Victory and Danger: Resisting Feminism's Amenability to Serving Security Council Politics,' in Gina Heathcote and Dianne Otto (eds.), *Rethinking Peacekeeping, Gender Equality and Collective Security*, (Palgrave Macmillan, 2014): 157–172.

41 Haraway, above note 2.

42 See: Michel Foucault, trans. Thomas Keenan, 'Is It Really Important to Think?' in Michel Foucault, *The Will to Knowledge: The History of Sexuality Volume 1*, (Penguin, 1976), p. 96.

43 See, for example: Rosi Braidotti, *Posthuman Knowledge*, (Polity Press, 2019).

44 Marieke de Goede, 'Engagements All the Way Down,' *Critical Studies on Security* (2020) 8(2): 101–115, p. 105.

45 Ibid., p. 106 – author's own emphasis.

46 Ibid.

47 See: Louise Amoore and Paul Langley, 'Ambiguities of Global Civil Society,' *Review of International Studies* (2004) 30(1): 89–110.

are able to live outside the powerful exploitative frames that structure the global order. While it is important to search for alternative epistemologies, alternative ways of living, of being free beyond these constraints,[48] as researchers, most of us are complicit in the structures we critique. To draw on Louise Amoore's words, 'there is no great refusal'.[49] Our lives as critical thinkers are constantly caught between resistance and compliance and, as such, we must search for 'a plurality of resistances'.[50]

In the following paragraphs, drawing on my analysis of the debates on LAWS in the previous chapter, I offer proposals on how to engage with debates on military technologies from a posthuman feminist perspective. Given the tensions feminists face between resistance and compliance, two sets of proposals are outlined. The first set focuses on compliance methods, i.e. proposals inspired by posthuman feminism that use existing international legal frameworks or ideas already circulating in international law. The second set of proposals is written in resistance mode, looking beyond international law towards alternative posthuman feminist imaginaries of human-technological relationships, drawing on theories such as xenofeminism, data feminism and Indigenous knowledge as applied to AI. While two sets of proposals are outlined, this is not to suggest that resistance and compliance are a binary. As noted above, a plurality of resistances 'spread over time and space at varying densities'[51] are required. This chapter is written in that spirit, seeking to provide multiple, sometimes contradictory proposals as a means of resistance. I conclude with some reflections on how this chapter speaks back to the resistance and compliance debate.

A Posthuman Feminist Approach to Regulating Military Technologies: Seeking to Transform International Law from Within

In the previous chapter, drawing on my analysis of existing and emerging military technologies and of the legal and ethical debates that surround LAWS, I came to several conclusions. One conclusion was the need to centre the relationship between the human and the machine when assessing how and whether machines should be involved in life/death decision-making. Second, I argued that, while autonomous systems are the central focus of the LAWS debate, the distinctions between autonomy and automation are unclear. I therefore argued that autonomy and automation work in continuum with one another. Finally, I questioned the focus on meaningful human control in relation to LAWS, noting that the bar for meaningful human

---

48 For an excellent study of epistemologies of freedom beyond liberal legalism, including a focus on queer theory and epistemologies of the global south, see: Ratna Kapur, *Gender, Alterity and Human Rights: Freedom in a Fishbowl*, (Edward Elgar, 2018).

49 See: Louise Amoore, 'There Is No Great Refusal,' in Marieke Goede (ed.), *International Political Economy and Poststructural Politics*, (Palgrave Macmillan, 2006): 255–274.

50 Michel Foucault, *The Will to Knowledge: The History of Sexuality Volume 1*, (Penguin, 1976), p. 96.

51 Ibid., p. 96.

control has already been set so low as applied to systems already in use that, in the end, there is a risk that meaningful human control may become meaningless.[52]

In this section, I bring these conclusions into conversation with existing practice and literature on how to regulate LAWS, focusing on several issues including: the lack of democratic accountability in the review of weapons process, the inability of IHL to adequately regulate LAWS, the inadequacy of arms control frameworks in addressing the nuances in regulating new and emerging military technologies and the problems posed by trying to regulate the future – that is, to regulate technologies that do not yet exist. I conclude by seeking alternative ways to regulate these technologies, ways that may allow more complex discussions of the ethical issues that arise to be had alongside debates on autonomy and automation and human and machinic connections.

As I outlined in the previous chapter, a series of diplomatic meetings on the regulation of LAWS have been held since 2014 under the auspice of the CCW, with the GGE, who have been mandated to formalise discussions and draft regulations, being set up in 2016.[53] There is no precise definition of LAWS as of yet, but ongoing debates currently centre the concept of meaningful human control. While, in 2019, the GGE produced 11 (non-binding) Guiding Principles,[54] progress to create binding law is slow.[55]

Various proposals have been put forward on how to regulate LAWS. For example, some argue that IHL is already adequate to regulate LAWS. This is a position that some members of the GGE have also taken,[56] and a position I critiqued in the previous chapter. The GGE continues to focus strongly on upholding IHL when it comes to regulating LAWS, this being a key element of the Guiding Principles produced in 2019.[57] Another related view that is taken by some parties to the CCW is that LAWS may be regulated under the review of weapons.[58]

---

52 Ingvild Bode and Tom Watts, 'Meaning-*less* Human Control: Lessons from Air Defence Systems on meaningful human Control for the Debate on AWS,' Centre for War Studies 2021, https://drone-wars.net/wp-content/uploads/2021/02/DW-Control-WEB.pdf (last accessed 11 July 2022), p. 3.

53 Report of the 2016 Informal Meeting of Experts on Lethal Autonomous Weapons Systems (LAWS) 2016 Session, CCW/CONF.V/2, Annex 14.

54 Meeting of the High Contracting Parties to the Convention on Prohibitions or Restrictions on the Use of Certain Conventions Weapons Which May Be Deemed to be Excessively Injurious or to Have Indiscriminate Effects, 13–15 November 2019, CCW MSP/2019/9, Annex III.

55 For a discussion of the effectiveness of multilateral forums in regulating LAWS, see: Amandeep S. Gill, 'The Changing Role of Multilateral Forums in Regulating Armed Conflict in the Digital Age,' *International Review of the Red Cross* (2020), 103(913): 261–285.

56 Human-Machine Interaction in the Development, Deployment and Use of Emerging Technologies in the Area of Lethal Autonomous Weapons Systems, Submitted by the United States, CCW/GGE.2/2018/P.4, p. 6–7.

57 Report on 2019 Meeting of the High Contracting Parties to the Convention on Prohibitions or Restrictions on the Use of Certain Conventional Weapons Which May Be Deemed to Be Excessively Injurious or to Have Indiscriminate Effects 2019, CCW/MSP/2019/9, Annex III.

58 Meeting of the High Contracting Parties to the Convention on Prohibitions or Restrictions on the Use of Certain Conventional Weapons Which May Be Deemed to Be Excessively Injurious or to Have Indiscriminate Effects, CCW/MSP/2015/WP.2.

The legal requirement to review weapons has its origins in Article 36 of the First Additional Protocol to the Geneva Conventions.[59] This provision obliges all states to apply a robust review of weapons before a new weapon is deployed. On the face of it, it seems like the review of weapons could be a good place to embed a more nuanced analysis of the regulation of LAWS and other means and methods of warfare. However, there are various issues with relying solely on the review of weapons. First, these reviews are limited to systems that are defined as weapons systems under IHL. This means that HETs are not included in the review of weapons because HETs involve enhancing the human as opposed to being a distinct weapon system. As HETs become more advanced, the distinction between an enhanced soldier and a weapons system may become less clear. However, HETs do not come under the review of weapons, thereby limiting the remit of any review.[60] In addition, while some have argued that the review of weapons is customary international law,[61] others argue differently, pointing out another significant flaw in relying on the review of weapons to regulate military technologies; that Article 36 is known to be implemented by only a handful of states.[62] Furthermore, the review of weapons is conducted at a domestic level. These reviews are conducted privately, without public scrutiny, with national security interests often being invoked as a justification for secrecy. As Palo Kalmanovitz argues, this is problematic, as '[s]ecrecy under the guise of national security undermines the clearest incentive for effective regulation, namely naming and shaming before public opinion'.[63] Given the various ethical concerns that surround LAWS, transparency will be necessary when regulating them.[64] Weapons reviews that occur behind closed doors do not meet these requirements. Finally, the review is limited in scope, requiring states to conduct a

---

59 Protocol Additional to the Geneva Conventions of 12 August 1949, and Relating to the Protection of Victims of International Armed Conflicts, 8 June 1977, 1125 U.N.T.S. 3, 8 June 1977, Article 36.

60 See: Rain Liivoja and Luke Chircop, 'Are Enhanced Warfighters Weapons, Means, or Methods of Warfare?' *International Law Studies* (2018) 94: 161–185; Heather A. Harrison Dinniss and Jann K. Kleffner, 'Soldier 2.0: Military Human Enhancement and International Law,' *International Law Studies* (2016) 92: 432–482, p. 436–439; Noam Lubell and Katya Al-Khateeb, 'Cyborg Soldiers: Military Use of Brain-Computer Interfaces and the Law of Armed Conflict,' in Laura Dickenson and Eiki Berg (eds.), *Big Data and Armed Conflict*, (Oxford University Press, forthcoming 2023).

61 See: Michael N. Schmitt and Jeffrey S. Thurnher, '"Out of the Loop": Autonomous Weapon Systems and the Law of Armed Conflict,' *Harvard National Security Journal* (2013) 4: 231–281, p. 271; Kobi Leins, *New War Technologies and International Law: The Legal Limits to Weaponising Nanomaterials*, (Cambridge University Press, 2022), p. 19–20.

   Others have argued that Article 36 is 'arguably' customary international law. See: Daragh Murray, *Practitioners' Guide to Human Rights Law in Armed Conflict*, (Oxford University Press, 2017), p. 172.

62 See: Natalia Jevglevskaja, 'Weapons Review Obligation under Customary International Law,' *International Law Studies* (2018) 24: 186–221.

63 Palo Kalmanovitz, 'Judgement, Liability and the Risks of Riskless Warfare,' in Nehal Bhuta et al. (eds.), *Autonomous Weapons Systems: Law, Ethics, Policy*, (Cambridge University Press, 2016): 145–163, p. 146.

64 Sarah Knuckey, 'Autonomous Weapons Systems and Transparency: Towards an International Dialogue,' in Nehal Bhuta et al. (eds.), *Autonomous Weapons Systems: Law, Ethics, Policy* (Cambridge University Press, 2016): 164–184; Kalmanovitz, Ibid.

review of a system's compatibility with existing IHL. This is distinct from asking whether new and additional concerns for IHL may be raised by a said weapon.[65] While IHL does set some clear standards, the ultimate concern that structures the LAWS debate is whether we want machines to make life/death decisions and, if so, how much decision-making are we willing to accept? This is a deeply ethical question, and one which, as I argued in the previous chapter, cannot be addressed by applying IHL alone. Rather, in line with the Martens Clause and its public con-science requirement,[66] it is evident that discussions about reviewing weapons must be held publicly. It becomes clear that weapons reviews that occur behind closed doors cannot be the central focus for those seeking to devise ways to regulate LAWS and other military technologies.

The second means proposed to regulate LAWS is arms control and the possibility of banning or regulating systems either through the CCW or through a new treaty. However, arms control processes tend to be set up in particular ways. One method of arms control limits the numbers of a said weapon that states are allowed to own, with the Anti-Ballistic Missile Treaty or the Treaty on Conventional Armed Forces in Europe being examples of this.[67] The second method is the use of a ban. This can include a complete ban, as happened with blinding lasers,[68] or a definitional ban – as proposed by the use of meaningful human control to regulate LAWS. The Treaty on the Non-Proliferation of Nuclear Weapons provides an additional model. This Treaty bans nuclear weapons for the majority of states yet permits them for five 'nuclear-weapon states',[69] this framework being put in place due to the particular political circumstances that surrounded that Treaty. Overall, systems in arms con-trol treaties have either been banned or numerically limited. If a system is neither banned nor limited, it is allowed, subject to its compatibility with IHL.

The above-mentioned arms control frameworks are inadequate to regulate LAWS. This is because, as I outlined in the previous chapter, the nuances between autonomy and automation and the relationship between the human and the machine are complex. These nuances reflect, in part, why the CCW debates on the regu-lation of LAWS have been ongoing for almost a decade. LAWS present a different set of issues to those posed by the systems regulated in the above-mentioned arms control treaties. This is because their very definition is at the heart of the discussion of a ban. While many treaties require interpretations of their terms, for a ban of

---

65 See: Nehal Bhuta et al., 'Present Futures: Concluding Reflections and Open Questions on Autonomous Weapons Systems,' Nehal Bhuta et al. (eds.), *Autonomous Weapons Systems: Law, Ethics, Policy* (Cambridge University Press, 2016): 347–383, p. 380.

66 The Martens Clause is found in several treaties relating to international humanitarian law but was incorporated into the body of the main 1949 Geneva Conventions as well as in the First Additional Protocol. See: Protocol Additional …, above note 59.

67 Treaty on the Limitation of Anti-Ballistic Missile Systems, 26 May 1927; Treaty on Conventional Armed Forces in Europe, 19 November 1990.

68 Protocol on Blinding Laser Weapons (Protocol IV to the 1980 Convention on Certain Conventional Weapons) 13 October 1995.

69 Treaty on the Non-Proliferation of Nuclear Weapons, 5 March 1970. These nuclear-weapon states being: the US, Russia, the UK, China and France.

LAWS to be meaningful, these terms will have to be defined in advance to avoid a race to the bottom. This is especially the case given how states are already beginning to define meaningful human control. For example, Bode and Watts have argued that the way 'automated and autonomous features have already been integrated into the critical functions of air defence systems' means that 'in some situations, human control has become effectively meaningless',[70] with operators sometimes being given less than six seconds to come to a decision.[71] In short, Bode and Watts warn that the standard for meaningful human control has already been set so low that it would render any use of this term in regulating LAWS meaningless, unless stringently negotiated.

Furthermore, I contended in the previous chapter that seeking to define autonomy and thereby to distinguish it from automation is futile, arguing, through an examination of weapons systems in current use, that autonomy and automation work in continuum with one another. Defining autonomy as distinct from automation risks setting the standard so high for machine decision-making that, in the end, almost nothing may be covered under a ban. However, any ban of LAWS will have to ban autonomous systems specifically, either by defining autonomy or by defining meaningful human control. This is because states are not going to be willing to sign a treaty that challenges the distinctions between autonomy and automation because more nuanced understanding of these terms may in fact end up banning systems they already use and want to continue using. In the meantime, machines are already contributing to the making of life/death decisions, this being the central ethical question of concern that is not being adequately addressed in any of the above-mentioned proposals to regulate LAWS.

Another key issue raised by ongoing attempts to regulate LAWS is temporality. As Sara Kendall notes, 'human law lacks the optics to apprehend what lies beyond its reach'.[72] LAWS regulations will need to apply to technologies that do not yet exist. However, the effectiveness of any regulation as applied to future technologies cannot be measured without knowing what those technologies will be.[73] HETs are a good example here. While HETs would not be covered under a ban on LAWS, as they develop, the point at which meaningful human control is retained will come under question.

However, recognising the temporal limitations to the regulation of LAWS does not mean that the necessary and complex ethical questions that surround their regulation should not be asked. The US has used the temporal argument to justify a cautious approach to LAWS regulation, arguing that we should not 'make hasty judgments about the value or likely effects of emerging or future technologies'.[74]

---

70 Bode and Watts, above note 52, p. 3.

71 Ibid., p. 39.

72 Sara Kendall, 'Law's End: On Algorithmic Warfare and Humanitarian Violence,' in Max Liljefors et al. (eds.), *War and the Algorithm*, (Rowman & Littlefield, 2019): 105–125, p. 105.

73 See: Bhuta et al., above note 65, p. 363; Gill, above note 55, p. 266.

74 US Opening Statement at the Group of Government Experts (GGE) on Lethal Autonomous Weapons Systems, 9 April 2018.

In short, a cautionary approach to regulating the future could also be used to justify inaction. The debate on LAWS is deeply politicised. Critiques of attempts to regulate LAWS risk being co-opted by more conservative voices, this harking back to the discussion of the take-up of certain feminist ideas and not others in the outline of feminist engagements with the WPS agenda above.

As noted in the Introduction to this volume, this book seeks to exemplify how gender theory, and specifically posthuman feminism, can be used to re-think the legal regulation of areas of the law that are not usually associated with being areas of feminist engagement. One such proposal that clearly comes from the posthuman feminist analysis outlined in the previous chapter is the need to see autonomy-agency and the human–machine as relational continuums. This is something Lucy Suchman and Jutta Weber have similarly highlighted, drawing on the work of posthuman feminist scholars such as Karen Barad to argue for an understanding of agency as relational to be made central to the debate on LAWS. Therefore, they argue,

> [a]pplied to weapons systems, this means that the question is less about automation versus autonomy than it is about what new forms of agency are enabled by contemporary configurations of war fighting and with what political, ethical, moral and legal consequences.[75]

In a similar vein, Hin-Yan Liu argues for the need to see LAWS as 'networks',[76] while Williams equally finds value in turning to relational epistemologies.[77]

The current frameworks in place that could be applied to regulate LAWS and other military technologies cannot encompass these relational understandings of the human and the machine, autonomy and automation. Nor can they necessarily ensure that they will be able to adequately regulate all future military technologies. This is because a ban will require precise definitions to operate effectively. A defined ban, however, risks creating categories of weapons that are allowed and those that are not. By defining what is/is not allowed, the wider ethical question of how much we want to delegate life/death decisions to machines will be pushed aside, the focus shifting instead to discussions of the legal and technical definitions of whatever standards are set. Precise definitions create binary modes of thought, restricting the

---

75 Lucy Suchman and Jutta Weber, 'Human-Machine Autonomies,' in Nehal Bhuta et al. (eds.), *Autonomous Weapons Systems: Law, Ethics, Policy* (Cambridge University Press, 2016): 75–102, p. 102.

76 Hin-Yan Liu, 'From the Autonomy Framework towards Networks and Systems Approaches for 'Autonomous' Weapons Systems,' *Journal of International Humanitarian Legal Studies* (2019) 10(1): 89–110.

  Bourne has also argued this more broadly in relation to arms control. See: Mike Bourne, 'Cyborgs, Control and Transformation: Posthumanist Arms Control and Disarmament,' in Erika Cudworth et al. (eds.), *Posthuman Dialogues in International Relations*, (Routledge, 2016): 216–234.

77 John Williams, 'Locating LAWS: Lethal Autonomous Weapons, Epistemic Space, and "Meaningful Human Control",' *Journal of Global Security Studies* (2021) 6(4): 1–18.

  For a wider discussion on whether robots should have rights and relationality, see: Josh Gellers, *Rights for Robots: Artificial Intelligence, Animal and Environmental Law*, (Routledge, 2020).

possibility of relational thinking. This is not, of course, only a problem that is raised in this context – as we shall see in the next chapter, while there have been many calls for relational ontologies to be embedded into international environmental law, putting these theories into practice remains a challenge. Overall, this is a problem with international law more widely and its Eurocentric understanding of what the law is. International law requires definitions and clearly defined subjects to function in a way that, as we shall see in the coming chapters, other understandings of the law do not. While there is a need for alternative understandings of what the law is and can be, in this chapter, I wish, in 'compliance' mode, to now turn to analysing existing provisions in international law that can be used to shift the paradigm. Here, I seek incremental change with the aim of fostering a regulatory system for weapons, using existing models in international law, that can at least better, if not fully, account for relational understandings of the human and the machine, autonomy and automation.

One possible way that some of the necessary nuances outlined in this and the previous chapter could be brought into practice is through an ethical balancing system. While arms control processes generally require definitions of a weapon to be banned (or, in the case of LAWS, will require a definition of meaningful human control), there are mechanisms in place in other areas of international law that deal with weapons regulation in a slightly less binary way. The Biological Weapons Convention (BWC) provides one possible starting point. The BWC effectively bans the use of biological weapons, including their stockpiling and transfer.[78] Central to the Convention is collaboration between states.[79] Noting that some biological discoveries could have a dual use, i.e. could be used commercially but also as a weapon, the BWC seeks to balance the need to not hamper scientific and economic development alongside the need to ban certain biological weapons.[80] The BWC is interesting in terms of how it has been applied in some states. While there is no international verification protocol (attempts at creating one have been ongoing since 1994[81] but states have failed to agree on such a process,[82] this being a key downfall in terms of oversight and enforceability), national implementation measures are required.[83] These measures vary in form, yet some of them provide a starting point to think through what a more nuanced system of ethical balancing could look like. In particular, control lists provide an interesting framework when thinking about the regulation of new and emerging military technologies.

---

78 Convention on the Prohibition of the Development, Production and Stockpiling of Bacteriological (Biological) and Toxin Weapons and on Their Destruction, 10 April 1972.
79 Ibid. See, for example, Article 5 and Article 10(1).
80 Ibid., Article 10(2).
81 Special Conference of the States Parties to the Convention on the Prohibition of the Development, Production and Stockpiling of Bacteriological (Biological) and Toxin Weapons and on Their Destruction, Final Report, 1994, BWC/SPCONF/1.
82 This was again considered in 2019 but, in the end, it was concluded that it was not practical. See: Chairperson of the 2019 Meeting of Experts on Institutional Strengthening of the Convention, 4 October 2019, Summary Report, BWC/MSP/2019/MX.5/2.
83 Security Council Resolution 1540, 28 April 2004, S/RES/1540, Article 4, para. 2.

Control lists are regularly reviewed lists of dangerous biological agents and toxins. These lists are drafted with dual use in mind, i.e. the fact that some agents could be used for medical purposes *and* as weapons. Control lists are interesting for the present purpose because they require a balance to be struck between competing interests, relying on discussions of the various contextual concerns as opposed to decisions needing to be made on whether or not something fits within a defined ban.[84] Unfortunately, the BWC is largely seen as establishing a weak compliance framework due to a lack of institutional support and the absence of a formal verification regime to monitor compliance. Furthermore, 'many States have yet to adopt necessary measures to give effect to certain obligations'.[85] However, the idea of control lists provides an interesting model for the present discussion on how to regulate military technologies including and beyond LAWS. This is because control lists allow for systems to be considered in context. This means that the issues relevant to each system and the central ethical questions around human-machine life/death decision-making can be considered in context each time, as applied to each system and its own unique attributes. Furthermore, a model whereby each system is discussed and the ethics of deploying it are weighed up each time a new system is created seems much more sensible when seeking to regulate technologies that do not yet exist — this model allows for flexibility as technologies develop over time.

The BWC is not the only blueprint here. Gill, for example, calls for a 'regular technology discussion (not a review mechanism) at the CCW so that policy measures can be considered for updating in light of future technology breakthroughs'.[86] While this may be a good starting point, to adequately regulate each system and discuss the legal and ethical concerns that arise accordingly, a more robust framework that analyses each technology in context is needed. These reviews must go beyond the scope of existing weapons reviews, meaning that discussions must include and go beyond IHL compliance, allowing for ethical deliberations to occur in line with the obligations under the Martens Clause. These discussions must also be public, ensuring that decisions are not made by powerful states behind closed doors and that 'public conscience' is meaningfully considered. Unfortunately, such a proposal is unlikely to come to fruition any time soon, given the lack of consensus already present at the CCW alongside the likelihood that states would quash any proposal to make reviews public in the name of national security.[87]

---

84 See: National Implementation Measures Programme, Biological Weapons Convention, Report on National Implementing Legislation, VERTIC, 2016), p. 12–13.

85 Ibid., p. 16. For a wider discussion of verification and implementation of the BWC, see: Sonia Drobysz, 'Verification and Implementation of the Biological and Toxin Weapons Convention,' *The Nonproliferation Review* (2020) 27:4–6: 487–497.

86 Gill, above note 55, p. 261.

87 For a wider discussion of the various different ways LAWS could be regulated, weighing up their feasibility, see: Rebecca Crootof, 'Regulating New Weapons Technology,' in Eric Talbot Jensen and Ronald T.P. Alcala (eds.), *The Impact of Emerging Technologies on the Law of Armed Conflict, Lieber Studies Volume 2*, (Oxford University Press, 2019): 3–25.

A Posthuman Feminist Approach to Regulating Military Technologies Beyond the Law: Xenofeminism, Data Feminism and Indigenous AI

While the previous section drew on my posthuman feminist analysis of LAWS to think about regulating military technologies using existing frameworks available in international law, in this section, noting the exclusionary humanism upheld by international law, I will turn to feminist and other critical theories of technology to reimagine human-technological relations. I thereby seek to understand whether and how these theories can apply to the regulation of military technologies. While, on the one hand, these ideas may seem unlikely to be applied in practice to debates on arms regulation, as noted at the start of this chapter, there is a need to think through modes of resistance that use existing structures of power, seeking to change the system from within, while retaining a focus on modes of resistance beyond those problematic power structures. This reflection is substantiated by the fact that, while engaging with the debate on the regulation of LAWS and other military technologies may prove fruitful, there is also a strong likelihood that attempts to regulate LAWS will fail. John Williams, for example, believes that 'efforts to ban the development and deployment of LAWS will fail',[88] and statements made by the former Indian Ambassador to the UN Conference on Disarmament and former Chair of the GGE on LAWS at the CCW in 2019 suggest a similar scepticism:

> The economic, political and security drivers for mainstreaming this suite of technologies into security functions are simply too powerful to be rolled back. There will be plenty of persuasive national security applications … [which will be used] to provide counterarguments against concerns about runaway robots or accidental wars caused by machine error.[89]

Indeed, the powerful structures in which the debates on the regulation of military technologies are embedded will hamper any meaningful legal change. This realist scepticism provides another reason why imaginaries beyond the law are necessary.

My analysis of LAWS thus far, while discussing questions of exclusionary humanism at certain key moments, has primarily focused on anthropocentric humanism, seeking to challenge the idea that humans are separate from and in control of their machines. In this section, I turn to ideas of technology that seek to move beyond exclusionary humanism, going back to the problems raised in the previous chapter around who is creating, regulating and deploying military technologies and who is not. After all, the people most likely to be subject to developments in military

---

88 John Williams, 'Effective, Deployable, Accountable: Pick Two': Regulating Lethal Autonomous Weapons Systems, E-International Relations, 2021, https://www.e-ir.info/2021/08/12/effective-deployable-accountable-pick-two-regulating-lethal-autonomous-weapons-system (last accessed 11 July 2022).

89 Amandeep Singh Gill, 'Artificial Intelligence and International Security: The Long View,' *Ethics & International Affairs* (2019) 33(2): 169–179, p. 175.

technologies are based in the global south, yet their voices are little heard in the debate on LAWS.[90] It is also key to remember that the majority of states that have called for a ban on LAWS thus far are from the global south. Furthermore, and as also discussed in the previous chapter, military technologies are already and will continue to be deployed in ways that are racialised, gendered and ableist.[91]

Critical scholars have long highlighted the exclusionary humanism that permeates technology. Scholars working on the intersection of black studies and technology have examined the fact that many people have never had access to the category of the "human", arguing that there are those that are more or less human than others, this being mediated through race, gender and coloniality.[92] As Zakiyyah Iman Jackson argues, 'the figure of 'man' … is a technology of slavery and colonialism that imposes its authority over "the universal" through a racialized deployment of force'.[93] However, many of these scholars, starting from the perspective that technologies are shaped by human culture, find hope in the possibility of being able to re-design human-technological relationships[94] through modes of generative justice[95] or through viral black feminist subversions.[96] In a similar vein, crip technoscience scholars, noting the assimilationist way that technology is often described as a means to either exclude disabled people or to 'fix' them,[97] seek 'practices of anti-assimilationist disability making and knowing', fostering 'material and social practices of disability world-building'.[98] This must include, as Aimi Hamraie and Kelly Fritsch argue: centring disabled people as knowers and makers; challenging the idea that technology allows 'access' and instead promoting a politics of anti-assimilation, one which de-centres able-bodiedness as the ideal; fostering relations between bodies, environments and tools; and centring disability justice.[99] As inspired by these visions

---

90 Williams, above note 77.

91 Ray Acheson, 'Autonomous Weapons and Patriarchy,' Campaign to Stop Killer Robots and Women's International League for Peace and Freedom 2020, https://reachingcriticalwill.org/images/documents/Publications/aws-and-patriarchy.pdf (last accessed 11 July 2022).

92 See: Katherine McKittrick (ed.), *Sylvia Wynter: On Being Human as Praxis*, (Duke University Press, 2014); Christina Sharpe, *In the Wake: On Blackness as Being*, (Duke University Press, 2016).

93 Zakiyyah Iman Jackson, 'Animal: New Directions in the Theorization of Race and Posthumanism,' *Feminist Studies* (2013) 29(3): 669–685, p. 640.

94 See: Ruha Benjamin, 'Discriminatory Design, Liberating Imagination,' in Ruha Benjamin (ed.), *Captivating Technology: Race, Carceral Technoscience, and Liberatory Imagination in Everyday Life*, (Duke University Press, 2019): 1–22.

95 See: Ron Eglash, 'Anti-Racist Technoscience: A Generative Tradition,' in Ruha Benjamin (ed.), *Captivating Technology: Race, Carceral Technoscience, and Liberatory Imagination in Everyday Life*, (Duke University Press, 2019): 227–251.

96 Ashleigh Greene Wade, '"New Genres of Being Human": Worldmaking through Viral Blackness,' *Journal of Black Studies and Research* (2017) 47(3): 33–44.
See also: Sareeta Amrute and Luis Felipe R. Murillo, 'Introduction: Computing in/from the South,' *Catalyst* (2020) 6(2): 1–23.

97 Gina Heathcote, 'War's Perpetuity: Disabled Bodies of War and the Exoskeleton of Equality,' *Australian Feminist Law Journal* (2018) 44(1): 71–91.

98 Kelly Fritsch et al,. 'Introduction to Special Section on Crip Technoscience,' *Catalyst* (2019) 5(1): 1–10, p. 2. See also: Alison Kafer, 'Crip Kind, Manifesting,' *Catalyst* (2019) 5(1): 1–37.

99 Aimi Hamraie and Kelly Fritsch, 'Crip Technoscience Manifesto,' *Catalyst* (2019) 5(1): 1–33.

of world-making, in this section I turn to alternative conceptualisations of technology, including feminist analyses and Indigenous knowledge as applied to AI, to understand what lessons can be learnt for those seeking to engage in debates on the regulation of new and emerging military technologies.

As Rosi Braidotti summarises, '[m]ost feminist technoscience studies scholars are social-constructivists who push the nature-culture continuum to its logical conclusion, mainly the equation of biology with technology'.[100] As I noted in the previous chapter, many feminist theories of technology are positive about technology's transformative potential. For example, Haraway sees promise in technology's ability to challenge the distinction between the human and the machine, noting the potential to be found in deconstructing exclusionary humanism in this way.[101] Likewise, xenofeminism argues that technology can be used to transform multiple gendered dichotomies such as nature/culture through, for example, providing reproductive technologies that allow women to escape the labour of reproduction.[102] In the previous chapter, I noted the need to nuance these arguments, highlighting the fact that technology is deeply embedded in structures of capitalism, sexism, racism, ableism and militarism. While many feminist theories of technology, such as xenofeminism, do not fully account for the links between technology and militarism, this does not mean that they cannot accommodate such concerns.[103]

Posthuman feminism, including xenofeminism, has developed several ways of re-configuring human-technological relationships, some of which can be used to think about the regulation of military technologies. For example, posthuman feminists are well aware that it matters who makes programming choices; 'it matters which figures figure figures, which systems systematize systems'.[104] Thus, as Haraway notes, '[w]e can be responsible for machines: *they* do not dominate or threaten us. We are responsible for boundaries; we are they'.[105] Science and technology are thereby described as sites of contestation where feminist intervention is required.

Noting that 'technology isn't inherently progressive', the xenofeminists call for an intervention in these choices,[106] seeing technology as an activist tool.[107] Xenofeminism thereby proposes a feminist ethics for the technomaterial world, seeking both to promote feminist interventions in the shaping of science and

100 Rosi Braidotti, *Posthuman Feminism*, (Polity Press, 2022), p. 152.

101 Donna Haraway, 'A Cyborg Manifesto,' in David Bell and Barbara M. Kennedy (eds.), *The Cybercultures Reader*, (Routledge, 2001): 291–324.

102 Helen Hester, *Xenofeminism*, (Polity Press, 2018). See also: Sophie Lewis, *Full Surrogacy Now: Feminism Against Family*, (Verso, 2021).

103 Emily Jones, 'Feminist Technologies and Post-Capitalism: Defining and Reflecting Upon Xenofeminism,' *Feminist Review* (2019) 123: 126–134.

104 Donna Haraway, 'Anthropocene, Capitalocene, Plantationocene, Chthulucene: Making Kin,' *Environmental Humanities* (2015) 6: 159–165, p. 160.

105 Haraway, above note 101, p. 215 – emphasis in the original.

106 Laboria Cuboniks, Xenofeminism: A Politics for Alienation, www.laboriacuboniks.net (last accessed 11 July 2022), Zero 0×02.

107 Ibid.

technology and working to ensure that any radical technological change is analysed and shaped by and through a feminist lens.

Taking an affirmative posthuman-xenofeminist perspective, one that pays attention to the interconnections between the human and the machine, the xenofeminist method of appropriating technology for feminist aims can be used to consider other ways of engaging with the regulation of military technologies. Given the lack of focus in xenofeminism on militarism, however, this xenofeminist approach must be read through feminist international legal work on anti-militarism.[108] Combining xenofeminist methods of seeking to develop and use technology for feminist aims, working to appropriate technology while creating a future from the present, manipulating, hacking and coding the system, alongside a commitment to anti-militarism, different proposals for tackling the ethical issues raised by new and emerging military technologies emerge.

One proposal that can be thought through in this register is engagements with technological design. Feminist theories show that technology is dependent on a set of programming choices which will shape machine intelligence as technology advances. What choices are made now will structure the future of machine intelligence, especially as we work towards creating ever more advanced AI systems. If the aim is to ensure that, for example, AI, when it does become intelligent, includes a complex, intersectional feminist ethics, in the hope that AI systems may actually refuse to participate in war at all, it is necessary to have posthuman feminist perspectives and xenofeminist infiltrations now to ensure that those ethics are programmed into these systems at an early stage of their development.

The proposal raises a series of questions around resistance and compliance. On the one hand, there is a need to resist the making of these technologies. The refusal of Google staff to work on developing AI for the US military in 2018 represents one possible way of resisting militaristic tendencies in technological development, with Google subsequently ending its contract with Project Maven in 2019[109] and releasing a series of ethical guiding principles for AI.[110] However, resistance methods are not always effective and while Google staff did have an impact, Google by no means ended all its work with the US military in 2019.[111]

Seeking to shape technological development thereby offers an alternative mode of engagement to refusal. Recent feminist work that seeks to understand how data science can be shaped by feminism may prove useful here. For example, in their book, *Data Feminism*, Catherine D'Ignazio and Lauren F. Klein outline a set of

---

108 Jones, above note 103.

109 Daisuke Wakabayashi and Scott Shane, 'Google will not Renew Pentagon Contract that Upset Employees, *The New York Times*, 1 June 2018, https://www.nytimes.com/2018/06/01/technology/google-pentagon-project-maven.html (last accessed 11 July 2022).

110 Google, Artificial Intelligence at Google: Our Principles, https://ai.google/principles (last accessed 11 July 2022).

111 Wired, 3 Years After the Maven Uproar, Google Cozies to the Pentagon, 18 November 2021, https://www.wired.com/story/3-years-maven-uproar-google-warms-pentagon/?msclkid=d-b6cdbf3afa111ecba983f2fce04d254 (last accessed 11 July 2022).

principles that can be used to embed intersectional feminism into data science and ethics. These principles are:

1. Examine power. Data feminism begins by analyzing how power operates in the world.
2. Challenge power. Data feminism commits to challenging unequal power structures and working toward justice.
3. Elevate emotion and embodiment. Data feminism teaches us to value multiple forms of knowledge, including the knowledge that comes from people as living, feeling bodies in the world.
4. Rethink binaries and hierarchies. Data feminism requires us to challenge the gender binary, along with other systems of counting and classification that perpetuate oppression.
5. Embrace pluralism. Data feminism insists that the most complete knowledge comes from synthesizing multiple perspectives, with priority given to local, Indigenous, and experiential ways of knowing.
6. Consider context. Data feminism asserts that data are not neutral or objective. They are the products of unequal social relations, and this context is essential for conducting accurate, ethical analysis.
7. Make labor visible. The work of data science, like all work in the world, is the work of many hands. Data feminism makes this labor visible so that it can be recognized and valued.[112]

While anti-militarism is not explicitly a part of these principles, it must be made central. After all, militarism is a central structure of power, pertaining to principles 1, 2 and 6. Furthermore, an anti-militarist perspective calls for attention to be paid to those living in conflict, as per principle 3. As examined in the previous chapter, military technologies are also deeply embedded in discrimination, with gendered and racialised stereotypes being used to make targeting decisions.[113] Furthermore, a feminist approach to military technology design will require pluralism and complex and multiple perspectives, as per principle 5. As highlighted in the previous chapter there is currently a lack of nuance present in debates on LAWS which seek to falsely separate the human from the machine and autonomy from automation. While the authors of *Data Feminism* do not directly discuss military technologies, these principles may also encompass the ethical questions raised by such technologies.

While seeking to engage in tech design may be one way of tackling some of the issues raised by military technologies, a second mode of engagement can be thought through in response to xenofeminism. That second mode is for feminists to help develop military technologies directly, seeking to make this process more 'ethical'. There are, however, great risks posed by this approach which could

112 Catherine D'Ignazio and Lauren F. Klein, *Data Feminism*, (MIT Press, 2020), p. 17–18.
113 See: Acheson, above note 91.

result in the legitimisation of the use of killing machines through claiming to make them more 'ethical'. While this mode of engagement could be seen as one method among many within the resistance and compliance paradigm, and while above, in my analysis of the resistance and compliance conundrum in feminist approaches to international law, I called for multiple approaches that seek to 'stay with the trouble' of working within the system of international law while also working outside of it, this proposal challenges that analysis. Developing military technologies is a big step away from seeking to get feminist ideas onto the agenda of the Security Council (even if that too, as discussed, comes with risks and co-optation). There is a limit to how far feminists can stay with the trouble when working within militaristic structures. While I have urged for multiple, and sometimes contradictory strategies to be adopted by feminist international lawyers, at some point these contradictory positions become too conflicting, to the point that one is not only legitimising oppressive structures of power but actually helping to maintain and construct these structures. The question remains, however, of where the line should be drawn. This is not something that is self-evident. It seems that working directly to develop military technologies *is*, however, a step too far, going against the grain of a feminist politics of anti-militarism. If resistance and compliance strategies are to be read as a continuum, there are also two ends to that continuum. From a feminist perspective, working to develop machines that kill lies too far at one end of the spectrum to be able to stay with.

Reflecting on black engagements with science and technology and underscoring centuries of medical experimentation on colonised and enslaved bodies, Benjamin calls for a reclamation of refusal, with refusal becoming a speculative practice, a way of imagining otherwise, seeking to centre a justice-orientated approach to science and technology.[114] Following Benjamin's call, a politics of refusal seems to be the only option when it comes to the question of whether or not to engage in the making of military technologies. This example shows that the tension between resistance and compliance cannot always be resolved. Feminist efforts are better placed, to follow Benjamin, in imagining otherwise and re-thinking how technology can be shaped and used in ways that seek to make alternative, more just worlds.

Another possible way to seek to tackle the issues raised by military technologies maps onto principle 5 of the *Data Feminism* principles above. This principle centres 'local, Indigenous, and experiential ways of knowing'. In relation to the regulation of military technologies, this principle also maps onto some of the debates discussed in the previous section around the need to find a more nuanced way of balancing the various ethical concerns raised by these technologies and the relationships and connections between humans and machines, autonomy and automation. Above, I addressed this by calling for a system of arms control that is less binary, less based on ban/allow, and more focused on the weighing up of multiple, relational connections and continuums.

---

114 Ruha Benjamin, 'Informed Refusal: Toward a Justice-Based Bioethics,' *Science, Technology, & Human Values* (2016) 61(6): 967–990.

Thinking more deeply about world-making through technology, another body of knowledge that may be turned to here is Indigenous AI.[115] There is much to be learnt from Indigenous knowledge in the field of technology. Thus far, I have argued that there is a need to acknowledge connections between the human and the machine, autonomy and automation. These relational continuums may be better addressed by turning away from Eurocentric binary legal frameworks, looking instead towards Indigenous knowledge. This is because 'Indigenous epistemologies are much better at respectfully accommodating the non-human', working to 'treat these new non-human kin respectfully and reciprocally – and not as mere tools, or worse, slaves to their creators'.[116]

The Indigenous Protocol and Artificial Intelligence Working Group, made up of a global group of primarily Indigenous experts, noting the 'long history of technological advances being used against Indigenous people', seeks to engage with technological shifts, working as 'vigorously as possible to influence its development in directions that are advantageous to us'.[117] Noting that technology has, until now, primarily been informed by a western frame, risking the upholding of various biases and, 'at worst' fostering the creation of 'relationships with [technologies] … that are akin to that of a master and slave',[118] the Working Group seeks to design new conceptual and practical approaches to the development of AI, drawing on Indigenous knowledge to shape their proposals.[119] While a single Indigenous knowledge does not exist, the work of this group has some core focal points, including a centring of relational understandings of technology and drawing on Indigenous knowledge that de-centres the human and focuses, rather, on the connections between humans and the material world.[120] This work clearly resonates with posthuman and new materialist work that likewise centres relational onto-epistemologies of technology.[121] The work of this group is ongoing but, in 2020, a series of Guidelines for Indigenous-Centred AI Design were put forward. These principles, to paraphrase, are:

115 For a discussion of why Indigenous design principle and governance is so needed here, particularly reflecting on Australian Aboriginal knowledge, see: Angie Abdilla, 'Beyond Imperial Tools: Future-Proofing Technology through Indigenous Governance and Traditional Knowledge Systems,' in Josh Harle et al. (eds.), *Decolonizing the Digital: Technology as Cultural Practice*, (Tactical Space Lab, 2018): 67–195.

116 Jason Edward Lewis et al., 'Making Kin with the Machines,' *Journal of Design Studies* (2018), published online 16 July 2018, n.p., https://doi.org/10.21428/bfafd97b (last accessed 11 July 2022).

117 Indigenous Protocol and Artificial Intelligence Working Group, 'Position Paper: Indigenous Protocol and Artificial Intelligence,' 30 January 2020, https://spectrum.library.concordia.ca/id/eprint/986506/7/Indigenous_Protocol_and_AI_2020.pdf (last accessed 11 July 2022), p. 6.

118 Ibid. p. 6

119 See: Indigenous Protocol and Artificial Intelligence Working Group, https://www.indigenous-ai.net (last accessed 11 July 2022).

120 See: Indigenous Protocol and Artificial Intelligence Working Group, above note 117; Lewis et al., above note 116.

121 See, for example, Goda Klumbytė and Claude Draude, 'New Materialist Informatics,' in Rosi Braidotti, Emily Jones and Goda Klumbytė (eds.), *More Posthuman Glossary*, (Bloomsbury, forthcoming 2023).

1. Locality — noting that Indigenous knowledge is often 'rooted in specific territories', this guideline calls for AI systems to be designed in partnership with specific Indigenous communities, connecting the local to the global.

2. Relationality and Reciprocity — focusing on the connections between humans and non-humans and the need to see AI systems as 'part of the circle of relationships', including the specific communities they are deployed in.

3. Responsibility, Relevance and Accountability — noting that AI systems developed with Indigenous communities should be responsible and accountable to them first and foremost.

4. Develop Governance Guidelines from Indigenous Protocols — protocols and governance frameworks for 'designing, building and deploying AI systems' must be developed out of 'ontological, epistemological and customary configurations of knowledge grounded in locality, relationality and responsibility'.

5. Recognise the Cultural Nature of all Computational Technology — which includes noting that technology is cultural and therefore there is a need for Indigenous-informed computational methods.

6. Apply Ethical Design to the Extended Stack — arguing for the need to centre an ethics of 'do-no-harm' through all stages of technological design and development.

7. Respect and Support Data Sovereignty — to ensure Indigenous peoples have and retain ownership over their data and the way their knowledge is used.[122]

This framework provides another way of thinking about human relationships to technology. Indigenous knowledge has not been centred enough in technological design. A lot can be learnt, including the need to understand technology as culturally embedded, to see connections between the human and the nonhuman and to seek to understand the relational nature of technologies, both between technologies and humans, as well as the web of connections technologies are situated in once deployed. While the Working Group does not address the link between technologies and militarism explicitly, it seems that guideline 6 and the 'do-no-harm' principle, read alongside the other calls for ethical stances to be taken in the rest of the guidelines, suggests very strongly that an Indigenous-informed perspective on AI design would indeed protest against the use of AI by the military, especially given the long history of violence perpetuated against Indigenous peoples by the very same militaries (such as the US and the UK) that are now seeking to use AI in their everyday operations.

---

122 See: Indigenous Protocol and Artificial Intelligence Working Group above note 117, p. 21–22.
    While these principles are outlined on pages 21–22, there are a series of other reflections in this document on how to design AI as informed by Indigenous knowledge. For example, for another blueprint, see: Suzanne Kite in discussion with Corey Stover et al., 'How to Build Anything Ethically,' in Indigenous Protocol and Artificial Intelligence Working Group, 'Position Paper: Indigenous Protocol and Artificial Intelligence,' 30 January 2020, https://spectrum.library.concordia.ca/id/eprint/986506/7/Indigenous_Protocol_and_AI_2020.pdf (last accessed 11 July 2022): 75–84.
    For a further discussion of Indigenous knowledge as applied to AI, see also: Lewis et al., above note 116.

While much can be learnt from Indigenous knowledge as applied to AI, any attempt to centre Indigenous voices must be taken with care, acknowledging the violence of settler colonialism. Furthermore, there are elements of Indigenous knowledge that are so complex, so plainly incommensurable with western humanist knowledge systems, and that come from such a long history of thought, that we, or rather I, as a white European, cannot ever begin to fully comprehend them. It is thereby to deep listening that we must turn to begin to understand these far more relational knowledges of the law, of technology and of the world.

Conclusion

In this chapter, drawing on my work in the previous chapter which critiqued the humanist underpinnings of the debate on the regulation of LAWS, I put forward a series of posthuman feminist inspired proposals for how critical feminists can engage with debates on the regulation of military technologies. In undertaking this work, I drew on debates in feminist approaches to international law around the tension between resistance and compliance, that is, seeking to resist the problematic framework that is international law versus working to foster positive change within and using that system, concluding that there is a need to see resistance and compliance, not as binary options but as a spectrum of choices. I argued for the need for multiple, sometimes contradictory interventions.

Following this, I put forward a series of posthuman feminist inspired proposals for regulating new and emerging military technologies. The first set of proposals, written in compliance mode, examined existing provisions in international law, using them to develop a more nuanced system for regulating these technologies. I proposed that a framework of ethical balancing may help address some of the concerns I have raised about the current way weapons are regulated. This framework would need to move beyond a system that seeks to define what is banned and what is allowed, allowing for more widely informed discussions to be had around whether and how we want to delegate life/death decisions to machines, ensuring that contextualised debates can continue as technologies develop. Furthermore, I argued that these debates need to be held in public if the values of public conscience and democratic accountability are to be embedded into these regulatory processes.

The second set of proposals were written more in resistance mode. Drawing on scholarship on race and technology, gender and technology (including posthuman feminism and xenofeminism) and crip technoscience, I noted that military technologies are by no means the only set of technologies that are based upon and apply in biased and discriminatory ways. I therefore turned to posthuman and data feminisms and Indigenous knowledge as applied to technology and AI to propose alternative framings for engaging with new technologies, including military technologies. In doing so, two main proposals and their accompanying tensions were discussed.

The first proposal was that feminists and other critical thinkers should engage with making and developing technology, including machine learning and AI. Drawing on projects that seek to apply Indigenous knowledge to AI, xenofeminism and data feminism, a set of guidelines and principles were outlined in this vein. I then brought these guidelines into conversation with the issues posed by military technologies to help think through how those principles may apply to that particular area.

The second proposal was the idea that feminists should possibly seek to shape the development and making of military technologies. At the beginning of this chapter, I argued for multiple solutions that work across the resistance and compliance continuum. However, the proposal for feminists to develop military technologies challenged this stance. While there is a need to stay with the trouble, to be at ease with contradictory approaches and seek multiple strategies, I concluded that working to make or support the making of killing machines was a step too far from the perspective of a feminist politics of anti-militarism. This is especially the case when having feminists working to develop these technologies would only serve to help legitimise their use. This example therefore required me to reassess my engagement with the resistance and compliance debate and the need for multiple, contradictory solutions, concluding that, while resistance and compliance should be seen, not as binary options but as a continuum, there are still always two opposite ends to a continuum. Working to develop military technologies is too far along the compliance side for comfort. While staying with the trouble maybe sometimes be necessary, the trouble is sometimes too troublesome to be able to stay with.

4

QUEERING THE NONHUMAN

Engaging International Environmental Law

Globally, groups are declaring that we have reached a 'climate emergency'.[1] Yet despite the increasingly dire warnings about biodiversity loss, environmental degradation and climate change, international environmental law has failed to produce the necessary solutions.[2] International environmental law, as discussed in Chapter 1, has operated to conceptually transform 'nature into resources',[3] with nature being rendered an object to be exploited for economic gain.[4] In response, this chapter draws on posthuman feminism, including queer theories of the nonhuman, in conversation with critical environmental law scholarship, to explore the possibility of an international environmental law that takes seriously the interests of nonhuman others, challenging the object/subject binary at the heart of the current legal framework and seeking more adequate legal solutions for the challenges of the current times.

As outlined in the Introduction to this volume, while feminist approaches to international law initially focused on a wide array of issues in international law, over the past few decades, this field of scholarship has come to focus primarily on issues that pertain to women's lived experiences, focusing principally on representation

---

1 William J. Ripple et al., 'World Scientists' Warning of a Climate Emergency,' *Bioscience* (2020) 70(1): 8–12.

2 Will Steffen et al., 'Planetary Boundaries: Guiding Human Development on a Changing Planet,' *Science (American Association for the Advancement of Science)* (2015) 347(6223): 736–747. See also: Louis J. Kotzé, 'Earth System Law for the Anthropocene: Rethinking Environmental Law alongside the Earth System Metaphor,' *Transnational Legal Theory* (2020) 11 (1–2): 75–104.

3 Sundhya Pahuja, 'Conserving the World's Resources?' in James Crawford and Martti Koskenniemi (eds.), *The Cambridge Companion to International Law*, (Cambridge University Press, 2015): 398–420, pp. 398–399.

4 Usha Natarajan and Kishan Khody, 'Locating Nature: Making and Unmaking International Law,' Leiden *Journal of International Law* (2014) 27(3): 573–593, p. 592.

DOI: 10.4324/9781003363798-5

and participation.[5] A similar pattern can be observed when looking at the field of gender and international environmental law: most of this work focuses either on the need to include women further in decision-making processes[6] or on the impacts of environmental degradation on women's lives.[7] Scholarship that focuses on how feminist theory can be used to re-think the masculinist underpinnings of international environmental law is few and far between. This scholarship has, however, started to emerge over the past few years.[8] This chapter adds to this emerging body of thought by bringing feminist approaches to international environmental law into conversation with posthuman feminist theory, including queer theories of the nonhuman, seeking posthuman ways to imagine international environmental law otherwise.

The chapter begins with an outline of some of the core elements of critical posthuman theories of neo-materialism, noting the focus in these theories on dismantling subject/object and nature/culture binaries and on understanding matter as an actant. This scholarship is brought into conversation with critical environmental law work which has begun to use posthuman theory to challenge legal anthropocentrism. Arguing that questions of class, patriarchy, ableism, racism and coloniality

5 Hilary Charlesworth, Gina Heathcote and Emily Jones, 'Feminist Scholarship on International Law in the 1990s and Today: An Inter-Generational Conversation,' *Feminist Legal Studies* (2019) 27: 79–93; Gina Heathcote, *Feminist Dialogues on International Law: Successes, Tensions, Futures*, (Oxford University Press, 2019).

6 See, for example: Keina Yoshida, 'The Protection of the Environment: A Gendered Analysis,' *Goettingen Journal of International Law* (2020) 10(1): 283–305; Rowena Maguire, 'Gender, Climate Change and the United Nations Framework Convention on Climate Change,' in Susan Harris Rimmer and Kate Ogg (eds.), *Research Handbook on Feminist Engagement with International Law*, (Edward Elgar, 2019): 63–80; Anne Rochette, 'Transcending the Conquest of Nature and Women: A Feminist Perspective on International Environmental Law,' in Doris Buss and Ambreena Manji (eds.), *International Law: Modern Feminist* Approaches, (Hart, 2005): 203–235; Karen Lesley Morrow, 'Tackling Climate Change and Gender Justice – Integral; not Optional,' *Oñati Socio-Legal Series* (2021) 11(1): 207–230; Carol Cohn and Claire Duncanson, 'Women, Peace and Security in a Changing Climate,' *International Feminist Journal of Politics* (2020) 22(5): 742–762.

7 See, for example: Maguire, Ibid.; Rochette, Ibid.; Rowena Maguire and Bridget Lewis, 'Women, Human Rights and the Global Climate Regime,' *Journal of Human Rights and the Environment* (2018) 9(1): 51–67; Jody M. Prescott, *Armed Conflict, Women and Climate Change*, (Routledge, 2019).

8 See: Katie Woolaston, 'Wildlife and International Law: Can Feminism Transform Our Relationship with Nature?' in Susan Harris Rimmer and Kate Ogg (eds.), *Research Handbook on Feminist Engagement with International Law*, (Edward Elgar, 2019): 44–62; Emily Jones and Dianne Otto, Thinking through Anthropocentrism in International Law: Queer Theory, Posthuman Feminism and the Postcolonial, LSE Women, Peace and Security blog (January 2020); Gina V. Heathcote, 'Feminism and the Law of the Sea: A Preliminary Inquiry,' in Irini Papanicolopulu (ed.), *Gender and the Law of the Sea*, (Brill, 2019): 83–105; Alice Ollino, 'Feminism, Nature and the Post-Human: towards a Critical Analysis of the International Law of the Sea Governing Marine Living Resources Management,' in Irini Papanicolopulu (ed.), *Gender and the Law of the Sea*, (Brill, 2019): 204–228; Dianne Otto and Anna Grear, 'International Law, Social Change and Resistance: A nBetween Professor Anna Grear (Cardiff) and Professorial Fellow Dianne Otto (Melbourne),' *Feminist Legal Studies* (2018) 26: 351–363; Karen Morrow, 'Perspectives on Environmental Law and the Law Relating to Sustainability: A Continued Role for Ecofeminism?' in Andreas Philippopoulos-Mihalopoulos (ed.), *Law and Ecology: New Environmental Foundations*, (Routledge, 2011): 126–152.

must remain at the forefront of attempts to transform international environmental law, I note the need to pay greater attention to which forms of posthumanism are being used in critical environmental law scholarship. The second part of this chapter thereby centres feminist and queer posthuman theories that have long worked to challenge intersectional structures of oppression when challenging anthropocentrism, using these theories to re-think international environmental law.

Queer theories of the nonhuman are drawn on, not only because these theories pay attention to the inequalities between humans while fostering human-nonhuman connections, but also because these theories avoid gender essentialism. Some strands of scholarship on gender and the environment are based upon the essentialist idea that feminist theory might have something to say about the environment because women are somehow more connected to nature. Queer theories actively rebuke this claim, working to dismantle the nature/culture binary. The anti-essentialism of queer theories of the nonhuman, held alongside their attentiveness to human inequalities, means that these theories can be used to provide a unique way of understanding international environmental law. Consequently, this chapter also contributes to scholarship on gender and international environmental law by applying queer theories of the environment to international law for the first time.

While, in Chapter 3, I noted the difficulty in applying posthuman feminism to debates on military technologies, given the tension between feminist ethics and militarism, the aims of the present chapter, read alongside the next, are to explore whether posthuman feminist theories may find more traction as applied to an area of the law that, on the face of it, sits less in tension with feminist values: international environmental law. Critical environmental law scholar Anna Grear argues that environmental law is a good place to start when applying posthuman or new materialist ideas to the law precisely because 'environmental law is closer than many forms of law to the materiality of the world and potentially responsive to materiality as an ethical matter'.[9] This chapter argues that posthuman feminist theories, which seek to dismantle hierarchies between humans (such as gender, race and class), while challenging the idea that the human sits in hierarchical superiority over all other entities, including matter and nonhumans,[10] can be used to destabilise the problematic and exclusionary anthropocentrism of the law.

However, the aim of this book is not only to use posthuman feminist theory to analyse international law, but also to design and foster legal change. While critical environmental law scholarship has already begun to re-imagine environmental law in theory, there is little work that applies these theories to legal practice. The next chapter, in line with this book's intention to bridge theory and practice, applies

---

9 Anna Grear, "Anthropocene, Capitalocene, Chthulucene': Re-Encountering Environmental Law and its "Subject" with Haraway and New Materialism,' in Louis J. Kotzé (ed.), *Environmental Law and Governance for the Anthropocene*, (Hart, 2017): 77–95, p. 94.

10 Rosi Braidotti, *The Posthuman*, (Polity Press, 2013); Rosi Braidotti, *Posthuman Knowledge*, (Polity Press 2019); Rosi Braidotti, *Posthuman Feminism*, (Polity Press, 2022).

queer posthuman feminist theories of the environment to international law, focusing on the emerging rights of nature movement.

Posthuman Theory and Environmental Law

In Chapter 1, I argued that international environmental law is anthropocentric, prioritising human interests, and particularly economic interests and the needs of the global north, over others, including the interests of the environment. I drew on a variety of examples to make this point, analysing the anthropocentrism inherent in each, from the principle of sustainable development to the field of human rights and the environment and beyond. Overall, I concluded that international environmental law views the environment as an object, this pattern justifying environmental exploitation and extraction.

In contrast, posthuman theory challenges the dichotomy between subject and object, questioning dominant understandings of subjectivity and stressing both the 'force of living matter' and the ways that nature-culture has always been complicated by techno-scientific discovery.[11] In this chapter, I will draw on a variety of posthuman theories of neo-materialism, from new materialism and feminist new materialism to theories of 'vibrant matter',[12] 'agential-realism'[13] or 'vitalist materialism',[14] to queer theories of the nonhuman,[15] in order to challenge the subject/object binary that lies at the heart of both western thought and, subsequently, international environmental law. I argue that these theories, if applied to international environmental law, provide a very different vision of what the law could be, in terms of its objectives, terms of reference and underlaying assumptions. This vision of the law, I argue, could provide a way to better rise to the contemporary challenges presented by climate change and environmental degradation.

As suggested, there are multiple strands of posthuman thought on neo-materialism. One example can be found in the work of Jane Bennett. Bennett, in her work on 'vibrant matter', challenges the binding of subjectivity to the fantasy of 'human uniqueness'[16] and the 'fantasy that "we" are really in charge of those "its"'.[17] Bennett thus re-centres matter as an 'actant',[18] re-thinking the idea that objects are the opposite of subjects through a focus on 'thing-power'.[19] Bennett notes that humans are part of a shared, 'vital materiality',[20] arguing that humans impact upon and are impacted on by things but also highlighting the fact that humans are, themselves,

11 Braidotti, 'The Posthuman,' Ibid, p. 3.
12 Jane Bennett, *Vibrant Matter*, (Duke University Press, 2010).
13 Karen Barad, *Meeting the Universe Halfway: Quantum Physics and the Entanglement of Matter and Meaning*, (Duke University Press, 2007).
14 Braidotti, 'The Posthuman,' above note 11, p. 55.
15 Noreen Giffney and Myra Hird (eds.), *Queering the Non/Human*, (Routledge, 2008).
16 Bennet, above note 13, p. Ix.
17 Ibid., p. x.
18 Ibid., p. viii.
19 Ibid., p. 2.
20 Ibid., p. 14.

'a particularly potent mix of minerals'.[21] Bennett thereby challenges the idea that agency is something held by humans alone but, rather, states that 'the locus of agency is always a human-nonhuman working group'.[22]

Posthuman theories centre the agency and vibrancy of matter, situating the cultural within a wider collective of human and nonhuman interactions. Theorists such as Bennet, alongside scholars such as feminist new materialist Vicky Kirby, therefore argue that the world is a network, a criss-crossing of multiple assemblages, both human and nonhuman in which nature and culture are overlapping as opposed to distinct.[23] As environmental law scholar Grear notes, '[o]ur relationships with our "environments" are never neutral, for we are unavoidably co-constituted by and with the "landscapes" or "spaces" we inhabit, not only in material, but in social and discursive dimensions'.[24] Humans adapt to their natural surroundings through, for example, using certain building materials in certain environments. In turn, nature responds to and adapts to humans,[25] climate change being the obvious example here. Humans and nonhumans are always situated in relation and connection to one another. In this sense, agency is never 'pure' nor absolute but rather, agency is always distributed and reliant upon its connection to other agential entities and beings, human and nonhuman alike.[26]

Critical posthuman theories of neo-materialism thereby challenge the subject/object dichotomy, re-centring the agency of things. As outlined in more detail in Chapter 1, the subject/object dichotomy is central in international environmental law. Dismantling this binary is core work when it comes to re-thinking international environmental law. The basic tenets of posthuman theories of neo-materialism, if applied to the law, could provide a way to re-think the anthropocentrism of the law, challenging the idea that humans are in domination over the environment and by extension, the justification of economies of extraction and exploitation. Thus, as Grear argues, 'If matter has escaped its imposed (imagined) inertia — if matter begins to evade categorisations, to over-spill linear conceptions of causality, to generate meanings — then matter necessarily challenges the previous *taken for granted* of environmental law'.[27] To apply posthuman feminisms to international environmental law, and to understand the added value of applying these theories, there is a need to

---

21 Ibid., p. 11.
22 Ibid., p. xvi.
23 Ibid.; Vicki Kirby, 'Natural Convers(at)ions: Or, What If Culture was Really Nature All Along?' in Stacy Alaimo and Susan Hekman (eds.), *Material Feminisms*, (Indiana University Press, 2008): 214–236, p. 225.

These scholars both draw on Actor-Network theory. See: Bruno Latour, *Reassembling the Social: An Introduction to Actor-Network Theory*, (Oxford University Press, 2007).
24 Anna Grear, 'Human Rights, Property and the Search for "Worlds Other,"' *Journal of Human Rights and the Environment* (2012) 3(2): 173–195, p. 195.
25 See: Christopher D. Stone, 'Should Trees Have Standing? – Toward Legal Rights for Natural Objects,' *Southern California Law Review* (1972) 45: 450–501, p. 471.
26 Stacy Alaimo, 'Trans-Corporeal Feminisms and the Ethical Space of Nature,' in Stacy Alaimo and Susan Hekman (eds.), *Material Feminisms*, (Indiana University Press, 2008): 237–264, p. 246.
27 Grear, above note 10, p. 92 – author's own emphasis.

briefly map relevant trends in environmental law scholarship. There is a strong body of critical environmental law literature that seeks to think through the anthropocentric tendencies of environmental law, a body of work that I can by no means provide a comprehensive overview of here. This scholarship has a long history, with much of it originating in literatures on earth jurisprudence or wild law.[28] Broadly, this work seeks to re-think human-nature relationships. Some of this work is explicitly posthuman or new materialist, and some of it is not. One strand of thought in this field is planetary justice literature, with scholars such as John S. Dryzek and Jonathan Pickering arguing that current conceptions of justice are based upon Holocene visions of justice. Dryzek and Pickering thereby call for new understandings of planetary justice. Their proposals include working to expand understandings of justice to include nonhumans, future generations and the Earth system as a whole and working towards collective approaches that foster links between humans and nature.[29] Similarly, earth system law, bringing the field of earth system governance to the legal sphere, seeks to reconceive law in a way that is more attuned to planetary boundaries and the connections between humans and their environments.[30] Furthermore, there is a strong body of work focusing on ecocentric or ecological law perspectives which seeks to re-think the connections between humans and nature.[31]

However, most interestingly for the purposes of this chapter, there is an emerging body of scholarship that brings posthuman and new materialist theory into conversation with environmental law. This is happening in a variety of ways, sometimes in conversation with some of the above-mentioned frames, sometimes not. For example, Marie-Catherine Petersmann, discussing earth system law, seeks to understand what re-thinking human-nonhuman relations may mean for this project.[32] Petersmann notes the need to challenge the dichotomies between human/nature, nature/culture,[33] in turn challenging environmental law's prioritisation of the

28 See: Thomas Berry, *The Great Work: Our Way into the Future* (Bell Tower, 1999); Cormac Cullinan, *Wild Law: A Manifesto for Earth Jurisprudence* (Green Books, 2003); Arne Naess, *Ecology of Wisdom*, (Penguin, 2016); Peter Burdon, *Earth Jurisprudence: Private Property and the Environment* (Routledge, 2017); Nicole Rogers and Michelle Maloney (eds.), *Law as if Earth Really Mattered* (Routledge, 2017); Peter Burdon, *Exploring Wild Law: The Philosophy of Earth Jurisprudence*, (Wakefield Press, 2011).

29 John S. Dryzek and Jonathan Pickering, *The Politics of the Anthropocene*, (Oxford University Press, 2018).

30 Louise J. Kotzé and Rakhyun E. Kim, 'Earth System Law: The Juridical Dimensions of Earth System Governance,' *Earth System Governance* (2019) 1: 1–12; Marie-Catherine Petersmann, 'Sympoietic Thinking and Earth System Law: The Earth, Its Subjects and the Law,' *Earth System Governance* (2021) 9: 1–8.

31 See, for example: Bron Taylor et al., 'The Need for Ecocentrism in Biodiversity Conservation,' *Conservation Biology* (2020) 34(5): 1089–1096; Massimiliano Montini, 'The Transformation of Environmental Law into Ecological Law,' in Kirsten Anker et al. (ed.), *From Environmental to Ecological Law*, (Routledge, 2021): 11–22.
   See also: Andreas Philippopoulos-Mihalopoulos, 'Critical; Environmental Law in the Anthropocene,' in Louise J. Kotzé (ed.), *Environmental Law and Governance for the Anthropocene*, (Bloomsbury, 2017): 117–135.

32 Petersmann, above note 31.

33 Ibid.

human subject. Emille Boulot and Joshua Sterlin take a similar approach, applying what they term the 'legal ontological turn' to look towards an environmental law for all beings, drawing parallels between this turn in law and ecological systems and Indigenous legal thinking.[34] However, posthuman and new materialist approaches to environmental law are also emerging as a stand-alone field. For example, Matt Harvey and Steve Vanderheiden draw on theories of the 'more-than-human' to question who speaks for nature in law,[35] while social scientists Nick J. Fox and Pam Alldred apply posthuman theory to challenge the sustainable development paradigm[36] and to re-think climate change policies.[37] Sam Adelman likewise uses new materialist concepts of agency and mattering to re-think climate justice,[38] while Petersmann applies posthuman theories to the concepts of responsibility and protection in international environmental law, calling for a shift towards what she terms response-abilities of care (drawing on Haraway's terminology).[39] Grear is a central voice in the field of posthuman and new materialist theory as applied to environmental law. She draws on the work of Bennett, Haraway and Alaimo, among others, to highlight human-nonhuman connections, fostering new legal imaginaries.[40] Furthermore, my own work has begun to explore whether posthuman theory may find some recourse to action through the rights of nature, reflecting on what the rights of nature movement may, in turn, learn from posthuman theory[41] – a theme I return to in the next chapter of this book.

While applying posthuman theory to environmental law is an exciting development, scholars in this field are drawing on a wide array of sometimes very different posthuman theories, at times conflating these theories and their radically different political agendas. For example, scholars draw on object orientated ontology alongside the work of critical posthuman theorists and even posthuman feminisms. The need to note the nuances and the very different political projects present in different strands of posthuman work is something I outlined in greater detail in the Introduction to this volume. There, I argued that some strands of posthuman theory, in focusing on objects and ontology, at times displace important questions

34 Emille Boulot and Joshua Sterlin, 'Steps Towards a Legal Ontological Turn: Proposals for Law's Place Beyond the Human,' *Transnational Environmental Law*, (2022) 11(1): 13–38.
35 Matt Harvey and Steve Vanderheiden, "For the Trees Have No Tongues': Eco-Feedback, Speech, and the Silencing of Nature,' *Journal of Human Rights and the Environment* (2021) 12: 38–58.
36 Nick J. Fox and Pam Alldred, 'Climate Change, Environmental Justice and the Unusual Capacities of Posthumans,' *Journal of Human Rights and the Environment* (2021) 12: 59–75.
37 Nick J. Fox and Pam Alldred, 'Re-Assembling Climate Change Policy: Materialism, Posthumanism, and the Policy Assemblage,' *British Journal of Sociology* (2020) 17(2): 269–283.
38 Sam Adelman, 'A Legal Paradigm Shift towards Climate Justice in the Anthropocene,' *Oñati Socio-Legal Series* (2021) 11(1): 44–68.
39 Marie-Catherine Petersmann, 'Response-Abilities of Care in More-Than-Human Worlds,' *Journal of Human Rights and the Environment* (2021) 12: 102–124.
40 Anna Grear, above note 10; Anna Grear, 'Resisting Anthropocene Neoliberalism: Towards New Materialism Commoning?' in Anna Grear and David Bollier (eds.), *The Great Awakening: New Modes of Life Amidst Capitalist Ruins*, (Punctum Books, 2020): 317–355.
41 Emily Jones 'Posthuman International Law and the Rights of Nature,' *Journal of Human Rights and the Environment* (2021) 12(0): 76–101.

of epistemology and the inequalities that exist between humans. Greater attention must be paid to which posthuman theories are being transposed to environmental law and which are not. In the next section, drawing on debates from within posthuman theories of the environment, and particularly on queer literatures that critique the lack of focus on the inequalities between humans within some strands of posthuman scholarship, I argue that queer theories of the nonhuman provide an important resource for those wishing to apply posthuman and new materialist theories to environmental law. These theories already provide a complex understanding of the need to hold the inequalities between multiple humans and nonhumans together, providing a strong blueprint from which critical environmental law scholarship seeking to engage with posthumanism can springboard.

Posthuman theories may have radical implications for international environmental law, offering the potential to challenge and possibly resolve some of the core tensions raised by critical international environmental law scholars. Fostering an environmental law that is receptive to the epistemic shift required to take account of the insights of posthuman theory might allow for the casting-aside of 'the eco-destructive assumptions and ideological closures of the Anthropocene-Capitalocene'[42] allowing, instead, for a more a liveable law of a different imaginary in which relations are tangled, tentacular and co-emergent: a law, to use Donna Haraway's words, for the Chthulucene.[43] This potential arises precisely because these theories challenge the same dominant western epistemological frames that underlie international environmental law, i.e. anthropocentrism, exclusionary humanism and the division of nature/culture and subject/object, offering instead a more empirically faithful account of 'the world'. However, posthuman theory, when transposed to international environmental law, must retain a focus on the inhuman and the less-than-human when seeking to re-centre the nonhuman. The next section turns to queer posthuman theories, examining how these theories provide a way to think about these different elements simultaneously.

Posthuman Feminism: Queering the Nonhuman

Bringing posthuman theory to environmental law can aid in re-thinking the anthropocentrism of the law, allowing the fostering of an environmental law otherwise. However, given the differences between posthuman theories, it matters which theories are applied.

While some of the posthuman theories I outlined above, and which I will continue to draw on in this and the next chapter, are not explicitly feminist, the work of Jane Bennett being an example here, I draw on them as part of my posthuman feminist convergence. As Rosi Braidotti outlines in brilliant detail in her genealogy of posthuman feminism, while many posthuman theories now neglect feminist theory, feminism was one of the central precursors of the posthuman turn.[44] Feminist

---

42 Grear, above note 10, p. 95.
43 Donna Haraway, *Staying with the Trouble: Making Kin in the Chthulucene*, (Duke University Press, 2016).
44 Braidotti, *Posthuman Feminism*, above note 11.

theory has greatly shaped critical posthuman theory. This can be exemplified by looking at the work of Bennett herself which, while not explicitly feminist, pays attention, not only to the exclusion of nonhuman others, but also to the real inequalities between humans.[45] It is this intersectional feminist ethics that sets the work of critical posthuman scholars, such as Bennett, aside from other posthuman scholars that take a much more conservative approach. My concern is that, in transposing posthuman theories to environmental law, the feminist history of the posthuman turn is being lost in translation. While much of the scholarship on posthumanism and environmental law does focus both on the need to de-centre the human subject in environmental law and the need to tackle the inequalities between humans, this emerging body of work has only tentatively begun to bring posthuman theory into conversation with environmental law. Meanwhile, posthuman feminism and queer theories of the nonhuman have already well theorised the need to think through the question of nonhuman alongside the inequalities that exist between humans. In this section, I argue that queer posthuman feminist theories, through their systematic attentiveness to the need to see the human, the nonhuman, the inhuman and the less than human as always contestable, as always embedded, not only in anthropocentrism but also gender, race, class and ableism, can be used to greatly inform critical environmental law scholarship.

A posthuman feminist politics of new materialism can be articulated by looking at the work of Braidotti in relation to debates on monism or the oneness of all matter. The oneness of living matter is a central idea in many neo-materialist or posthuman theories. These theories posit that all things are made, essentially, of the same stuff. The oneness of matter, as expressed in contemporary posthuman neo-materialisms through the work of scholars such as Bennett and Braidotti, however, has a much longer history which these scholars draw on in their philosophies. For example, the last century BC Roman philosopher and poet, Lucretius, discussed such ideas in his philosophical poem *De Rerum Natura* (On the Nature of Things), in which he describes an 'eternal substance'[46] or a 'solid singleness' [47] which holds all things together, from which all things are made.[48] We are all made of variations of the same elementary particles. Moving further along the timeline, similar ideas were put forward by seventeenth-century philosopher Spinoza who stated that: 'Any thing whatsoever, whether it be more perfect or less perfect, will always be able to persist in existing with that same force whereby it begins to exist, so that in this respect all things are equal'.[49] Spinoza therefore states that all things are 'animate, albeit in different degrees'.[50] Reflecting on human freedom and

---

45 Bennett, above note 13.
46 Lucretius, *On the Nature of Things*, trans. Cyril Bailey, (Oxford University Press, 1948 [1910]), Book I, ll. 237–266, p. 35.
47 Ibid., p. 45.
48 Ibid., Book I, II and III.
49 Benedictus de Spinoza, *The Ethics*, (Penguin, 1996 [1677]), p. 4 proposition 37, scholium 1, preface 4.
50 Ibid., pt 2 proposition 12 scholium 72.

consciousness, Spinoza submits that even a falling stone 'is endeavouring, as far as it can, to continue to move',[51] concluding that all things and beings are animate. As Spinoza scholar Hasana Sharp writes, all things possess the power 'to act and be acted upon' and all things possess 'a desire to preserve in being, to remain what it is, to preserve and enhance its life to the extent that its nature allows'.[52] Braidotti, drawing upon the work of Spinoza, thereby concludes that 'matter is one, driven by the desire for self-expression and ontologically free', being free, also, from the violence of dualistic thinking.[53]

French post-structuralist Gilles Deleuze, discussing the work of Spinoza, likewise puts forward a theory of matter which he defines as 'ontologically one, formally diverse'.[54] Such an understanding of the world inherently breaks down the idea that humans are subjects and everything else is object, noting the connections between humans and the wider material world and challenging any will to dominate or exploit. Material oneness does not, however, reduce everything to the same, at least not in posthuman feminist form. A rejection of dualism, including of nature/ culture does not mean all is reduced to one – this is the fallacy of the 'flat ontology' defended by object orientated ontology (OOO). In a posthuman feminist frame, everything becomes differentiated, modulated otherwise, designed along multiple axes. This is centrally important for posthuman feminism. After all, as Braidotti states, 'we are all in this together, but we are not one and the same'.[55] A statement calling for intersectional political action across differences, the materialist elements of Braidotti's philosophy can also be read here. We are all inter-connected, all made up of the same stuff, yet are also differently situated within that context, working across different spaces, temporalities, locations. We each have a different position in the world, a different relation to power and oppression. Braidotti's emphasis on the oneness of matter, drawing on scholars such as Spinoza and Deleuze, therefore poses a situated universalism made up of multiplicity, 'relocating difference outside the dialectical scheme'.[56] Such an understanding allows differences to be visualised and understood while inherently shifting from a paradigm of domination and hierarchy to one of shared connection and the collaborative 'relation to multiple others'.[57]

A posthuman feminist understanding of matter or the environment that seeks to re-think the subject/object binary necessarily includes an understanding of non-dualistic difference as central. This position compliments the way I have defined

---

51 Benedictus de Spinoza, trans. Samuel Shirley, *The Letters Epistile*, (Hackett Publishing, 1996): 58.
52 Hasana Sharp, 'The Force of Ideas in Spinoza,' *Political Theory* (2007) 35(6): 732–755, p. 740.
53 Braidotti, 'The Posthuman,' above note 11, p. 56.
54 Gilles Deleuze, trans. Martin Joughin, *Expressionism in Philosophy: Spinoza*, (Zone Books, 1990 [1968]), p. 66.
55 This is a phrase Braidotti uses throughout her work. However, see: Rosi Braidotti, '"We" Are In *This* Together, but We Are Not One and the Same,' *Journal of Bioethical Inquiry* (2020) 17: 465–468.
56 Braidotti, 'The Posthuman,' above note 11, p. 56.
57 Ibid., p. 56.

posthuman feminism throughout this book as a body of work that seeks to challenge, not only the centrality of the human in western thought (and therefore international law) but also the centrality of a particular vision of the human that is the white, middle-class, able-bodied, heterosexual man. There is another reason, however, why it matters so much which theories are being applied to environmental law. This relates to the debate in feminism on essentialism versus social constructivism. This issue can be reflected on by turning to discussions within feminist new materialism.

While feminist new materialist work discuses a wide array of issues, one central theme in this work is the limitations of social constructivist gender theory. In short, feminist new materialism argues that, in focusing on language, culture and discourse alone, matter has been left out of gender theory, having 'serious consequences for feminist theory and practice'.[58] Emphasising the deconstruction of binaries as a core feminist methodology, feminist new materialist thinkers note the need to also deconstruct the nature/culture divide upheld by social constructivist gender theory in its primary focus on the cultural.[59] This position is outlined by Vicky Kirby who states that, in 'arguing that these significations are cultural ascriptions with no essential truth',[60] gender theorists work to ensure that the question of nature or matter becomes '*entirely* displaced … it can have no frame of reference that isn't properly cultural'.[61] Everything, instead, becomes interpreted through discourse.[62] Karen Barad thereby argues that 'language has been granted too much power'.[63] Such representationalism, Barad argues, separates the world into words and things, ignoring the linkage between the two and leading Barad to conclude that 'the only thing that does not seem to matter anymore is matter'.[64] The problem for feminist new materialist thinkers, therefore, is the power given to discourse by social constructivist gender theories, this focus side-lining questions about the material world and reducing matter to *'thingification'*.[65] This thingification operates to dismiss

58 Stacy Alaimo and Susan Hekman, 'Introduction: Emerging Models of Materiality in Feminist Theory,' in Stacy Alaimo and Susan Hekman (eds.), *Material Feminisms*, (Indiana University Press, 2008): 1–19, p. 3.

59 Karen Barad, 'Posthumanist Performativity: Towards an Understanding of How Matter Comes to Matter,' in Stacy Alaimo and Susan Hekman (eds.), *Material Feminisms*, (Indiana University Press, 2008): 120–154; Alaimo, above note 28.

60 Kirby, above note 23, p. 220.

61 Ibid., p. 220 – emphasis in the original.

62 While this argument has been made recently by feminist new materialist thinkers, a similar critique has long been made by feminist scholars. For example, writing in 2002, Braidotti draws on both theories of materialism alongside psychoanalytic feminist theories to critique social constructionism and its silences. She states that 'it is important to move beyond the reductivism of social constructionism, which tends to underplay the continuity of factors that provide the empirical foundations of the subject and which are mostly related to biology, but also include affectivity and especially memory and desire' (Rosi Braidotti, *Metamorphoses: Towards a Materialist Theory of Becoming*, (Polity Press, 2002), p. 11–64 and particularly p. 62.

63 Barad, above note 59, p 120.

64 Ibid., p. 120.

65 Ibid., p. 130 – author's own emphasis.

matter as a site of knowledge and of subject formation. In contrast, feminist new materialism challenges the idea that subjects coincide solely with their representations, highlighting the thick materiality of bodies and the locations they inhabit. These thinkers therefore call for further attention to be paid to the agency of matter itself and to the materially embedded roots of all entities, humans included.[66]

Feminist new materialism seeks to challenge the nature/culture dualism by reasserting matter and the natural. However, considering how 'nature and "the natural" have long been waged against homosexuals, as well as women, people of color, and indigenous peoples',[67] it becomes clear that there are serious risks presented by essentialism when reasserting the natural. Furthermore, binarism raises its ugly head again – as women have traditionally been associated with nature and men with culture. By reasserting the natural as a feminist strategy, one risks proposing an essentialist position that reasserts nature as a feminine attribute, consequently suggesting that women are more closely related to the natural. The feminist new materialists are very aware of this risk, arguing that the fear of essentialism has led to a concerning 'flight from nature'.[68] Keeping the risks of essentialism at the forefront, while also seeking to engage with questions of matter, this group of scholars assert, instead, that there is a need to challenge the gendering of the nature/culture binary[69] and to de-link the false idea that women are inherently more connected to nature while simultaneously noting that nature-culture is a continuum.[70]

This debate is relevant for the present work which seeks to apply posthuman feminist ideas to international environmental law. This must be done with care and in a way that does not suggest that feminism is relevant because women are somehow more connected to nature. Rather, I argue that feminist theory, and particularly posthuman feminism, is relevant to this field because it provides an alternative vision for international environmental law, one which can be used to re-imagine international environmental law beyond its current anthropocentric frame. Feminist theory is therefore relevant, not because women are somehow more connected to nature and hence better placed to defend it, but because feminist theory is a complex, grounded, differential and deeply nuanced body of thought that can be used to re-think all areas of international law, not only areas that directly pertain to women's lives.

The risks of essentialism are clearly exposed by looking at some of the literature on gender and international environmental law. While much of this scholarship focuses on issues that pertain to women's lived experiences,[71] literature is emerging

---

66 Ibid., p. 122.
67 Stacy Alaimo, 'Eluding Capture: The Science, Culture, and Pleasure of "Queer" Animals,' in Catriona Mortimer Sandilands and Bruce Erickson (eds.), *Queer Ecologies: Sex, Nature, Politics, Desire*, (Indiana University Press, 2010): 51–72, p. 51.
68 Alaimo and Hekman, above note 59, p. 5.
69 Ibid., p. 5–6.
70 See: Stacy Alaimo and Susan Hekman (eds.), *Material Feminisms*, (Indiana University Press, 2008).
71 See, for example; Maguire, above note 7; Rochette, above note 7; Maguire and Lewis, above note 8; Prescott, above note 8; Christopher C. Joyner and George E. Little, 'It's Not Nice to Fool Mother Nature! The Mystique of Feminist Approaches to International Environmental Law,' *Boston University International Law Journal* (1994) 14: 223–266.

that applies feminist theory to re-think the masculinist underpinnings of this body of law.[72] However, there is also a body of work that relies on essentialising tropes around the idea that women are somehow more connected to nature in order to bring a feminist perspective to international environmental law. For example, Joyner and Little argue that women 'are more inclined than men to respect the human relationship to the environment', linking women to 'Mother Nature'.[73] While noting the risks of essentialism, Picado and Reid likewise ultimately conclude that 'women judges, as women, have a different relationship to nature'.[74] While they argue that this is not an ontological position but, rather, comes from women's constructed roles in society,[75] such thinking relies nonetheless on essentialist tropes and on ideas of gender as a binary system. Beyond feminist legal approaches, discussions of 'Mother Nature' can be seen in much of the wider scholarship on gender and the environment,[76] as well as environmental law scholarship that otherwise does not speak directly to the feminist literature.[77] Furthermore, as I will discuss in the next chapter, 'Mother Nature' continues to be used in some parts of the rights of nature movement, this concept being present because of a particular set of political factors (which I will discuss in that chapter).

The thorny issue of women's relationship to nature comes from wider feminist discussions on the environment within the realm of ecofeminism – ecofeminism being a body of feminist thought on the environment that emerged in the 1980s, coming to prominence in the 1990s. Some strands of ecofeminism certainly do portray an essentialised idea of women as connected to nature, linking women's oppression to nature's.[78] This is not to say, however, that all strands of ecofeminism do this or that ecofeminist thought must be rejected. As Val Plumwood notes,

72 See, for example, Woolaston, above note 9; Jones and Otto, above note 9; Heathcote, above note 9; Ollino, above note 9; Otto and Grear, above note 9; Morrow, above note 9.

73 Joyner and Little, above note 72, p. 248.

74 Johnathan A. Picado and Rebecca A. Reid, 'Mother Nature, Lady Justice,' *Open Judicial Politics* (2021), https://open.oregonstate.education/open-judicial-politics/chapter/mother-nature-lady-justice/#footnote-724-3 (last accessed 11 July 2022).

75 Ibid.

76 Cong Minh Huynh and Hong Hiep Hoang, 'Does a Free Market Economy Make Mother Nature Angry? Evidence from Asian Economies,' *Environmental Science and Pollution Research* (2021) 28(39): 55603–55614; Eric A. Goldstein, 'Mother Nature Knows Best: Fundamentals for Ensuring Safe Water Supply,' *Fordham Environmental Law Journal* (2001)12(3): 455–466; Mavra Bari, Manipulating Mother Nature: The Gendered Antagonism of Geoengineering, Heinrich Böll Stiftung 2020, https://eu.boell.org/en/2020/01/30/manipulating-mother-nature-gendered-antagonism-geoengineering (last accessed 11 July 2022).

77 See, for example: Richard J. Lazarus, 'Environmental Law After Katrina: Reforming Environmental Law by Reforming Environmental Lawmaking,' *Tulane Law Review* (2007) 81: 1019–1058; W. Earl Webster, 'How Can Mother Nature Get to Court the Status of the Standing Doctrine in Post Laidlaw Landscape?,' *Journal of Land, Resources, & Environmental Law* 27(2): 453–472; William J. Snape III, 'A Pattern of Ruling Against Mother Nature: Wildlife Species Cases Decided by Justice Kavanaugh,' *Sustainable Development Law & Policy* (2018) 19(1): 4–33.

78 For a history of ecofeminism, focusing on essentialism and seeking to move beyond it, see: Greta Gaard, 'Ecofeminism Revisited: Rejecting Essentialism and Re-Placing Species in a Material Feminist Environmentalism,' *Feminist Formations* (2011) 23(2): 26–53.

'ecological feminists differ on how and even whether women are connected to nature, on whether such connection is in principle sharable by men, [and] on how to treat the exclusion of women from culture'.[79] Thus, as Greta Gaard argues, there is still much to be learnt from ecofeminism.[80] However, gender essentialism must be avoided. The idea that women are somehow more connected to nature, as embodied in the figure of 'Mother Nature', upholds the gendered dichotomy of nature/culture as opposed to dismantling it.[81] There are clear undertones of biological determinism in this construction, with links being made between the gendered pregnant body[82] and the natural, reinforcing the patriarchal notion that women are 'natural' caregivers.[83] In contrast, queer scholarship on the environment begins with a rejection of gendered essentialisms, challenging the nature/culture binary.[84] Queer scholarship thereby holds promise for re-thinking international environmental law. This is first, because of its focus on the need to think through the nonhuman alongside inequalities between humans, and second, because this body of thought disrupts essentialised notions of gender that are present in some feminist literatures on environmental law.

While there are multiple queer approaches to the environment as I will come on to discuss, this field broadly argues that 'LGBTQ+ people have historically been placed on the side of the unnatural'.[85] These theories, much like some of the postcolonial and black studies literature I outlined in Chapter 1, seek to embrace the inhuman or the nonhuman as a site for radical transformation. Many of these theories subsequently align closely with posthuman feminism and its focus on the nonhuman and the need to challenge anthropocentrism. Queer theories of the environment thereby argue that engagements with the environment must not be underpinned by gendered binaries such as nature/culture but, rather, that engagements should actively seek to dismantle this gendered binary as part of a queer environmental politics.[86]

There are many strands of thought within what can be termed queer theories of the environment, including theories of queer ecology that call for the 'opening up of environmental understandings to explicitly non-heterosexual forms of relationship, experience and imagination' as a means to transform 'entrenched sexual and natural practices'.[87] This body of work also includes literatures that link queerness

79 Val Plumwood, *Feminism and the Mastery of Mature*, (Routledge, 1993), p. 8.

80 Gaard, above note 79.

81 Timothy Morton, 'Queer Ecology,' *PMLA* (2010) 125(2): 273–282, p. 274.

82 I use the word gendered here to note the fact that not all pregnant people are women.

83 For a queer analysis of the politics of 'reproductive futurism' and an insistence on focusing on the inhuman, see: Lee Edelman, *No Future: Queer Theory and the Death Drive*, (Duke University Press, 2004).

84 Alaimo, above note 68.

85 Braidotti, *Posthuman Feminism*, above note 11, p. 160.

86 See: Catriona Mortimer-Sandilands and Bruce Erickson, 'Introduction: A Genealogy of Queer Ecologies,' in Catriona Mortimer Sandilands and Bruce Erickson (eds.), *Queer Ecologies: Sex, Nature, Politics, Desire*, (Indiana University Press, 2010): 1–48.

87 Ibid., p. 3.

to the nonhuman or inhuman as a positive relation and resource.[88] Posthuman queer scholarship also seeks to challenge heteronormative assumptions in discussions of nature,[89] noting, for example, the diverse sexualities of animals.[90] Another research approach focuses on the queer politics of coalition building in and across the environmental movement.[91] However, for the purposes of this chapter, I draw primarily on queer theories of the nonhuman.[92] This is because these theories most closely align with my posthuman feminist focus in this chapter, and the wider book, on the need to reconfigure the nonhuman in international law.

Dana Luciano and Mel Y. Chen argue that there is little gain to be found for queer people in seeking to be included in the category of so-called 'humanity', which has always been exclusionary and based around the heterosexual, white, middle-class, male subject. They argue that queer studies should focus instead on nonhuman configurations as a site of disruption to the 'human' subject.[93] What needs to be transformed, in other words, is the very idea and ideal of the human and the kind of recognition and equality that can emerge within this notion. The counter-figuration of the nonhuman queer is thereby deeply tied to theories which note that some people have never been able to fully access the dominant vision of humanity. For example, in a similar fashion to Sylvia Wynter's analysis that many people have never had full access to humanity, including racialised and gendered subjects,[94] Gloria Anzaldúa links the queer to difference. Noting the 'heterosexual tribe's fear' of the queer subject, Anzaldúa analyses how the queer subject becomes

88 See, for example: Dana Luciano and Mel Y. Chen, 'Has the Queer ever been Human?' *GLQ: A Journal of Lesbian and Gay Studies* (2015) 21 (203): 183–207.

89 See: Nicole Seymour, *Strange Natures: Futurity, Empath, and the Queer Ecological Imagination*, (University of Illinois Press, 2013).

90 Bruce Bagemihl, *Biological Exuberance: Animal Homosexuality and Natural Diversity*, (Stonewall Inn Editions, 2000); Stacy Alaimo, above note 68.

91 Katie Hogan, 'Undoing Nature: Collation Building as Queer Environmentalism,' in Catriona Mortimer-Sandilands and Bruce Erikson (eds.), *Queer Ecologies: Sex, Nature, Politics Desire*, (Indiana University Press, 2010): 231–253.

92 See: Giffney and Hird, above note 16. This work also has a long history. For example, in 1991, Sandy Stone linked the dissonances formed around the transsexual body to Donna Haraway's promise of monsters. See: Sandy Stone, 'The Empire Strikes Back: A Posttranssexual Manifesto,' in Julia Epstein and Kristina Straub (eds.), *Body Guards: The Cultural Politics of Gender Ambiguity*, (Routledge, 1991): 280–304; Susan Stryker, 'My Words to Victor Frankenstein above the Village of Chamounix: Performing Transgender Rage,' *GLQ: A Journal of Lesbian and Gay Studies* (1993) 1(3): 237–254; J. M. Halberstam and Ira Livingston, *Posthuman Bodies*, (Indiana University Press, 1995).

93 Luciano and Chen, above note 89, p. 184.

94 Sylvia Wynter, 'Unsettling the Coloniality of Being/Power/Truth/Freedom: Towards the Human/After Man, Its Overrepresentation – An Argument,' *The New Centennial Review* (2003) 3(3): 257–337, p. 288. See also: Sylvia Wynter and Katherine McKittrick, 'Unparalleled Catastrophe for Our Species? Or, to Give Humanness a Different Future: Conversations,' in Katherine McKittrick (ed.), *Sylvia Wynter: On Being Human as Praxis*, (Duke University Press, 2015): 9–89; Sylvia Wynter, 'On How We Mistook the Map for the Territory, and Re-Imprisoned Ourselves in Our Unbearable Wrongness of Being, of Désêtre: Black Studies Toward the Human Project,' in Lewis R. Gordon and Jane Anna Gordon (eds.), *Not Only the Master's Tools : African-American Studies and Theory in Practice*, (Paradigm Publishers, 2006): 107–169.

marked as 'sub-human, inhuman, non-human'.[95] Anzaldúa thus proposes a mode of resistance through what she terms 'mestiza consciousness', making links between marginalised subjects and the land and fostering material connections between the human and the nonhuman,[96] this forming the 'onto-epistemology' of her New Mestiza.[97] Anzaldúa thereby sees 'dehumanization as an opportunity to reconstruct what it means to be human'.[98]

The onto-epistemology of Anzaldúa's New Mestiza finds resonance with some of the posthuman work I outlined above. Bennett, for example, argues that we are all made up of multiple bacteria and are, therefore, all an inherent mix of human and nonhuman.[99] In a similar vein Anzaldúa writes, 'You're all the different organisms and parasites that live on your body and also the ones who live in a symbiotic relationship to you … So who are you? You're not one single entity. You're a multiple entity'.[100] In this figuring of the queer subject, the human is not only unsettled but new possibilities are created. Many have never been fully human, including many racialised, gendered, sexualised, disabled and classed people. Queer posthuman perspectives thereby add another element to the inhuman and nonhuman paradigm, pointing out that humans were never all or solely human. Such a position challenges dominant hierarchies and accounts of the human, providing new ways of envisaging both humans and human-nature connections while also avoiding the essentialism that has permeated some strands of feminist environmental thought.

To summarise, the defining features of a queer posthuman feminist analysis of nature comprise of several key strands, starting from the need to challenge gendered binaries such as nature/culture and subject/object. Next comes a focus on the generative connections between humans and nonhumans and the agency of vibrant matter itself. Alongside this, the need to more adequately account for, and even reclaim, the nonhuman – i.e. all those who do not match the dominant vision of the human – are centred, both as a subject and as a site of knowledge. This does not, however, mean positioning the nonhuman as somehow beyond the human. Such a positioning would risk collapsing into the critiques I outlined in the Introduction to this volume concerning the fact that some theories of posthumanism, by focusing exclusively on an undifferentiated category of the nonhuman, ultimately displace and silence the enduring and real inequalities between humans. Such a slippage risks the reintroduction of the very 'Eurocentric transcendentalism this movement purports to disrupt'.[101] After all, as Luciano and Chen reflect:

---

95 Gloria Anzaldúa, *Borderlands/La Frontera: The New Mestiza*, (Aunt Lute Books, 2012), p. 40.

96 Ibid., p. 40.

97 Carlos Gallego, *Chicana/o Subjectivity and the Politics of Identity: Between Recognition and Revolution* (Palgrave, 2011), p. 74.

98 Luciano and Chen, above note 89, p. 186.

99 Bennett, above note 13.

100 Gloria Anzaldúa, quoted in Mikko Tuhkanen, 'Queer Hybridity,' in hrysanthi Niganni and Merl Storr (eds.), *Deleuze and Queer Theory*, (Edinburgh University Press, 2009): 92–114, p. 96.

101 Jackson in José Esteban Muñoz et al., 'Theorizing Queer Inhumanisms,' *GLQ: A Journal of Lesbian and Gay Studies*, (2015) 21 (2–3): 209–248, p. 215.

If we accept the framing of the nonhuman turn as a move "beyond" the merely human concerns of identity and alterity, we overlook how the very possibility of making a distinction between human and nonhuman has, historically, been constructed by the kind of actions and processes that we have named dehumanization.[102]

Rather than focusing solely on the nonhuman, therefore, there is a need for legal discourse to note the interconnections between naturalised nonhumans, technologised nonhumans and de-humanised humans. This extra layer of complexity can result in highlighting points of solidarity between the nonhuman and the less/more/other/-than-human, without conflating their differences of location and power. In short, a queer posthuman feminist politics cannot be satisfied by simply looking beyond the human, as doing so would risk silencing 'the very histories of dehumanization too often overlooked in celebratory posthumanisms'.[103] A focus on the status of dehumanised humans, moreover, is a necessary corrective to theories and practices that pose equality as the only possible form of recognition for nonhuman entities. Queer posthuman feminist theories of the nonhuman do much more than just displace the human but, rather, explore the multiple new forms of interconnection between and across the inhuman or nonhuman categories, in a manner that avoids dialectical oppositions. The in/non/post-human, in other words, should not become an anti-humanity. This allows for multiple struggles by turning these categories into various and variable vectors of the inhuman, the nonhuman, the less than human and the beyond human to be held together without conflation. This can result in a plurality of political positions, creating a politics of '*being-with*'[104] or, to use Haraway's language, a companion species politics of kin and kind.[105]

Queer theories of the nonhuman have a lot to contribute to critical environmental law scholarship, speaking back to the need to focus on human inequalities alongside questions of the nonhuman. They introduce more depth and complexity, and produce more highly defined categories of legal subjects, objects and spheres of intervention. Furthermore, these theories have the potential to add to the field of gender and international environmental law, providing a queer feminist model that can be used to challenge the anthropocentrism of international environmental law that steers clear of problematic gender essentialisms.

---

102 Luciano and Chen, above note 89, p. 195. See also Jackson and Puar in Ibid.
103 Luciano and Chen, Ibid., p. 196.
104 José Esteban Muñoz in José Esteban Muñoz et al. above note 102, p. 210 – emphasis in the original.
105 See: Donna Haraway, 'Companion Species, Mis-Recognition, and Queering Worlding,' in Noreen Giffney and Myra J. Hird (eds.), *Queering the Non-Human*, (Routledge, 2016): xxii-xxvi, p. xxiv.

Conclusion

In Chapter 1, I argued that international environmental law is anthropocentric, separating human, nonhuman, and environmental interests into discretely demarcated legal spheres, while prioritising human interests over all others. In this chapter, I built on this analysis, seeking to show how posthuman feminism can be used to re-think the anthropocentric assumptions of international environmental law. This move requires a balancing act across multiple pitfalls: I first stressed the need to retain a focus on redressing inequalities between humans, while pursuing an analysis of the position and question of the nonhuman in environmental law. Second, I exposed the risks presented by feminist engagements with international environmental law that centre women as inherently closer to or more connected to nature. In contrast, and rejecting this essentialising position, I argued that queer feminist posthuman theories of the environment, if applied in international environmental law, may provide a promising blueprint for re-imagining the law otherwise. These theories reject the nature/culture binary and the idea that women are somehow more connected to nature. Rather, these theories draw transformative links between the queer subject as other and the already-othered nonhuman subject. This approach calls for a re-thinking of anthropocentrism and of the nature/culture divide from the perspective of a larger and far more diverse range of nonhuman and less-than-human others. This can be fruitful for international environmental law.

Having thought through and presented a queer posthuman feminist paradigm for imagining international environmental law otherwise and being mindful of this book's aim to bridge theory and practice, in the next chapter, I apply these theories to an emerging area of environmental law: the rights of nature. There are some inherent similarities in the aims of posthuman feminism and the rights of nature movement, in that both seek to challenge who or what the legal subject is. I therefore turn to consider whether the rights of nature may provide one way to apply posthuman feminism to international law, analysing what can be learnt by thinking about the rights of nature and posthuman feminist theory together.

5

THE SUBJECTIVITY OF MATTER

The Rights of Nature in International Law

So far, I have argued for the need to challenge the anthropocentric and exclusionary humanisms that underly international law. In Chapter 1, I outlined how international law, despite being primarily formally based on nonhuman legal subjects, such as the state, ultimately upholds elite human interests in a way that sustains and reinforces global inequalities. In the same chapter, I argued that international law is stubbornly anthropocentric, prioritising human interests over nonhuman interests. I then moved on, in Chapters 2 and 3, to apply posthuman feminism to debates on the regulation of military technologies, noting that exclusionary and anthropocentric humanisms also haunt this area of international law, and to seek alternative posthuman feminist inspired legal futures. I concluded by noting the difficulties feminist international lawyers face when managing the tension between resistance and compliance, that is, when seeking to make positive change within and by using international law while also needing to resist and think beyond it.

In Chapter 3, I questioned how far feminists can engage with debates on the regulation of military technologies given that regulation ultimately justifies the use of some of these necro-technologies. This, I argued, sits in tension with the strong history of anti-militarism in feminist thought. The aim of the present chapter, however, is to explore whether posthuman feminist theories may find more traction when applied to international environmental law. As I noted in the previous chapter, critical environmental law scholar Anna Grear argues that environmental law is a good place to start when trying to apply posthuman or new materialist ideas to the law precisely because 'environmental law is closer than many forms of law to the materiality of the world and potentially responsive to materiality as an ethical matter'.[1]

---

1 Anna Grear, '"Anthropocene, Capitalocene, Chthulucene": Re-encountering Environmental Law and Its "Subject" with Haraway and New Materialism,' in Louis J. Kotzé (ed.), *Environmental Law and Governance for the Anthropocene*, (Hart, 2017): 77–95, p. 94.

DOI: 10.4324/9781003363798-6

Following this line of thought, and in line with this book's intention to bridge theory and practice, this chapter seeks to understand how posthuman feminist theories of the environment may be used to re-think the anthropocentrism of international environmental law.

In the previous chapter, building on my analysis in Chapter 1 where I argued that international environmental law is stubbornly anthropocentric, I used posthuman feminisms, including queer theories of the nonhuman, alongside critical environmental law scholarship to imagine an international environmental law otherwise. Drawing on my conclusions, in this chapter I turn to examining whether the emerging rights of nature (RoN) movement may provide a way to bring these posthuman feminist ideas into being in practice.

RoN were described in 2017 by the now UN Special Rapporteur on Human Rights and the Environment, David R. Boyd, as 'a legal revolution that could save the world'.[2] While nature has been recognised as having rights in over 27 countries in every continent,[3] RoN have yet to be adopted within international law.[4] However, there is increasing international interest in doing so, and this chapter argues that those seeking to apply posthuman feminist theory to international environmental law might find some useful alliances with RoN approaches. At the same time, it is also argued that posthuman feminist theories can provide some insights for RoN. This chapter subsequently outlines the potentials in RoN from a posthuman feminist perspective, while addressing the limitations and highlighting the barriers faced when working within, albeit seeking to change, the liberal humanist and anthropocentric framework that is international law.

Indigenous peoples have played a central role in ensuring the recognition of RoN in many domestic jurisdictions.[5] While some posthuman theories and some strands of Indigenous thought have commonalities,[6] there are also divergences, with

2 David R. Boyd, *The Rights of Nature: A Legal Revolution that Could Save the World*, (EWC Press, 2017).
3 See: Craig M. Kauffman and Pamela L. Martin, *The Politics of the Rights of Nature: Strategies for Building a More Sustainable Future*, (MIT Press, 2021), p. 31.
4 See: Harriet Harden-Davies et al., 'Rights of Nature: Perspectives for Global Ocean Stewardship,' *Marine Policy* (2020) 122: 1–11.
5 Erin O'Donnell et al., 'Stop Burying the Lede: The Essential Role of Indigenous Law(s) in Creating Rights of Nature,' *Transnational Environmental Law* (2020) 9(3): 403–427.
   On the links between indigenous thought and Earth jurisprudence, see: Kirsten Anker, 'Ecological Jurisprudence and Indigenous Relational Ontologies,' in Kirsten Anker et al. (eds.), *From Environmental to Ecological Law*, (Routledge, 2021): 104–118.
6 See: Simone Bignall and Daryle Rigney, 'Indigeneity, Posthumanism and Nomad Thought: Transforming Colonial Ecologies,' in Rosi Braidotti and Simone Bignall (eds.), *Posthuman Ecologies*, (Rowman & Littlefield, 2019): 159–182; Simone Bignall er al., 'Three Ecosophies for the Anthropocene: Environmental Governance, Continental Posthumanism and Indigenous Expressivism,' *Deleuze Studies* (2016) 10(4): 455–478; Jerry Lee Rosiek et al., 'The New Materialisms and Indigenous Theories of Non-Human Agency: Making the Case for Respectful Anti-Colonial Engagement,' *Qualitative Inquiry* (2020) 26(3–4): 331–346; Karen Malone et al., 'Shimmering with Deborah Rose: Posthuman Theory-Making with Feminist Ecophilosophers and Social Ecologists,' *Australian Journal of Environmental Education* (2020) 36(2): 129–145; Kim Tallbear in José Esteban Muñoz et al., 'Theorizing Queer Inhumanisms,' *GLQ: A Journal of Lesbian and Gay Studies*, (2015) 21(2–3): 209–248.

Indigenous theories and practices being multiple and differing. It should be noted that not all Indigenous peoples support a RoN approach. Some Australian Nations have, for example, rejected the approach, calling instead for stronger Indigenous environmental governance through 'Caring for Country'.[7] While much work needs to be done to bring Indigenous and posthuman thought together, noting cross-overs and differences, such a project lies outside the scope of the present chapter, which focuses on why posthuman feminism should engage with the RoN movement and what RoN might also learn from such engagements.[8] However, this chapter does engage with Indigenous perspectives when examining the potentials and pitfalls of RoN as applied in international law, focusing on the problems in transferring Indigenous informed applications of RoN and connections between people and place to international law.

While RoN have yet to be transposed to international law, momentum is building. However, RoN provisions have been applied in different ways in different contexts. It is therefore key to understand the different ways RoN have been applied when seeking to think through their possible application to international law. This chapter begins by mapping existing RoN provisions and their similarities and differences. I then go on to analyse these different provisions and the possible application of RoN to international law from a posthuman feminist perspective, identifying an array of potentials and pitfalls. Here, I discuss the tensions present when bringing legal provisions intimately connected to place to the universal, questioning what that means in the context of global inequalities. I also consider whether a framework of rights can encompass the posthuman feminist

---

7 Virginia Marshall, 'Removing the Veil from the "Rights of Nature": The Dichotomy between First Nations Customary Rights and Environmental Legal Personhood,' *Australian Feminist Law Journal* (2019) 45(2): 233–248.

　　It is also important to note that 'Caring for Country' is a rich and complex concept. Deborah Bird Rose's work on the many meanings of Country exemplifies this well. See: Deborah Bird Rose, 'Country,' in *Nourishing Terrains: Australian Aboriginal Views of Landscape and Wilderness*, (Australian Heritage Commission, 1996), p. 6. Pelizzon and Kennedy also discuss the many meanings of Country. See; Alessandro Pelizzon and Jade Kennedy, 'Welcome to Country: Legal Meanings and Cultural Implications,' *Australian Indigenous Law Review* (2012) 16(2): 58–69, p. 65–66.

8 For more on Indigenous perspectives on RoN, see: Jacinta Ruru, 'Listening to Papatūānuku: A Call to Reform Water Law,' *Journal of the Royal Society of New Zealand/Aotearoa* (2019) 48(2–3): 215–224; Todd A. Eisenstadt and Karleen Jones West, *Who Speaks for Nature? Indigenous Movements, Public Opinion and the Petro-State in Ecuador*, (Oxford University Press, 2019); Iván Darió Vargas-Roncancio, 'Conjuring Sentiment Beings and Relations in Law,' in Kirsetn Anker et al. (eds.), *From Environmental to Ecological Law*, (Routledge, 2021): 119–134; Kirsti Luke in Hal Crimmel and Issac Goeckeritz, 'The Rights of Nature in New Zealand: Conversations with Kirsti Luke and Christopher Finlayson,' *ILSE: Interdisciplinary Studies in Literature and Environment* (2020) 27(3): 563–577.

　　On Indigenous legal theory and the environment (though not necessarily from a RoN perspective), see: Aaron Mills, 'Aki, Anishianaabek, kaye tahsh Crown,' *Indigenous Law Journal* (2010) 9(1): 107–213 (here, on concepts of relationships with land and natural resources); and Steve Hemming et al., 'Indigenous Nation Building for Environmental Futures: Murrundi Flows through Ngarrindjeri Country,' *Australasian Journal of Environmental Management* (2019) 26(3): 216–235 (here, on Indigenous Nation (re-)building and water management).

complexity of the agency of matter and of co-emergent relations between humans and nonhumans. Furthermore, I discuss tensions around the ability of the law and of humans to represent nature. The chapter thereby concludes with a discussion on the difficulties and risks in applying theory to practice and the tension between resistance and compliance. I then turn, in the final and concluding chapter of the book, to discuss the potentials and limitations of applying posthuman feminism to international law more broadly, focusing on the issues presented by the constraints of liberal legalism.

The Rights of Nature and Nature's Legal Personality

As I outlined in the previous chapter, while there are many wonderful theoretical pieces written on how to think environmental law otherwise, there is little work that applies these theories to practice. In parallel, over the past few decades, nature has begun to be recognised both as having rights and as being a legal person in certain contexts.[9] RoN laws are 'emerging in response to extreme pressure on ecosystems, and on communities that live and rely on them'.[10] The call for the environment to have legal rights and/or personhood, allowing it to bring claims in law on behalf of 'itself', could challenge the anthropocentrism of international environmental law.

While rights approaches and legal personality approaches are distinct, in this chapter, I use the terminology of RoN to refer to both, distinguishing accordingly where necessary. This is done not to conflate the two but rather as a way of bringing multiple perspectives and provisions into conversation with one another. There are many differences in RoN provisions, not only in terms of rights versus personality models but also within these two categories, with there being, for example, multiple definitions of rights. I therefore use the language of RoN to discuss many different approaches, this allowing me to analyse each of these approaches when thinking about their possible transposition to international law.

The RoN movement has much in common with posthuman feminist theories and critical environmental law scholarship. A RoN approach has the potential to provide a more integrated account of the environment, with RoN laws challenging 'the values of dominant political and economic systems, which view humans as

---

9 Post-anthropocentric conceptions of environmental governance have a long history. Much is left to be said about the relationship between these bodies of thought and RoN. See, e.g. Christopher D. Stone, *Should Trees Have Standing? Law, Morality and the Environment* (Oxford University Press, 3rd edn, 2010); Thomas Berry, *The Great Work: Our Way into the Future* (Bell Tower, 1999); Cormac Cullinan, *Wild Law: A Manifesto for Earth Jurisprudence* (Green Books, 2003); Arne Naess, *Ecology of Wisdom*, (Penguin, 2016); Peter Burdon, *Earth Jurisprudence: Private Property and the Environment* (Routledge, 2017); Nicole Rogers and Michelle Maloney (eds.), *Law as if Earth Really Mattered* (Routledge, 2017); Peter Burdon, *Exploring Wild Law: The Philosophy of Earth Jurisprudence*, (Wakefield Press, 2011).

10 Craig M. Kauffman and Linda Sheehan, 'The Rights of Nature: Guiding our Responsibilities through Standards,' in Stephen Turner et al. (eds.), *Environmental Rights: The Development of Standards*, (Cambridge University Press, 2019): 342–366, p. 343.

separate from nature, treat the elements of nature as objects for human exploitation, and prioritize exponential economic growth over ecosystem functioning'.[11] This aim aligns with posthuman feminist and queer theories and the call for a greater understanding of the connection between human and nonhuman entities. RoN laws may allow for nature to be legally seen as an actant, challenging human–nonhuman relations. RoN provisions, as applied to international environmental law, may therefore be one way to tackle some of the shortcomings of this body of law, including its anthropocentrism. However, the effectiveness of RoN in achieving these objectives will depend on how nature and its rights are defined.

RoN have been recognised in a variety of domestic contexts in multiple different ways[12] but have yet to be implemented at the international level.[13] The closest international law has come to recognising RoN was in the negotiations on the zero draft of the Post-2020 Global Biodiversity Framework. While the final Post-2020 Global Biodiversity Framework includes a call to focus on the 'harmony with nature',[14] this referring to the UN Harmony with Nature initiative led by Bolivia, the original zero draft, released in August 2020, included more specific language on RoN, including language around the need to '[c]onsider and recognize, where appropriate, the rights of nature' alongside discussions of the need to focus on the rights of 'Mother Earth'.[15] This language, if included, would have made the framework the first international treaty to recognise RoN. However, this language was subsequently removed.[16]

Some states have, however, begun to push for the international recognition of RoN. In 2009, the Bolivian President called on the UN General Assembly (UNGA) to adopt a Universal Declaration of the Rights of Mother Earth (UDRME).[17] In 2010, Bolivia hosted the World People's Conference on Climate Change and the Rights of Mother Earth where around 35,000 people from over 140 countries[18] wrote the citizens' UDRME.[19] The text asserts the rights of nature, which includes the role of humans and pays particular attention to the multiple power dynamics that structure the climate change debate, calling for the 'decolonization

---

11 Ibid., p. 356.

12 Boyd, above note 2.

13 For an overview and analysis of how RoN provisions have emerged, see: Kauffman and Martin, above note 3.

14 Convention on Biological Diversity, Open Ended Working Group on the Post-2020 Global Biodiversity Framework, Second Meeting, 6 January 2020, CBD/WG2020/2/3.

15 Convention on Biological Diversity, Update of the Zero Draft of the Post-2020 Global Biodiversity Framework, 17 August 2020, CBD/POST2020/PREP/2/1.

16 Convention on Biological Diversity, Open Ended Working Group on the Post-2020 Global Biodiversity Framework, 29 March 2020, CBD/WG2020/3/L.2.

17 Evo Morales, 'Address by H.E. Mr. Evo Morales Ayma, the President of the Plurinational State of Bolivia,' 64th Session of the General Assembly of the United Nations, 2009.

18 Stats on delegates from: Kauffman and Sheehan, above note 10, p. 347.

19 World People's Conference on Climate Change and the Rights of Mother Earth, April 22 2010, Bolivia, People's Agreement.

of the atmosphere' while noting the links between the ways that the environment is exploited and capitalist and patriarchal structures.[20]

At the UN level, annual intergovernmental negotiations have been held since 2009 on constructing a non-anthropocentric understanding of sustainable development. Several UN General Assembly Resolutions and UN Secretary General Reports have now been produced that call for the recognition of RoN.[21] A series of UNGA Interactive Dialogues have also been held on Harmony with Nature.[22] In 2015, the UNGA called for the creation of an expert report on 'Earth Jurisprudence', establishing a global network of experts.[23] The Expert Report on Earth Jurisprudence that followed was released in 2016.[24] The Report recognises the 'fundamental legal rights of ecosystems and species to exist, thrive and regenerate'.[25] In 2017, the UNGA Dialogue focused on applying Earth Jurisprudence to the Sustainable Development goals.[26]

In terms of setting international standards, the jurisprudence of the citizen-led International Tribunal for the Rights of Nature, which applies the UDRME to real cases, is also of interest.[27] The Tribunal was established by the Global Alliance for the Rights of Nature (GARN) in 2014. The aim is to create a space where people can 'speak on behalf of nature'.[28] The Tribunal has held five hearings, while Regional Chambers of the Tribunal have conducted further hearings. Although peoples' tribunals have played a significant role in international law in the past, these Tribunals follow quite a different model in that, rather than applying existing international law, they apply a new model, that is RoN, *to* international law. While this jurisprudence is of interest, as a civil society initiative, it is not binding.

One trend that can be observed from the above overview of the limited international legal engagement with RoN is the repeated focus on the rights of Mother Earth. The focus on this concept comes, in part, from Bolivia's attempt to get RoN on the global agenda, with Pachamama (Mother Earth) being a central component in Indigenous knowledges of peoples of the Andes. While Mother Earth means many different things to many different people, the focus on Mother Earth as applied globally, is concerning. Mother Earth, in a western context, is often used to promote the essentialising idea that women are more connected to nature than men – a notion

20 Ibid. For a wider history of the UDRME, see: Paola Villavicencio and Louis J. Kotzé, 'Living in Harmony with Nature? A Critical Appraisal of the Rights of Mother Earth in Bolivia,' *Transnational Environmental Law* (2018) 7(3): 397–424.
21 For a full list of these, see; UN Harmony with Nature, UN Documents on Harmony with Nature, http://harmonywithnatureun.org/unDocs (last accessed 11 July 2022).
22 See; UN Harmony with Nature, Interactive Dialogues of the General Assembly, www.harmonywithnatureun.org/dialogues (last accessed 11 July 2022).
23 United Nations, UNGA Res A/RES/70/208 (2015), 3–4.
24 United Nations, UNGA Res A/71/266 (2016).
25 Ibid., p. 7.
26 UNGA, Report of the Secretary-General on UN Harmony with Nature, 19 July 2017, A/72/175.
27 Rights of Nature Tribunal, https://www.rightsofnaturetribunal.org (last accessed 11 July 2022).
28 Rights of Nature Tribunal, About Us, https://www.rightsofnaturetribunal.org/about-us (last accessed 11 July 2022).

that I critiqued in the previous chapter. While the concept of Mother Earth has multiple meanings, there is a need to be wary of the transposition of this concept to international law. As Mihnea Tănăsescu argues, the adoption of gendered language would be a 'blow to indigenous conceptions, which are much more multidimensional and variegated'.[29] Transposing Mother Earth to the Eurocentric framework of international law risks losing those multidimensional aspects, transforming the concept into an essentialising, one dimensional and watered-down version of the original.

Despite the above developments, RoN have yet to be seriously considered within international law. To understand what RoN could include and exclude as applied to international law, there is a need to analyse their application in domestic law. In the following paragraphs, I thereby outline some of the ways RoN have been designed and applied, analysing these models from a posthuman feminist perspective.

Indigenous peoples have been central in obtaining RoN in various contexts. For example, Indigenous peoples played a key role in the recognition of RoN in Ecuador's 2008 Constitution.[30] The Constitution 'celebrates' nature, with nature being defined as *Pachamama*, referring to the sacred deity revered by Indigenous peoples of the Andes.[31] In Aotearoa/New Zealand, Indigenous peoples have also played a vital role in the recognition of the legal personality of nature. Here, legal personality has been recognised through two agreements which came about following negotiation processes with local Māori activists, (the Whanganui *Iwi* in relation to the Whanganui River or Te Awa Tupua and the Tūhoe *Iwi* in relation to the Te Urewera Forest).[32] While this instance of recognition is often seen as part of the wider RoN movement, rights have not actually been recognised in Aotearoa/New Zealand. Rather, a different model was adopted based on legal personality, one that was seen to better fit the worldview of the people involved. Therefore, while a broad approach is often taken in the wider RoN movement to bring cases such as Aotearoa/New Zealand and Ecuador together under the same umbrella, this ignores real differences between the two places. This, in turn, conflates the very different bodies of knowledge and political strategies that informed each instance of recognition.

However, Indigenous people have not been involved in all instances of RoN recognition. While RoN started off very much as an Indigenous-led movement, increasingly, RoN are being recognised in other places too. For example, Indigenous groups are not involved in the proposed 'right of nature' bill in the Philippines,[33] nor

---

29 Mihnea Tănăsescu, *Understanding the Rights of Nature: A Critical Introduction*, (Transcript Publishing, 2022), p. 116.
30 See: Eisenstadt and Jones West, above note 8.
31 Republic of Ecuador, Constitution of 2008, trans. Georgetown University, Preamble, https://pdba.georgetown.edu/Constitutions/Ecuador/english08.html (last accessed 11 July 2022).
32 Te Awa Tupua (Whanganui River Claims Settlement) Act 2017 Aotearoa/(New Zealand); Te Urewera Act 2014 (Aotearoa/New Zealand).
33 L. Chavez, Philippine Bill Seeks to Grant Nature the Same Legal Rights as Humans, Mongaby, 2019, https://news.mongabay.com/2019/08/philippine-bill-seeks-to-grant-nature-the-same-legal-rights-as-humans/#:~:text=A%20coalition%20in%20the%20Philippines,confer%20legal%20personhood%20on%20nature.&text=The%20bill%20is%20part%20of,their%20protection%20amid%20intensifying%20threats (last accessed 11 July 2022).

in the recognition of RoN in India (subsequently stayed by the Supreme Court).[34] It is clear, however, that Indigenous legalities have been central in the recasting of legal concepts that has led to the emergence of the recognition of RoN.[35]

In 2008, Ecuador became the first country to recognise RoN constitutionally. Ecuador's Constitution outlines nature rights as being inherent to the Earth itself, a legal recognition and status that applies nationally (this being the same model Chile proposed in 2022 to be adopted in its new Constitution, the text of the Constitution being rejected by the Chilean people later the same year).[36] This broad national coverage differs from provisions in other countries, which focus on specific ecosystems.[37] For example, in Aotearoa/New Zealand, the Whanganui River (Te Awa Tupua) and the Te Urewera Forest have had their legal personality recognised.[38] Here, the relevant laws define the boundaries of the two ecosystems and therefore legal personality is recognised only in relation to these two specific areas — not nationwide. Approaches that focus on specific ecosystems as opposed to applying RoN nationally are more common in application of RoN in domestic law, with the High Court of Uttarakhand in India, for example, originally recognising the legal personhood of Ganges and Yamuna Rivers alone,[39] and with the Supreme Court of Bangladesh having upheld the rights of all rivers in Bangladesh in 2020.[40]

From a posthuman feminist perspective, recognition of RoN within a bounded area alone runs the risk of perpetuating the fragmentation of environments (depending on the construction of 'an area'). The development of posthuman feminist theory-informed international RoN standards would require an entanglement-responsive approach that recognises the juridical implications of distributed agency and interconnection. Seeing nature as agentic, and accounting for the intimate connections between humans and 'environments' would address some of the core problems outlined in Chapter 1 concerning international environmental law, namely its anthropocentric underpinnings and its fragmented nature. Arguably, this kind of agency and connection must be recognised globally. Recognising RoN within a bounded area alone denies such interconnections beyond those boundaries. At the same time, as I will discuss in the next section, there are various issues that arise when one takes RoN, an initially Indigenous instigated movement, out of its connection to place.

---

34 First recognised by the High Court of Uttarakhand in: *Mohd. Salim v. State of Uttarakhand and Others* (Writ Petition (PIL) No. 126 of 2014, (March 20, 2017) with the decision being stayed by the Supreme Court of India later that year. See: *The State of Uttarakhand and Orgs v Mohd. Salim & Ors.*, Supreme Court of India, Petition for Special Leave to Appeal No. 016879/2017.

35 See: O'Donnell et al., above note 5.

36 See: Earth Law Center, Seeking Rights of Nature in Chile's Constitution, https://www.earth-lawcenter.org/chile (last accessed 11 July 2022).

37 Kauffman and Sheehan, above note 10, p. 344.

38 Te Awa Tupua Act, above note 32.

39 See above note 34.

40 Appellate Division of the Supreme Court of Bangladesh, upholding the 2019 decision of the High Court (in Writ Petition No. 13989) 2020.

RoN provisions differ in their content, but they do share at least one key commonality: the linking of the health and well-being of the environment to that of the people who live there such that the provisions allow people to bring legal claims on behalf of nature. In coming to the Te Awa Tupua Agreement, for example, the Whanganui *Iwi* argued that they are connected to the environment they live in and that the river is alive, an ancestor. The Te Awa Tupua Act recognises the river as a legal person with 'all the rights, powers, duties and liabilities of a legal person'.[41] To uphold the river's interests, a guardian body (*Tu Pou Tupua*) must be appointed and is authorised to speak on behalf of the river.[42] The guardian body is made up of one *Iwi* representative and one Crown representative. The river and the people are deemed to be inseparable,[43] meaning that harming the river is, by law, harming the *Iwi*. Similarly, the Te Urewera Act recognises Māori ties to the forest and the Māori view that the forest is a living being. This Act also created a board to serve as the guardian of the forest's interests, recognising the legal personality of Te Urewera.[44]

Similarly, in Ecuador, the Constitution states that humans are an inherent part of nature, linking RoN to the right to a healthy environment.[45] Furthermore, Article 71 of the Constitution states that all 'persons, communities, peoples and nations can call upon public authorities to enforce the rights of nature'.[46] In the US, where over 40 state-based (regional) level RoN laws have been adopted,[47] RoN provisions link local communities to nature. RoN in the US therefore tend to be linked to community rights, with nature being framed as being integral to human welfare.[48]

Bolivia adopted a similar model. While Bolivia's Constitution does not recognise the rights of nature per se, it focuses instead on an 'environmental right' that must be granted to 'individuals and collectives of present and future generations, as well as to other living things'.[49] While this provision differs from the wording in the

---

41 Te Awa Tupua Act, above note 32.
42 Ibid.
43 Ibid., Article 69(2).
44 For a further discussion of this context see: Kauffman and Sheehan, above note 10, p. 354–345.
　　For more both on this specific case and on the rights of rivers, see; Erin O'Donnell, *Legal Rights for Rivers: Competition, Collaboration and Water Governance*, (Routledge, 2020). See also: Boyd, above note 2, p.131–157.
45 Republic of Ecuador, above note 31.
46 Ibid., Article 71.
47 By mid-2017, at least 43 US local governments had adopted some form of RoN ordinances. Craig Kauffman and Pamela Martin compiled data on these cases. See footnote 9 in Kauffman and Sheehan, above note 10.
48 See, for example: City of Pittsburgh, Code of Ordinances, Title 6, art 1, ch 618, 'Marcellus Shale Natural Gas Drilling Ordinance' (2010), https://library.municode.com/pa/pittsburgh/codes/code_of_ordinances?nodeId=COOR_TITSIXCO_ARTIRERIAC_CH618MASHNAGADR (last accessed 11 July 2022).
　　For more on this, see: Kauffman and Sheehan, Ibid., p. 346–347.
49 Constitution of the Plurinational State of Bolivia, 2009, Article 33.

Ecuadorian Constitution (as discussed in more detail below), it importantly still offers humans the possibility of bringing legal claims on behalf of 'living things'.[50]

The focus on community or people's rights within RoN and on humans bringing claims on behalf of nature is, in the end, a human-centred approach. It might be assumed, therefore, that a posthuman feminist approach would necessarily read this human focus as anthropocentric. However, posthuman feminist theory suggests, not the displacement of culture for or by nature but, rather, the need to focus on the nature-culture continuum.[51] By teasing out the entanglements between humans, nonhumans, and 'the environment', a more reciprocal dynamic can be made central for the law. There will be a need to balance these sometimes competing interests. However, this will need to be done from a starting point that does not, *ab initio*, assume them to exist in atomistic competition or to pre-exist such enquiry as privileged agentic subject versus objectified matter.

RoN provisions have been applied through different means, in different contexts. One clear division discernible, as noted above, is the difference between models that recognise the rights of nature (as in Ecuador) and provisions that recognise nature's legal personality. In Aotearoa/New Zealand a legal personality model has been used. This is because the *Iwi* do not emphasise the concept of rights, for them nature is not property but rather a living, 'spiritual' entity as well as a 'physical entity',[52] an ancestor.[53] Accordingly, the concept of guardianship was promoted. The preference for the guardianship approach, in part, explains the difference between provisions in Aotearoa/New Zealand and, say, Ecuador.[54] The different models result in different procedures. Unlike Ecuador's RoN laws, Aotearoa/New Zealand's laws do not award inherent rights. Rather, legal personality is instilled in the river and forest. This grants the river and the forest (through their guardians) procedural access rights in Aotearoa/New Zealand's legal system but does not give them special rights per se. The natural systems therefore have the mediated right to petition the court or to receive reparations, for example, but they do not have the right to be protected in and of themselves.[55]

The differences in the way RoN provisions have been designed also impacts what happens when RoN clash with other rights. For example, while the Bolivian Constitution provides for environmental rights that can be claimed by all, this sits

---

50 Ibid., Article 34. For a wider discussion of the context of Bolivia, see: Villavicencio and Kotzé, above note 20.

51 Donna Haraway, 'A Cyborg Manifesto: Science, Technology, and Socialist-Feminism in the Late Twentieth Century,' in *Simians, Cyborgs and Women: The Reinvention of Nature* (Free Association Books,1991): 149–181, p. 151; Cecilia Åsberg, 'Feminist Posthumanities in the Anthropocene: Forays into the Postnatural,' *Journal of Posthuman Studies* (2017) 1(2): 185–204.

52 Te Awa Tupua Act, above note 32, Article 13(a).

53 Craig M. Kauffman, 'Managing People for the Benefit of the Land: Practicing Earth Jurisprudence in Te Urewera, New Zealand/Aotearoa,' *ILSE: Interdisciplinary Studies in Literature and Environment* (2020) 27(1): 578–595.

54 See: Craig M. Kauffman and Pamela L. Martin, 'Constructing Rights of Nature Norms in the US, Ecuador, and New Zealand/Aotearoa,' *Global Environmental Politics*, (2018) 18(4): 43–62, p. 57.

55 See: Kauffman and Sheehan, above note 10, p. 346.

in contrast to another provision in a different section of the Constitution which sets out the 'essential purposes and functions of the State', one of these functions being:

> To promote and guarantee the responsible and planned use of natural resources, and to stimulate their industrialization through the development and strengthening of the productive base in its different dimensions and levels, as well as to preserve the environment for the welfare of present and future generations.[56]

The tension between economic development and the protection of nature is by no means an easy tension to resolve. However, as Paola Villavicencio and Louis J. Kotzé highlight, the way the Constitution is drafted creates a system whereby:

> instead of pursuing ecologically sensitive ways to go about this, the legal framework actively enables the state to promote the industrialization of natural resources as 'a national priority'. Indeed, the exploitation of natural resources is explicitly defined as one of the purposes and functions of the state.[57]

Ecuador, being one of the first states to recognise RoN, has some of the most developed jurisprudence in this area. However, as in Bolivia, the recognition of RoN in Ecuador has in practice been highly contested and environmental damage remains rampant, particularly in relation to industrial activity and oil extraction.[58] Many provisions have yet to be adequately defined and applied.

Under the Constitution of Ecuador, nature has 'the right to integral respect for its existence and for the maintenance and regeneration of its life cycles, structures, functions and evolutionary processes'.[59] In addition, it is stated that '[n]ature has the right to be restored' and that the state 'shall apply preventative and restrictive measures on activities that might lead to the extinction of species, the destruction of ecosystems and the permanent alteration of natural cycles'.[60] Nature rights are not, however, absolutely protected. The Constitution situates sustainable development as core, seeking to balance environmental needs against development needs.[61] Central, however, is Article 395.4, which states that, 'In the event of doubt about the scope of legal provisions for environmental issues, it is the most favourable interpretation of their effective force for the protection of nature that shall prevail'.[62] This, however, is not always the outcome, and RoN laws have, since 2008, developed within a highly politicised context.[63]

---

56 Constitution of the Plurinational State of Bolivia, above note 49, Article 9(6).
57 Villavicencio and Kotzé, above note 20, p. 417. Referencing the Constitution (about note 49) at Articles 9.6, 316.6, and 355.
58 For more on the tension between the recognition of RoN and mineral mining in Ecuador, see: Eisenstadt and Jones West, above note 8. On Bolivia, where oil and gas exploration has also been extended despite RoN provisions, see: Villavicencio and Kotzé, above note 20, p. 418.
59 Republic of Ecuador, above note 31, Article 71.
60 Ibid., Articles 72 and 73.
61 See, for example, Ibid., Article 395. See also: Article 408.
62 Ibid., Article 395.4.
63 Kauffman and Sheehan, above note 10, p. 349.

Nevertheless, despite contestation, there are signs of progress. Several cases have established a standard that killing any animal that is part of an endangered species constitutes a RoN violation.[64] Other judgements have focused on government construction projects, concluding that such projects cannot impede the ability of ecosystems or species to regenerate.[65] The disruption of migration and breeding patterns has also been ruled as violating RoN[66] and the government has been ordered to control illegal mining.[67] RoN have furthermore been enforced in other contexts, for example, in 2011, following the government's removal of several shrimp companies from ecological reserves, one company sought to sue the government, arguing that their removal infringed their economic interests and their property rights and the right to work.[68] In 2015, the Constitutional Court ruled on this case, declaring that because natural rights are transversal, they impact on all other rights, including property rights. The Court stated that all actions of the state and individuals must be in accordance with the rights of nature,[69] proclaiming that this position reflects 'a biocentric vision that prioritizes nature in contrast to the classic anthropocentric conception in which the human being is the centre and measure of all things, and where nature was considered a mere provider of resources'.[70] The courts in Ecuador have therefore sought to use RoN to challenge anthropocentrism with the transversal application of RoN and their ability to challenge other rights. While such approaches and standards could provide key normative inspirations when setting global RoN standards, it is salutary that the setting of standards in Ecuador took considerable effort, especially when it came to challenging economic interests,[71] and that this struggle is still very much ongoing.[72]

---

64 See, for example: Judgment No. 09171-2015-0004, Ninth Court of Criminal Guarantees, Guayas Province, Republic of Ecuador (23 April 2015) 55–59. See also: Ibid., p. 350. And: Judgment No. 2003-2014 – C.T., National Court of Justice, Specialized Chamber of Criminal, Military Criminal, Criminal Police and Transit Cases, Republic of Ecuador (7 September 2014).

65 Judgment No. 11121-2011-0010, Provincial Court of Justice, Loja Province, Republic of Ecuador (30 March 2011).

66 Judgment No. 269 – 2012, Civil and Mercantile Court, Galápagos Province, Republic of Ecuador (28 June 2012).

67 Constitutional Protective Action No. 0016-2011, Twenty-Second Criminal Court, Pichincha Province, Republic of Ecuador (20 May 2011).

68 Judgment No. 166-15-SEP-CC, Case No. 0507-12-EP, Constitutional Court of Ecuador, Republic of Ecuador (20 May 2015) 2.

69 Ibid., 12.

70 Ibid., 10 – trans. from Kauffman and Sheehan, above note 10, p. 353.

71 For more on this see: Kauffman and Sheehan, Ibid., p. 357.

72 For more on this evolving history and the various challenges faced in Ecuador, see: Craig M. Kauffman and Pamela L. Martin, *The Politics of Rights of Nature: Strategies for Building a More Sustainable Future*, (MIT Press, 2021). RoN laws in Ecuador are still developing. For example, in 2014, RoN were codified into a new Penal Code and Ecuador's 2018 Environmental Code also included RoN provisions. While these are promising steps, unfortunately both Codes remain vague at the level of application. See: Republic of Ecuador, Penal Code, Organic Law, 2014; Republic of Ecuador, Environmental Code, 2018. With thanks to Craig Kauffman for his insights on the Penal and Environmental Code in Ecuador. See also: Kauffman and Sheehan, Ibid., p. 353–354. For a more detailed analysis of the various RoN cases brought through the Ecuadorian court system, see: Kauffman and Martin, Ibid., p. 79–116.

In Aotearoa/New Zealand, the Te Awa Tupua Act does not derogate from existing private rights in the Whanganui River.[73] The Act states that any actor, public or private, must 'have particular regard to' the interests of the river[74] and must recognise the values of the Te Awa Tupua, which include treating the river as a living entity.[75] As Craig M Kauffman and Linda Sheehan note, through giving legal personhood to nature (but not giving nature rights per se), the Aotearoa/ New Zealand system has been set up so that 'decisions on how to balance the rights of ecosystems against the rights of other legal persons (e.g. individuals and corporations) in a given situation will need to be made'.[76] As of writing, these provisions have yet to be tested through the courts. This is not to suggest, however, that a rights-based approach is preferable. After all, a legal personality model was adopted in Aotearoa/New Zealand because it was seen as a better approximation of Māori understandings of the link between people and place, as transposed into the settler-colonial legal system of Aotearoa/New Zealand. Currently, the hierarchy of rights between these multiple competing interests is unclear. Standards will probably develop over time, much as in Ecuador. These Acts, therefore, while being key for Māori rights, are carefully constructed to ensure that they are framed around the neo/liberal legal order. The Acts allow for recognition through a legal personhood framework, thereby drawing on the existing options with New Zealand's settler-colonial legal framework, avoiding the outright prioritisation of RoN over, for example, corporate rights to exploit nature.[77] It remains to be seen how a court would rule in the instance of a clash between property rights and nature rights.

A key emerging RoN standard in the US that might prove central when seeking to set out posthuman feminist theory informed international RoN standards is the right of nature to flourish.[78] Kauffman and Sheehan argue that:

> the right to flourish switches the emphasis from preventing permanent damage to ensuring some level of well-being for an ecosystem. This would require a more restrictive definition of which human impacts are acceptable, and thus stricter standards based on measurements of the well-being of ecosystems.[79]

---

73 The situation of the forest is a little different as it was formerly a national park. For more on this see: Kauffman and Martin, above note 54, p. 52.

74 Te Awa Tupua Act, above note 32, Article 15(3).

75 Ibid., Article 13.

76 Kauffman and Sheehan, above note 10, p. 354.

77 Emily Jones and Dianne Otto, Thinking through Anthropocentrism in International Law: Queer Theory, Posthuman Feminism and the Postcolonial, LSE Women, Peace and Security blog (January 2020).

78 Kauffman and Sheehan, above note 10, p. 347. See, for example: Ordinance of the City Council of Santa Monica Establishing Sustainability Rights, 12 March 2012, https://www.smgov.net/ departments/council/agendas/2013/20130312/s2013031207-C-1.htm#:~:text=(a)%20All%20 residents%20of%20Santa,sustainable%20climate%20that%20supports%20thriving> (last accessed 11 July 2022).

79 Kauffman and Sheehan, above note 10, p. 347.

The right to flourish is somewhat similar to the 'right to restoration' provided for in Bolivia's 2010 Law of the Rights of Mother Earth (a statutory law which built on Bolivia's Constitution).[80] However, arguably flourishing goes well beyond restoration. The right to flourish could be a step towards recognising nature's full agency in a way that is more akin to posthuman feminist understandings of the agency of matter. Such a right would contrast with the more limited understanding of nature's legally defined rights, which does not inherently allow for a wider understanding of the agency of matter itself.

It is clear from this review that RoN challenge powerful political and economic interests, making the question of their implementation highly politicised. The recognition of RoN globally could be one way of potentially dismantling the subject/object dichotomy at the heart of international environmental law. RoN could also provide a way to challenge the more top-down, state-led approach taken within international environmental law, allowing multiple stakeholders to have a greater say in environmental protection. While there is clearly growing international interest in RoN, the question of standards and implementation remains a lively field of contestation. However, domestic examples of application, such as the ones outlined above, could, and arguably do, suggest standards that could be considered as models for a way forward.

Potentials and Risks

There are clearly many points of resonance between RoN and posthuman feminist theory. Both seek to recognise the agency of nature-matter. Both therefore call into question the subject/object binary that underpins western thought, challenging human exceptionalism. However, while links between RoN and posthuman theory have been suggested,[81] from a legal perspective, it is not a given that a RoN approach will inherently produce a posthuman feminist approach to international environmental law. These projects, while related, are distinct and posthuman feminist theory and RoN have not yet extensively been brought into mutual conversation.[82] In the next section, I will analyse the potentials and risks of a posthuman feminist theory informed RoN approach, focusing on the issues that arise in relation to universalism and global inequalities, the difficulty in but the need to redefine

---

80 Article 7, Law 071 of the Rights of Mother Earth, 21 Dec. 2010; an English version of the law can be found at: http://181.224.152.72/~embajad5/wp-content/uploads/2017/12/rights-of-mother-earth.pdf.

81 See, for example, artist Ursula Biemann and architect Paulo Tavares' fantastic project on 'Forest Law.' See: Ursula Biemann and Paulo Tavares: BAK (2015) *Frieze*, Issue 175, https://www.frieze.com/article/ursula-biemann-paulo-tavares (last accessed 3 October 2022). Similarly, Jessie Hohmann, while not discussing RoN, does note the potential for new materialism to push rights beyond the more than human. See: Jessie Hohmann, 'Diffuse Subjects and Dispersed Power: New Materialist Insights and Cautionary Lessons for International Law,' *Leiden Journal of International Law* (2021) 34: 585–606.

82 Though I have begun to undertake this work. See: Emily Jones 'Posthuman International Law and the Rights of Nature,' *Journal of Human Rights and the Environment* (2021) 12(0): 76–101.

rights in international law, issues of representation and the impossibility of exiting liberal legalism.

Universalism, Global Inequalities and the Meaning of Rights

Since sovereign will[83] and the lack of a universal system for environmental protection are two of the core challenges faced in international environmental law, it is tempting to think that seeking to create a universal RoN frame for environmental protection is required. After all, for RoN to have a global impact, they need to be applied globally and not just to specific areas, for example, a river. However, there are tremendous problems with the concept of universalism that could haunt any application of RoN. Feminist and postcolonial theorists have long problematised international law's claim to be universal (and its purported neutrality), noting how this universalism both disguises and reproduces the gendered and racialised power hierarchies upheld by the law.[84] As outlined in Chapter 1, many international legal principles were created at a time when much of the world was colonised and when only European states had a say on what international law was.[85] Thinking specifically about Indigenous peoples, although they have long interacted between peoples and nations, often 'going beyond the nation-state in order to advance their position and pursue justice',[86] they were and often still are excluded from shaping, making and participating in international law.[87]

International environmental law has, to some extent, already sought to tackle the problems posed by the structural injustices associated with universalism, most notably when seeking to balance environmental protection with the economic needs of different actors with varying levels of economic power.[88] Many provisions have been built into international environmental law that seek to manage this tension. For example, the concept of common but differentiated responsibility underpins many environmental law treaties, seeking to ensure that the economic

---

83 For example, Aguila and Viñuales argue that State sovereignty and the lack of State will to push forward on environmental issues in a more radical way is a central reason why the provisions in the Global Pact for the Environment will probably not go beyond existing provisions in international environmental law. See: Yann Aguila and Jorge E. Viñuales, 'A Global Pact for the Environment: Conceptual foundations' *Review of European, Comparative and International Environmental Law* (2019) 28(1): 3–12, p. 8.

84 See: Antony Anghie, *Imperialism, Sovereignty and the Making of International Law* (Cambridge University Press, 2012); Hilary Charlesworth and Christine Chinkin, *The Boundaries of International Law: A Feminist Analysis* (Manchester University Press, 2000).

85 Antony Anghie, 'Finding the Peripheries: Sovereignty and Colonialism in Nineteenth-Century International Law,' *Harvard International Law Journal* (1999) 40(1): 1–71.

86 Mark McMillan and Sophie Rigney, 'The Place of the First Peoples in the International Sphere: A Logical Starting Point for the Demand for Justice by Indigenous Peoples,' *Melbourne University Law Review* (2016) 39(3) 981–1002, p. 992.

87 S. James Anaya, *Indigenous Peoples in International Law* (Oxford University Press, 2nd edn, 2000); Ibid., p. 994–997.

88 See: Shawkat Alam et al. (eds.), *International Environmental Law and the Global South* (Cambridge University Press, 2015).

development needs of some states are balanced against the wealth of others when deciding differing responsibilities to address climate change. The principle of sustainable development, likewise, and as discussed in Chapter 1, seeks to balance the supposed need to exploit natural resources in a manner that is sustainable and in which economic objectives are taken into consideration to ensure that states, and especially states with stronger development needs, can continue to draw on their natural resources.[89] However, as I concluded in Chapter 1, such approaches ultimately allow environmental exploitation to continue,[90] with sustainable development being, ultimately, an oxymoron.[91]

As I argued in Chapter 3, drawing on feminist approaches to international law and the resistance and compliance conundrum, there are risks posed by seeking to challenge the liberal framework of the law from within. By calling upon legal constructs so intimately and ultimately depending upon an anthropocentric, individualistic account of the legal subject,[92] by trying to work within the system, even when seeking to include a new subject (such as nature), one risks merely extending the existing paradigm without challenging it sufficiently. Feminist approaches to international law provide a good example here. As discussed in Chapter 3, while feminist approaches have been successful in adding women's concerns to existing international legal frames, such as within the Women, Peace and Security agenda, the transformative elements of feminist approaches that seek to challenge the gendered foundations of the international legal system have been somewhat left behind in the focus on the inclusion of women.[93] In other words, by calling for inclusion without a wider paradigm shift, there is a risk, as Braidotti argues (in relation to the inclusion of animals as subjects), that '[h]umanism is actually being reinstated uncritically under the aegis of species [and materialist] egalitarianism'.[94]

---

89 Sustainable development' is made up of several components, including the general need to exploit resources in a manner which is 'sustainable,' the need to preserve resources for future generations, the equitable use of resources between states and the need to consider economic and development objectivities. Sustainable development concretised recently through its use in the 2015 Paris Agreement to the UN Framework Convention on Climate Change (UNFCCC) and the 2017 Resolution of the UN General Assembly, 'Our Ocean, Our Future: Call to Action.' See: United Nations, UNGA Res A/Res/71/312 (2017). See also: Ruth Gordon, 'Unsustainable Development' in Shawkat Alam et al. (eds.), *International Environmental Law and the Global South* (Cambridge University Press, 2015): 50–73.

90 On the politics of international environmental law from a global north/south perspective, calling for a more nuanced understanding of global north/south relations in international environmental law (IEL), see: Usha Natarajan and Kishan Khoday, 'Locating Nature: Making and Unmaking International Law,' *Leiden Journal of International Law* (2014) 27(3): 573–593.

91 Ibid., p. 589.

92 On the legal subject, see: Ngaire Naffine, 'Women and the Cast of Legal Persons,' in Jackie Jones et al., (eds.), *Gender, Sexualities and Law*, (Routledge, 2011): 15–25; Anna Grear, "Sexing the Matrix': Embodiment, Disembodiment and the Law – towards the Re-Gendering of Legal Rationality,' in Jackie Jones et al., (eds.), *Gender, Sexualities and Law*, (Routledge, 2011): 39–52.

93 Hilary Charlesworth, Gina Heathcote and Emily Jones, 'Feminist Scholarship on International Law in the 1990s and Today: An Inter-Generational Conversation,' *Feminist Legal Studies* (2019) 27: 79–93.

94 Rosi Braidotti, *The Posthuman*, (Polity Press, 2013), p. 78–79.

Such a concern is particularly relevant when thinking about RoN and the concept of rights. Rights have been framed in international law in a particular way. International human rights law defines which rights an individual can claim. Understandings of rights beyond these frames cannot be claimed through this body of law.[95] In addition, human rights law primarily focuses on the individual subject and its claim to egalitarianism. This focus silences the broader collective structures of oppression in which rights violations occur, including patriarchy, colonialism and capitalism.[96] While there have been attempts to disrupt this model of rights bearing, with the Inter-American human rights system leading the way in this regard,[97] human rights continue to uphold a particular vision of freedom that is liberal, gendered and Eurocentric.[98]

A similar argument is made in queer scholarship on the nonhuman, as I outlined in Chapter 4. For example, Dana Luciano and Mel Y. Chen argue that there is little gain to be found for queer people in seeking to be included in the category of so-called 'humanity', which has always been exclusionary and based around the heterosexual, white, middle-class, cis male subject. They thereby argue that queer studies should focus instead on nonhuman configurations as a site of disruption to the 'human' subject.[99] This body of thought argues that any attempt to better account for the nonhuman must also retain a focus on the status of dehumanised humans. This focus provides a necessary corrective to theories and practices that pose equality as the only possible form of recognition of nonhuman entities. Queer posthuman feminist theories of the nonhuman do much more than just displace the human, rather, they explore the multiple new forms of interconnection between and across the inhuman or nonhuman categories, in a manner that avoids dialectical oppositions. This can result in a plurality of political positions, creating a politics of '*being-with*'.[100] Given these insights, rather than focusing solely on the nonhuman, or on the rights of nature, there is a need for the law to note the interconnections between humans and nonhumans. This extra layer of complexity can result in highlighting points of solidarity between the nonhuman and the less/more/other/-than-human, without conflating their differences of location and power.

In short, there is a risk that calling for nature to be recognised as a subject within the current legal system, perhaps particularly at the international level, will reinforce or legitimise the very same system that makes such resort necessary. International law, including international environmental law but also international human rights

---

95 Ratna Kapur, *Gender, Alterity and Human Rights: Freedom in a Fishbowl*, (Edward Elgar, 2018).

96 Emily Jones, 'Gender and Reparations: Seeking Transformative Justice,' in Carla Ferstman and Mariana Goetz (eds.), *Reparations for Victims of Genocide, War Crimes and Crimes Against Humanity: Systems in Place and Systems in the Making*, (Brill, 2020): 86-118.

97 Ibid.

98 Kapur, above note 95.

99 Dana Luciano and Mel Y. Chen, 'Has the Queer ever been Human?,' *GLQ: A Journal of Lesbian and Gay Studies* (2015) 21 (203): 183-207, p. 184.

100 José Esteban Muñoz in José Esteban Muñoz et al., 'Theorizing Queer Inhumanisms,' *GLQ: A Journal of Lesbian and Gay Studies*, (2015) 21(2–3): 209–248, p. 210 – emphasis in the original.

law, which most powerfully determines how rights are currently understood at the international level, is based on anthropocentric and exclusionary humanist values, perpetuating global inequalities both between humans themselves, and between humans and nonhumans. There is a risk, therefore, that RoN, when brought to international law, may simply be transposed in a way that does not challenge the problems of international law but merely greenwashes it.

Thinking more directly about RoN and greenwashing or 'window dressing', a similar concern has been raised by Paola Villavicencio and Louis J. Kotzé when discussing the application of RoN in Bolivia. These authors point out that, while the Constitution and supplementary Law on the Rights of Mother Earth were both symbolically key in Bolivia, fostering 'a significant elevation of the popular social and political profile of Bolivia as a global champion (at least on paper)',[101] the Bolivian government did not, in response to these laws, approve new legislation. Furthermore, Villavicencio and Kotzé also highlight that Bolivia did not repeal major laws that are inconsistent with provisions on RoN.[102] Thus, these authors continue, '[a]rguably, Bolivia's efforts have had greater epistemic, symbolic and political impact outside its borders than within',[103] leading to suspicion as to whether these laws were actually 'attempts to window-dress ongoing environmental destruction and the exploitation of nature and of indigenous people'.[104] Overall, it is clear that RoN must be used, not only to recognise RoN in and of themselves, but that a more radical understanding is required, one that actively challenges the normative underpinnings of the way international law constitutes the environment as an economic resource.

One way in which RoN can be thought of beyond the liberal individual subject would be through challenging the meaning of rights themselves. Rights have predominantly been applied in law to bounded, individual legal subjects.[105] Christopher Garver, for example, questions whether rights of nature (as rights) can be radical enough to create an ecological law.[106] It is relatively clear that if RoN are framed through current dominant legal understandings of rights, their impact will be limited. However, rights can be re-thought. As Iván Darío Vargas-Roncancio asks, drawing on ethnographic research focusing on Indigenous cosmovisions: what happens if rights are granted 'to relationships instead of substances and or/persons?'.[107] Arguably, if rights are granted to relationships, the framing shifts. Rights are currently balanced against one another, a framing that for RoN 'essentially equips

101 Villavicencio and Kotzé, above note 20, p. 415.

102 Ibid., p. 416.

103 Here the authors are referring to Bolivia's global attempts to get RoN on the agenda through, for example, the UDRME and the Harmony with Nature programme.

104 Villavicencio and Kotzé, above note 20, p. 416.

105 Kapur, above note 95. On the limits of human rights and re-imagining them from a new materialist perspective, see: Anna Grear, 'Human Rights and New Horizons? Thoughts toward a New Juridical Ontology,' *Science, Technology & Human Values* (2018) 43(1): 129–145.

106 Garver, above note 167.

107 Vargas-Roncancio, above note 8, p. 122.

nature for battle with other rights holders'.[108] Clearly, existing liberal conceptions of rights are part of the currently dominant 'divisive, reductionist and atomistic' system that does not account for the interconnections between matter, humans and nonhumans.[109] However, if rights are granted to relationships, the framing of relational dynamics opens up, promising a shift beyond the problematic theoretical underpinnings of existing applications of rights.[110] RoN, if so conceived and adequately developed both theoretically and jurisprudentially, have the potential not only to challenge the anthropocentrism of international environmental law, but to address the entire way in which law and jural relations are currently understood.[111]

Another concern in relation to universalism arises when thinking about the transposition of RoN, initially an Indigenous instigated and led movement, to international law. As discussed above, Indigenous peoples have played a key role in the recognition of RoN. These instances of recognition come from specific connections to place that cannot be transposed globally.[112] For RoN to be truly transformative, connections between people and place must be central in their application, it being no coincidence that existing instances of RoN recognition focus heavily on community rights, with humans ultimately being needed to represent nature's claims in law effectively. This provides a challenge for international law and its universalising, top-down nature, as can be exemplified by looking at some existing attempts to bring RoN to the international legal realm, such as the recognition of rights of 'Mother Nature'. These attempts to bring a thin version of Indigenous ideas from one place to a global arena must be resisted and a focus on people as connected to place must be retained.[113] RoN are radical because of the Indigenous knowledges that have inspired and instigated the movement, with connections between law and place being central in many strands of Indigenous thought.[114]

Indigenous Anishinaabe (Canadian) legal scholar Aaron Mills argues for what he terms 'rooted constitutionalism', that is, an understanding of law that is deeply entwined with place. Mills states that he 'prefer[s] to speak of rooted constitutionalism and not indigenous constitutionalism', stating that he makes this 'choice

---

108 Geoffrey Garver, 'Are rights of nature radical enough for ecological law?,' in Kirsten Anker et al. (eds.), *From Environmental to Ecological Law*, (Routledge, 2021): 90–103, p. 91.

109 Ibid., p. 91.

110 On the liberal underpinnings of rights and alternative framings, see: Kapur, above note 95.

111 Youfatt makes a similar argument, noting the need to emphasise the connections between the human and nonhuman. Youfatt, however, calls for legal personhood to be considered, not rights, suggesting that legal personhood has a stronger protentional to recognise such connections. However, if rights are framed in relation, it seems rights framings could indeed fit Youfatt's framing too. See: Rafi Youfatt, 'Personhood and the Rights of Nature: The New Subjects of Contemporary Earth Politics,' *International Political Sociology* (2017) 11: 1–16.

112 With thanks to Elizabeth Macpherson, Julia Dehm and Jérémie Gilbert for the discussions that informed this perspective.

113 Tănăsescu, above note 29, Elizabeth Macpherson et al., 'Where Ordinary Laws Fall Short: 'Riverine Rights' and Constitutionalism,' *Griffith Law Review* (2021) 0: 1–36.

114 See: Samantha Muller et al., 'Indigenous Sovereignties: Relational Ontologies and Environmental Management,' *Geographical Research* (2019) 57(4): 399–410.

precisely to place the emphasis where it ought to be: on the kind of constitutionalism at issue, and not on the identity of the subjects who bear it'.[115] In terms of what a rooted constitutionalism means, Mills states that 'rootedness is available to anyone willing to sustain it'.[116] He continues that:

> Rooted peoples understand this to be how Earth community functions, and as such, they find themselves in always-already existing networks of mutual aid. In reproducing its logic in their own communities, rooted peoples constitute themselves in and through Earth (hence 'rooted').[117]

Rooted constitutionalism thereby centres relationships between peoples and place, replacing the idea of the liberal individual (an idea that permeates Eurocentric international law, as outlined in Chapter 1) by focusing instead on the community and ties of kinship.[118] It is hard to imagine a rooted international law, given international law's universalising tendencies. Such an approach may, in fact, require a move away from international law, fostering instead a global law based on transnational pluralities.

The issue of universalism is by no means unique to international law. Zakiyyah Iman Jackson, for example, raises concerns with the universalism of posthuman theory, arguing that if posthuman theory fails to challenge this universalism, it risks once again centring the figure of the Western Man.[119] This is a point I discussed in more detail in the Introduction to this volume and in the previous chapter, highlighting the need to focus on critical theories of posthuman feminism, including queer theories of the nonhuman, that refuse to side-line dehumanised humans when thinking about the nonhuman. These theories thus hold both struggles together, in connection with one another. Following this blueprint, it becomes clear that the recognition of RoN in international law, while holding potential, cannot alone challenge the anthropocentrism and exclusionary humanism upheld by and through international law. RoN can only be one part of a much wider picture which must, for example, include the challenging of existing economic power imbalances.

Who Represents Nature?

Posthuman feminist theories, from vibrant matter to feminist new materialism, to theories of the oneness of matter, to queer theories of the nonhuman, all exemplify the need to further break down the nature/culture binary that has been upheld

---

115 Aaron Mills, 'A Preliminary Sketch of Anishinaabe (a Species of Rooted) Constitutionalism,' *Rooted* (2021) 1(1): 2–7, p. 3.

116 Ibid.

117 Ibid., p. 4.

118 Ibid., p. 4. For more on human-nonhuman kinship relations, see: Darcey Lindberg, 'Excerpts from Nêhiyaw Âskiy Wiyasiwêwina: Plains Cree Earth Law and Constitutional/Ecological Reconciliation,' *Rooted* (2021) 1(1): 10–16.

119 Zakiyyah Iman Jackson, 'Animal: New Directions in the Theorization of Race and Posthumanism,' *Feminist Studies* (2013) 39(3): 669–685.

by western thought. There is a need to re-centre the agency of matter itself, as to fail to do so is to paint an incomplete picture. However, while the picture may be more complete when matter is no longer side-lined, humans are still painting the picture. The same concern applies to RoN. If RoN are to be upheld in law, humans must represent nature's claims on its behalf. Humans can seek to represent nature drawing on a variety of tools, which may include, for example, Earth jurisprudence or the application of scientific knowledge. However, these tools are by no means neutral, and they do not always provide clear answers. Take the application of scientific knowledge: while the application of the 'right to science' to international environmental law may, as Anna-Maria Hubert argues, create a more 'effective, equitable and democratically legitimate and accountable process',[120] exactly what science says for the purpose of understanding what is best for nature is contestable. To give a concrete example of how science, despite drawing on a variety of recognised methods to ensure rigour, is contestable, one can look to deep-sea mining. While deep-sea mining, or what is termed 'exploitation', has not yet been legally authorised, the Mining Code, which would authorise such exploitation, is currently under draft.[121] There is an obligation under international law to ensure that adequate environmental impact assessments (EIAs) are conducted before mining can go ahead.[122] Scientists argue, however, that the standards currently set for conducting EIAs are too low,[123] noting how the measures used to conduct EIAs in international waters lag behind international standards applicable to other environments and within other areas of international law.[124] There is no defined minimum scope for conducting a valid EIA in international law.[125] Accordingly, while EIAs have been conducted,[126] the concern is that the standards set when conducting such EIAs are inadequate.[127] Commenting specifically on the EIAs that have been

120 Anna-Maria Hubert, 'The Human Right to Science and Its Relationship to International Environmental Law,' *European Journal of International Law* (2020) 31(2): 625–656, p. 625.

121 See: International Seabed Authority, The Mining Code, https://www.isa.org.jm/miningcode (last accessed 11 July 2022).

122 *Pulp Mills on the River Uruguay* (Argentina v Uruguay), International Court of Justice, Judgment of 20 April 2010. More specifically in relation to the Law of the Sea, the need for EIAs was affirmed in: *Responsibilities and Obligations of States Sponsoring Persons and Entities with Respect to Activities in The Area*, International Tribunal for the Law of the Sea, Advisory Opinion of 1 February 2011, para 124–150.

123 Holly J. Niner et al., 'Deep-Sea Mining with No Net Loss of Biodiversity – An Impossible Aim,' *Frontiers in Marine Science* (2018) 5: 1–12; Flora and Fauna International, 'The Risks and Impacts of Deep-Sea Mining to Marine Ecosystems,' https://cms.fauna-flora.org/wp-content/uploads/2020/03/FFI_2020_The-risks-impacts-deep-seabed-mining_Executive-Summary.pdf (last accessed 11 July 2022), p. 7; Jennifer M. Durden et al., 'Environmental Impact Assessment Process for Deep-Sea Mining in "The Area",' *Marine Policy* (2018) 87: 194–202.

124 Harden-Davies et al., above note 4.

125 Pulp Mills on the River Uruguay, above note 122, para 205.

126 See: Bundesanstalt für Geowissenschaften und Rohstoffe, Environmental Impact Assessment, 2018, https://isa.org.jm/files/files/documents/EIA_BGR_0.pdf (last accessed 11 July 2022); Global Sea Mineral Resources, Environmental Impact Assessment, 2018, https://www.isa.org.jm/minerals/environmental-impact-assessments (last accessed 11 July 2022).

127 Harden-Davies et al., above note 4.

conducted on deep-sea mining, marine scientists have argued that these EIAs lack the 'statistical power' required in order to be deemed adequate or accurate.[128]

What the above example shows is that it is not always clear what is best for nature. While one group of scientists might argue that any harm to ecosystems caused by deep-sea mining will be minimal, another challenges that stance. This lack of certainty makes it difficult for humans to represent nature at all. From a post-human feminist perspective, this dilemma becomes ever more complex. As feminist new materialist scholar Vicky Kirby has argued, to 'represent nature' is to risk re-inscribing a humanist and anthropocentric blueprint through a human framing of what nature is and wants. As Kirby states, nature does not need a 'human scribe to represent itself, to mediate or translate its identity'.[129] Nature is self-organising and has a language of its own, comprised of a series of networks.[130] Yet if the law is to protect nature's rights, nature will require human representation. This is a problem: humans do not always know what is best for nature[131] and are tied to humanist and anthropocentric blueprints of thought when working within the dominant Eurocentric framework of international law. This representational necessity presents a conundrum: if 'the world' really is 'a witty agent' with an 'independent sense of humor',[132] as Haraway argues, how can that wit, that agency, ever be fully understood by humans, let alone represented by them in court?

Bennett, when discussing the need to create a political system that includes matter, is likewise all too aware of this dilemma concerning human understanding and representation. '[T]hing power', she states, is that which 'we cannot know' and which 'refuses to dissolve completely into the milieu of human knowledge'.[133] Posthuman feminism therefore presents an impossibility: the need to include matter/nature in understandings of the world and the impossibility of humans ever being able to fully understand it. However, while there is something about matter that will always exceed human knowledge, this does not mean that matter should remain side-lined or objectified.[134] Rather, posthuman feminist theory points to the need to remain 'perceptually open', to accept that not all can be known but to seek to know and understand what can.[135]

Queer theories of the nonhuman are not presented with quite the same tension. As outlined in the previous chapter, these theories begin with the premise that there is a need to understand various forms of inhumanity, including the nonhuman but also to make links between the nonhuman and those humans who have long been

---

128 Niner et al., above note 123, p. 7. On both the inadequacies of existing processes, as well as proposals on how to make the process more robust, see: Durden et al., above note 123.
129 Vicki Kirby, 'Natural Convers(at)ions: Or, What if Culture was Really Nature All Along?' in Stacy Alaimo and Susan Hekman (eds.), *Material Feminisms*, (Indiana University Press, 2008): 214–236, p. 232.
130 Ibid.
131 Ibid..
132 Donna Haraway, *Simians, Cyborgs and Women: The Reinvention of Nature* (Routledge, 1991), p. 199.
133 Jane Bennett, *Vibrant Matter*, (Duke University Press, 2010), p. 3.
134 Ibid.
135 Ibid., p. 14.

deemed to be less-than-human. Furthermore, the dilemma of representation does not seem to be so central in the minds of the Indigenous peoples who instigated instances of RoN recognition, or at least not in the same way. While Indigenous knowledge is vast and differs greatly between different groups, a central focus in many strands of Indigenous thought is on relationships between humans and non-humans.[136] Many Indigenous peoples reject the idea of the ownership of nature and the notion, prominent in international law, that nature is merely a resource to be exploited. Rather, looking to Aotearoa/New Zealand, for example, the Tūhoe *Iwi* state that nature is not and cannot be property. As the CEO of Te Uru Taumatua (the organisation representing the Tūhoe *Iwi*), Kirsti Luke, argued in 2013:

> Ownership and the owning of Te Urewera has been a mechanism to destroy belonging and care, and therefore community. Ownership granted entitlement without having earned it ... Ownership does not value kinship with the things around us ... it breeds very transactional relationships between humans and the land ...[137]

In this instance, to respect this non-ownability, a legal personality model was applied: no one owned Te Urewera, and legal personality was deployed as 'an imperfect approximation of recognizing the forest as a whole, living, spiritual being ... the best possibility within a European legal framework'.[138] In this sense, what Kirsti Luke proposed here, is not that humans seek to represent nature, with nature then becoming the unrepresentable subject, but, rather, that human *relationships* to nature are transformed from one of domination to one of relational connection.

What these reflections highlight is that RoN is not merely an ecocentric approach but, rather, the binary upheld in some of the literature on RoN and ecocentric law between an idealised environment and humans, between ecocentrism and anthropocentrism, needs to be re-thought. RoN laws require humans to represent nature, re-thinking human-nature relationships. As Braidotti argues, 'we need to devise a new vocabulary, with new figurations to refer to the elements of our posthuman embodied and embedded subjectivity'.[139] RoN may indeed be one of those new figurations, but RoN are certainly not free of human involvement. Rather, RoN hold potential, not because they focus purely on nature, but because they require human-nonhuman relationships to be re-thought.

136 The idea of relationality is central in many other strands of Indigenous thought. For example, Canadian-based Indigenous legal scholars Aaron Mills and Darcey Lindberg both centre relationality in their work.,Meanwhile Muller, Hemming and Rigney, writing from Australia note the importance of relationality and 'reciprocal responsibilities' when it comes to Indigenous approaches to environmental management. See: Mills, above note 115; Muller et al., above note 114.

137 Kirsti Luke, Presentation at the United Nations Interactive Dialogue of the General Assembly on Harmony with Nature, United Nations Headquarters, New York, Monday, 23 April 2018 – as quoted in Kauffman, above note 53, p. 6.

138 Kauffman Ibid., p. 7.

139 Braidotti, above note 94, p.82.

Conclusion

In Chapter 1, I outlined how international environmental law is anthropocentric, separating human and nonhuman interests into different legal spheres and ultimately prioritising human interests over all others, particularly the economic interests of certain elite humans in the global north. In Chapter 4, I sought an international environmental law otherwise, bringing posthuman feminist theories of neo-materialisms, including queer theories of the nonhuman, into conversation with critical environmental law scholarship. This book, however, not only aims to develop a posthuman feminist framework for analysing international law but also seeks to understand how posthuman feminism can be applied in practice. In that vein, this chapter drew on the work in previous chapters to argue that those seeking to apply posthuman feminist legal theory could greatly benefit from engaging with RoN approaches, noting some of the links between their respective aims and, in particular, the focus on the subjectivity of the nonhuman. To foster this reflection, I outlined some developing RoN standards in various domestic jurisdictions, with an eye towards the development of international standards, given this book's focus on international law. In turn, I sought to understand what RoN could learn from posthuman feminist theory, including queer theories of the nonhuman, seeking to understand the usefulness of posthuman feminism as applied.

Drawing on the lessons learnt from domestic applications of RoN, several key challenges were highlighted. One challenge was the core tension between economic interests and nature's rights. I then discussed some of the broader issues that haunt the application of both RoN and posthuman feminist theory in international law, focusing on the challenges presented by representation, universalism, the conceptualisation of rights and liberal legalism. Noting the problems with promoting universal concepts in an unequal world, I highlighted the need to situate RoN within the wider context of global economic inequalities, emphasising the need to challenge global economic imbalances. Furthermore, noting that many instances of RoN recognition have come about through Indigenous activism, I argued that the connection between people and place must not be lost when transposing RoN to international law. RoN provisions, I thereby argued, must be used, not merely to give rights to nature, but to transform understanding of rights in international law. RoN provisions have the potential to challenge the anthropocentrism of international law, but they will only do so if they are applied in a way that seeks to transform international law. Part of the reason RoN are so promising is because they call for human-nature relationships to be re-thought. That relational connection must not be lost in any transposition to international law. Given this and the need to retain a focus on people and place, I therefore concluded that some hope may be found by turning to international environmental law's transnational structure.

On the question of representation and whether nature can ever be truly represented by humans, I drew on posthuman feminism to argue that there is a need to remain 'perceptually open'[140] and to devise new vocabularies,[141] recognising the limits of the RoN project, while seeking to promote imaginative change. Noting that many strands of Indigenous thought focus, not on whether and how humans can represent nature but, rather, on human relationships to nature, I thereby challenged binary understandings of ecocentric versus anthropocentric perspectives. Rather than idealising 'Mother Nature', there is a need to reconfigure human relationships to nature. Such an approach would be transformative if applied in international law, and it is because of its focus on relationality that, I argued, RoN holds much potential.

While the tensions present here differ from those in my discussions of the regulation of military technologies, where the focus was on the conflict between militarism and feminist ethics, other tensions, ones that also map onto the resistance and compliance continuum, are clearly present when seeking to apply posthuman feminism to international environmental law. As I outlined above, there are always risks in working within the liberal legal system in that, by working within the system and seeking to improve it, one risks legitimising it. This is a problem that all critical thinkers face when seeking to apply critical thought; there is a risk that part of the radicality of that thought will be lost in its application. In Chapter 3, I suggested that critical change must occur within international law but that this change must be held alongside attempts to imagine the system otherwise. However, I also noted that there are limits as to how far one can work within a normatively oppressive system, the limitation I identified in that chapter being working within structures that enforce and uphold militarism. While the tensions and limitations here are not so stark, they are still very much present when thinking about environmental law. Overall, despite the tensions, I have argued that recognising RoN is a strong place to start when seeking to re-think international environmental law in a posthuman feminist register.

In the next and concluding chapter, I delve into the conundrum of resistance and compliance in more detail, questioning whether there is a possible exit from liberal legalism and searching for posthuman feminist modes of understanding beyond the anthropocentric and exclusionary humanist constraints of international law.

---

140 Bennett, above note 133, p. 14.
141 Ibid., p. 82.

6

POSTHUMAN FEMINISM

Reworlding Exits from Liberal Legalism

I hope that this book has successfully proven to any uncertain international lawyer that feminist approaches to international law can be used to evaluate a range of issues in international law, providing unique and much-needed analyses of some of the most pressing issues of our times. Chapter 1 explored the exclusionary humanism and anthropocentrism that underlies international law through an analysis of the legal subject and of how international law currently regulates the environment. Seeking to outline the specific contributions of posthuman feminism to the analysis and re-shaping of international law, Chapter 2 examined the humanist and anthropocentric ideologies that underpin debates on the regulation of LAWS. Here, I argued that the normative underpinnings of the debate on LAWS create false distinctions between autonomous and automated technologies and the human and the machine. This, I argued, works to ensure that the debate on LAWS focuses on LAWS alone, glossing over the fact that other technologies are already helping to make life/death decisions. This focus on autonomy without a more complex account of the nuances and degrees of agency between autonomy and automation, works to de-centre the core ethical question that *should* be at the heart of the LAWS debate, that being, do we want machines to make life/death decisions? In response to this complex dilemma, Chapter 3 outlined a series of posthuman feminist inspired proposals on how to regulate military technologies otherwise.

Chapter 4, springboarding from my analysis of international environmental law in Chapter 1, examined whether and to what extent a posthuman feminist framework and here, specifically, queer theories of the nonhuman, can be deployed to challenge and re-think the anthropocentric bias of international environmental law. Chapter 5 went on to apply these conceptual revisions to the emerging rights of nature movement. I argued that those seeking to apply posthuman feminist legal theory could greatly benefit from engaging with the RoN movement, noting some

DOI: 10.4324/9781003363798-7

of the links and resonances between the aims of this movement and posthuman feminism. I concluded that chapter by discussing some of the issues that haunt the application of both the RoN and posthuman feminist theory to international law, focusing on the challenges presented by representation, universalism and liberal legalism.

As I argued in the Introduction, a core facet of posthuman feminism is interdisciplinarity. In this book, I drew on scholarship from philosophy, science and technology studies, queer and feminist theories, marine biology, postcolonial and critical race theories, computer science, critical disability studies, cultural and media studies, Indigenous onto-epistemologies, critical legal theory, political science and beyond. These literatures were used to speak back to international law and feminist approaches to it, providing a holistic account of the underlying exclusionary humanism and anthropocentrism of international law.

I set out to write this book with two main aims in mind. First, I wanted to show that feminist approaches to international law can be used to analyse a broad range of areas of international law. I did this through my evaluation of legal personality, of the way international law regulates the environment, and of the debates on the regulation of military technologies. My second goal was to examine how posthuman feminism could be used both to analyse international law, and to design and foster legal change. Throughout my analyses, a series of tensions emerged in relation to this aim. One central challenge surfaced time and again, namely the tension between theory and practice, resistance and compliance. As a consequence, in this final and concluding chapter, I will analyse this tension in more detail, seeking multiple posthuman feminist pathways for reworlding international law.

Practice and Theory, Resistance and Compliance

Noting that posthuman theory has, until now, mostly been a theoretical and philosophical project, one of the central aims of this book was to apply posthuman feminist theory in practice, using it to propose concrete international legal change. This notion permeated each chapter though came to the fore in Chapter 3. In this chapter, I discussed feminist approaches to international law and the resistance and compliance conundrum. This conundrum refers to the systemic tension feminists are caught between when working with(in) international law. Here, there is a debate over whether feminists should seek legal change from within the terms of the law itself or, rather, whether there is a need instead to look beyond the law,[1] given international law's exclusionary humanist and anthropocentric underpinnings. Thinking through this conundrum in reference to my conclusions in Chapter 2, where I examined the humanist ideas that underpin the debate on the regulation of military technologies, I thereby came up with two sets of proposals for re-thinking military technology regulation in Chapter 3. The first set of proposals

---

1 Sari Kouvo and Zoe Pearson, (eds.), *Feminist Perspectives on Contemporary International Law: Between Resistance and Compliance?* (Hart, 2014).

were framed within the terms of existing international legal frameworks and institutions, re-thinking or expanding them with the aim of fostering a more posthuman notion of human-machine connections. While I made some concrete suggestions for legal change in this first set of proposals, these proposals were inherently limited by the framework of international law within which I sought to design them. In summary, these proposals, while being radical compared to the framework currently in place, ended up being far more conservative than I had initially hoped. Furthermore, in the process of outlining these proposals, I felt a sense of unease in applying feminist theory to regulate military technologies, given feminism's long history of a politics of anti-militarism. In short, regulating these technologies ultimately means marking some military technologies as legal, this outcome sitting in tension with a feminist politics of anti-militarism. As I outlined in that chapter, this inherent tension between wanting to work within international law but then having to accept international law's constraints when doing so is a wider tension that is presented when seeking to bring theory to practice. Feeling frustrated with this outcome, the second half of the chapter went on to seek posthuman feminist solutions to the regulation of military technologies beyond the limited framework that is international law, turning to theories such as data feminism and Indigenous AI to do so. While these solutions resonate more strongly than the first set of proposals with the critical aims of posthuman feminism, in this section I struggled to speak back to international law. In short, I struggled to remain within international law because to do so is to accept international law's limitations and to work at least partially within its normative underpinnings.

I developed the theme of resistance and compliance further in Chapters 4 and 5 where I discussed the international legal regulation of the environment, seeking posthuman feminist inspired ideas for moving international law beyond its current anthropocentrism. While the tensions present here differ from those in my discussions of the regulation of military technologies, where the focus was on the tension between militarism and feminist ethics, other tensions, ones that also map onto the resistance and compliance conundrum, emerged in these chapters. One central tension that arose focused on the risks of working within international law's (neo)liberal legal framework, noting that, through working within the system and seeking to improve it, one risks legitimising the system itself. While in Chapter 3 I suggested that critical change must occur both within a system as well as from outside to be effective, the conclusions of Chapters 3 and 5 led me to question this position. It is this questioning that I will now explore in more detail.

No Exit from Liberal Legalism

As I outlined in the Introduction and in Chapter 1, feminist legal scholars have shown that the subject of international law is the liberal subject of exclusionary humanism. He is male, white, heterosexual, able-bodied, speaking a standard language, mostly English, and middle-class.[2] Adding to this analysis, I argued in Chapter 1 that international law is also based on a series of anthropocentric assumptions. In short, the subject of international law, I argued, is indeed very much the exclusionary human/Anthropos, with nonhuman entities such as the environment and nonhuman animals, being rendered as mere objects in international law.

Speaking specifically about international human rights law, postcolonial feminist international lawyer Ratna Kapur has argued that human rights, likewise, are centred around the liberal subject, working to limit the ability of human rights to provide the freedom they promise. Kapur thereby argues that: 'rights interventions occur within and against already established normative and material frameworks, namely, conventional racial, cultural, sexual and civilizational arrangements that inform both the ideology and apparatus of human rights'.[3] Kapur argues that human rights foster a system in which 'the entitled subject, the rights-seeking subject' is painted at the expense of erasing other freedom-seeking subjects.[4] Kapur argues that the liberal ideologies that underpin international human rights law, alongside the way this body of law has been touted as an emancipatory tool, have worked to create an understanding of freedom in liberal terms that has become so pervasive that it actually restricts and invisiblises understandings of freedom beyond the liberal fishbowl. In a similar vein, and adding to Kapur's analysis of human rights, in Chapter 1 I argued that not only are human rights based on liberalism and exclusionary humanism but they are also intrinsically anthropocentric. Here, I drew on the example of the recent global recognition of a right to a healthy, clean and sustainable environment to highlight how human rights, even when engaging with environmental issues, ultimately prioritise human interests over the interests of the environment and nonhuman others.

The limited, culturally specific frame of freedom promoted by human rights has an impact not only at the imaginary level, when thinking about what freedom is and can possibly be, but also at the material level, with liberal (and, I would thereby add, exclusionary humanist and anthropocentric) ideas of freedom having become a tool for governance. For example, Kapur uses the case study of the debates over the

---

2 See: Rose Parfitt, 'Theorizing Recognition and International Personality,' in Anne Orford and Florian Hoffman (eds.), *The Oxford Handbook of the Theory of International Law*, (Oxford University Press, 2016), 583–599, p. 583; Anna Grear, '"Sexing the Matrix": Embodiment, Disembodiment and the Law – towards the Re-Gendering of Legal Rationality,' in Jackie Jones et al. (eds.), *Gender, Sexualities and Law*, (Routledge, 2011): 39–52; Ngaire Naffine, 'The Body Bag,' in Ngaire Naffine and Rosemary Owens (eds.), *Sexing the Subject of Law*, (LBC Information Services, 1997): 73–93.

Anna Grear, 'Deconstructing Anthropos: A Critical Legal Reflection on "Anthropocentric" Law and Anthropocene Humanity,' *Law and Critique* (2015) 26(3): 225–249, p. 225; Hilary Charlesworth, 'The Sex of the State in International Law,' in Ngaire Naffine and Rosemary Owens (eds.), *Sexing the Subject of Law*, (LBC Information Services, 1997): 251–268.

3 Ratna Kapur, *Gender, Alterity and Human Rights: Freedom in a Fishbowl*, (Edward Elgar, 2018), p. 15.

4 Ibid, p. 15.

veil to outline how human rights, despite being seen and often used as an emanci-patory tool, are used as a mode of governance.

Many feminists have advocated for the banning of the veil, or what is more commonly though not always accurately termed the hijab,[5] arguing that this piece of clothing is a symbol of women's oppression. Legal bans of the veil have thus followed. Cases questioning these bans have consequently been brought to the European Court of Human Rights (ECtHR) which has upheld these bans.[6] While, as noted, the legal sanctioning against this piece of clothing is often articulated in terms of women's rights, this so-called feminist perspective ignores the fact that the veil has many meanings. While, indeed, the veil can be imposed as a form of oppression, the veil is also worn by some out of choice, being a symbol of freedom for many.[7] The veil cases and the wider debates on the veil and women's human rights exemplify how human rights, despite claiming to be promoting the universal human rights of all, are deeply political in terms of who is included and excluded. In this instance, a colonial gaze can clearly be seen in the argument that a particular piece of clothing inherently restrains a woman's freedom.[8] 'Muslims', Kapur thus notes, 'continue to be conceptualized as the embodiment of a threatening alterity, and always as incommensurable with the liberal values which are the substrate of human rights discourse'.[9] Unveiling therefore becomes a form of governance,[10] excluding some from the universal humanity human rights claim to promote[11] while forcing others to submit to be able to access the 'freedom' human rights prescribes them.

It is clear from this example that human rights law, while claiming to provide a universal framework of freedom for all, is in fact a deeply political governance tool. The problem with human rights, however, is not only its use as a tool for govern-ance but its universal claims. Human rights have become one of the most dominant accounts of freedom in the global order over the past century. In becoming such

5 As Kapur states; 'I use the term "veil" as a generic category that includes its various manifesta-tions – the hijab, jilbab, abaya, niqab, burqa and chador – each version of the garment encoded with particular meaning for its adherents, proponents and opponents, and serving as both topos and target of national and regional socio-politics as well as global geo-politics.' Ibid, p. 120.

6 See, *Dakir v* Belgium, Appl. No. 4619/12, 11 July 2017; *Sahin v Turkey*, Appl. no. 4474/98, 10 November 2005; *S.A.S. v France*, Appl. no. 4835/11, 1 July 2014. For an analysis of these cases see Ratna Kapur, 'Alterity, gender Equality and the Veil' in Ratna Kapur, *Gender, Alterity and Human Rights: Freedom in a Fishbowl*, (Edward Elgar, 2018): 120–150.

7 Saba Mahmood, *Politics of Piety: The Islamic Revival and the Feminist Subject*, (Princeton University Press, 2004).

8 Kapur, above note 3.

9 Ibid., p. 132.

10 Ibid., p. 130.

11 Of course, 'humanity' has only ever been inscribed to some in international law. See, Kojo Koram, '"Satan is Black" – Frantz Fanon's Juridico-Theology of Racialisation and Damnation,' *Law, Culture and the Humanities* (2017): 1–20; Ayça Çubukçu, 'Thinking Against Humanity,' *London Review of International Law* (2017) 5(2): 251–267; Antony Anghie, 'Finding the Peripheries: Sovereignty and Colonialism in Nineteenth Century International Law,' *Harvard International Law Journal*, (1999) 40: 1–71.

a powerful discourse however, as Kapur notes, human rights have worked to limit the very idea of what freedom is and can be to what is envisaged as freedom within human rights alone. Frames beyond this fishbowl of freedom are accordingly not only given less priority but are portrayed as unimaginable and erased.[12] Accounts of freedom which are excluded by the human rights project, for example and following Kapur, include accounts of religious freedom and women's agency which lie beyond the liberal mindset, including the wearing of the veil by choice.[13]

While Kapur's work is written in specific reference to human rights law, her argument can be applied to international law more generally. In this book, I have argued that international law is based upon exclusionary humanism and anthropocentrism. I examined how these ideological underpinnings likewise, through international law, become tools for governance. For example, I argued in Chapters 2 and 3 that the exclusionary humanism that underpins debates on the regulation of military technologies works to falsely separate the human from the machine. This is concerning, not only because it presents an inaccurate account of how technologies work with and are part of the human, but also because these humanist underpinnings ultimately limit debate on the regulation of these technologies: at the same time as people are working to ban LAWS, systems which do not yet exist, an array of technologies are being deployed, and machines are already making life/death decisions. Furthermore, as I argued in Chapters 1, 4 and 5, the anthropocentric ideas that underpin the international legal regulation of the environment work to ensure that even emancipatory struggles that seek to tackle the climate crisis, such as human rights and the environment or international environmental law itself, are ultimately restricted by their own anthropocentrism and their constant prioritisation of human needs over the interests of the nonhuman.

Given this picture, the question becomes, how can critical feminist international lawyers begin to re-think international law beyond the constraints of the exclusionary humanism and anthropocentrism, given that these ideas are so much a part of the international legal structure? This question once again harks back to the resistance and compliance discussion within feminist approaches to international law. As I discussed in Chapter 3, while feminist approaches have been successful in adding women's concerns to existing international legal frames, such as within international human rights law or through the Women, Peace and Security agenda, the transformative elements of feminist approaches which seek, for example, to challenge the gendered foundations of the international legal system itself, have been left behind in the focus on the inclusion of women.[14] In other words, by calling for inclusion without a wider paradigm shift, there is a risk, as Braidotti argues (in

---

12 Kapur, above note 3.
13 Ibid., p. 120.
14 Hilary Charlesworth, Gina Heathcote and Emily Jones, 'Feminist Scholarship on International Law in the 1990s and Today: An Inter-Generational Conversation,' *Feminist Legal Studies* (2019) 27(1): 79–93.

relation to the inclusion of animals as subjects), that '[h]umanism is actually being reinstated uncritically under the aegis of species [and materialist] egalitarianism'.[15]

The tension between resistance and compliance is a theme I returned to in Chapter 5, where I examined the rights of nature. While I concluded there that there is much hope to be found in the emerging RoN movement, which has the potential to challenge some of the anthropocentric norms that underpin international environmental law, I also raised a series of concerns about bringing the RoN to the international realm. One of those concerns related to the liberal limits of international law. In short, I argued that there is a need to ensure that we do not just add nature and stir, as was done, to some extent, with women. I concluded that chapter by calling for further substantial engagements with the RoN movement by critical international legal scholars. This is needed now, as the RoN begin to gain traction. This engagement is required to ensure that nature is not merely added as a rights holding subject, extending the liberal paradigm without actually changing it. Rather, I argued, the RoN momentum must be used to transform international law into a legal system that is better able to address environmental issues.

However, I am by no means the first person to have come up against the limits of liberal legalism when trying to think international law in a more critical register. This is, for example, a central theme in critical human rights literature. While there is a vast body of fantastic literature in this field, Kapur's work is key. This is because Kapur does not merely criticise human rights but, unlike others, she seeks to imagine freedom otherwise. Kapur works to re-think freedom beyond a liberal register through focusing on an array of non-liberal theories, drawing on, for example, Eve Kosofsky Sedgwick's and Michel Foucault's works on Mahayana Buddhism and the Shia Islam underpinnings of the Iranian Revolution respectively,[16] and the tradition of non-dualism found in the Indian philosophy of Advaita.[17] Kapur also draws on several examples of case studies or figures who have sought freedom in non-liberal registers. For example, she tells the story of Lalla, a fourteenth-century Kashmiri woman who renounced marriage and material life and wandered naked while undertaking a process of self-reflection and meditation through, in part, a turn to mystic poetry.[18] Ultimately, in searching for freedom beyond the liberal fishbowl, Kapur looks well beyond the law.

While Kapur finds hope in looking towards spiritual practices that primarily draw on epistemologies of the global south, I made a similar move in this book through my use of posthuman feminism. For example, in Chapter 3, I sought posthuman feminist approaches to the legal regulation of military technologies by turning away from the law. Here, I turned instead to critical works such as Indigenous and feminist perspectives on AI. This shift away from the law in Chapter 3, however, represents a wider tension that emerged throughout the writing of this book.

---

15 Rosi Braidotti, *The Posthuman*, (Polity Press, 2013), p. 78–79.
16 Kapur, above note 3, p. 180–209.
17 Ibid.
18 Ibid.

While I have sought to apply posthuman feminist theory to practice, using posthuman feminism both to analyse international law and to seek legal change, at times, I have struggled with the latter objective. In Chapter 3, my turning away from the law followed an attempt to work within the law. However, I found only limited recourse for change in existing legal instruments. Similarly, in Chapter 5, I found recourse to hope in the RoN movement, while also noting that any attempt to bring this movement to international law risks a watering down of the transformative elements of it. While I have sought to provide suggestions for legal change throughout the book, seeking to balance methods of resistance and compliance by attempting to find modes for change from within the law while also working to imagine international law otherwise, in the last and final section of this book, I turn to focus in more detail on that otherwise. Here, I provide some brief reflections on what a posthuman feminist international law that does not have to work within the constraints of the current legal framework may look like.

Reworlding as Practice

Throughout this book, I have sought to apply posthuman feminist theories. While, at times, I have made proposals for legal change, at other times I have struggled to stay within international law when seeking to re-think it. However, while feminist international lawyers have long found themselves caught between resistance and compliance, and while I have found myself caught between this conundrum at various moments throughout this book, it is also key to note that resistance and compliance are not binary modes of engagement. Rather, there is a need to seek solutions from within international law *and* to resist international law's normative pull, working towards an international law otherwise. These methods for seeking change flow into one another. For example, one way to change international law can be to work within it. While working within international law, as I have discussed throughout the book, potentially offers fewer radical solutions that one may hope for otherwise, incremental change is one way of seeking transformation, and incremental change can occur with a larger goal in mind.

Furthermore, while I have attempted to understand what posthuman feminism can add to practice, theory and practice are likewise not binary opposite approaches. Reworlding, imagining worlds otherwise, is also a practice,[19] and one that is vitally important. This is a point queer theorist José Esteban Muñoz makes, highlighting the power of reworlding through his concept of the brown commons. This 'commons of brown people, places, feelings, sounds, animals, minerals, flora, and other objects',[20] is defined by Muñoz as fostering 'a process of thinking, imag-

---

19 Donna Haraway, *Staying with the Trouble: Making Kin in the Chthulucene*, (Duke University Press, 2016).
20 José Esteban Muñoz, 'Preface: Fragment from the *Sense of Brown* Manuscript,' *GLQ: A Journal of Lesbian and Gay Studies* (2018) 24(4): 395–397, p. 395.

ining otherwiseness'.[21] The importance, and practice, of 'imagining otherwiseness' has also been examined, in a different context, by feminist historian Joan Wallach Scott, who identifies the potential for radical change in fantasy. For Scott, while the concepts of the symbolic order 'provide the language through which identities are formed, the unconscious foundations on which social practices are implemented ... fantasy enables challenge and change'.[22] Reworlding is a practice, one that enables the construction of futures otherwise.

The importance of reworlding has been made clear throughout the writing of this book. This point was perhaps most clearly analysed, however, in Chapter 5, where I reflected on the problems of recognising the RoN when rights themselves, in international law, are understood in such a limited, liberal way. Here, I concluded by arguing that there is a need to remain 'perceptually open'[23] and to devise new vocabularies,[24] recognising the limits of the rights project while seeking transformative change. Grietje Baars has drawn a similar conclusion in their work on political economy and international law. Baars likewise concludes by calling for models of emancipation to be sought beyond the law, noting that freedom under the law is already bounded, already prescribed and therefore already limited, or, in Baars' words, 'forever deferred'.[25] In this vein, this last section offers some brief reflections on what reworlding international law could look like in a posthuman feminist mode. These reflections are tentative. A project of reworlding is not one that I could possibly endeavour to undertake alone. Rather, I offer some initial thoughts in the hope of sparking further, collaborative work and conversations.

One core theme that has emerged through this book is the need to transform international law to foster more attentiveness to relationality. I have shown how international law upholds exclusionary humanist and anthropocentric ideas about the connections between humans and nonhumans, calling for an international law that is able to think these connections otherwise. For example, as I argued in Chapter 3, the legal debates on lethal autonomous weapons systems are centred around a false distinction that is made between the human and the machine. I thereby called for more complex understandings of the human and the machine as being in connection to one another, noting that such an understanding will be required if our increasingly complex military technologies are to be adequately regulated.

Moving on to Chapters 4 and 5, relationality once again came to the forefront. Drawing on queer theories of the nonhuman that emphasise the links between

21 José Esteban Muñoz, "The Brown Commons: The Sense of Wildness" (Paper presented at the Annual Convention of the American Studies Association, San Juan, Puerto Rico, 16 November 2012). Quote taken from Dana Luciano and Mel Y. Chen, 'Has the Queer ever been Human?' *GLQ: A Journal of Lesbian and Gay Studies* (2015) 21(203): 183–207, p. 192.
22 Joan Wallach Scott, *The Fantasy of Feminist History*, (Duke University Press, 2012), p. 18.
23 Jane Bennett, *Vibrant Matter*, (Duke University Press, 2010), p. 14.
24 Braidotti, above note 15, p. 82.
25 Grietje Baars, *The Corporation, Law and Capitalism: A Radical Perspective on the Role of Law in the Global Economy*, (Brill, 2019), p. 5.

marginalised human and nonhuman subjects, I asked whether recognising nature's rights may be one way to begin to challenge the object/subject binary that permeates international environmental law. I concluded that, while the RoN movement holds much promise for re-thinking international law's anthropocentrism, for the movement to be fully transformative, it will need to transform the meaning of rights in international law. Drawing on the work of Indigenous scholars such as Aaron Mills,[26] alongside the work of Iván Vargas-Roncancio, I subsequently argued that one way of reconceiving rights might be through defining rights in relational ways.[27] An international law that understands connections between humans and nature, people and place, I argued, has the potential to radically transform human relationships to our environments.

Not only can posthuman feminism embrace such dynamics of reciprocity, it also renders visible deeper, more complex levels of entanglement: humans and nonhumans are situated in co-emergent relationalities. In this sense, agency is never 'pure' or 'absolute' but rather, agency is always distributed, always conditioned by entanglements between agential 'beings', human and nonhuman alike.[28] This, however, is a world where, as Haraway writes, '[n]othing is connected to everything; everything is connected to something'.[29] The repercussions of such relationalities directly challenge international law's imagined separation of humans and nonhumans, be that in relation to technology, the environment or other spheres of legal regulation. This does not mean, however, that all agential beings, whether human or nonhuman, are the same. While there may be 'affinities across … differences', differences remain.[30] As I argued in the Introduction, this is what separates posthuman feminism from some of the other theories of posthumanism, some of which seek to render subjects flat or horizontal.[31] Seeking to visibilise the nonhuman in the law does not mean that all subjects should be seen in equal terms. As Jane Bennett argues, the 'political goal of a vital materialism is not the perfect equality of actants, but a polity with more channels of communication between members'.[32] As I have argued throughout the book, the real inequalities between humans and between humans and nonhumans must be central in this reworlding of international law, ensuring that, in working to challenge anthropocentrism, exclusionary humanism is not left unchallenged.

Yet posthuman feminist theory is not the only, nor the first body of work to think through human-nonhuman relations in a more complex manner. For example, as I

26 Aaron Mills, 'A Preliminary Sketch of Anishinaabe (a Species of Rooted) Constitutionalism,' *Rooted* (2021) 1(1): 2–7, p. 4.
27 Iván Darío Vargas-Roncancio, 'Conjuring Sentient Beings and Relations in Law,' in Kirsten Anker et al. (eds.), *From Environmental to Ecological Law*, (Routledge, 2021): 119–134, p. 122.
28 Bennett, above note 23.
29 Haraway, above note 19, p. 31.
30 Bennett, above note 23, p. 104.
31 See my critique of, for example, some strands of new materialism, OOO and transhumanism in the Introduction.
32 Bennett, above note 23, p. 104.

noted in Chapter 5, while the RoN movement has gained traction precisely because this movement offers a 'new' solution, this solution is far from new. While RoN approaches may be 'new' to Eurocentric legal thought, this movement was developed by Indigenous thinkers, being based upon a millennia of Indigenous knowledge. It is precisely, as I argued in Chapter 5, the relational elements of the RoN and the focus on connections between people and place, that has proven to be so radical. Furthermore, it is no coincidence that I also ended Chapter 3, on military technologies, by turning to Indigenous work on AI. Indigenous onto-epistemologies, across their multiple differences, offer a more complex understanding of the world than the cannon of western thought. Violent western colonialism has long silenced these voices, through genocide, acts of everyday violence and political and epistemological erasure. It is clear, in this context, that the same body of western thought which committed and justified such atrocious acts, that same body of thought that has created a violent, colonial, exploitative capitalist world order whereby we are now facing urgent environmental challenges, cannot resolve the problems it has created in its current form. Likewise international law, being a Eurocentric legal framework and having played a central role in creating the world we now live in, justifying colonialism and logics of extraction and exploitation, cannot, as it is, get us out of this mess. In seeking to think international law otherwise, a lot may be gained by listening to and learning from Indigenous voices. Indigenous knowledge has a long history, providing a set of complex, nuanced and often differing ideas among different peoples. Much has yet to be gained from centring these voices. However, any attempt to centre Indigenous voices must be taken with care, acknowledging the histories of violence that permeate any discussion while also recognising that there are elements of Indigenous knowledge that are so complex, that come from such a long history of thought, that we, or rather I, as a white European, cannot ever begin to fully comprehend. It is thereby to deep listening that we must turn in seeking to begin to understand these far more complex knowledges of the law and of the world.[33]

Indigenous jurisprudence and posthuman feminist onto-epistemologies may provide one way of reworlding international law. However, a central problem remains: international law is a tool for governance. It is hard to imagine international law in any other way. While international law could expand to better include nonhuman entities and while it could place a greater focus on relationality, even under these models, it would still be a mode of governance. Given this, it may in fact be the case that reworlding international law ultimately requires abandoning international law altogether. Marxist legal theorist Pashukanis made this argument, concluding that a truly radical legal theory will, in the end, result in a 'withering away' of the law.[34] Indeed, this may be the only way to think international law in a

---

33 On understanding and listening to multiple Indigenous ways of legal knowing, see: Jill Stauffer, "You People Talk from Paper': Indigenous Law, Western Legalism, and the Cultural Viability of Materials,' *Law, Text, Culture* (2019) 23: 40–57.

34 Evgeny B. Pashukanis, 'Economics and Legal Regulation' in Piers Beirne and Robert Sharlet (eds.), *Pashukanis: Selected Writings on Marxism and Law*, (Academic Press London, 1980), p. 268–69.

genuinely radical way. Any engagement with international law, whether one seeks to work within it or to imagine an international law otherwise, will always be a mode of compliance, working with(in) a system which, in a radical future, cannot exist. Yet while withering away may be the end goal, there will be many steps to get there. Multiple contradictory standpoints[35] will be required, searching beyond what is known while being attentive to the constraints of the now. In the meantime, in this book I have sought to make some tentative solutions as to how we, those of us who are all in this together but who are not one and the same,[36] can use posthuman feminism to work towards reworlding international law at multiple levels. In doing so, I have exemplified how feminism, and specifically posthuman feminism, can be used to analyse all areas of international law, fostering a more just system for human and nonhuman subjects alike.

35 Donna Haraway, 'A Cyborg Manifesto,' in David Bell and Barbara M. Kennedy (eds.), *The Cybercultures Reader*, (Routledge, 2001): 291–324.
36 This is a phrase Braidotti uses throughout her work. However, see: Rosi Braidotti, '"We" Are In *This* Together, But We Are Not One and the Same,' *Journal of Bioethical Inquiry* (2020) 17: 465–468.

BIBLIOGRAPHY

Books and Journal Articles

Abdilla, Angie, 'Beyond Imperial Tools: Future-Proofing Technology through Indigenous Governance and Traditional Knowledge Systems,' in Josh Harle et al. (eds.), *Decolonizing the Digital: Technology as Cultural Practice*, (Tactical Space Lab, 2018): 67–195.

Adelman, Sam, 'A Legal Paradigm Shift towards Climate Justice in the Anthropocene,' *Oñati Socio-Legal Series* (2021) 11(1): 44–68.

Aeronautics and Space Engineering Board et al., *The Global Positioning System: A Shared National Asset*, (National Academies Press, 1995).

Aerospace Industries Association (AIA), '2021 Facts and Figures,' 2021, https://www.aia-aerospace.org/wp-content/uploads/2021-Facts-and-Figures-U.S.-Aerospace-and-Defense.pdf (last accessed 27 September 2022).

Aguila, Yann and Viñuales, Jorge E., 'A Global Pact for the Environment: Conceptual Foundations,' *Review of European, Comparative and International Environmental Law* (2019) 28(1): 3–12.

Alaimo, Stacy, *Exposed: Environmental Politics and Pleasures in Posthuman Times*, (University of Minnesota Press, 2016).

Alaimo, Stacy, *Bodily Natures: Science, Environment, and the Material Self*, (Indiana University Press, 2010a).

Alaimo, Stacy, 'Eluding Capture: The Science, Culture, and Pleasure of "Queer" Animals,' in Catriona Mortimer Sandilands and Bruce Erickson (eds.), *Queer Ecologies: Sex, Nature, Politics, Desire*, (Indiana University Press, 2010b): 51–72.

Alaimo, Stacy, 'Trans-Corporeal Feminisms and the Ethical Space of Nature,' in Stacy Alaimo and Susan Hekman (eds.), *Material Feminisms*, (Indiana University Press, 2008): 237–264.

Alaimo, Stacy and Hekman, Susan, 'Introduction: Emerging Models of Materiality in Feminist Theory,' in Stacy Alaimo and Susan Hekman (eds.), *Material Feminisms*, (Indiana University Press, 2008a): 1–19.

Alaimo, Stacy and Hekman, Susan, (eds.), *Material Feminisms*, (Indiana University Press, 2008b).

Alam, Sawkat et al., (eds.), *International Environmental Law and the Global South*, (Cambridge University Press, 2015).

Almagro, Maria Martin de, 'Producing Participants: Gender, Race, Class, and Women, Peace and Security,' *Global Society* (2018) 32(4): 395–414.

Amaro, Ramon, *The Black Technical Object: On Machine Learning and the Aspiration of Black Being*, (MIT Press, 2022).

Amaro, Ramon, 'Afrofuturism,' in Rosi Braidotti and Maria Hlavajova (eds.), *Posthuman Glossary*, (Bloomsbury, 2018).

Amoore, Louise, *Cloud Ethics: Algorithms and the Attributes of Ourselves and Others*, (Duke University Press, 2020).

Amoore, Louise, 'Algorithmic War: Everyday Geographies of the War on Terror,' *Antipode* (2009) 41(1): 49–69.

Amoore, Louise, 'There Is No Great Refusal,' in Marieke Goede (ed.), *International Political Economy and Poststructural Politics*, (Palgrave Macmillan, 2006): 255–274.

Amoore, Louise and Langley, Paul, 'Ambiguities of Global Civil Society,' *Review of International Studies* (2004) 30(1): 89–110.

Amrute, Sareeta and Murillo, Luis Felipe R., 'Introduction: Computing in/from the South,' *Catalyst* (2020) 6(2): 1–23.

Anaya, S. James, *Indigenous Peoples in International Law* (Oxford University Press, 2nd edn, 2000).

Anghie, Antony, *Imperialism, Sovereignty and the Making of International Law* (Cambridge University Press, 2012).

Anghie, Antony, 'Finding the Peripheries: Sovereignty and Colonialism in Nineteenth Century International Law,' *Harvard International Law Journal*, (1999) 40: 1–71.

Anker, Kirsten, 'Ecological Jurisprudence and Indigenous Relational Ontologies,' in Kirsten Anker et al. (eds), *From Environmental to Ecological Law*, (Routledge, 2021): 104–118.

Anzaldúa, Gloria, *Borderlands/La Frontera: The New Mestiza*, (Aunt Lute Books, 2012).

Arkin, Ronald, 'Lethal Autonomous Systems and the Plight of the Non-Combatant,' *AISB Quarterly* (2013): 137–236.

Arkin, Ronald 'The Case for Ethical Autonomy in Unmanned Systems,' *Journal of Military Ethics* (2010) 9(4): 332–341.

Arkin, Ronald, *Governing Lethal Behaviour in Autonomous Robots* (Routledge, 2009).

Arvidsson, Matilda, 'The Swarm that We Already Are: Artificially Intelligent (AI) Swarming "Insect Drones", Targeting and International Humanitarian Law in a Posthuman Ecology,' *Journal of Human Rights and the Environment* (2020) 11(1): 114–137.

Arvidsson, Matilda, 'Targeting, Gender, and International *Posthumani*tarian Law and Practice: Framing the Question of the Human in International Humanitarian Law,' *Australian Feminist Law Journal* (2018) 44(1): 9–28.

Asaro, Peter, '*Jus nascendi*, Robotic Weapons and the Martens Clause' in Ryan Calo et al. (eds), *Robot Law*, (Edward Elgar Publishing, 2016): 367–386.

Asaro, Peter, 'On Banning Autonomous Weapons Systems: Human Rights, Automation, and the Dehumanization of Lethal Decision-Making,' *International Review of the Red Cross* (2012) 94(886): 687–709.

Åsberg, Cecilia, 'Feminist Posthumanities in the Anthropocene: Forays into the Postnatural,' *Journal of Posthuman Studies* (2017) 1(2): 185–204.

Åsberg, Cecilia, 'The Timely Ethics of Posthumanist Gender Studies,' *Feministische Studien* (2013) 31(1): 7–12.

Åsberg, Cecilia and Braidotti, Rosi, (eds.), *A Feminist Companion to the Posthumanities*, (Springer International, 2018a).

Åsberg, Cecilia and Braidotti, Rosi, 'Feminist Posthumanities: An Introduction' in Cecilia Åsberg and Rosi Braidotti (eds.), *A Feminist Companion to the Posthumanities*, (Springer International, 2018b): 1–22.

Åsberg, Cecilia and Lykke, Nina, 'Feminist Technoscience Studies,' *European Journal of Women's Studies* (2010) 17(4): 299–305.

Atapattu, Sumudu and Gonzalez, Carmen G., 'The North-South Divide in International Environmental Law', in Sawkat Alam et al. (eds.), *International Environmental Law and the Global South*, (Cambridge University Press, 2015): 1–20.

Atapattu, Sumudu A. et al., 'Intersections of Environmental Justice and Sustainable Development: Framing the Issues,' in Sumudu A. Atapattu et al. (eds.), *The Cambridge Handbook of Environmental Justice and Sustainable Development*, (Cambridge University Press, 2021): 1–20.

Baars, Grietje, *The Corporation, Law and Capitalism: A Radical Perspective on the Role of Law in the Global Economy*, (Brill, 2019).

Baars, Grietje, 'From the Dutch East India Company to the Corporate Bill of Rights: Corporations and International Law,' in Ugo Mattei and John D. Haskell (eds.), *Research Handbook on Political Economy and Law*, (Edward Elgar, 2017a): 260–279.

Baars, Grietje, '#Lesbiansarehot: On Oil, Imperialism, and What It Means to Queer International Law,' *feminists@law* (2017b) 7(1): 1–9.

Baars, Grietje, '"It's not Me, It's the Corporation": The Value of Corporate Accountability in the Global Political Economy,' *London Review of International Law* (2016) 4(1): 127–163.

Bagemihl, Bruce, *Biological Exuberance: Animal Homosexuality and Natural Diversity*, (Stonewall Inn Editions, 2000).

Barad, Karen, 'Posthumanist Performativity: Toward an Understanding of How Matter Comes to Matter,' in Stacy Alaimo and Susan Hekman (eds), *Material Feminisms*, (Indiana University Press, 2008): 120–154.

Barad, Karen, *Meeting the Universe Halfway: Quantum Physics and the Entanglement of Matter and Meaning*, (Duke University Press, 2007).

Barad, Karen, 'Posthumanist Performativity: Toward an Understanding of How Matter Comes to Matter,' *Signs* (2003) 28(3): 801–831.

Baxi, Upendra, *Human Rights in a Posthuman World*, (Oxford University Press, 2009).

Baxi, Upendra, 'Voice of Suffering and the Future of Human Rights,' *Transnational Law and Contemporary Problems* (1998): 315–325.

Beard, Jack M., 'Autonomous Weapons and Human Responsibilities' (2014) 45(3): 617–681.

Beckett, Jason, 'Creating Poverty,' in Anne Orford and Florian Hoffmann (eds.), *The Oxford Handbook of the Theory of International Law*, (Oxford University Press, 2016): 985–1010.

Belcher, Oliver et al., 'Hidden Carbon Costs of the "Everywhere War": Logistics, Geopolitical Ecology, and the Carbon Boot-Print of the US Military,' *Transactions of the Institute of British Geographers* (2020) 45(1): 65–80.

Benjamin, Ruha, 'Discriminatory Design, Liberating Imagination,' in Ruha Benjamin (ed.), *Captivating Technology: Race, Carceral Technoscience, and Liberatory Imagination in Everyday Life*, (Duke University Press, 2019): 1–22.

Benjamin, Ruha, *Race After Technology*, (Polity Press, 2019).

Benjamin, Ruha, 'Informed Refusal: Toward a Justice-Based Bioethics,' *Science, Technology, & Human Values* (2016) 61(6): 967–990.

Bennett, Jane, *Vibrant Matter*, (Duke University Press, 2010).

Bernbach, John C. and Cheever, Federico, 'Sustainable Development and Its Discontents,' *Transnational Environmental Law* (2015) 4(2): 247–287.

Berry, Thomas, *The Great Work: Our Way into the Future* (Bell Tower, 1999).

Bertotti, Sara et al., *The Law of War and Peace: A Gender Analysis, Volume One*, (Bloomsbury, 2021).

Bhuta, Nehal et al., 'Present Futures: Concluding Reflections and Open Questions on Autonomous Weapons Systems,' Nehal Bhuta et al. (eds.), *Autonomous Weapons Systems: Law, Ethics, Policy* (Cambridge University Press, 2016): 347–383.

Bianchi, Andrea, *International Law Theories: An Inquiry into Different Ways of Thinking*, (Oxford University Press, 2017).

Bickford, Andrew, *Chemical Heroes: Pharmacological Supersoldiers in the US Military*, (Duke University Press, 2020).

Biemann, Ursula and Tavares, Paulo: BAK (2015) *Frieze*, Issue 175, https://www.frieze.com/article/ursula-biemann-paulo-tavares (last accessed 3 October 2022).

Bignall, Simone, 'Relational Sovereignty,' in Rosi Braidotti, Emily Jones and Goda Klumbytė (eds.), *More Posthuman Glossary*, (Bloomsbury, forthcoming 2023).

Bignall, Simone and Rigney, Daryle, 'Indigeneity, Posthumanism and Nomad Thought: Transforming Colonial Ecologies,' in Rosi Braidotti and Simone Bignall (eds.), *Posthuman Ecologies*, (Rowman & Littlefield, 2019): 159–182.

Bignall, Simone et al., 'Three Ecosophies for the Anthropocene: Environmental Governance, Continental Posthumanism and Indigenous Expressivism,' *Deleuze Studies* (2016) 10(4): 455–478.

Bird Rose, Deborah, 'Country,' in *Nourishing Terrains: Australian Aboriginal Views of Landscape and Wilderness*, (Australian Heritage Commission, 1996).

Blanchard, Eric, 'The Technoscience Question in Feminist International Relations: Unmanning the US War on Terror,' in J. Ann Tickner Laura Sjoberg (eds.), *Feminism and International Relations: Conversations About the Past, Present, and Future*, (Routledge, 2011): 146–165.

Blanco, Elena and Grear, Anna, 'Personhood, Jurisdiction and Injustice: Law Colonialities and the Global Order,' *Journal of Human Rights and the Environment* (2019) 10(1): 86–117.

Bo, Marta, 'Autonomous Weapons and the Responsibility Gap in Light of the *Mens Rea* of the War Crime of Attacking Civilians in the ICC Statute,' *Journal of International Criminal Justice* (2021) 19(2): 275–299.

Bogost, Ian, *Alien Phenomenology, or What's It Like to be a Thing?* (Minnesota University Press, 2012).

Borras, Saturnino M. Jr. et al., 'Towards a Better Understanding of Global Land Grabbing: An Editorial Introduction,' *The Journal of Peasant Studies* (2011) 38(2): 209–216.

Bostrom, Nick, 'In Defence of Posthuman Dignity,' *Bioethics* (2005), 19(3): 202–214.

Boulot, Emille and Sterlin, Joshua, 'Steps Towards a Legal Ontological Turn: Proposals for Law's Place Beyond the Human,' *Transnational Environmental Law*, (2022) 11(1): 13–38.

Bourke, Joanna, 'Killing in a Posthuman World: The Philosophy and Practice of Critical Military History,' in Bolette Blaagaard and Iris van der Tuin (eds.), *The Subject of Rosi Braidotti: Politics and Concepts*, (Bloomsbury, 2004): 29–37.

Bourne, Mike, 'Cyborgs, Control and Transformation: Posthumanist Arms Control and Disarmament,' in Erika Cudworth et al. (eds.), *Posthuman Dialogues in International Relations*, (Routledge, 2016): 216–234.

Boyd, David R., *The Rights of Nature: A Legal Revolution that Could Save the World*, (EWC Press, 2017).

Braidotti, Rosi, *Posthuman Feminism*, (Polity Press, 2022).

Braidotti, Rosi, '"We" Are in *This* Together, but We Are Not One and the Same,' *Journal of Bioethical Inquiry* (2020) 17: 465–468.

Braidotti, Rosi, 'A Theoretical Framework for the Critical Posthumanities,' *Theory, Culture & Society* (2019a) 36(6): 31–61.

Braidotti, Rosi, *Posthuman Knowledge*, (Polity Press, 2019b).

Braidotti, Rosi, *The Posthuman*, (Polity Press, 2013).

Braidotti, Rosi, *Metamorphoses: Towards a Materialist Theory of Becoming*, (Polity Press, 2002).

Braidotti, Rosi and Fuller, Matthew, 'The Posthumanities in an Era of Unexpected Consequences,' *Theory, Culture & Society* (2019) 36(6): 3–29.

Braidotti, Rosi, and Hlavajova, Maria (eds.), *Posthuman Glossary*, (Bloomsbury, 2018).

Braidotti, Rosi and Hlavajova, Maria, 'Introduction,' in Rosi Braidotti and Maria Hlavajova (eds.), *The Posthuman Glossary*, (Bloomsbury, 2018): 1–14.

Braidotti, Rosi and Jones, Emily, 'Critical Posthuman Theory,' in Rosi Braidotti, Emily Jones and Goda Klumbytė (eds.), *More Posthuman Glossary*, (Bloomsbury, forthcoming 2023): 28–30.

Braidotti, Rosi et al., (eds.), *More Posthuman Glossary*, (Bloomsbury, forthcoming 2023).

Brown, Clare, 'The Use of ICTs in Conflict and Peacebuilding: A Feminist Analysis,' *Australian Feminist Law Journal* (2018) 44(1): 137–153.

Brown, Wendy, *Politics Out of History*, (Princeton University Press, 2001).

Burdon, Peter, *Earth Jurisprudence: Private Property and the Environment* (Routledge, 2017).

Burdon, Peter, *Exploring Wild Law: The Philosophy of Earth Jurisprudence*, (Wakefield Press, 2011).

Burke, Anthony, 'The Absent Presence of Biodiversity in International Law,' *International Political Sociology* (2019) 13: 333–351.

Buss, Doris and Manji, Ambreena, 'Introduction,' in Doris Buss and Ambreena Manji (eds.), *International Law: Modern Feminist Approaches*, (Hart, 2014): 1–16.

Butler, Judith, *Frames of War: When is Life Grieveable?* (Verso, 2009).

Butler, Judith, 'Contingent Foundations: Feminism and the Question of "Post-Modernism"' in Judith Butler and Joan W. Scott (eds.), *Feminists Theorize the Political*, (Routledge, 1992): 3–21.

Calhoun, Laurie, *We Kill Because We Can*, (Zed Books, 2016).

Carvalho, Juliana Santos de, 'A "Male" Future: An Analysis of the Gendered Discourses Regarding Lethal Autonomous Weapons,' *Amsterdam Law Forum* (2018) 2: 41–61.

Cassese, Antonio, *International Law*, (Oxford University Press, 2nd edn, 2005).

Catts, Oron, 'Biological Arts/Living Arts,' in Rosi Braidotti and Maria Hlavajova (eds.), *Posthuman Glossary*, (Bloomsbury, 2018): 66–68.

Chace, Calum, *The Economic Singularity: Artificial Intelligence and the Death of Capitalism*, (Three Cs, 2016).

Chamayou, Grégoire, trans. Janet Lloyd, *A Theory of the Drone* (The New Press, 2015).

Charlesworth, Hilary, 'Talking to Ourselves? Feminist Scholarship in International Law,' in Sari Kouvo and Zoe Pearson (eds.), *Feminist Perspectives on Contemporary International Law: Between Resistance and Compliance?* (Hart, 2014): 17–32.

Charlesworth, Hilary, 'The Sex of the State in International Law,' in Ngaire Naffine and Rosemary Owens (eds.), *Sexing the Subject of Law*, (LBC Information Services, 1997): 251–268.

Charlesworth, Hilary, 'Cries and Whispers: Responses to Feminist Scholarship in International Law,' *Nordic Journal of International Law* (1996) 65: 557–568.

Charlesworth, Hilary, 'Feminist Critiques of International Law and Their Critics,' *Third World Legal Studies* (1995) 13(1): 1–16.

Charlesworth, Hilary and Chinkin, Christine, *The Boundaries of International Law: A Feminist Analysis*, (Manchester University Press, 2000).

Charlesworth, Hilary, Chinkin, Christine, and Wright, Shelley, 'Feminist Approaches to International Law,' *American Journal of International Law* (1991) 85(4): 613–645.

Charlesworth, Hilary, Heathcote, Gina and Jones, Emily, 'Feminist Scholarship on International Law in the 1990s and Today: An Inter-Generational Conversation,' *Feminist Legal Studies* (2019) 27: 79–93.

Charnovitz, Steve, 'Nongovernmental Organizations and International Law,' *American Journal of International Law* (2017) 100(2): 348–372.

Chimni, B.S., *International Law and the World Order: A Critique of Contemporary Approaches*, (Cambridge University Press, 2nd edn, 2017).

Chimni, B.S., 'Capitalism, Imperialism, and International Law in the Twenty-First Century,' *Oregon Review of International Law* (2012) 14(1): 17–45.

Chinkin, Christine, 'Gendered Perspective to the International Use of Force,' *Australian Yearbook of International Law* (1992) 12: 279–293.

Chinkin, Christine et al., '*Bozkurt* Case, aka the *Lotus Case (France v Turkey)*: Ships that Go Bump in the Night,' in Loveday Hodson and Troy Lavers (eds.), *Feminist Judgments in International Law*, (Bloomsbury, 2019): 27–51.

Chinkin, Christine and Kaldor, Mary, *International Law and New Wars*, (Cambridge University Press, 2017).

Choat, Simon, 'Science, Agency and Ontology: A Historical Materialist Response to New Materialism,' *Political Studies* (2017) 66(4): 1027–1042.

Choe, Jaehoon et al., 'Transcranial Direct Current Stimulation Modulates Neuronal Activity and Learning in Pilot Training,' *Frontiers in Human Neuroscience* (2016) 10(34): 1–25.

Cockburn, Cynthia, *From Where We Stand: War, Women's Activism and Feminist Analysis*, (Zed Books, 2007).

Cohn, Carol and Duncanson, Claire, 'Women, Peace and Security in a Changing Climate,' *International Feminist Journal of Politics* (2020) 22(5): 742–762.

Clark, Lindsay C., 'Grim Reapers: Ghostly Narratives of Masculinity and Killing in Drone Warfare,' *International Feminist Journal of Politics* (2018) 20(4): 602–623.

Clarke, Kamari Maxine and Kendall, Sara, 'The Beauty ... is that It Speaks for Itself': Geospatial Materials as Evidentiary Matters,' *Law Text Culture* (2019) 23: 91–118.

Cohn, Carol, 'Sex and Death in the Rational World of Defence Intellectuals,' *Signs*, (1987), 12(4): 687–718.

Cohn, Carol et al., 'Women, Peace and Security: Resolution 1325,' *International Feminist Journal of Politics* (2004) 6(1): 130–140.

Conaghan, Joanna, 'Feminism, Law and Materialism: Reclaiming the Tainted Realm,' in Margaret Davies and Vanessa Munro (eds.), *The Ashgate Research Companion to Feminist Legal Theory*, (Routledge, 2013): 31–50.

Craven, Matt, '"Other Spaces": Constructing the Legal Architecture of a Cold War Commons and the Scientific-Technical Imaginary of Outer Space,' *European Journal of International Law* (2019) 30(2): 547–572.

Craven, Matthew, 'What Happened to Unequal Treaties? The Continuities of Informal Empire,' *Nordic Journal of International Law* (2005) 74: 335–382.

Crawford, James, *The Creation of States in International Law*, (Oxford University Press, 2006).

Crimmel, Hal and Goeckeritz, Issac, 'The Rights of Nature in New Zealand: Conversations with Kirsti Luke and Christopher Finlayson,' *ILSE: Interdisciplinary Studies in Literature and Environment* (2020) 27(3): 563–577.

Crootof, Rebecca, 'Regulating New Weapons Technology,' in Eric Talbot Jensen and Ronald T.P. Alcala (eds.), *The Impact of Emerging Technologies on the Law of Armed Conflict, Lieber Studies Volume 2*, (Oxford University Press, 2019): 3–25.

Çubukçu, Ayça, 'Thinking Against Humanity,' *London Review of International Law* (2017) 5(2): 251–267.

Cudworth, Erika and Hobden, Steve, 'The Posthuman Way of War,' *Security Dialogue* (2015) 46(6): 513–529.

Cullinan, Cormac, *Wild Law: A Manifesto for Earth Jurisprudence* (Green Books, 2003).

Cusato, Eliana, *The Ecology of War and Peace: Marginalising Slow and Structural Violence in International Law*, (Cambridge University Press, 2021).

Cusato, Eliana, 'International Law, the Paradox of Plenty and the Making of Resource-Driven Conflict,' *Leiden Journal of International Law* (2020) 33(3): 649–666.

Daggett, Cara, 'Drone Disorientations: How "Unmanned" Weapons Queer the Experience of Killing in War,' *International Feminist Journal of Politics* (2015) 17(3): 361–379.

Danielsen, Dan, 'Corporate Power and Global Order,' in Anne Orford (ed.), *International Law and Its Others*, (Cambridge University Press, 2006): 85–99.

Davies, Lisa and Stern, Jessica, 'WPS and LGBTI Rights,' in Sara E. Davies and Jacqui True (eds.), *The Oxford Handbook of Women, Peace, and Security*, (Oxford University Press 2019): 658–668.

Davies, Margaret, *Law Unlimited*, (Routledge, 2017).

Deckha, Maneesha, 'Toward a Postcolonial, Posthumanist Feminist Theory: Centralizing Race and Culture in Feminist Work on Nonhuman Animals,' *Hypatia* (2012) 27(3): 527–545.

Deleuze, Gilles, trans. Martin Joughin, *Expressionism in Philosophy: Spinoza*, (Zone Books, 1990 [1968]).

Delphy, Christine, trans. Diana Leonard, 'A Materialist Feminism is Possible,' *Feminist Review* (1980) 4: 79–105.

Dickinson, Laura A., 'Lethal Autonomous Weapons Systems: The Overlooked Importance of Administrative Accountability,' in Eric Talbot and Ronald T.O. Alcala (eds.), *The Impact of Emerging Technologies on the Law of Armed Conflict*, (Oxford University Press, 2019): 69–97.

D'Ignazio, Catherine and Klein, Lauren F., *Data Feminism*, (MIT Press, 2020).

Drobysz, Sonia, 'Verification and Implementation of the Biological and Toxin Weapons Convention,' *The Nonproliferation Review* (2020) 27:4–6: 487–497.

Dryzek, John S. and Pickering, Jonathan, *The Politics of the Anthropocene*, (Oxford University Press, 2018).

Dunne, P., 'The Political Economy of Military Expenditure: An Introduction,' *Cambridge Journal of Economics* (1990) 14: 395–404.

Dupuy, Pierre-Marie and Vierucci, Luisa, (eds.), *NGOs in International Law: Efficiency in Flexibility?* (Edward Elgar, 2008).

Durden, Jennifer M. et al., 'Environmental Impact Assessment Process for Deep-Sea Mining in "The Area",' *Marine Policy* (2018) 87: 194–202.

Edelman, Lee, *No Future: Queer Theory and the Death Drive*, (Duke University Press, 2004).

Edelman, Marc et al., (eds.). *Global Land Grabs: History, Theory and Method*, (Routledge, 2015).

Edelman, Marc et al., 'Global Land Grabs: Historical Processes, Theoretical and Methodological Implications and Current Trajectories,' *Third World Quarterly* (2013) 34(9): 1517–1531.

Eglash, Ron, 'Anti-Racist Technoscience: A Generative Tradition,' in Ruha Benjamin (ed.), *Captivating Technology: Race, Carceral Technoscience, and Liberatory Imagination in Everyday Life*, (Duke University Press, 2019): 227–251.

Eisenstadt, Todd A. and Jones West, Karleen, *Who Speaks for Nature? Indigenous Movements, Public Opinion and the Petro-State in Ecuador*, (Oxford University Press, 2019).

Engle, Karen, *The Grip of Sexual Violence in Conflict*, (Stanford University Press, 2020).

Engle, Karen, 'Feminist Governance and International Law: From Liberal to Carceral Feminism,' in Janet Halley et al. (eds.), *Governance Feminism: Notes from the Field*, (Minnesota University Press, 2019): 3–20.

Engle, Karen et al., 'Feminist Approaches to International Law,' in Jeffrey N. Dunoff and Mark A. Pollack (eds.), *International Legal Theory: Foundations and Frontiers*, (Cambridge University Press, 2022): 174–195.

Eslava, Luis, *Local Space, Global Life: The Everyday Operation of International Law and Development*, (Cambridge University Press, 2015).

Eubanks, Virgina, *Automating Inequality: How High-Tech Tools Profile, Police, and Punish the Poor*, (St Martin's Press, 2018).

Fanon, Frantz, trans Constance Farringdon, *The Wretched of the Earth*, (Grove Press, 1963).

Federman, Cary, 'Constructing Kinds of Persons in 1886: Corporate and Criminal,' *Law and Critique* (2003) 14(2): 167–189.

Fellmeth, Aaron Xavier, 'Feminism and International Law: Theory, Methodology, and Substantive Reform,' *Human Rights Quarterly* (2000) 22(3): 658–733.

Ferrando, Francesca, *Philosophical Posthumanism*, (Bloomsbury, 2020).

Foucault, Michel, *The Order of Things*, (Routledge, 2001 [1966]).

Foucault, Michel, trans. Thomas Keenan, 'Is It Really Important to Think?' in Michel Foucault, *The Will to Knowledge: The History of Sexuality Volume 1*, (Penguin, 1976a).

Foucault, Michel, *The Will to Knowledge: The History of Sexuality Volume 1*, (Penguin, 1976b).

Fox, Nick J. and Alldred, Pam, 'Climate Change, Environmental Justice and the Unusual Capacities of Posthumans,' *Journal of Human Rights and the Environment* (2021) 12: 59–75.

Fox, Nick J. and Alldred, Pam, 'Re-Assembling Climate Change Policy: Materialism, Posthumanism, and the Policy Assemblage,' *British Journal of Sociology* (2020) 17(2): 269–283.

Fraser, Nancy, 'Feminism, Capitalism, and the Cunning of History,' *New Left Review* (2009) 56: 97–117.

Fritsch, Kelly et al., 'Introduction to Special Section on Crip Technoscience,' *Catalyst* (2019) 5(1): 1–10.

Gaard, Greta, 'Ecofeminism Revisited: Rejecting Essentialism and Re-Placing Species in a Material Feminist Environmentalism,' *Feminist Formations* (2011) 23(2): 26–53.

Gallego, Carlos, *Chicana/o Subjectivity and the Politics of Identity: Between Recognition and Revolution* (Palgrave, 2011).

Gandorfer, Daniela, 'Introduction to Research Handbook on Law and Literature. What is your Power?,' in Peter Goodrich and Daniela Gandorfer (eds.), *Research Handbook on Law and Literature*, (Edward Elgar, 2022): 1–13.

Gardham, Judith, 'A Feminist Analysis of Certain Aspects of International Humanitarian Law,' *Australian Yearbook of International Law* (1988) 12: 265–278.

Garver, Geoffrey, 'Are Rights of Nature Radical Enough for Ecological Law?,' in Kirsten Anker et al. (eds.), *From Environmental to Ecological Law*, (Routledge, 2021): 90–103.

Gathii, James T., 'Good Governance as a Counterinsurgency Agenda to Oppositional and Transformative Social Projects in International Law,' *Buffalo Human Rights Law Review* (1999) 5: 107–174.

Gellers, Josh, *Rights for Robots: Artificial Intelligence, Animal and Environmental Law*, (Routledge, 2020).

Giffney, Noreen, and Hird, Myra J., 'Introduction: Queering the Non/Human,' in Noreen Giffney and Myra Hird (eds.), *Queering the Non/Human*, (Routledge, 2008): 1–16.

Giffney, Noreen, and Hird, Myra J., (eds.), *Queering the Non/Human* (Routledge, 2008).

Gilani, Sabrina, 'Bionic Bodies, Posthuman Violence and the Disembodied Criminal Subject,' *Law and Critique* (2021) 32: 171–193.

Gill, Amandeep S., 'The Changing Role of Multilateral Forums in Regulating Armed Conflict in the Digital Age,' *International Review of the Red Cross* (2020), 103(913): 261–285.

Gill, Amandeep Singh, 'Artificial Intelligence and International Security: The Long View,' *Ethics & International Affairs* (2019) 33(2): 169–179.

Ginsberg, Matt, *Essentials of Artificial Intelligence*, (Morgan Kaufmann, 2013).

Gleeson, Jules Joanne and O'Rourke, Elle, (eds.), *Transgender Marxism*, (Pluto Press, 2021).

Goede, Marieke de, 'Engagements All the Way Down,' *Critical Studies on Security* (2020) 8(2): 101–115.

Goldstein, Eric A., 'Mother Nature Knows Best: Fundamentals for Ensuring Safe Water Supply,' *Fordham Environmental Law Journal* (2001) 12(3): 455–466.

Gonzalez, Carmen G., 'Racial Capitalism and the Anthropocene,' in Sumudu A. Atapattu et al. (eds.), *The Cambridge Handbook of Environmental Justice and Sustainable Development*, (Cambridge University Press, 2021): 72–85.

Goodley, Dan et al., Katherine, 'Posthuman Disability Studies,' *Subjectivity* (2014) 7: 342–361.

Gordon, Ruth, 'Unsustainable Development,' in Shawkat Alam et al. (eds.), *International Environmental Law and the Global South*, (Cambridge University Press, 2015): 50–73.

Grear, Anna, 'Legal Imaginaries and the Anthropocene: "Of" and "For",' *Law and Critique* (2020) 31: 351–366.

Grear, Anna, 'Resisting Anthropocene Neoliberalism: Towards New Materialism Commoning?,' in Anna Grear and David Bollier (eds.), *The Great Awakening: New Modes of Life Amidst Capitalist Ruins*, (Punctum Books, 2020): 317–355.

Grear, Anna, 'Human Rights and New Horizons? Thoughts toward a New Juridical Ontology,' *Science, Technology and Human Values* (2018) 43(1): 129–145.

Grear, Anna, '"Anthropocene, Capitalocene, Chthulucene": Re-Encountering Environmental Law and Its "Subject" with Haraway and New Materialism,' in Louis J. Kotzé (ed.), *Environmental Law and Governance for the Anthropocene*, (Hart, 2017): 77–95.

Grear, Anna, 'Deconstructing Anthropos: A Critical Legal Reflection on 'Anthropocentric' Law and Anthropocene 'Humanity',' *Law and Critique* (2015) 26(3): 225–249.

Grear, Anna, 'Human Rights, Property and the Search for "Worlds Other,"' *Journal of Human Rights and the Environment* (2012) 3(2): 173–195.

Grear, Anna, '"Sexing the Matrix": Embodiment, Disembodiment and the Law – towards the Re-Gendering of Legal Rationality,' in Jackie Jones et al. (eds.), *Gender, Sexualities and Law*, (Routledge, 2011): 39–52.

Grear, Anna, *Redirecting Human Rights: Facing the Challenge of Corporate Legal Humanity*, (Palgrave Macmillan, 2010).

Greene Wade, Ashleigh, '"New Genres of Being Human": Worldmaking through Viral Blackness,' *Journal of Black Studies and Research* (2017) 47(3): 33–44.

Guardiola-Rivera, Oscar, 'Return of the Fetish: A Plea for a New Materialism,' *Law and Critique* (2007) 18: 275–307.

Hagen, Jamie J., 'Queering Women, Peace and Security,' *International Affairs* (2016) 92(2): 313–332.

Halberstam, J.M. and Livingston, Ira, *Posthuman Bodies*, (Indiana University Press, 1995).

Halley, Janet, 'Introducing Governance Feminism,' in Janet Halley et al., *Governance Feminism: An Introduction*, (Minnesota University Press, 2018a): ix–xxi.

Halley, Janet et al., *Governance Feminism: An Introduction*, (Minnesota University Press, 2018b).

Hammond, Daniel N., 'Autonomous Weapons and the Problem of State Accountability,' *Chicago Journal of International Law* (2015) 15: 652–687.

Hamraie, Aimi and Fritsch, Kelly, 'Crip Technoscience Manifesto,' *Catalyst* (2019) 5(1): 1–33.

Haraway, Donna, 'Companion Species, Mis-Recognition, and Queering Worlding,' in Noreen Giffney and Myra J. Hird (eds.), *Queering the Non-Human*, (Routledge, 2016a): xxiii–xxvi.

Haraway, Donna, *Staying with the Trouble: Making Kin in the Chthulucene*, (Duke University Press, 2016b).

Haraway, Donna, 'Anthropocene, Capitalocene, Plantationocene, Chthulucene: Making Kin,' *Environmental Humanities* (2015) 6: 159–165.

Haraway, Donna, 'The Promises of Monsters: A Regenerative Politics for Inappropriate/d Others,' in *The Haraway Reader*, (Routledge, 2004): 63–124.

Haraway, Donna, 'A Cyborg Manifesto,' in David Bell and Barbara M. Kennedy (eds.), *The Cybercultures Reader*, (Routledge, 2001): 291–324.

Haraway, Donna, 'A Cyborg Manifesto: Science, Technology, and Socialist-Feminism in the Late Twentieth Century,' in Donna Haraway, *Simians, Cyborgs and Women: The Reinvention of Nature* (Free Association Books, 1991): 149–181.

Haraway, Donna, *Simians, Cyborgs and Women: The Reinvention of Nature*, (Routledge, 1991).

Harden-Davies, Harriet et al., 'Rights of Nature: Perspectives for Global Ocean Stewardship,' *Marine Policy* (2020) 122: 1–11.

Harman, Graham, *Tool-Being: Heidegger and the Metaphysics of Objects*, (Open Court, 2002).

Harris, Angela P., 'Toward a Law and Political Economy Approach to Environmental Justice,' in Sumudu A. Atapattu et al. (eds.), *The Cambridge Handbook of Environmental Justice and Sustainable Development*, (Cambridge University Press, 2021): 453–469.

Harris Rimmer, Susanand Ogg, Kate, (eds.), *Research Handbook of Feminist Engagement with International Law*, (Edward Elgar, 2019).

Harvey, Matt and Vanderheiden, Steve, '"For the Trees Have No Tongues": Eco-Feedback, Speech, and the Silencing of Nature,' *Journal of Human Rights and the Environment* (2021) 12: 38–58.

Heathcote, Gina, *Feminist Dialogues on International Law: Successes, Tensions, Futures*, (Oxford University Press, 2019a).

Heathcote, Gina, 'Security Council Resolution 2242 on Women, Peace and Security: Progressive Gains or Dangerous Developments?,' *Global Society* (2018a) 32(4): 374–394.

Heathcote, Gina, 'War's Perpetuity: Disabled Bodies of War and the Exoskeleton of Equality,' *Australian Feminist Law Journal* (2018b) 44(1): 71–91.

Heathcote, Gina, 'LAWS, UFOs and UAVs: Feminist Encounters with the Law of Armed Conflict,' in Dale Stephens and Paul Babie (eds.), *Imagining Law: Essays in Conversation with Judith Gardham*, (University of Adelaide Press, 2017): 153–170.

Heathcote, Gina, *The Law on the Use of Force: A Feminist Analysis*, (Routledge, 2012).

Heathcote, Gina V., 'Feminism and the Law of the Sea: A Preliminary Inquiry,' in Irini Papanicolopulu (ed.), *Gender and the Law of the Sea*, (Brill, 2019b): 83–105.

Hemming, Steve et al., 'Indigenous Nation Building for Environmental Futures: Murrundi Flows through Ngarrindjeri Country,' *Australasian Journal of Environmental Management* (2019) 26(3): 216–235.

Henkin, Louis, 'The Mythology of Sovereignty,' in *State Sovereignty: The Challenge of a Changing World: Proceedings of the 1992 Conference of the Canadian Council on International Law*, (Canadian Council of International Law Proceedings, 1992).

Hennessey, Rosemary and Ingraham, Chrys, 'Introduction: Reclaiming Anticapitalist Feminism,' in Rosemary Hennessey and Chrys Ingraham (eds.), *Materialist Feminism: A Reader in Class, Difference and Women's Lives*, (Routledge 1997): 1–14.

Hester, Helen, *Xenofeminism*, (Polity Press, 2018).

Heyns, Christof and Borden, Tess, 'Unmanned Weapons: Looking for the Gender Dimensions,' in Fionnuala Ní Aoláin et al. (eds.) *The Oxford Handbook of Gender and Conflict*, (Oxford University Press, 2018): 376–389.

Hodson, Loveday, 'Mermaids and Utopias: The High Seas as Feminist Space?' in Irini Papanicolopulu (ed.), *Gender and the Law of the Sea*, (Brill, 2019): 122–143.

Hodson, Loveday and Lavers, Tory, (eds.), *Feminist Judgments in International Law*, (Bloomsbury, 2019).

Hogan, Katie, 'Undoing Nature: Collation Building as Queer Environmentalism,' in Catriona Mortimer-Sandilands and Bruce Erikson (eds.), *Queer Ecologies: Sex, Nature, Politics Desire*, (Indiana University Press, 2010): 231–253.

Hohmann, Jessie, 'Diffuse Subjects and Dispersed Power: New Materialist Insights and Cautionary Lessons for International Law,' *Leiden Journal of International Law* (2021) 34: 585–606.

Hohmann, Jessie and Joyce, Daniel, *International Law's Objects*, (Oxford University Press, 2018).

Hubert, Anna-Maria, 'The Human Right to Science and Its Relationship to International Environmental Law,' *European Journal of International Law* (2020) 31(2): 625–656.

Hulme, Karen, *War Torn Environment: Interpreting the Legal Threshold* (Brill, 2004).

Humphreys, Stephen and Otomo, Yoriko, 'Theorizing International Environmental Law,' in Anne Orford and Florian Hoffman (eds), *The Oxford Handbook of the Theory of International Law*, (Oxford University Press, 2016): 797–819.

Huynh, Cong Minh and Hoang, Hong Hiep, 'Does a Free Market Economy Make Mother Nature Angry? Evidence from Asian Economies,' *Environmental Science and Pollution Research* (2021) 28(39): 55603–55614.

Jackson, Zakiyyah Iman, 'Outer Worlds: The Persistence of Race in Movement "Beyond the Human,"' *GLQ: A Journal of Lesbian and Gay Studies* (2015) 21(2–3): 215–218.

Jackson, Zakiyyah Iman, 'Animal: New Directions in the Theorization of Race and Posthumanism,' *Feminist Studies* (2013) 39(3): 669–685.

Jasanoff, Sheila, 'Future Imperfect: Science, Technology, and the Imaginations of Modernity,' in Sheila Jasanoff and Sang Hyun Kim (eds.), *Dreamscapes of Modernity: Sociotechnical Imaginaries and the Fabrication of Power*, (University of Chicago Press, 2015): 1–33.

Jevglevskaja, Natalia, 'Weapons Review Obligation under Customary International Law,' *International Law Studies* (2018) 24: 186–221.

Johns, Fleur, 'Theorizing the Corporation in International Law,' in Anne Orford and Florian Hoffmann (eds.), *The Oxford Handbook of the Theory of International Law* (Oxford University Press, 2016): 635–654.

Johnson, Tom, 'Legal History and The Material Turn,' in Markus D. Dubber and Christopher Tomlins (eds.), *The Oxford Handbook of Legal History*, (Oxford University Press, 2018): 497–514.

Jones, Emily, 'Posthuman International Law and the Rights of Nature,' *Journal of Human Rights and the Environment* (2021) 12(0): 76–101.

Jones, Emily, 'Gender and Reparations: Seeking Transformative Justice,' in Carla Ferstman and Mariana Goetz (eds.), *Reparations for Victims of Genocide, War Crimes and Crimes Against Humanity: Systems in Place and Systems in the Making*, (Brill, 2020): 86–118.

Jones, Emily, 'Feminist Technologies and Post-Capitalism: Defining and Reflecting Upon Xenofeminism,' *Feminist Review* (2019) 123: 126–134.

Jones, Emily, 'A Posthuman-Xenofeminist Analysis of the Discourse on Autonomous Weapons Systems and Other Killing Machines,' *Australian Feminist Law Journal* (2018) 44(1): 93–118.

Joyner, Christopher C. and Little, George E., 'It's Not Nice to Fool Mother Nature! The Mystique of Feminist Approaches to International Environmental Law,' *Boston University International Law Journal* (1994) 14: 223–266.

Kafer, Alison, 'Crip Kind, Manifesting,' *Catalyst* (2019) 5(1): 1–37.

Käll, Jannice, 'The Materiality of Data as Property,' *Harvard International Law Journal Frontiers* (2020) 61: 1–11.

Käll, Jannice, 'A Posthuman Data Subject? The Right to be Forgotten and Beyond,' *German Law Journal* (2017) 18(5): 1145–1162.

Kalmanovitz, Palo, 'Judgement, Liability and the Risks of Riskless Warfare,' in Nehal Bhuta et al. (eds.), *Autonomous Weapons Systems: Law, Ethics, Policy*, (Cambridge University Press, 2016):147–163.

Kamieński, Lucasz, *Shooting Up: A History of Drugs and War*, (Oxford University Press, 2016).

Kang, Hyo Yoon, 'Law's Materiality: Between Concrete Matters and Abstract Forms, or How Matter Becomes Material,' in Andreas Philippopoulos-Mihalopoulos (ed.), *Routledge Handbook for Law and Theory*, (Routledge, 2018): 453–474.

Kang, Hyo Yoon and Kendall, Sara, 'Legal Materiality,' in Simon Stern et al. (eds.), *The Oxford Handbook of Law and Humanities*, (Oxford University Press, 2019b): 21–38.

Kang, Hyo Yoon and Kendall, Sara (eds.), Special Issue on Legal Materiality, *Law Text Culture* (2019a) 43. 1–293.

Kapur, Ratna, *Gender, Alterity and Human Rights: Freedom in a Fishbowl*, (Edward Elgar, 2018).

Kapur, Ratna, 'Gender, Sovereignty and the Rise of a Sexual Security Regime in International Law and Postcolonial India,' *Melbourne Journal of International Law* (2014) 14(2): 317–345.

Kapur, Ratna, 'The Tragedy of Victimization Rhetoric: Resurrecting the "Native" Subject in International/Post-Colonial Feminist Legal Politics,' *Harvard Human Rights Journal* (2002) 15(1): 1–38.

Kauffman, Craig M., 'Managing People for the Benefit of the Land: Practicing Earth Jurisprudence in Te Urewera, New Zealand/Aotearoa,' *ILSE: Interdisciplinary Studies in Literature and Environment* (2020) 27(1): 578–595.

Kauffman, Craig M. and Martin, Pamela L., *The Politics of the Rights of Nature: Strategies for Building a More Sustainable Future*, (MIT Press, 2021).

Kauffman, Craig M. and Martin, Pamela L., 'Constructing Rights of Nature Norms in the US, Ecuador, and New Zealand/Aotearoa,' *Global Environmental Politics*, (2018) 18(4): 43–62.

Kauffman, Craig M. and Sheehan, Linda, 'The Rights of Nature: Guiding Our Responsibilities through Standards,' in Stephen Turner et al. (eds), *Environmental Rights: The Development of Standards*, (Cambridge University Press, 2019): 342–366.

Kazan, Helene, 'The Architecture of Slow, Structural, and Spectacular Violence and the Poetic Testimony of War,' *Australian Feminist Law Journal* (2018) 44(1): 119–136.

Kendall, Sara, 'Law's End: On Algorithmic Warfare and Humanitarian Violence,' in Max Liljefors et al. (eds.), *War and the Algorithm*, (Rowman & Littlefield, 2019): 105–125.

Kendall, Sara, 'Cartographies of the Present: "Contingent Sovereignty" and Territorial Integrity,' in Martin Kuijer and Wouter Werner (eds.), *Netherlands Yearbook of International Law* (2016) 47: 83–105.

Kennedy, David, *A World of Struggle: How Power, Law and Expertise Shape Global Political Economy*, (Princeton University Press, 2016).

Keshavarz, Mahmoud, and Parsa, Amin, 'Targeted by Persuasion: Military Uniforms and the Legal Matter of Killing in War,' *Law Text Culture* (2019) 23: 223–239.

Kinsella, Helen M., 'Gendering Grotius,' *Political Theory*, (2006) 34(2): 161–191.

Kirby, Vicki, 'Natural Convers(at)ions: Or, What If Culture was Really Nature All Along?' in Stacy Alaimo and Susan Hekman (eds.), *Material Feminisms*, (Indiana University Press, 2008): 214–236.

Klumbytė, Goda and Draude, Claude, 'New Materialist Informatics,' in Rosi Braidotti et al. (eds.), *More Posthuman Glossary*, (Bloomsbury, forthcoming 2023).

Knop, Karen, 'Here and There: International Law in Domestic Courts,' *N.Y.U. Journal of International Law and Politics* (1999–2000) 32: 501–535.

Knop, Karen, 'Why Rethinking the Sovereign State is Important for Women's International Human Rights Law,' in Rebecca J. Cook (ed.), *Human Rights of Women*, (Pennsylvania University Press, 1994): 153–164.

Knox, Robert, 'Marxist Approaches to International Law,' in Anne Orford and Florian Hoffmann (eds.), *The Oxford Handbook of the Theory of International Law*, (Oxford University Press, 2016a): 306–326.

Knox, Robert, 'Valuing Race? Stretched Marxism and the Logic of Imperialism,' *London Review of International Law* (2016b) 4(1): 81–126.

Knox, Robert, 'Strategy and Tactics,' *Finnish Yearbook of International Law* (2010) 21: 193–229.

Knuckey, Sarah, 'Autonomous Weapons Systems and Transparency: Towards an International Dialogue,' in Nehal Bhuta et al. (eds.), *Autonomous Weapons Systems: Law, Ethics, Policy* (Cambridge University Press, 2016): 164–184.

Koram, Kojo, '"Satan is Black" – Frantz Fanon's Juridico-Theology of Racialisation and Damnation,' *Law, Culture and the Humanities* (2017): 1–20.

Koskenniemi, Martti, *International Law and the Far Right: Reflection of Law and Cynicism*, Annual T.M.C Asser Lecture Series (T.M.C. Asser Press, 2019).

Koskenniemi, Martti, *From Apology to Utopia. The Structure of International Legal Argument*, (Cambridge University Press, 2005 [1989]).

Kotzé, Louis J., 'Earth System Law for the Anthropocene: Rethinking Environmental Law alongside the Earth System Metaphor,' *Transnational Legal Theory* (2020) 11(1–2): 75–10.

Kotzé, Louise J. and Kim, Rakhyun E., 'Earth System Law: The Juridical Dimensions of Earth System Governance,' *Earth System Governance* (2019) 1: 1–12.

Kouvo, Sari and Pearson, Zoe, (eds.), *Feminist Perspectives on Contemporary International Law: Between Resistance and Compliance?* (Hart, 2014).

Laboria Cuboniks, *The Xenofeminist Manifesto*, (Verso, 2018).

Lang, Andrew, 'Purse Seine Net,' in Jessie Hohmann and Daniel Joyce (eds.), *International Law's Objects*, (Oxford University Press, 2018): 377–386.

Latour, Bruno, *Reassembling the Social: An Introduction to Actor-Network Theory*, (Oxford University Press, 2007).

Latour, Bruno, *Pandora's Hope: Essays on the Reality of Science Studies*, (Harvard University Press, 1999).

Lazarus, Richard J., 'Environmental Law After Katrina: Reforming Environmental Law by Reforming Environmental Lawmaking,' *Tulane Law Review* (2007) 81: 1019–1058.

Leach, James, 'Documents against "Knowledge"; Immanence and Transcendence and Approaching Legal Materials,' *Law Text Culture* (2019) 23: 16–39.

Leins, Kobi, *New War Technologies and International Law: The Legal Limits to Weaponising Nanomaterials*, (Cambridge University Press, 2022).

Lewis, Holly, *The Politics of Everybody: Feminism, Queer Theory and Marxism at the Intersection*, (Zed Books, 2016).

Lewis, Jason Edward et al., 'Making Kin with the Machines,' *Journal of Design Studies* (2018), published online 16 July 2018, n.p., https://doi.org/10.21428/bfafd97b (last accessed 11 July 2022).

Lewis, Sophie, *Full Surrogacy Now: Feminist Against the Family*, (Verso, 2021).

Liivoja, Rain and Chircop, Luke, 'Are Enhanced Warfighters Weapons, Means, or Methods of Warfare?' *International Law Studies* (2018) 94: 161–185; Heather A. Harrison Dinniss and Jann K. Kleffner, 'Soldier 2.0: Military Human Enhancement and International Law,' *International Law Studies* (2016) 92: 432–482.

Lijnzaard, Liesbeth, 'The UN Fish Sticks Agreement as a Metaphor, or the Law of the Sea as a Gendered Process,' in Irini Papanicolopulu (ed.), *Gender and the Law of the Sea*, (Brill, 2019): 149–161.

Lindberg, Darcey, 'Excerpts from Nêhiyaw Âskiy Wiyasiwêwina: Plains Cree Earth Law and Constitutional/Ecological Reconciliation,' *Rooted* (2021) 1(1): 10–16.

Liu, Hin-Yan, 'From the Autonomy Framework towards Networks and Systems Approaches for "Autonomous" Weapons Systems,' *Journal of International Humanitarian Legal Studies* (2019) 10(1): 89–110.

Liu, Hin-Yan, 'Refining Responsibility: Differentiating Two Types of Responsibility Issues Raised by Autonomous Weapons Systems,' in Nehal Bhuta et al. (eds.), *Autonomous Weapons Systems: Law, Ethics, Policy* (Cambridge University Press, 2016): 325–344.

Lubell, Noam and Al-Khateeb, Katya, 'Cyborg Soldiers: Military Use of Brain-Computer Interfaces and the Law of Armed Conflict,' in Laura Dickenson and Eiki Berg (eds.), *Big Data and Armed Conflict*, (Oxford University Press, forthcoming 2023).

Lucas, George R., 'Automated Warfare,' *Stanford Law & Policy Review* (2001) 25(2): 317–340.

Luciano, Dana, and Chen, Mel Y., 'Has the Queer ever been Human?,' *GLQ: A Journal of Lesbian and Gay Studies* (2015) 21(203): 183–207.

Lucretius, *On the Nature of Things*, trans. Cyril Bailey, (Oxford University Press, 1948 [1910]).

Lustig, Doreen, *Veiled Power: International Law and the Private Corporation 1996–1981*, (Oxford University Press, 2020).

Lykke, Nina, 'Passionately Posthuman: From Feminist Disidentifications to Postdisciplinary Posthumanities,' in Cecilia Åsberg and Rosi Braidotti (eds.), *A Feminist Companion to the Posthumanities*, (Springer International, 2018): 23–33.

MacCormack, Patricia, *The Ahuman Manifesto: Activism for the End of the Anthropocene*, (Bloomsbury, 2020).

Macpherson, Elizabeth et al., 'Where Ordinary Laws Fall Short: "Riverine Rights"' and Constitutionalism,' *Griffith Law Review* (2021) 0: 1–36.

Maguire, Rowena, 'Gender, Climate Change and the United Nations Framework Convention on Climate Change,' in Susan Harris Rimmer and Kate Ogg (eds.), *Research Handbook on Feminist Engagement with International Law*, (Edward Elgar, 2019): 63–80.

Maguire, Rowena and Lewis, Bridget, 'Women, Human Rights and the Global Climate Regime,' *Journal of Human Rights and the Environment* (2018) 9(1): 51–67.

Mahmood, Saba, *Politics of Piety: The Islamic Revival and the Feminist Subject*, (Princeton University Press, 2004).

Malone, Karen et al., 'Shimmering with Deborah Rose: Posthuman Theory-Making with Feminist Ecophilosophers and Social Ecologists,' *Australian Journal of Environmental Education* (2020) 36(2): 129–145.

Malone, Linda A., 'Environmental Justice Reimagined through Human Security and Post-Modern Ecological Feminism: A Neglected Perspective on Climate Change,' *Fordham International Law Journal* (2015) 38(5):1445–1472.

Manjikian, Mary, 'Becoming Unmanned: The Gendering of Lethal Autonomous Warfare Technology,' *International Feminist Journal of Politics* (2014) 16(1): 48–65.

Margulies, Peter, 'The Other Side of Autonomous Weapons: Using Artificial Intelligence to Enhance IHL Compliance,' in Eric Talbot and Ronald T.O. Alcala (eds.), *The Impact of Emerging Technologies on the Law of Armed Conflict*, (Oxford University Press, 2019): 147–174.

Mark, Gregory A., 'The Personification of the Business Corporation in American Law,' *University of Chicago Law Review* (1987) 54(4): 1441–1483.

Marks, Susan, *A False Tree of Liberty: Human Rights in Radical Thought*, (Oxford University Press, 2019).

Marks, Susan, 'Four Human Rights Myths,' in David Kinley et al. (eds.), *Human Rights: Old Problems, New Possibilities*, (Edward Elgar, 2013): 217–235.

Marks, Susan, 'Human Rights and Root Causes,' *Modern Law Review* (2011) 74: 57–78.

Marks, Susan, 'False Contingency,' *Current Legal Problems* (2009) 62: 1–21.

Marshall, Virginia, 'Removing the Veil from the "Rights of Nature": The Dichotomy between First Nations Customary Rights and Environmental Legal Personhood,' *Australian Feminist Law Journal* (2019) 45(2): 233–248.

Masters, Cristina, 'Bodies of Technology: Cyborg Soldiers and Militarized Masculinities,' *International Feminist Journal of Politics* (2005) 7(1): 112–132.

Mayur, Carl J., 'Personalizing the Impersonal: Corporations and the Bill of Rights,' *Hastings Law Journal* (1990) 41(3): 577–667.

Mbembe, Achille, *Necropolitics*, (Duke University Press, 2019).

Mbembe, Achille, trans. Libby Meintjes, 'Necropolitics,' *Public Culture*, 2003, 15(1): 11–40.

McClimtock, Anne, *Imperial Leather: Race, Gender and Sexuality in the Colonial Context*, (Routledge, 1995).

McCorquodale, Robert, 'The Individual and the International Legal System,' in Malcom Evans (ed.), *International Law*, (Oxford University Press, 5th edn, 2018): 259–288.

McFarland, Tim, *Autonomous Weapons Systems and the Law of Armed Conflict*, (Cambridge University Press, 2020).

McKittrick, Katherine (ed.), *Sylvia Wynter: On Being Human as Praxis*, (Duke University Press, 2014).

McMillan, Mark and Rigney, Sophie, 'The Place of the First Peoples in the International Sphere: A Logical Starting Point for the Demand for Justice by Indigenous Peoples,' *Melbourne University Law Review* (2016) 39(3) 981–1002.

McNeil, Maureen, *Feminist Cultural Studies of Science and Technology*, (Routledge, 2007).

McNeilly, Kathryn, 'Documents and Time in International Human Rights Law Monitoring: Artefacts, Objects, Things,' in Kathryn McNeilly and Ben Warwick (eds.), *The Time and Temporalities of International Human Rights Law*, (Bloomsbury, 2022): 85–102.

Meili, Mario, *Towards a Gay Communism: Elements of a Homosexual Critique*, (Pluto Press, 2002).

Meir, Michael W., 'Emerging Technologies and the Principle of Distinction: A Further Blurring of the Lines Between Combatants and Civilians,' in Eric Talbot and Ronald T.O. Alcala (eds.), *The Impact of Emerging Technologies on the Law of Armed Conflict*, (Oxford University Press, 2019): 211–234.

Miéville, China, *Between Equal Rights: A Marxist Theory of International Law*, (Pluto Press, 2006).

Mills, Aaron, 'A Preliminary Sketch of Anishinaabe (a Species of Rooted) Constitutionalism,' *Rooted* (2021) 1(1): 2–7.

Mills, Aaron, 'Aki, Anishianaabek, kaye tahsh Crown,' *Indigenous Law Journal* (2010) 9(1): 107–213.

Miranda, Robbin A. et al., 'DARPA-Funded Efforts in the Development of Novel Brain-Computer Interface Technologies,' *Journal of Neuroscience Methods* (2015) 244: 52–67.

Mitchell, Audra, "Posthuman Security': Reflections from an Open-ended Conversation,' in Clara Eroukhmanoff and Matt Harker (eds.), *Reflections on the Posthuman in International Relations*, (E-International Relations Publishing, 2017): 10–18.

Montini, Massimiliano, 'The Transformation of Environmental Law into Ecological Law,' in Kirsten Anker et al. (ed.), *From Environmental to Ecological Law*, (Routledge, 2021).

Moore, Jason, 'The Capitalocene, Part I: On the Nature and Origins of Our Ecological Crisis,' *The Journal of Peasant Studies* (2017) 44(3): 594–630.

Morrow, Karen, 'Perspectives on Environmental Law and the Law Relating to Sustainability: A Continued Role for Ecofeminism?' in Andreas Philippopoulos-Mihalopoulos (ed.), *Law and Ecology: New Environmental Foundations*, (Routledge, 2011): 126–152.

Morrow, Karen Lesley, 'Tackling Climate Change and Gender Justice – Integral; not Optional,' *Oñati Socio-Legal Series* (2021) 11(1): 207–230.

Mortimer-Sandilands, Catriona and Erickson, Bruce, 'Introduction: A Genealogy of Queer Ecologies,' in Catriona Mortimer Sandilands and Bruce Erickson (eds.), *Queer Ecologies: Sex, Nature, Politics, Desire*, (Indiana University Press, 2010): 1–48.

Morton, Timothy, 'Queer Ecology,' *PMLA* (2010) 125(2): 273–282.

Muller, Samantha, et al., 'Indigenous Sovereignties: Relational Ontologies and Environmental Management,' *Geographical Research* (2019) 57(4): 399–410.

Muñoz, José Esteban, 'Preface: Fragment from the *Sense of Brown* Manuscript,' *GLQ: A Journal of Lesbian and Gay Studies* (2018) 24(4): 395–397.

Muñoz, José Esteban et al., 'Theorizing Queer Inhumanisms,' *GLQ: A Journal of Lesbian and Gay Studies*, (2015) 21(2–3): 209–248.

Murray, Daragh, *Practitioners' Guide to Human Rights Law in Armed Conflict*, (Oxford University Press, 2017).

Mussawir, Edward, 'A Modification in the Subject of Right: Deleuze, Jurisprudence and the Diagram of Bees in Roman Law,' in Rosi Braidotti and Simone Bignall (eds.), *Posthuman Ecologies: Complexity and Process after Deleuze*, (Rowman & Littlefield, 2019): 243–263.

Naess, Arne, *Ecology of Wisdom*, (Penguin, 2016).

Naffine, Ngaire, 'Women and the Cast of Legal Persons,' in Jackie Jones et al. (eds.), *Gender, Sexualities and Law*, (Routledge, 2011): 15–25.

Naffine, Ngaire, 'The Body Bag,' in Ngaire Naffine and Rosemary Owens (eds.), *Sexing the Subject of Law*, (LBC Information Services, 1997): 73–93.

Nagel, Joane, *Gender and Climate Change: Impacts, Science, Policy*, (Routledge, 2016).

Natarajan, Usha, 'Third World Approaches to International Law (TWAIL) and the Environment,' in Andreas Philippopoulos-Mihalopoulos and Victoria Brooks (eds.), *Research Methods in Environmental Law: A Handbook*, (Edward Elgar, 2017): 207–235.

Natarajan, Usha and Khoday, Kishan, 'Locating Nature: Making and Unmaking International Law,' *Leiden Journal of International Law* (2014) 27(3): 573–593.

Neimanis, Astrida, 'Bodies of Water, Human Rights and the Hydrocommons,' *TOPIA: Canadian Journal of Cultural Studies* (2009) 21: 161–182.

Nesiah, Vasuki, 'Gender and Forms of Conflict: The Moral Hazards of Dating the Security Council,' in Fionnuala Ní Aoláin et al. (eds.), *The Oxford Handbook of Gender and Conflict*, (Oxford University Press, 2018): 289–302.

Nesiah, Vaskui, 'The Ground Beneath Her Feet: TWAIL Feminisms,' in Antony Anghie et al. (eds.), *The Third World and International Order*, (Brill, 2003): 133–143.

Newton, Michael and May, Larry, *Proportionality in International Law*, (Oxford University Press, 2014).

Ní Aoláin, Fionnuala, 'The "War on Terror" and Extremism: Assessing the Relevance of the Women, Peace and Security Agenda,' *International Affairs* (2016) 9(2): 275–291.

Nijman, Janne Elisabeth, *The Concept of International Legal Personality: An Inquiry into the History and Theory of International Law*, (Asser Press, 2004).

Niner, Holly J. et al., 'Deep-Sea Mining with No Net Loss of Biodiversity – An Impossible Aim,' *Frontiers in Marine Science* (2018) 5: 1–12.

Ninic, Miroslav and Cusack, Thomas R., 'The Political Economy of US Military Spending,' *Journal of Peace Research* (1979) 6(2): 101–115.

Noble, Safiya Umoja, *Algorithms of Oppression: How Search Engines Reinforce Racism*, (New York University Press, 2018).

Noll, Gregor, 'War by Algorithm: The End of War?,' in Max Liljefors et al. (eds.), *War and the Algorithm*, (Rowman & Littlefield, 2019): 75–104.

Noll, Gregor, 'Weaponising Neurotechnology: International Humanitarian Law and the Loss of Language,' *London Review of International Law* (2014) 2(2): 201–231.

Noyes, John E., 'The Common Heritage of Mankind: Past, Present, and Future,' *Denver Journal of International Law and Policy*, (2011) 40: 447–471.

O'Connell, Mark, *To Be a Machine: Adventures Among Cyborgs, Utopians, Hackers and the Futurists Solving the Modest Problem of Death*, (Granta, 2017).

O'Donnell, Erin, *Legal Rights for Rivers: Competition, Collaboration and Water Governance*, (Routledge, 2020).

O'Donnell, Erin et al., 'Stop Burying the Lede: The Essential Role of Indigenous Law(s) in Creating Rights of Nature,' *Transnational Environmental Law* (2020) 9(3): 403–427.

Ollino, Alice, 'Feminism, Nature and the Post-Human: Towards a Critical Analysis of the International Law of the Sea Governing Marine Living Resources Management,' in Irini Papanicolopulu (ed.), *Gender and the Law of the Sea*, (Brill, 2019): 204–228.

Orford, Anne, 'Theorizing Free Trade,' in Anne Orford and Florian Hoffmann (eds.), *The Oxford Handbook of the Theory of International Law*, (Oxford University Press, 2016): 701–737.

Orford, Anne, *Reading Humanitarian Intervention: Human Rights and the Use of Force in International Law*, (Cambridge University Press, 2008).

Orford, Anne, 'Muscular Humanitarianism: Reading the Narratives of the New Interventionism,' *European Journal of International Law* (1999) 10(4): 679–711.

Otomo, Yoriko, *Unconditional Life: The Postwar International Law Settlement*, (Oxford University Press, 2016).

Otomo, Yoriko, 'Of Mimicry and Madness: Speculations on the State,' *Australian Feminist Law Journal* (2014) 28(1): 53–76.

Otomo, Yoriko and Mussawir, Edward, (eds.), *Law and the Question of the Animal*, (Routledge, 2013).

Otto, Dianne, 'Contesting Feminism's Institutional Doubles: Troubling the Security Council's Women, Peace and Security Agenda,' in Janet Halley et al. (eds.), *Governance Feminism: Notes from the Field*, (Minnesota University Press, 2019): 200–229.

Otto, Dianne, 'Women, Peace and Security: A Critical Analysis of the Security Council's Vision,' in Fionnuala Ní Aoláin et al. (eds.), *The Oxford Handbook of Gender and Conflict*, (Oxford University Press, 2018): 106–118.

Otto, Dianne, 'Feminist Approaches to International Law,' in Anne Orford and Florian Hoffman (eds.), *Oxford Handbook of International Legal Theory*, (Oxford University Press, 2016): 488–504.

Otto, Dianne, 'Queering Gender [Identity] in International Law,' *Nordic Journal of Human Rights* (2015) 33(4): 299–318.

Otto, Dianne, 'Beyond Stories of Victory and Danger: Resisting Feminism's Amenability to Serving Security Council Politics,' in Gina Heathcote and Dianne Otto (eds.), *Rethinking Peacekeeping, Gender Equality and Collective Security*, (Palgrave Macmillan, 2014): 157–172.

Otto, Dianne, 'International Human Rights Law: Towards Rethinking Sex/Gender Dualism,' in Margaret Davies and Vanessa E. Munro (eds.), *The Ashgate Research Companion to Feminist Legal Theory*, (Routledge, 2013): 197–216.

Otto, Dianne, 'The Security Council's Alliance of Gender Legitimacy: The Symbolic Capital of Resolution 1325' in Hilary Charlesworth and Jean-Marc Coicaud (eds.), *Fault Lines of International Legitimacy* (Cambridge University Press, 2010): 239–287.

Otto, Dianne and Grear, Anna, 'International Law, Social Change and Resistance: A n Between Professor Anna Grear (Cardiff) and Professorial Fellow Dianne Otto (Melbourne),' *Feminist Legal Studies* (2018) 26: 351–363.

Özsu, Umut, 'Grabbing Land Legally: A Marxist Analysis,' *Leiden Journal of International Law* (2019) 32: 215–233.

Pahuja, Sundhya, 'Conserving the World's Resources?,' in James Crawford and Martti Koskenniemi (eds.), *The Cambridge Companion to International Law*, (Cambridge University Press, 2015): 398–420.

Paige, Tamsin Phillipa, 'The Maintenance of Heteronormativity,' in Dianne Otto (ed.), *Queering International Law: Possibilities, Alliances, Complicities, Risks*, (Routledge, 2018): 91–109.

Papanicolopulu, Irini, (ed.), *Gender and the Law of the Sea*, (Brill, 2019).

Parfitt, Rose, *The Process of International Legal Production: Inequality, Historiography, Resistance*, (Cambridge University Press, 2019).

Parfitt, Rose, 'Theorizing Recognition and International Personality,' in Anne Orford and Florian Hoffmann (eds.), *The Oxford Handbook of the Theory of International Law* (Oxford University Press, 2016): 583–599.

Parisi, Luciana, 'Automated Thinking and the Limits of Reason,' *Cultural Studies ↔ Critical Methodologies* (2016) 16(5): 471–481.

Parsley, Connal, 'Automating Authority: The Human and Automation in Legal Discourse on the Meaningful Human Control of Lethal Autonomous Weapons Systems,' in Shane Chalmers and Sundhya Pahuja, *Routledge Handbook of International Law and the Humanities*, (Routledge, 2021): 432–445.

Pashukanis, Evgeny B., 'Economics and Legal Regulation,' in Piers Beirne and Robert Sharlet (eds.), *Pashukanis: Selected Writings on Marxism and Law*, (Academic Press London, 1980a).

Pashukanis, Evgeny B., 'The General Theory of Law and Marxism,' in Piers Beirne and Robert Sharlet (eds.), *Pashukanis: Selected Writings on Marxism and Law*, (Academic Press London, 1980b).

Pasquale, Frank, *The Black Box Society: The Secret Algorithms that Control Money and Information*, (Harvard University Press, 2015).

Pelizzon, Alessandro and Kennedy, Jade, 'Welcome to Country: Legal Meanings and Cultural Implications,' *Australian Indigenous Law Review* (2012) 16(2): 58–69.

Petersmann, Marie-Catherine, 'Response-Abilities of Care in More-Than-Human Worlds,' *Journal of Human Rights and the Environment* (2021a) 12: 102–124.

Petersmann, Marie-Catherine, 'Sympoietic Thinking and Earth System Law: The Earth, Its Subjects and the Law,' *Earth System Governance* (2021b) 9: 1–8.

Philippopoulos-Mihalopoulos, Andreas, 'Critical; Environmental Law in the Anthropocene,' in Louise J. Kotzé (ed.), *Environmental Law and Governance for the Anthropocene*, (Bloomsbury, 2017): 117–135.

Philippopoulos-Mihalopoulos, Andreas, 'Flesh of the Law: Material Legal Metaphors,' *Journal of Law and Society* (2016) 43: 45–65.

Philippopoulos-Mihalopoulos, Andreas, *Spatial Justice: Body, Lawscape, Atmosphere*, (Routledge, 2015).

Picado, Johnathan A. and Reid, Rebecca A., 'Mother Nature, Lady Justice,' *Open Judicial Politics* (2021), https://open.oregonstate.education/open-judicial-politics/chapter/mother-nature-lady-justice/#footnote-724-3 (last accessed 11 July 2022).

Piggott-McKellar, Annah E., et al., 'Moving People in a Changing Climate: Lessons from Two Case Studies in Fiji,' *Social Sciences* (2019) 8(133): 1–17.

Pilloud, Claude and Pictet, Jean, 'Protocol I – Article 57 – Precautions in Attack,' in Yves Sandoz et al. (eds.), *Commentary on the Additional Protocols of 8 June 1977 to the Geneva Conventions on 12 August 1949*, (Martinus Nijhoff, 1987): 677–690.

Plumwood, Val, *Feminism and the Mastery of Mature*, (Routledge, 1993).

Portmann, Roland, *Legal Personality in International Law*, (Cambridge University Press, 2010).

Pottage, Alain, 'The Materiality of What?,' *Journal of Law and Society* (2012) 39: 167–183.

Prescott, Jody M., *Armed Conflict, Women and Climate Change*, (Routledge, 2019).

Pufendorf, Samuel von, *De Iure Naturae et Gentium*, Libri Octo, Vol. I, 1688.

Puscas, Ioana Maria, 'Military Human Enhancement,' in William H. Boothby (ed.), *New Technologies and the Law in War and Peace*, (Cambridge University Press, 2018):182–229.

Quiroga-Villamarín, Daniel Ricardo, 'Beyond Texts? Towards a Material Turn in the Theory and History of International Law,' *Journal of the History of International Law* (2020a) 23: 466–500.

Quiroga-Villamarín, Daniel R., 'Domains of Objects, Rituals of Truth: Mapping Intersections between International Legal History and the New Materialisms,' *International Politics Reviews* (2020b) 8: 129–151.

Quiroga-Villamarín, Daniel R., 'Normalising Global Commerce: Containerisation, Materiality, and Transnational Regulation (1956–68),' *London Review of International Law* (2020c) 8(3): 457–477.

Ranganathan, Surabhi, 'Ocean Floor Grab: International Law and the Making of an Extractive Imaginary,' *European Journal of International Law* (2019) 30(2): 573–600.

Redgwell, Catherine, 'International Environmental Law,' in Malcolm D. Evans (ed.), *International Law*, (Oxford University Press, 5th edn, 2018): 675–716.

Ripple, W.J. et al., 'World Scientists' Warning of a Climate Emergency,' *Bioscience* (2020) 70(1): 8–12.

Rittich, Kerry, 'The Future of Law and Development: Second Generation Reforms and the Incorporation of the Social,' *Michigan Journal of International Law* (2004) 26(1): 199–243.

Rochette, Anne, 'Transcending the Conquest of Nature and Women: A Feminist Perspective on International Environmental Law,' in Doris Buss and Ambreena Manji (eds.), *International Law: Modern Feminist Approaches*, (Hart, 2005): 203–235.

Roff, Heather M., 'Gendering a Warbot,' *International Feminist Journal of Politics* (2016) 18(1): 1–18.

Rogers, Nicole and Maloney, Michelle (eds.), *Law as if Earth Really Mattered* (Routledge, 2017).

Rosiek, Jerry Lee et al., 'The New Materialisms and Indigenous Theories of Non-Human Agency: Making the Case for Respectful Anti-Colonial Engagement,' *Qualitative Inquiry* (2020) 26(3–4): 331–346.

Ruru, Jacinta, 'Listening to Papatūānuku: A Call to Reform Water Law,' *Journal of the Royal Society of New Zealand/Aotearoa* (2019) 48(2–3): 215–224.

Ruskola, Teemu, 'Raping Like a State,' *UCLA Law Review* (2009–10) 57: 1477–1536.

Saif, Atef Abu, *The Drone Eats with Me: A Gaza Diary*, (Beacon Press, 2016).

Salter, Mark B., (ed.), *Making Things International 2: Catalysts and Reactions*, (Minnesota University Press, 2016).

Salter, Mark B., (ed.), *Making Things International 1: Circuits and Motion*, (Minnesota University Press, 2015).

Sands, Philippe and Peel, Jacqueline, *Principles of Environmental Law*, (Cambridge University Press, 4th edn, 2018).

Sandvik, Kristin Bergtora, 'Technology, Dead Male Bodies, and Feminist Recognition: Gender ICT Harm,' *Australian Feminist Law Journal* (2018) 44(1): 49–69.

Sartor, Giovanni and Omicini, Andrea, 'The Autonomy of Technological Systems and Responsibilities for Their Use,' in Nehal Bhuta et al. (eds.), *Autonomous Weapons Systems: Law, Ethics, Policy*, (Cambridge University Press, 2016): 39–74.

Saxon, Dan, 'A Human Touch: Autonomous Weapons, DoD Directive 3000.09 and the Interpretation of "Appropriate Levels of Human Judgment over Force,"' in Nehal Bhuta et al. (eds.), *Autonomous Weapons Systems:, Ethics, Policy Law* (Cambridge University Press, 2016): 185–208.

Schippers, Birgit, 'Towards a Posthumanist Conception of Human Rights?', in Birgit Schippers (ed.), *Critical Perspectives on Human Rights*, (Rowman & Littlefield, 2019): 63–82.

Schmitt, Michael N. and Thurnher, Jeffrey S., '"Out of the Loop": Autonomous Weapon Systems and the Law of Armed Conflict,' *Harvard National Security Journal* (2013) 4: 231–281.

Schuppli, Susan, *Material Witness: Media, Forensics, Evidence*, (MIT Press, 2020).

Scott, Joan Wallach, *The Fantasy of Feminist History*, (Duke University Press, 2012).

Seymour, Nicole, *Strange Natures: Futurity, Empath, and the Queer Ecological Imagination*, (University of Illinois Press, 2013).

Sharkey, Noel, 'Staying in the Loop: Human Supervisory Control of Weapons,' in Nehal Bhuta et al. (eds.), *Autonomous Weapons Systems:, Ethics, Policy Law* (Cambridge University Press, 2016): 23–38.

Sharp, Hasana, 'The Force of Ideas in Spinoza,' *Political Theory* (2007) 35(6): 732–755.

Sharpe, Christina, *In the Wake: On Blackness as Being*, (Duke University Press, 2016).

Shaw, Ian, 'Predator Empire: The Geopolitics of US Drone Warfare,' *Geopolitics* (2013) 18(3): 536–559.

Shaw, Ian Graham Ronald and Majed, Akhter, 'The Unbearable Humanness of Drone Warfare in FATA, Pakistan,' *Antipode* (2011) 44(4): 1490–1509.

Sheldon, Rebekah, 'Form / Matter / Chora: Objected-Orientated Ontology and Feminist New Materialism,' in Richard Grusin (ed.), *The Nonhuman Turn* (Minnesota University Press, 2015): 193–222.

Simons, Penelope, 'International Law's Invisible Hand and the Future of Corporate Accountability for Violations of Human Rights,' *Journal of Human Rights and the Environment* (2013) 3(1): 5–43.

Simpson, Gerry, *Great Powers and Outlaw States: Unequal Sovereigns in the International Legal Order*, (Cambridge University Press, 2004).

Sjoberg, Laura and Gentry, Caron E., *Mothers, Monsters, Whores: Women's Violence in Global Politics*, (Zed Books, 2007).

Smelik, Anneke, 'Wearable Technology,' in Rosi Braidotti and Maria Hlavajova (eds.), *Posthuman Glossary*, (Bloomsbury, 2018): 455–458.

Snape III, William J., 'A Pattern of Ruling Against Mother Nature: Wildlife Species Cases Decided by Justice Kavanaugh,' *Sustainable Development Law & Policy* (2018) 19(1): 4–33.

Sousa Santos, Boaventura de, 'The Alternative to Utopia is Myopia,' *Politics & Society* (2020) 48(4): 567–584.

Sparrow, Robert, 'Robots and Respect: Assessing the Case Against Autonomous Weapon Systems,' *Ethics and International Affairs* (2016) 30(1): 93–116.

Spinoza, Benedictus de, *The Ethics*, (Penguin, 1996a [1677]).

Spinoza, Benedictus de, trans. Samuel Shirley, *The Letters Epistile*, (Hackett Publishing, 1996b).

Stauffer, Jill, '"You People Talk from Paper": Indigenous Law, Western Legalism, and the Cultural Viability of Law's Materials,' *Law, Text, Culture* (2019) 23: 40–57.

Steffen, Will et al., 'Planetary Boundaries: Guiding Human Development on a Changing Planet,' *Science (American Association for the Advancement of Science)* (2015) 347(6223): 1259855–1259855.

Stone, Christopher D., *Should Trees Have Standing? Law, Morality and the Environment* (Oxford University Press, 3rd edn, 2010).

Stone, Christopher D., 'Should Trees Have Standing? – Toward Legal Rights for Natural Objects,' *Southern California Law Review* (1972) 45: 450–501.

Stone, Sandy, 'The Empire Strikes Back: A Posttranssexual Manifesto,' in Julia Epstein and Kristina Straub (eds.), *Body Guards: The Cultural Politics of Gender Ambiguity*, (Routledge, 1991): 280–304.

Storr, Cait, '"Space is the Only Way to Go": The Evolution of the Extractivist Imaginary of International Law,' in Shane Chalmers and Sundhya Pahuja (eds.), *Routledge Handbook of International Law and the Humanities*, (Routledge, 2021): 290–301.

Stryker, Susan, 'My Words to Victor Frankenstein above the Village of Chamounix: Performing Transgender Rage,' *GLQ: A Journal of Lesbian and Gay Studies* (1993) 1(3): 237–54.

Suchman, Lucy, 'Algorithmic Warfare and the Reinvention of Accuracy,' *Critical Studies on Security* (2020) 8(2): 175–187.

Suchman, Lucy and Weber, Jutta, 'Human-Machine Autonomies,' in Nehal Bhuta et al. (eds.), *Autonomous Weapons Systems: Law, Ethics, Policy*, (Cambridge University Press, 2016): 75–102.

Swartz, Leslie, 'Cyborg Anxieties: Oscar Pistorius and the Boundaries of What It Means to Be Human,' *Disability & Society* (2008) 23(2): 187–190.

Tănăsescu, Mihnea, *Understanding the Rights of Nature: A Critical Introduction*, (Transcript Publishing, 2022).

Taylor, Bron et al., 'The Need for Ecocentrism in Biodiversity Conservation,' *Conservation Biology* (2020) 34(5): 1089–1096.

Taylor, Carol A. and Bayley, Annouchka, (eds.), *Posthumanism and Higher Education*, (Palgrave Macmillan, 2019).

Taylor, Carol A. and Hughes, Christina, (eds.), *Posthuman Research Practices in Education*, (Palgrave Macmillan, 2016).

Tesón, Fernando R., 'Feminism and International Law: A Reply,' *Virginia Journal of International Law* (1992–1993) 33: 647–684.

Teubner, Gunther, 'Rights of Non-Humans? Electronic Agents and Animals as New Actors in Politics and Law,' *Journal of Law and Society* (2006) 33: 497–521.

Tuhkanen, Mikko, 'Queer Hybridity,' in Chrysanthi Niganni and Merl Storr (eds.), *Deleuze and Queer Theory*, (Edinburgh University Press, 2009): 92–114.

Turner, Stephen J., *A Global Environmental Right*, (Routledge, 2014).

Tzanakopoulos, Antonios, 'The Right to Be Free from Economic Coercion,' *Cambridge Journal of International and Comparative Law* (2015) 4(3): 616–633.

Tzouvala, Ntina, *Capitalism as Civilisation: A History of International Law*, (Cambridge University Press, 2020).

Tzouvala, Ntina, 'A False Promise? Regulating Land-Grabbing and the Post-Colonial States,' *Leiden Journal of International Law* (2019) 32(2): 235–253.

Vargas-Roncancio, Iván Darió, 'Conjuring Sentient Beings and Relations in Law,' in Kirsetn Anker et al. (eds.), *From Environmental to Ecological Law*, (Routledge, 2021): 119–134.

Venzke, Ingo, 'The Law of the Global Economy and the Spectre of Inequality,' *London Review of International Law* (2021) 9(1): 111–134.

Venzke, Ingo and Heller, Kevin Jon (eds.), *Contingency in International Law: On the Possibility of Different Legal Histories*, (Oxford University Press, 2021).

Villavicencio, Paola and Kotzé, Louis J., 'Living in Harmony with Nature? A Critical Appraisal of the Rights of Mother Earth in Bolivia,' *Transnational Environmental Law* (2018) 7(3): 397–424.

Watson, Irene, 'Buried Alive,' *Law and Critique* (2002) 13: 253–269.

Webster, W. Earl, 'How Can Mother Nature Get to Court the Status of the Standing Doctrine in Post Laidlaw Landscape?,' *Journal of Land, Resources, & Environmental Law* 27(2): 453–472.

Weiss, Cornelia, 'Creating UNSCR 1325: Women Who Served as Initiators, Drafters, and Strategists,' in Rebecca Adami and Dan Plesch (eds.), *Women and the UN: A New History of Women's International Human Rights*, (Routledge, 2021): 139–160.

Whyte, Jessica, *The Morals of the Market: Human Rights and the Rise of Neoliberalism*, (Verso, 2019).

Wilcox, Lauren, 'Drones, Swarms and Becoming-Insect: Feminist Utopias and Posthuman Politics,' *Feminist Review* (2017) 116: 25–45.

Wilcox, Lauren, 'Embodying Algorithmic War: Gender, Race and the Posthuman in Warfare,' *Security Dialogue* (2016) 48(1): 1–18.

Wilcox, Lauren, 'Drone Warfare and the Making of Bodies out of Place,' *Critical Studies on Security* (2015) 3(1): 127–131.

Williams, John, 'Locating LAWS: Lethal Autonomous Weapons, Epistemic Space, and "Meaningful Human Control,"' *Journal of Global Security Studies* (2021a) 6(4): 1–18.

Woolaston, Katie, 'Wildlife and International Law: Can Feminism Transform Our Relationship with Nature?,' in Susan Harris Rimmer and Kate Ogg (eds.), *Research Handbook on Feminist Engagement with International Law*, (Edward Elgar, 2019): 44–62.

Wynter, Sylvia, 'On How We Mistook the Map for the Territory, and Re-Imprisoned Ourselves in Our Unbearable Wrongness of Being, of Désêtre: Black Studies Toward the Human Project,' in Lewis R. Gordon and Jane Anna Gordon (eds.), *Not Only the Master's Tools: African-American Studies and Theory in Practice*, (Paradigm Publishers, 2006): 107–169.

Wynter, Sylvia, 'Unsettling the Coloniality of Being/Power/Truth/Freedom: Towards the Human/After Man, Its Overrepresentation – An Argument,' *The New Centennial Review* (2003) 3(3): 257–337.

Wynter, Sylvia and McKittrick, Katherine, 'Unparalleled Catastrophe for Our Species? Or, to Give Humanness a Different Future: Conversations,' in Katherine McKittrick (ed.), *Sylvia Wynter: On Being Human as Praxis*, (Duke University Press, 2015): 9–89.

Youfatt, Rafi, 'Personhood and the Rights of Nature: The New Subjects of Contemporary Earth Politics,' *International Political Sociology* (2017) 11: 1–16.

Young, Iris Marion, *Justice and the Politics of Difference*, (Princeton University Press, 1990).

Yoshida, Keina, 'The Protection of the Environment: A Gendered Analysis,' *Goettingen Journal of International Law* (2020) 10(1): 283–305.

Websites, Blog Posts and News Reports

Bari, Mavra, Manipulating Mother Nature: The Gendered Antagonism of Geoengineering, Heinrich Böll Stiftung 2020, https://eu.boell.org/en/2020/01/30/manipulating-mother-nature-gendered-antagonism-geoengineering (last accessed 11 July 2022).

Barson, Ilinca, Research Reveals Inherent AI Gender Bias: Quantifying the Accuracy of Vision/ Facial Recognition on Identifying PPE Masks, Wunderman Thompson 2021, https:// www.wundermanthompson.com/insight/ai-and-gender-bias (last accessed 11 July 2022).

Bowcott, Owen, UK Opposes International Ban on Developing 'Killer Robots', *The Guardian*, 13 April 2015.

Brewster, Thomas, Project Maven: Startups Backed by Google, Peter Thiel, Eric Schmidt and James Murdoch are Building AI and Facial Recognition Surveillance Tools for the Pentagon, Forbes, 8 September 2021, https://www.forbes.com/sites/

thomasbrewster/2021/09/08/project-maven-startups-backed-by-google-peter-thiel-eric-schmidt-and-james-murdoch-build-ai-and-facial-recognition-surveillance-for-the-defense-department/?sh=4f29385a6ef2 (last accessed 11 July 2022).

Bundesanstalt für Geowissenschaften und Rohstoffe, Environmental Impact Assessment, 2018, https://isa.org.jm/files/files/documents/EIA_BGR_0.pdf (last accessed 11 July 2022).

Burns, Janet, Google Employees Denounce Company's Military Drone Work in Letter to CEO, Forbes 10 April 2018a, https://www.forbes.com/sites/janetwburns/2018/04/10/google-employees-denounce-companys-military-drone-work-in-letter-to-ceo/?sh=20e1ace1ef0d (last accessed 11 July 2022).

Burns, Janet, Google Employees Resign over Company's Pentagon Contract, Ethical Habits, Forbes, 14 May 2018b, https://www.forbes.com/sites/janetwburns/2018/05/14/google-employees-resign-over-firms-pentagon-contract-ethical-habits/?sh=5d74f1874169 (last accessed 11 July 2022).

Chavez, L., Philippine Bill Seeks to Grant Nature the Same Legal Rights as Humans, Mongaby, 2019, https://news.mongabay.com/2019/08/philippine-bill-seeks-to-grant-nature-the-same-legal-rights-as-humans/#:~:text=A%20coalition%20in%20the%20Philippines,confer%20legal%20personhood%20on%20nature.&text=The%20bill%20is%20part%20of,their%20protection%20amid%20intensifying%20threats (last accessed 11 July 2022).

Climate Diplomacy, Protest Against the Senhuile-Senethanol Project in Senegal, https://climate-diplomacy.org/case-studies/protest-against-senhuile-senethanol-project-senegal#fact_sheet_toc-actors (last accessed 11 July 2022).

Climate Emergency and Declaration and Mobilisation in Action, Climate Emergency Declaration Datasheet, https://www.cedamia.org/global (last accessed 11 July 2021).

Davies, Sara E. and True, Jacquie, From Pillars to Progress in Women, Peace and Security, LSE Blog, 26 November 2018, https://blogs.lse.ac.uk/wps/2018/11/26/from-pillars-to-progress-in-women-peace-and-security (last accessed 11 July 2022).

Earth Law Center, Seeking Rights of Nature in Chile's Constitution, https://www.earthlawcenter.org/chile (last accessed 11 July 2022).

Ecological Law and Governance Association, Oslo Manifesto, https://elgaworld.org/oslo-manifesto (last accessed 11 July 2022).

eMacula, Applications, https://www.emacula.io/home/applications (last accessed 11 July 2022).

Gerszon Mahler, Daniel et al., Updated Estimates of the Impact of COVID-19 on Global Poverty: Turning the Corner on the Pandemic in 2021?, World Bank Blogs, 24 June 2021, https://blogs.worldbank.org/opendata/updated-estimates-impact-covid-19-global-poverty-turning-corner-pandemic-2021 (last accessed 11 July 2022).

Global Greengrants Fund, Why the Environmental Justice Movement Must Include Persons with Disabilities, 18 March 2019, www.greengrants.org/2019/03/18/disability-and-environment (last accessed 11 July 2022).

Global Sea Mineral Resources, Environmental Impact Assessment, 2018, https://www.isa.org.jm/minerals/environmental-impact-assessments (last accessed 11 July 2022).

Global Security, Patriot Advanced Capability-3, www.globalsecurity.org/space/systems/patriot-ac-3.htm (last accessed 11 July 2022a).

Global Security, Samsung Techwin SGR-A1 Sentry Guard Robot, www.globalsecurity.org/military/world/rok/sgr-a1.htm (last accessed 11 July 2022b).

Google, Artificial Intelligence at Google: Our Principles, https://ai.google/principles (last accessed 11 July 2022).

GRAIN, Seized: The 2008 Landgrab for Food and Financial Security, 24 October 2008, www.grain.org/article/entries/93-seized-the-2008-landgrab-for-food-and-financial-security (last accessed 11 July 2022).

HRL Laboratories, HRL Demonstrates the Potential to Enhance the Human Intellect's Existing Capacity to Learn New Skills, 2016, www.hrl.com/news/2016/0210 (last accessed 11 July 2022).

Human Rights Watch, Stopping Killer Robots: Country Positions on Banning Full Autonomous Weapons and Retaining Human Control, 10 August 2020, https://www.hrw.org/report/2020/08/10/stopping-killer-robots/country-positions-banning-fully-autonomous-weapons-and#_ftn12 (last accessed 11 July 2022).

Indigenous Protocol and Artificial Intelligence Working Group, https://www.indigenous-ai.net (last accessed 11 July 2022).

International Committee of the Red Cross (ICRC), Position on Autonomous Weapons Systems, 12 May 2021, https://www.icrc.org/en/document/icrc-position-autonomous-weapon-systems (last accessed 11 July 2022).

International Seabed Authority, The Mining Code, https://www.isa.org.jm/miningcode (last accessed 11 July 2022).

Jones, Emily and Otto, Dianne, Thinking through Anthropocentrism in International Law: Queer Theory, Posthuman Feminism and the Postcolonial, LSE Women, Peace and Security blog (January 2020), www.lse.ac.uk/women-peace-security/assets/documents/2020/Final-Jones-and-Otto-Anthropocentrism-Posthuman-Feminism-Postcol-and-IL-LSE-WPS-Blog-2019-002.pdf (last accessed 29 September 2022).

Kamagai, Jean, A Robotic Sentry for Korea's Demilitarized Zone IEEE, Spectrum, 2007, http://spectrum.ieee.org/robotics/military-robots/a-robotic-sentry-for-koreas-demilitarized-zone (last accessed 11 July 2022).

Kiulian, Artur, Elon Musk and Mark Zuckerberg are Arguing about AI – but They're Both Missing the Point, Entrepreneur, 2017, https://www.entrepreneur.com/article/297861 (last accessed 11 July 2022).

Laboria Cuboniks, Xenofeminism: A Politics for Alienation, www.laboriacuboniks.net (last accessed 11 July 2022).

Moyes, Richard, Key Elements of Meaningful Human Control, Article 36, April 2016, www.article36.org/wp-content/uploads/2016/04/MHC-2016-FINAL.pdf (last accessed 11 July 2022).

Natarajan, Usha and Dehm, Julia, Where is the Environment? Locating Nature in International Law, TWAILR, 2019, https://twailr.com/where-is-the-environment-locating-nature-in-international-law (last accessed 11 July 2022).

Pax for Peace, Religious Leaders Call for a Ban on Killer Robots, 12 November 2014, https://www.paxforpeace.nl/stay-informed/news/religious-leaders-call-for-a-ban-on-killer-robots (last accessed 11 July 2022).

Raytheon, Boomerang, www.raytheon.co.uk/capabilities/products/boomerang (last accessed 11 July 2022).

Rights of Nature Tribunal, https://www.rightsofnaturetribunal.org (last accessed 11 July 2022).

Stockholm International Peace Research Institute (SIPRI), Military Expenditure Database, https://milex.sipri.org/sipri (last accessed 11 July 2022).

Stockton, Nick, Woman Controls a Fighter Jet Sim Using Only Her Mind, WIRED, 5 March 2015, https://www.wired.com/2015/03/woman-controls-fighter-jet-sim-using-mind (last accessed 11 July 2022).

The Algorithmic Justice League, https://www.ajlunited.org (last accessed 11 July 2022).

Tucker, Patrick, It's Now Possible to Telepathically Communicate with a Drone Swarm, Defence One, 6 September 2018, https://www.defenseone.com/technology/2018/09/its-now-possible-telepathically-communicate-drone-swarm/151068 (last accessed 11 July 2022).

UN Harmony with Nature, Interactive Dialogues of the General Assembly, www.harmonywithnatureun.org/dialogues (last accessed 11 July 2022a).

UN Harmony with Nature, UN Documents on Harmony with Nature, http://harmonywithnatureun.org/unDocs (last accessed 11 July 2022b).

United Nations High Commissioner for Refugees (UNHCR), Climate Change and Disaster Displacement, https://www.unhcr.org/uk/climate-change-and-disasters.html (last accessed 11 July 2022).

Vilmer, Jean-Baptiste Jeangène, Terminator Ethics: Should We Ban 'Killer Robots'?, Ethics and International Affairs, 2015, https://www.ethicsandinternationalaffairs.org/2015/terminator-ethics-ban-killer-robots (last accessed 11 July 2022).

Vinge, Vernor, The Coming Technological Singularity: How to Survive in the Post-Human Era, Paper presented at Vision 21: Interdisciplinary Science and Engineering in the Era of Cyberspace Conference, NASA Lewis Research Centre, 1993, NASA Publication CP-10129, https://ntrs.nasa.gov/archive/nasa/casi.ntrs.nasa.gov/19940022855.pdf (last accessed 11 July 2022).

Wakabayashi, Daisuke and Shane, Scott, Google will not Renew Pentagon Contract that Upset Employees, *The New York Times*, 1 June 2018, https://www.nytimes.com/2018/06/01/technology/google-pentagon-project-maven.html (last accessed 11 July 2022).

Williams, John, 'Effective, Deployable, Accountable: Pick Two': Regulating Lethal Autonomous Weapons Systems, E-International Relations, 2021b, https://www.e-ir.info/2021/08/12/effective-deployable-accountable-pick-two-regulating-lethal-autonomous-weapons-system (last accessed 11 July 2022).

Wired, 3 Years After the Maven Uproar, Google Cozies to the Pentagon, 18 November 2021, https://www.wired.com/story/3-years-maven-uproar-google-warms-pentagon/?msclkid=db6cdbf3afa111ecba983f2fce04d254 (last accessed 11 July 2022).

Wolfrum, Rüdiger, Common Heritage of Mankind, Max Planck Encyclopaedias of International Law, https://opil.ouplaw.com/view/10.1093/law:epil/9780199231690/law-9780199231690-e1149 (last accessed 11 July 2022).

Reports

Acheson, Ray, 'Autonomous Weapons and Gender-Based Violence,' Campaign to Stop Killer Robots and Women's International League for Peace and Freedom 2020a, https://reachingcriticalwill.org/images/documents/Publications/aws-and-gbv.pdf (last accessed 11 July 2022).

Acheson, Ray, 'Autonomous Weapons and Patriarchy,' Campaign to Stop Killer Robots and Women's International League for Peace and Freedom 2020b, https://reachingcriticalwill.org/images/documents/Publications/aws-and-patriarchy.pdf (last accessed 11 July 2022).

Aerospace Industries Association, '2021 Facts and Figures,' 2021, https://www.aia-aerospace.org/wp-content/uploads/2021-Facts-and-Figures-U.S.-Aerospace-and-Defense.pdf (last accessed 27 September 2022).

Bode, Ingvild and Watts, Tom, 'Meaning-*less* Human Control: Lessons from Air Defence Systems on Meaningful Human Control for the Debate on AWS,' Centre for War Studies 2021, https://dronewars.net/wp-content/uploads/2021/02/DW-Control-WEB.pdf (last accessed 11 July 2022).

Cummings, M.L., 'Artificial Intelligence and the Future of Warfare,' Chatham House, 2017.

Department of Defense (DoD) Defense Science Board, 'The Role of Autonomy in DoD Systems,' Task Force Report, 2012, https://irp.fas.org/agency/dod/dsb/autonomy.pdf (last accessed 11 July 2022).

Flora and Fauna International, 'The Risks and Impacts of Deep-Sea Mining to Marine Ecosystems,' https://cms.fauna-flora.org/wp-content/uploads/2020/03/FFI_2020_The-risks-impacts-deep-seabed-mining_Executive-Summary.pdf (last accessed 11 July 2022).

Hawley, John K., 'Patriot Wars: Automation and the Patriot Air and Missile Defense System, Voices from the Field,' Center for New American Security, 2017.

Human Rights Watch, 'Losing Humanity: The Case Against Killer Robots,' 2012, https://www.hrw.org/report/2012/11/19/losing-humanity/case-against-killer-robots (last accessed 28 September 2022).

Indigenous Protocol and Artificial Intelligence Working Group, 'Position Paper: Indigenous Protocol and Artificial Intelligence,' 30 January 2020, https://spectrum.library.concordia.ca/id/eprint/986506/7/Indigenous_Protocol_and_AI_2020.pdf (last accessed 11 July 2022).

Intergovernmental Science-Policy Platform on Biodiversity and Ecosystem Services (IPBES), 'The Global Assessment Report on Biodiversity and Ecosystem Services: Summary for Policymakers,' 2019, https://ipbes.net/sites/default/files/2020-02/ipbes_global_assessment_report_summary_for_policymakers_en.pdf (last accessed 11 July 2022).

Intergovernmental Panel on Climate Change (IPCC), 'Summary for Policymakers,' IPCC Special Report on the Ocean and Cryosphere in a Changing Climate, 2019, https://www.ipcc.ch/srocc/chapter/summary-for-policymakers/ (last accessed 29 September 2022).

International Committee of the Red Cross (ICRC), 'Autonomous Weapon Systems: Implications of Increasing Autonomy in the Critical Functions of Weapons,' Geneva, 2016, https://www.icrc.org/en/publication/4283-autonomous-weapons-systems (last accessed 29 September 2022).

Kite, Suzanne in discussion with Corey Stover, Melita Stover Janis and Scott Benesiinaabandan, 'How to Build Anything Ethically,' in Indigenous Protocol and Artificial Intelligence Working Group, 'Position Paper: Indigenous Protocol and Artificial Intelligence,' 30 January 2020, https://spectrum.library.concordia.ca/id/eprint/986506/7/Indigenous_Protocol_and_AI_2020.pdf (last accessed 11 July 2022): 75–84.

Ministry of Defence, 'Human-Machine Teaming,' Joint Concept Note 1/18, 2018.

National Aeronautics and Space Administration (NASA), 'The Artemis Accords: Principles for a Safe, Peaceful, and Prosperous Future,' 2020, https://www.nasa.gov/specials/artemis-accords/img/Artemis-Accords-v7_print.pdf (last accessed 11 July 2022).

National Implementation Measures Programme, Biological Weapons Convention, Report on National Implementing Legislation, VERTIC, 2016.

National Security Commission on Artificial Intelligence, 'Final Report,' March 2021, https://www.nscai.gov/wp-content/uploads/2021/03/Full-Report-Digital-1.pdf (last accessed 11 July 2022).

Nolte, Kerstin, Chamberlain, Wytske and Giger, Markus, 'International Land Deals for Agriculture: Fresh Insights from the Land Matrix: Analytical Report II,' Centre for Development and Environment, University of Bern, and German Institute of Global and Area Studies, University of Pretoria, Bern Open Publishing, 2016, www.landmatrix.org/media/filer_public/ab/c8/abc8b563-9d74-4a47-9548-cb59e4809b4e/land_matrix_2016_analytical_report_draft_ii.pdf (last accessed 11 July 2022).

Oxfam International, 'Time to Care: Unpaid and underpaid care work and the Global Inequality Crisis,' 20 January 2020.

The International Human Rights and Conflict Resolution Clinic, Stanford Law School and Global Justice Clinic and New York University School of Law, 'Living Under Drones: Death, Injury and Trauma to Civilians from US Drone Practices in Pakistan,' 2012.

Union Bank of Switzerland (UBS), 'Riding the Storm: Market Turbulence Accelerates Diverging Fortunes,' *Billionaires Insight* 2020, www.ubs.com/content/dam/static/noindex/ wealth-management/ubs-billionaires-report-2020-spread.pdf (last accessed 28 September 2022).

World Bank, 'Rising Global Interest in Farmland: Can It Yield Sustainable and Equitable Benefits?' World Bank, 2011, https://documents1.worldbank.org/curated/ en/998581468184149953/pdf/594630PUB0ID1810Box358282B01PUBLIC1.pdf (last accessed 28 September 2022).

Speeches

Muñoz, José Esteban, 'The Brown Commons: The Sense of Wildness,' Paper presented at the Annual Convention of the American Studies Association, San Juan, Puerto Rico, 16 November 2012).

Treaties and Other International Legal Instruments

Gerritson, Rupert, (ed.), trans. Peter Reynders, 'A Translation of the Charter of the Dutch East India Company (Verenigde Oostindische Compagnie or VOC): Granted by the States General of the United Netherlands, 20 March 1602,' Australia on the Map Division of the Australasian Hydrographic Society Canberra (2009).

The Treaty of Nanking, 29 August 1842.

Convention Respecting the Law and Customs of War on Land and Its Annex: Regulations Concerning the Laws and Customs of War on Land, 26 January 1910.

League of Nations, Covenant of the League of Nations, 28 April 1919.

Treaty on the Limitation of Anti-Ballistic Missile Systems, 26 May 1927.

Montevideo Convention on the Rights and Duties of States, 26 December 1933.

United Nations, Statute of the International Court of Justice, 18 April 1946.

United Nations, UNGA Res A/RES/375 (1949).

United Nations General Assembly (UNGA), International Covenant on Civil and Political Rights, 16 December 1966a, U.N.T.S. vol. 999.

United Nations General Assembly (UNGA), International Covenant on Economic, Social and Cultural Rights, 16 December 1966b, U.N.T.S. vol. 993.

United Nations General Assembly (UNGA), The Treaty on Principles Governing the Activities of States in the Exploration and Use of Outer Space, Including the Moon and Other Celestial Bodies (The Outer Space Treaty), 27 January 1967, UNGA Resolution 2222 (XXI).

United Nations General Assembly (UNGA), 1968, UNGA Res 2398, A/RES,2398 (XXII).

United Nations, Vienna Convention on the Law of Treaties, 23 May 1969, U.N.T.S. vol. 1155.

Treaty on the Non-Proliferation of Nuclear Weapons, 5 March 1970.

United Nations General Assembly (UNGA), Resolution 2749, Declaration of Principles Governing the Seabed and the Ocean Floor, and the Subsoil Thereof, beyond the Limits of National Jurisdiction, 17 December 1970, UNGA 118, A/RES/2749 (XXV).

Convention on the Prohibition of the Development, Production and Stockpiling of Bacteriological (Biological) and Toxin Weapons and on Their Destruction, 10 April 1972.

United Nations General Assembly, Stockholm Declaration, United Nations Conference on the Human Environment, 15 December 1972, A/RES/2994.

United Nations, UNGA Res A/RES/3171 (1973).

Protocol Additional to the Geneva Conventions of 12 August 1949, and Relating to the Protection of Victims of International Armed Conflicts, 8 June 1977, 1125 U.N.T.S. 3, 8 June 1977.

UNGA, Agreement Governing the Activities of States on the Moon and Other Celestial Bodies (The Moon Agreement), 18 December 1979, UNGA Resolution 34/68.

Convention on Certain Conventional Weapons, 10 October 1980, 1342 U.N.T.S. 137.

UN General Assembly, Convention on the Law of the Sea, 10 December 1982.

Protection of Global Climate for Present and Future Generations of Mankind, UNGA Res 43/53, 6 December 1988, GAOR 43rd Session Supp. 49 vol. 1, 133.

Treaty on Conventional Armed Forces in Europe, 19 November 1990.

United Nations, Convention on Biological Diversity, 5 June 1992, 1760, U.N.T.S. vol. 69.

Agreement Relating to the Implementation of Part XI of the United Nations Convention on the Law of the Sea of 10 December 1982, adopted 28 July 1994, 1836 U.N.T.S. 3.

Special Conference of the States Parties to the Convention on the Prohibition of the Development, Production and Stockpiling of Bacteriological (Biological) and Toxin Weapons and on Their Destruction, Final Report, 1994, BWC/SPCONF/1.

Protocol on Blinding Laser Weapons (Protocol IV to the 1980 Convention on Certain Conventional Weapons) 13 October 1995.

UN General Assembly, Rome Statute of the International Criminal Court, 17 July 1998 ISBN No. 92-9227-227-6.

Security Council Resolution 1325, 31 October 2000, S/RES/1325.

Security Council Resolution 1540, 28 April 2004, S/RES/1540.

Koskenniemi, Martti, 'Fragmentation of International Law: Difficulties Arising from the Diversification and Expansion of International Law,' International Law Commission 2006, A/CN.4/l.682.

Security Council Resolution 1820, 18 June 2008, S/RES/1820.

Evo Morales, 'Address by H.E. Mr. Evo Morales Ayma, the President of the Plurinational State of Bolivia,' 64th Session of the General Assembly of the United Nations, 2009.

Security Council Resolution 1888, 30 September 2009, S/RES/1888.

Security Council Resolution 1889, 5 October 2009, S/RES/1889.

World People's Conference on Climate Change and the Rights of Mother Earth, 22 April 2010, Bolivia, People's Agreement.

Security Council Resolution 1960, 16 December 2010, S/RES/1960.

UN General Assembly, Report of the Special Rapporteur on Extrajudicial, Summary or Arbitrary Executions, 9 April 2013, A/HRC/23/47.

Security Council Resolution 2106, 24 June 2013, S/RES/2106.

Security Council Resolution 2122,18 October 2013, S/RES/2122.

Convention on Certain Conventional Weapons, Meeting of State Parties, 25 November 2014, CCW/MSP/2014.

UN Human Rights Council, Report of the Special Rapporteur on Extreme Poverty and Human Rights, Philip Alston, 27 May 2015, A/HRC/29/31.

Security Council Resolution 2242, 13 October 2015, S/RES/2242.

Conference of the Parties, Adoption of the Paris Agreement, 12 December 2015, U.N. Doc. FCCC/CP/2015/L.9/Rev.1.

Meeting of the High Contracting Parties to the Convention on Prohibitions or Restrictions on the Use of Certain Conventional Weapons Which May Be Deemed to Be Excessively Injurious or to Have Indiscriminate Effects, 27 January 2016, CCW/MSP/2015/WP.2.

United Nations, UNGA Res A/RES/70/208 (2015).

General Statement made by Ambassador Michael Biontino, Representing Germany, Swiss Ambassador's Conference, Security in Uncertainty: New Approaches to Disarmament, Arms Control and Non-Proliferation, 26 January 2016.

Report of the 2016 Informal Meeting of Experts on Lethal Autonomous Weapons Systems (LAWS) 2016 Session, CCW/CONF.V/2.

United Nations, UNGA Res A/71/266 (2016).

United Nations, UNGA Res A/Res/71/312 (2017).

UNGA, Report of the Secretary-General on UN Harmony with Nature, 19 July 2017, A/72/175.

Human-Machine Interaction in the Development, Deployment and Use of Emerging Technologies in the Area of Lethal Autonomous Weapons Systems, Submitted by the United States, 28 August 2018, CCW/GGE.2/2018/P.4.

US Opening Statement at the Group of Government Experts (GGE) on Lethal Autonomous Weapons Systems, 9 April 2018.

Kirsti Luke, Presentation at the United Nations Interactive Dialogue of the General Assembly on Harmony with Nature, United Nations Headquarters, 23 April 2018.

United Nations, UNGA Res A/Res/72/277 (2018).

UN General Assembly, Report of UN Secretary General, Gaps in International Environmental Law and Environment-Related Instruments: Towards a Global Pact for the Environment, 30 November 2018, A/73/419.

Report of the Special Rapporteur on Human Rights and the Environment, 'Issue of Human Rights Obligations Relating to the Enjoyment of a Safe, Clean, Healthy and Sustainable Environment,' Human Rights Council, 8 January 2019, A/HRC/40/55.

Security Council Resolution 2467, 23 April 2019, S/RES/2467.

UN Human Rights Council, Report of the Special Rapporteur on Extreme Poverty and Human Rights: Visit to the United Kingdom of Great Britain and Northern Ireland, 30 May 2019a, A/HRC/41/39.

UN Human Rights Council, Report of the Special Rapporteur on Extreme Poverty and Human Rights: Climate Change and Poverty, 17 July 2019b, A/HRC/41/39.

Chairperson of the 2019 Meeting of Experts on Institutional Strengthening of the Convention, 4 October 2019, Summary Report, BWC/MSP/2019/MX.5/2.

Security Council Resolution 2493, 29 October 2019, S/RES/2493.

Meeting of the High Contracting Parties to the Convention on Prohibitions or Restrictions on the Use of Certain Conventions Weapons Which May Be Deemed to be Excessively Injurious or to Have Indiscriminate Effects, 13–15 November 2019, CCW MSP/2019/9.

Report on 2019 Meeting of the High Contracting Parties to the Convention on Prohibitions or Restrictions on the Use of Certain Conventional Weapons Which May Be Deemed to Be Excessively Injurious or to Have Indiscriminate Effects, 13–15 November 2019, CCW/MSP/2019/9.

Convention on Biological Diversity, Open Ended Working Group on the Post-2020 Global Biodiversity Framework, Second Meeting, 6 January 2020a, CBD/WG2020/2/3.

Convention on Biological Diversity, Open Ended Working Group on the Post-2020 Global Biodiversity Framework, 29 March 2020b, CBD/WG2020/3/L.2.

Convention on Biological Diversity, Update of the Zero Draft of the Post-2020 Global Biodiversity Framework, 17 August 2020c, CBD/POST2020/PREP/2/1.

United Nations General Assembly (UNGA), Resolution Adopted by the Human Rights Council on the Human Rights to a Clean, Healthy and Sustainable Environment 18 October 2021, A/HRC/48/13.

United Nations General Assembly (UNGA), The Human Right to a Clean, Healthy and Sustainable Environment 26 July 2022, A/76/L.75.

Domestic and Regional Laws, Policies and Statements
Bolivia

Constitution of the Plurinational State of Bolivia, 2009.
Law 071 of the Rights of Mother Earth, 21 Dec. 2010. An English version of the law can be found at: http://181.224.152.72/~embajad5/wp-content/uploads/2017/12/rights-of-mother-earth.pdf (last accessed 11 July 2022).

Ecuador

Republic of Ecuador, Constitution of 2008, trans. Georgetown University, Preamble, https://pdba.georgetown.edu/Constitutions/Ecuador/english08.html (last accessed 11 July 2022).
Constitutional Protective Action No. 0016-2011, Twenty-Second Criminal Court, Pichincha Province, Republic of Ecuador (20 May 2011).
Republic of Ecuador, Penal Code, Organic Law, 2014.
Republic of Ecuador, Environmental Code, 2018.

European Parliament

European Parliament Resolution on the Use of Armed Drones 25 February 2014 2014/2567 (RSP).
European Parliament Resolution on Autonomous Weapons Systems 12 September 2018 2018/2752(RSP).
European Parliament, 'Guidelines for Military and Non-Military Use of Artificial Intelligence: Press Release,' 20 January 2021, https://www.europarl.europa.eu/news/en/press-room/20210114IPR95627/guidelines-for-military-and-non-military-use-of-artificial-intelligence (last accessed 11 July 2022).

Aotearoa/New Zealand

Te Urewera Act 2014.
Te Awa (Whanganui River Claims Settlement) Act Tupua 2017.

Russia

Russian Federation, Potential Opportunities and Limitations of Military Uses of Lethal Autonomous Weapons Systems: Working Paper Submitted by the Russian Federation, UN Doc. CCW/GGE.1/2019/WP.1, 15 March 2019.

United Kingdom of Great Britain and Northern Ireland

UK Ministry of Defence, The UK Approach to Unmanned Aircraft Systems Joint Doctrine Note 2/11 (30 March 2011).

Ministry of Defence, Letter to Maiara Folly, 4 January 2021, https://article36.org/wp-content/uploads/2021/01/UK-govt-reply-2020-LAWS.pdf (last accessed 11 July 2022).

United States of America

City of Pittsburgh, Code of Ordinances, Title 6, art 1, ch 618, 'Marcellus Shale Natural Gas Drilling Ordinance' (2010), https://library.municode.com/pa/pittsburgh/codes/code_of_ordinances? nodeId=COOR_TITSIXCO_ARTIRERIAC_CH618MASHNAGADR (last accessed 11 July 2022).

Ordinance of the City Council of Santa Monica Establishing Sustainability Rights, 12 March 2012, https://www.smgov.net/departments/council/agendas/2013/20130312/s2013031207-C-1.htm#:~:text=(a)%20All%20residents%20of%20Santa,sustainable%20climate%20that%20supports%20thriving (last accessed 11 July 2022).

U.S. Department of Defense, Autonomy in Weapons Systems, Directive 3000.09 (21 November 2012).

Robert O. Work, 'Establishment of an Algorithmic Warfare Cross-Functional Team (Project Maven),' Memorandum from the US Deputy Secretary of Defense, 26 April 2017, https://www.govexec.com/media/gbc/docs/pdfs_edit/establishment_of_the_awcft_project_maven.pdf (last accessed 11 July 2022).

US Federal Register, 'Encouraging International Support for the Recovery and Use of Space Resources,' Executive Order 13914 of 6 April 2020, https://www.federalregister.gov/documents/2020/04/10/2020-07800/encouraging-international-support-for-the-recovery-and-use-of-space-resources (last accessed 11 July 2022).

International Law Cases

Case of the SS Lotus (Judgment), 1927 PCIJ Series A No. 10.

Jurisdiction of the Courts of Danzig, Advisory Opinion, 1928, *PCIJ, Ser B, No 15*.

Trial of Major War Criminals Before the International Military Tribunal, Judgement: The Law of the Charter, International Military Tribunal for Germany, 1 October 1946.

Reparation for Injuries Suffered in the Service of the United Nations (Advisory Opinion), International Court of Justice,11 April 1949, ICJ Rep 174, ICGJ 232 (ICJ 1949).

Legality of the Threat or Use of Nuclear Weapons (Advisory Opinion), International Court of Justice, 8 July 1996, I.C.J. Reports 1996.

Prosecutor v Kupreškić (Judgment) (International Criminal Tribunal for the Former Yugoslavia, Trial Chamber, Case No IT-95-16, 14 January 2000.

Pulp Mills on the River Uruguay (Argentina v Uruguay), International Court of Justice, 2006 ICJ Rep 113.

Pulp Mills on the River Uruguay (Argentina v Uruguay), International Court of Justice, Judgment of 20 April 2010.

Responsibilities and Obligations of States Sponsoring Persons and Entities with Respect to Activities in The Area, International Tribunal for the Law of the Sea, Advisory Opinion of 1 February 2011.

European Court of Human Rights Cases

Sahin v Turkey, Appl. no. 4474/98, 10 November 2005.

S.A.S. v France, Appl. no. 4835/11, 1 July 2014.

Dakir v Belgium, Appl. no. 4619/12, 11 July 2017.

Domestic Law Cases

Bangladesh

Appellate Division of the Supreme Court of Bangladesh, upholding the 2019 decision of the High Court (in Writ Petition No. 13989) 2020.

Ecuador

Judgment No. 11121-2011-0010, Provincial Court of Justice, Loja Province, Republic of Ecuador (30 March 2011).

Judgment No. 269–2012, Civil and Mercantile Court, Gala´pagos Province, Republic of Ecuador (28 June 2012).

Judgment No. 2003-2014 – C.T., National Court of Justice, Specialized Chamber of Criminal, Military Criminal, Criminal Police and Transit Cases, Republic of Ecuador (7 September 2014).

Judgment No. 09171-2015-0004, Ninth Court of Criminal Guarantees, Guayas Province, Republic of Ecuador (23 April 2015).

Judgment No. 166-15-SEP-CC, Case No. 0507-12-EP, Constitutional Court of Ecuador, Republic of Ecuador (20 May 2015).

India

Mohd. Salim v. State of Uttarakhand and Others (Writ Petition (PIL) No. 126 of 2014 (March 20, 2017).

The State of Uttarakhand and Orgs v Mohd. Salim & Ors., Supreme Court of India, Petition for Special Leave to Appeal No. 016879/2017.

United States of America

County of Santa Clara v Southern Pacific Railroad, 118 US 394 (1886).

INDEX

ableism 70, 76, 101, 102, 111–112, 118
accountability 69–70, 107, 148; democratic 93, 108
Acheson, R. 70
Adelman, S. 23, 116
Advaita 159
Africa 45; Ghana 62
agency of matter 13, 16, 17, 19, 121, 125, 131, 141, 148
agential beings 162
agential realism 11, 113
agricultural practices 47
ahuman 11
air defence systems 71–72, 78, 96
Alaimo, S. 116
Alldred, P. 23, 116
Alston, P. 40
Amoore, L. 74, 92
amphetamines 79
Anghie, A. 31
animals 46, 47, 59, 124, 143, 159; capitalism 43; endangered species 139; healthy environment 53; legal status of 18, 23; nature, rights of 139; wildlife 7
anthropocentrism 1, 8, 10, 11, 13–15, 19, 24, 27–28, 31, 112, 123, 154, 156, 158, 162; colonialism, land grabbing and 27–28, 43–46; of international (environmental) law 25, 46–55, 114, 117, 126; language 25; marine living resources 8; military technologies 58, 59, 61, 63, 76; nature, rights of 129, 131–133, 135, 137, 139, 143, 145–147, 149–152; post- 9, 15

anti-humanisms 11
Anzaldúa, G. 124–125
Aotearoa/New Zealand 134–137, 140, 150
Arkin, R. 65–66
armed conflict 8; exoskeletons 8, 22, 59, 81; see also drone warfare; international humanitarian law (IHL); military technologies
arms control 95–96, 100; Biological Weapons Convention (BWC) 98–99; Convention on Certain Conventional Weapons (CCW), see separate entry
arms market 88
Article 36 (NGO) 76
artificial intelligence (AI) 20, 57–58, 68; black box dilemma 74; data collection and racial and gender bias 70; design 11; general 75; intersectional feminist ethics 103; machine learning 75; xenofeminism, data feminism and Indigenous knowledge as applied to 100–108
Arvidsson, M. 22
Asaro, P. 76
Åsberg, C. 61
Asia 45; see also individual countries
Australian Nations 130
Austria 58, 64
automation 20; false binary line between automated and autonomous systems see lethal autonomous weapons systems (LAWS)

Baars, G. 36–37, 54, 161
Bangladesh 135

Barad, K. 14, 77, 97, 120
Baxi, U. 23–24
Beckett, J. 41
Benjamin, R. 63, 105
Bennett, J. 14, 113–114, 116–118, 125, 149, 162
big data 8, 78
billionaire wealth 40
biofuel 44–45
biological determinism 123
biological diversity 51–52; Post-2020 Global Biodiversity Framework: zero draft 132
Biological Weapons Convention (BWC) 98–99
bionic body 18
Biontino, M. 73
Bode, I. 78, 96
bodies marked as targetable: military uniforms 18
Bolivia 132, 133, 136–138, 141, 145
Boomerang gunfire location system 81
Boulot, E. 23, 116
Boyd, D.R. 129
Braidotti, R. 10, 12–15, 19, 42, 45–46, 62, 102, 117–119, 143, 150, 158–159
brain-computer interface applications 81–82
Buddhism 159

capitalism 20, 45–46, 54, 90, 144, 163; colonialism, exclusion and 38–43; gender and 39–40; race and 39, 43; sustainable development 49; technology and 62, 63, 102
capitalocene 43; anthropocene- 117
carceral feminism 89
care work, unpaid 40
Chamayou, G. 78
Charlesworth, H. 2–4, 34
Chen, M.Y. 124–126, 144
Chile 135
China 31–32
Chinkin, C. 2–3
Chthulucene 117
civil society 87, 90, 133
Clarke, K.M. 18–19
climate change 7, 23, 44–47, 113, 114; common but differentiated responsibility 142–143; cryosphere change 46; displacement 47; and poverty 43, 47; and women 47; World People's Conference on Climate Change and the Rights of Mother Earth (2010) 132–133

climate justice 23, 116
coercion, economic and political 32
colonial gaze 157
colonialism 12, 34, 49, 54, 101, 108, 142, 144, 163; anthropocentrism, land grabbing and 27–28, 43–46; capitalism, exclusion and 38–43; corporation 36; role of documents in governance 18; state sovereignty 31–32, 34
coloniality 101, 111–112
commodification and international law 20
common but differentiated responsibility 142–143
common concern of mankind 50
common heritage of humankind 50–51
compliance see resistance and compliance
computer science 10
Conaghan, J. 17, 19
consent, state 29–32, 37
constitutionalism, rooted 146–147
contingency and international law 20
Convention on Biological Diversity (CBD) 51–52
Convention on Certain Conventional Weapons (CCW) 64, 95, 99; Group of Governmental Experts (GGE) 66–67, 70–71, 93
corporations: accountability 36–37; co-construction in international law of state and 37; nature, rights of 140; nonhuman and international law 27, 28, 30, 35–37, 45
counter-terrorism 24, 87; gender and racial profiling 66
COVID-19 pandemic 40
Craven, M. 32, 51
crip: technoscience 101; theory 14
critical animal studies 10
critical disability studies 10, 11, 22
critical environmental studies 10, 110–112, 115, 117, 126, 128, 131
critical human rights 159
critical international law 30, 159
critical legal theory 11
critical posthumanism 12–15, 91, 116, 118
critical race theory 10, 14
Çubukçu, A. 41–42
cultural and media studies 10–11
culture/nature binary 61, 102, 111, 112, 114, 115, 117, 119–121, 123, 125, 127, 137, 147–148
customary international law 48–49, 67–69, 94
cyborg 61; soldier 63, 80

data collection 78, 81
data feminism: principles 103–105;
   xenofeminism, Indigenous AI and 85,
   100–108
data, posthuman 16
data sovereignty 107
Davies, M. 17, 19
Davies, S.E. 88
decision-making 95–97; algorithmic
   programming 74; cycles in micro-seconds
   79; drone strikes 77–78, 83; expert
   decision-makers 30; human enhancement
   technologies (HETs) 80, 81, 83; inclusion
   of women in 3, 7, 9, 86, 111; Patriot and
   SGR-A1 systems 74, 83; Women, Peace
   and Security (WPS) agenda 86
defining posthuman feminism 9–15
Deleuze, G. 119
development, right to 24
D'Ignazio, C. 103–104
disabilities, people with 47, 101, 125
disarmament 85, 88
discrimination 9, 60, 104
distinction, principle of 67
do-no-harm ethics 107
domestic courts 29
drone warfare 8, 56, 59, 60, 62, 76, 83;
   gender and 22, 60, 78; machine learning
   to enhance targeting 57–58; pattern
   of life analyses 77–78; race and 22, 78;
   swarming drones 22, 82
Dryzek, J.S. 115
Dutch East India Company 36, 37

e-waste 62
earth system law 115–116
ecocentric or ecological law 115, 145, 150
ecofeminism 122–123
Ecuador 134–139
emotion(s) 80; and embodiment 104
Enlightenment 12, 20, 24
environment 162; capitalism's role in
   objectification of 43; climate change
   see separate entry; legal status of 18;
   marginalisation of gendered, raced and
   classed subjects and exploitation of 8, 23;
   military and greenhouse gases 57; right
   to healthy environment 53–54, 136, 156
environmental impact assessments (EIAs)
   148–149
environmental law 11, 16, 20, 22–23,
   26, 98, 110–113, 127, 158;
   anthropocentrism of international
   25, 46–55, 114, 117, 126; feminist
   approaches to international 6–8; nature,

rights of see separate entry; posthuman
   feminism: queering the nonhuman
   117–126, 127; posthuman theory and
   113–117; subject/object binary 54, 110,
   111, 113, 114, 117, 119, 125, 137, 141
essentialism 87, 112, 120–123, 125–127,
   133–134
ethical balancing system 98–99, 105, 108
Eurocentric transcendentalism 14, 125
European Court of Human Rights
   (ECtHR) 157
European Union: Parliament 65
exoskeletons 8, 22, 59, 81
expert decision-makers 30

failed states 34–35
Fanon, F. 41
feminist approaches: to international law
   2–6, 9, 11; to environment and military
   technologies in international law 6–9
feminist psychoanalytic analysis 5
flat ontology 119
food production 44, 47
force, law on use of 3, 5
forensic architecture group 19
Foucault, M. 41, 91, 159
Fox, N.J. 23, 116
fragmentation 48, 52–53, 135
France 42
Fraser, N. 89
Fritsch, K. 101

Gaard, G. 123
Garver, C. 145
gender binary 5–6, 40, 104, 122, 123
gender equality: WPS agenda 86
genealogy of posthuman legal theory 16–20
Geneva Conventions, Additional Protocol
   I: art 35, 67; art 36 65, 94–95; art 57(2)
   67–68
geospatial materials 18–19
Ghana 62
Gill, A.S. 99, 100
Global Alliance for the Rights of Nature
   (GARN) 133
Global Pact for the Environment 52
global south 34, 35, 40, 45, 47, 58, 62, 64,
   76, 101, 159
globalisation 12
Goede, M. de 91
Gonzalez, C.G. 43
Google 57–58, 103
governance feminism 91
Grear, A. 8, 23, 24, 35–36, 54, 112, 114,
   116, 128

green washing 145
greenhouse gases 57
Grotius, H. 33
guardianship and nature 137

Halley, J. 5, 91
Hamraie, A. 101
Haraway, D. 43, 55, 61–62, 85, 91, 102, 116, 117, 126, 149, 162
hard law: soft and 7; treaties, *see separate entry*
Harvey, M. 23, 116
Hawley, J. 71
healthy environment, right to 53–54, 136, 156
Heathcote, G. 5, 7–8, 22, 23, 30
Henkin, L. 34
high seas 50, 53
hijab 157, 158
histories, international legal 21
Hohmann, J. 20–21
Holy See 58, 64
HRL: Information & System Sciences Laboratory 82
Hubert, A.-M. 148
human enhancement technologies (HETs) 58, 79–83, 96; defining 80n159, 81; review of weapons 94
human in/on/out of the loop 73–75, 77
human and machine *see* lethal autonomous weapons systems (LAWS)
human rights 5, 20, 22–24, 29, 144–145, 156–158; business and 37; corporations 37; enforcement of 41; environment and 52–54, 136, 156, 158; freedom 144, 157–158, 159; governance tool 157; lethal autonomous weapons systems 66; status quo 89–90
Human Rights Watch 64
human-nonhuman relations 11, 19, 20, 23, 24, 30, 77, 107, 114–116, 125, 126, 131, 132, 144, 146, 149–150, 162–163
humanism 12, 14, 19, 158–159; -as-statism 52; exclusionary 1, 10, 13, 15, 27–28, 31, 41–44, 46, 54, 55, 61, 63, 76, 101, 102, 117, 144, 145, 147, 154, 155–156, 158, 162; military technologies 58; ultra- 12
humanitarian intervention 5

indeterminacy thesis of international law 30
India 135
Indigenous: bounded territory 34; communities and climate change 46;

cosmovisions 145; knowledge 18, 104–108, 133–134, 146, 150, 163; legal thinking 116, 135, 137, 140; onto-epistemologies 11, 22, 106, 163; peoples and international law 142; peoples and rights of nature 129–130, 133–141, 145, 146, 150, 163; peoples and state 34; xenofeminism, data feminism and Indigenous knowledge as applied to AI 85, 100–108
individualism 36, 58
industrialisation 38, 43, 138
inequalities 12–14, 21, 58, 117, 118, 125, 127; between states 31–32, 58; international law perpetuates existing societal 33; nonhuman and international law 27, 31–33, 35, 38–41, 49–50, 54; queer theories of the nonhuman 112, 117, 118, 123, 126; reworlding 162; universalism, meaning of rights and 141–147
Inter-American human rights system 144
interdisciplinary method 10–11, 27, 154
International Committee of the Red Cross (ICRC) 71, 76
International Covenant on Civil and Political Rights (ICCPR) 52
International Covenant on Economic Social and Cultural Rights (ICESCR) 52
international criminal law 37, 70; trials 18–19
international economic law 41, 49
international humanitarian law (IHL) 3, 8, 22, 59; gendered and racialised assumptions 66; lethal autonomous weapons systems 65–71, 93–95, 99; review of weapons 93–95, 99
international institutions 4–5, 6–7
International Organisation for Standardisation (ISO) 21
international organisations 28–30
international relations 22, 30, 91
International Tribunal for the Rights of Nature 133
intersectional feminist theory 10, 14, 15, 19, 22
Iranian Revolution 159
Islam 157, 159

Jackson, Z.I. 14, 101, 147
Japan 31–32
Johns, F. 36
Joyce, D. 20–21
Joyner, C.C. 122

Kalmanovitz, P. 94
Kapur, R. 5, 156–158, 159
Kauffman, C.M. 140
Kendall, S. 18–19, 96
Kennedy, D. 30
Keshavarz, M. 18
Khoday, K. 49–50
Kirby, V. 114, 120, 149
Klein, L.F. 103–104
Knox, R. 39, 90
Koskenniemi, M. 41
Kotzé, L.J. 138, 145
Kouvo, S. 85, 89

Lalla 159
land grabbing, anthropocentrism and
    colonialism 27–28, 43–46
Land Matrix 44, 45
language 24–25
Latour, B. 77
law of the sea 6–8, 23
law and space 17–19
Leach, J. 18
League of Nations Mandate System 42
learning complex skills 82
legal geographies 17
legal subject of international law: classed,
    gendered and white 35
Leins, K. 81
lethal autonomous weapons systems
    (LAWS) 9, 22, 56–60, 83, 158, 161;
    autonomy and meaningful human
    control 71–79; definitions 57, 64, 93,
    95–98; gender and 60, 66; human
    enhancement technologies (HETs)
    79–83; legal and ethical debates on
    64–71; regulating see resistance and
    compliance; techno-utopianism or
    militarised masculinity 61–63
LGBTIQ+ persons 86, 123
liberal internationalism 12
liberal legalism, no exit from 155–160
Little, G.E. 122
Liu, H.-Y. 97
Luciano, D. 124–126, 144
Lucretius 118
Luke, K. 150
Lustig, D. 37
Lykke, N. 61

McFarland, T. 69
machine and human see lethal autonomous
    weapons systems (LAWS)
machines and bodies 18

Mahayana Buddhism 159
Malaysia 45
Manjikian, M. 63
marine biology 10
marine living resources 8
Marks, S. 89
Martens Clause 68–69, 95, 99
Marxism 21–22, 39
Masters, C. 63
materials and objects 18–21
Mbembe, A. 62
Miéville, C. 39
militarism 63, 102, 103, 107; anti- 85, 88,
    103–105, 109
military spending 56–57
military technologies 11, 16, 20, 25–26,
    158, 161; feminist approaches to
    international law on 8–9; gendered
    underpinnings: world of 62–63; lethal
    autonomous weapons systems (LAWS)
    see separate entry; regulating see resistance
    and compliance
military uniforms 18
Mills, A. 146–147, 162
mining: deep-sea 148–149; illegal 139
monism 118
Montevideo Convention 33, 34
Moore, J. 43
Mother Earth 132–134, 141, 145; Universal
    Declaration of the Rights of (UDRME)
    132–133
Mother Nature 122, 123, 146, 152
Muñoz, J.E. 160–161
Muslims 157, 159

naming and shaming 94
nanotechnologies 81
Natarajan, U. 49–50
national security 94, 99, 100
nature, rights of 18, 23, 26, 116, 128–
    131, 151–152, 159, 160; nature's
    legal personality and 131–141, 150;
    reworlding 161–162; universalism,
    global inequalities and meaning of
    rights 141–147; who represents nature
    147–150
nature/culture binary 61, 102, 111, 112,
    114, 115, 117, 119, 120, 121, 123, 125,
    127, 137, 147–148
neocolonialism 34, 35
neoliberal ideologies 38–39
Nesiah, V. 5
new materialisms 11, 13–15, 17, 20–24,
    106, 111–116, 118, 120–121

new technologies 20; artificial intelligence (AI) *see separate entry*; military technologies, *see separate entry*
New Zealand 58, 64, 134–137, 140, 150
Nijman, J.E. 29
Noble, S.U. 70
nomadic peoples 34
non-dualism 159
non-governmental organisations (NGOs) 4–5, 30, 76, 87–88
non-state groups 34–35
nonhuman and international law 25, 27–28, 54–55; anthropocentrism of environmental law 46–54; capitalism, colonialism and exclusion 38–43; colonialism, anthropocentrism and land grapping 27–28, 43–46; international law not posthuman 28–38
North Korea: sentry gun (SGR-A1) 72, 74, 83
nuclear weapons 95

object-orientated ontology (OOO) 14, 21, 116
objects and materials 18–21
Ollino, A. 8, 23
Oman 57
Orford, A. 5, 38–39
Otomo, Y. 5
Otto, D. 5–6, 8, 23, 88, 90–91
outer space law 50–51
outlaw states 34–35
Oxfam International 40

Papanicolopulu, I. 6
Papua New Guinea 18
Parfitt, R. 34
Parsa, A. 18
participation 8, 86; representation and 5, 110–111
Pashukanis, E.B. 39, 163
patriarchy 40, 42, 70, 90, 111–112, 123, 133, 144
Patriot system 71–74, 83
Pearson, Z. 85, 89
personality, legal 28–30, 33–36; rights of nature and nature's 131–141, 150
Petersmann, M.-C. 23, 115–116
Phalanx 72
pharmaceuticals 79–81
Philippines 134
Philippopoulos-Mihalopoulos, A. 17–19
philosophy 10, 12; Advaita 159; Lucretius 118
Picado, J.A. 122
Pickering, J. 115

pilot training 82
planetary justice 115
plants 46
Plumwood, V. 122–123
pluralism 104
policing of sexuality and gender 88
political economy 38–39, 40, 161
political science 11, 63
politics of ontological becoming, posthuman 22
pollution 57
Portmann, R. 30
postcolonial feminism 3, 5, 89
postcolonial theory 10, 14, 22, 123, 142
postdisciplinary method 10
posthuman feminism, defining 9–15
posthuman legal theory: genealogy of 16–20; and international law 20–24
posthuman theory 9, 11–12, 17, 59, 147, 162; environmental law and 113–117
poverty 40, 41, 43, 46, 47, 70
prevention, principle of 48n157
profiling 77–78, 81; gender and race 66, 78
proportionality 66
psychoanalytic analysis, feminist 5
Pufendorf, S. von 33–34

queer theory/ies 10, 14, 15, 22, 132, 144; ecology 123; inhuman or less-than-human nature of the queer subject 42; of the nonhuman 8, 16, 111–113, 123–127, 147, 149–150, 161–162; reworlding 160–161
Quiroga-Villamarín, D.R. 21

racism 14, 38, 43, 90, 102, 111–112
Ranganathan, S. 51
reciprocity 107, 137, 162
refugees 8, 70
Reid, R.A. 122
relationality 7, 20, 97–98, 107, 152, 161–163; *see also* human-nonhuman relations
relationships, rights granted to 145–146
representation 3, 9, 88; participation and 5, 110–111
reproductive technologies 61, 102
resistance and compliance 11, 25–26, 84–85, 108–109, 143, 154–155, 158–160, 163–164; control lists 98–99; ethical balancing system 98–99, 105, 108; feminist strategies in international law: between 85–92; regulating beyond law 92, 100–108, 155, 159–160, 163; review of weapons 93–95, 99; seeking

to transform international law from within 92–99, 154–155; temporal limitations 96
reworlding as practice 160–164; no exit from liberal legalism 155–160
Rio Conference on Environment and Development (1992) 48
Rochette, A. 7
Ruskola, T. 34
Russia 67

Salter, M.B. 21
satellite imagery 18–19
Saudi Arabia 57
Saxon, D. 79
Schippers, B. 24
Schuppli, S. 19
science and technology 11, 102–103, 105; nanotechnologies 81; studies 10, 12, 91; techno-utopianism, *see separate entry*
Scott, J.W. 161
seabed, deep 50, 51
secrecy 94
security studies 62–63
Sedgwick, E.K. 159
Senegal 44–45
sentry gun: SGR-A1 72, 74, 83
sexism 102
sexual violence in conflict 5, 87
Sharp, H. 119
Sheehan, L. 140
Sheldon, R. 14
shipping containers 21
Simpson, G. 34
social constructivism 102, 120–121
social theory 21
socio-legal theory 17
soft law 7, 49
South Korea: sentry gun (SGR-A1) 72, 74, 83
sovereign equality 31–32, 37, 39
sovereign state 3, 5; defined territory 34; gendered and racialised 33–35, 37–38; natural resources 7, 51–52, 138; nonhuman and international law 28–35, 37–38, 45, 51–52; state, concept of the 33
Special Rapporteur: on extreme poverty and human rights 43; on human rights and environment 53; on summary or arbitrary executions 64
Spinoza, B. de 118–119
Sterlin, J. 23, 116
stimulant tablets 79
Stockholm Declaration (1972) 48n150, 52

structural bias feminism 5
Suchman, L. 97
sustainable development 23, 49–51, 116, 133, 143

Tănăsescu, M. 134
techno-utopianism 59; or militarised masculinity 61–63
technological advancement 12, 57, 61
terra nullius 42
terrorism 24, 66, 87
third world approaches to international law (TWAIL) 21
tort law 70
training 82
transcranial direct current stimulation project 82
transhumanism 11, 12–14, 21
transparency 94
treaties 3; environment 47, 50–52, 142–143; unequal 31–32; *see also individual treaties*
True, J. 88
Turner, S.J. 54
Tzouvala, N. 38, 39

United Kingdom 40, 42, 107; lethal autonomous weapons systems 64, 67, 75–76
United Nations: Environment Programme (UNEP) 48; General Assembly 48, 53; Human Rights Council 53; nature, rights of 133; Security Council's Women, Peace and Security agenda 5, 84, 86–91, 97, 143, 158; Special Rapporteur, *see separate entry*
United States 22, 107; corporation as legal person 35–36; Defense Advanced Research Projects Agency (DARPA) 80–81; human enhancement technologies (HETs) 79, 80–81, 82; lethal autonomous weapons systems 64, 76, 78, 96; Military Defense Science Board 78; military spending 57; nature, rights of 136, 140–141; Project Maven: machine learning to enhance targeting 57–58, 103
Universal Declaration of the Rights of Mother Earth (UDRME) 132–133
Universal (Hu)man 14
universalism, global inequalities and meaning of rights 141–147

Vanderheiden, S. 23, 116
Vargas-Roncancio, I.D. 145, 162
veil 157, 158

vibrant matter 14, 16, 20, 113–114, 125
Vienna Convention on the Law of Treaties
1969 (VCLT) 32
Villavicencio, P. 138, 145
Vilmer, J.-B.J. 66, 73–74
Vinge, V. 79
vitalist materialism 113
vulnerabilities of women 8

Watts, T. 78, 96
wearable military technologies 81
Weber, J. 97
Wilcox, L. 22, 78
wildlife 7
Williams, J. 76, 97, 100

window dressing 145
Wolfrum, R. 50
Women, Peace and Security (WPS) agenda
5, 84, 86–91, 97, 143, 158
Women's International League for Peace
and Freedom (WILPF) 85, 87–88
Woolaston, K. 7
World Bank 44
Wright, S. 3
Wynter, S. 41, 124

xenofeminism 61–62, 92; data feminism,
Indigenous AI and 85, 100–108

Young, I.M. 33